Psychology Revivals

Empathy II

When the late Heinz Kohut defined psychoanalysis as the science of empathy and introspection, he sparked a debate that has animated psychoanalytic discourse ever since. What is the relationship of empathy to psychoanalysis? Is it a constituent of analytical technique, an integral aspect of the therapeutic action of analysis, or simply a metaphor for a mode of observation better understood via 'classical' theory and terminology? The dialogue about empathy, which is really a dialogue about the nature of the analytic process, continues in this two-volume set, originally published in 1984.

In Volume I, several illuminating attempts to define empathy are followed by Kohut's essay, 'Introspection, Empathy, and the Semicircle of Mental Health.' Kohut's paper, in turn, ushers in a series of original contributions on 'Empathy as a Perspective in Psychoanalysis.' The volume ends with five papers which strive to demarcate an empathic approach to various areas of artistic endeavour, including the appreciation of visual art.

Volume II continues the dialogue with a series of developmental studies which explore the role of empathy in early child care at the same time as they chart the emergence of the young child's capacity to empathize. In the concluding section, 'Empathy in Psychoanalytic Work,' contributors and discussants return to the arena of technique. They not only theorize about empathy in relation to analytic understanding and communication, but address issues of nosology, considering how the empathic vantage point may be utilized in the treatment of patients with borderline and schizophrenic pathology.

In their critical attention to the many dimensions of empathy – philosophical, developmental, therapeutic, artistic – the contributors collectively bear witness to the fact that Kohut has helped to shape new questions, but not set limits to the search for answers. The product of their efforts is an anatomical exploration of a topic whose relevance for psychoanalysis and psychotherapy is only beginning to be understood.

Empathy II

Edited by
Joseph D. Lichtenberg
Melvin Bornstein
Donald Silver

Routledge
Taylor & Francis Group
LONDON AND NEW YORK

First published in 1984
by The Analytic Press

This edition first published in 2014 by Routledge
27 Church Road, Hove, BN3 2FA

Simultaneously published in the USA and Canada
by Routledge
711 Third Avenue, New York, NY 10017

Routledge is an imprint of the Taylor & Francis Group, an informa business

Publisher's Note
The publisher has gone to great lengths to ensure the quality of this reprint but points out that some imperfections in the original copies may be apparent.

Disclaimer
The publisher has made every effort to trace copyright holders and welcomes correspondence from those they have been unable to contact.

A Library of Congress record exists under ISBN: 088163011X

ISBN: 978-0-415-71849-3 (hbk)
ISBN: 978-1-315-86973-5 (ebk)

EMPATHY II

Edited by
Joseph Lichtenberg, M.D.
Melvin Bornstein, M.D.
Donald Silver, M.D.

THE ANALYTIC PRESS
1984

Distributed by
LAWRENCE ERLBAUM ASSOCIATES, PUBLISHERS
Hillsdale, New Jersey London

The Analytic Press

Distributed solely by

Lawrence Erlbaum Associates, Inc., Publishers
365 Broadway
Hillsdale, New Jersey 07642

Library of Congress Cataloging in Publication Data
Main entry under title:
Empathy.

(Psychoanalytic inquiry book series ; v. 3)
Includes bibliographies and indexes.
1. Empathy. 2. Psychoanalysis. I. Lichtenberg, Joseph. II. Bornstein, Melvin. III. Silver, Donald. IV. Series. [DNLM: 1. Empathy. 2. Psychoanalytic therapy. 3. Art. 4. Physician—Patient relations. W1 PS3427F v. 3 / WM 460.5.C5]
BF575.E55E45 1984 152.4 84–2862
ISBN 0–88163–006–3 (set)
ISBN 0–88163–010–1 (v. 1)
ISBN 0–88163–011–X (v. 2)

Printed in the United States of America
10 9 8 7 6 5 4 3 2 1

Contents

Acknowledgment

These two volumes on Empathy are the result of many individual talents. Pietro Castelnuovo-Tedesco responded to the potential in the 1982 issues of *Psychoanalytic Inquiry* by suggesting that some might easily lend themselves to expansion into book form. Evelyne Schwaber recommended that we extend the issue entitled On Empathy. She most generously contributed her ideas and her time. Dr. Schwaber, Arthur Malin and Alan Skolnikoff had served as Consulting Editors for the papers in On Empathy which provided the conceptual core for the books.

Aided by Ann Appelbaum, Warren Poland was the central organizer of the section on empathy in the arts. Donald Silver, with the tireless assistance of his secretary Joan Berry, was co-editor of On Empathy and the organizer of the section on developmental aspects. Melvin Bornstein, co-editor of On Empathy, handled the lion's share of coordinating the remaining sections on definition, perspective and clinical work. His secretary, Joanne Piatek, has given her unstinting devotion to the small and large tasks of this enterprise. Charlotte Lichtenberg took an active part in the conceptual editing of a number of the papers and offered skilled advice and counsel throughout the project.

We are indebted to Betty Kohut and Thomas Kohut for their help in arranging for Dr. Kohut's extremely valuable contribution to appear in this volume. And we are grateful to the Editors of the *International Journal and Review* who gave permission for its re-issue.

As anyone who has produced a book knows, the final product rests on two pillars: the creative qualities of the contributors and the painstaking skills of the publisher and his staff. The brilliant array of authors whose papers and discussions comprise the book have been universally cooperative and patient. Their faith in our project has been matched by the optimism of Lawrence Erlbaum, publisher of the Analytic Press. Under Mr. Erlbaum's direction, the staff of the Analytic Press has given practical meaning to our dream of a broad, thorough coverage of the complex subject of empathy. Many people have contributed—especially Beverly Byrne in production, Judith Abrams in publicity and Joe Petrowski in distribution. Most of all we are indebted to Sue Heinemann. Not only did she copy edit each paper, but her suggestions enabled us to solve many of the problems of organizing so vast a number of papers into two volumes—each of which could stand alone, but which together, we believe, constitute a unique treatment of an important psychoanalytic subject.

Joseph D. Lichtenberg

IV

DEVELOPMENTAL ASPECTS OF EMPATHY

Introductory Remarks

DONALD SILVER, M.D.

CONSIDER THE RECENT MOVIE *E.T.* In this science-fiction version of the classic tale of a boy and his dog, an unhappy 10-year-old, who has recently lost his father, encounters and befriends a gnome of a creature, who has been left behind by a group of fellow explorers from a distant planet. Eliot, the fatherless boy, and E.T., the extraterrestrial gremlin separated from his companions, share a common feeling of abandonment and isolation under trying circumstances. Lacking any prior knowledge of one another, these two "aliens" are immediately drawn together out of their mutual recognition of each other's neediness.

It is the community of feeling between E.T. and Eliot that renders each protagonist openly receptive to the overtures of the other. In itself, however, this affective resonance posits nothing more than the traditional scenario of "boy loves dog; dog loves boy." The film actually depicts much more in that we see the genetic unfolding of the conditions for meaningful dialogue between the two protagonists via their intense efforts to establish a shared language. Through an exhaustive series of trial-and-error efforts, we see E.T. and Eliot striving to reach, engage, and understand one another, with the ultimate achievement of an interactive mutual empathy.

In its depiction of the evolution of affective resonance into a shared language, *E.T.* metaphorically telescopes the usual situation of the mother and her newborn. Here, too, a matrix of mutual need and a readiness to interrelate evolve into a shared language only after the concerted efforts of each member of the dyad to move beyond a simple communion of feeling. But here, too, the shared language presupposes a foundation of shared affective experience. Like E.T. and Eliot, that is, the mother and her infant must initially depend on reciprocal affective cueing. The language of mother and infant, like the language of Eliot and E.T., is anchored in, and proceeds from, the resonance of affect.

In significant ways, then, the moving depiction of the deepening relationship between Eliot and E.T. typifies the epigenetic unfolding of the infant's capacity for empathic interchange. Congruent with the message of the film, we may posit two major conditions for empathic development. First, the mother and her infant must have a mutuality of affect. At the level of earliest infancy, the achievement of such mutuality hinges on the mother's ability to cultivate an empathic environment for the infant by thinking and behaving in a manner synchronous with what the infant is experiencing. Under optimal circumstances, the mother "reads" her infant's affective signals accurately and responds to them appropriately. Appropriate responses, in this context, are responses consonant with the experiential requirements of the infant's neediness. Thus, the mother who senses her infant is hungry, but prepares food too hot for the infant to ingest comfortably, is correctly "reading" her baby's distress from hunger, but responding in a way that is antithetical to the child's need. Conversely, the mother who accurately "reads" her infant's anger, correctly infers that the baby is tired, and puts her child to bed, is responding appropriately—i.e., she is responding from a vantage point consonant with the infant's own "interests." The mother's cultivation of an adequately empathic environment results in a community of feeling with her infant akin to the affective resonance of Eliot and E.T.

If the infant's own empathic capacity is to unfold, however, the community of feeling must motivate the two partners to establish a common language that promotes more nuanced and reciprocally meaningful interactions. It falls to the mother to spur this development by conveying to the infant an accurate understanding of what the needy infant has affectively conveyed to her. Such communication not only reinforces the infant's efforts to signal the mother, but, over time, imparts to the infant a deeper comprehension of the matrix through which his (or her) needs are comprehended and addressed. By reinforcing her convergent response to the infant's affective cues with appropriate verbalization, the mother provides the infant with the anlagen of self-understanding; the infant learns to understand himself "auto-empathically" following the mother's verbal confirmations of her own empathic ministrations. The offshoot of this development is the emergence of the child's own empathic capacity in the period of representational thinking. We see early glimmerings of this capacity in the nursery when, for example, the toddler picks up a stuffed animal and verbally informs himself (or someone else), "Teddy hungry" or "Teddy bed."

The two-phase schema sketched above gives an overview of the process of empathic development in the infant. The contributors in this section—Virginia Demos, William S. Condon, Anni Bergman and Arnold Wilson, and Elsie Broussard—offer illuminating insights into the various constituents of this process. By drawing on a few selected aspects of their presentations, I hope to clarify my own view of how empathy gets started in the infant.

To begin with, from William Condon's wide-ranging consideration of the intertwining of communication and our relation to the world, we can tease out several points with particular pertinence for the development of empathy. In explicating the notion of "entrainment," he essentially deals with the psychobiological anlagen out of which the affective resonance between mother and infant emerges. A primary concern, we might say, is with the matrix of communion that subtends empathic development. In accord with the intriguing research that Condon reports, this communion matrix may be understood as a synchronized perceptual system. The mother's mental attitude toward her infant, her body tone, and the timbre of her voice collectively embody a coherent communicational system in which the infant, exquisitely in tune with the mother, is necessarily embedded. In Condon's depiction of the mother-infant dyad as an ecological system, so to speak, we see evidence of the infant's marvelous inborn capacity to reach out and engage the object with which he is in communion; we also see the substratum out of which mother and infant eventually undertake intense efforts to develop a shared language.

Anni Bergman and Arnold Wilson, drawing on Margaret Mahler's developmental framework, reinforce the importance of the mother-infant matrix out of which the infant's capacity for empathy emerges. What strikes me in their observations is the suggestion that the child's ability to empathize is a phase-specific achievement, occurring at about 18 months, when representational thinking and symbolic fantasy emerge. This is to argue that the ability to empathize emerges at the very time when the child acquires the cognitive equipment to apprehend both his own "separateness" and the autonomous psychic states of the other. On the other hand, this empathic capacity, while contingent on representational thinking, is developmentally rooted in prerepresentational pleasures experienced during the stage of symbiotic reciprocity, as Bergman and Wilson indicate. It is during this time that the infant learns selective cueing, based on apprehension of the "other's" preferences.

Virginia Demos, for her part, contributes to our understanding of the second phase of my proposed schema by exploring the relationship of "affect" to the development of a shared language between mother and infant. Drawing on the work of Silvan Tomkins, she elaborates the notion of "affective resonance" as a significant constituent of the empathic exchanges of mother and infant. Following Tomkins, Demos understands affect as a biologically innate response to external or internal excitation that has organizing properties with respect to the type of excitation being experienced. Affects, in this sense, amplify and transcribe the perception of stimuli into moods or states of being that are meaningful to the "stimulated" infant. As amplified simulations of stimuli, Demos observes, affects are infectious and tend to be transmitted from the infant experiencing the affect to the caregiver observing the infant; they thereby become communications to the infant's caregiver. This "affect linkage" is the basis of empathy in the adult; by implication, the empathic response engendered by this linkage promotes the development of the infant's own empathic responsiveness. In delineating the various components of infantile affective experience to which the adult may empathize and which are conjointly implicated in the infant's sense of being empathically understood, I believe that Demos makes an important contribution to the phenomenology of the empathic exchange.

Elsie Broussard provides a contrasting but equally telling vantage point for evaluating the quality of the shared language between mother and child. In contrast to Demos' focus on affect as the nexus from which empathic sensibilities radiate, Broussard examines empathy from the standpoint of the mother's self-esteem. Her longitudinal data suggest that, as the mother's feelings about herself vary, so do the child's feelings about himself. Mothers who have positive self-images and positive feelings about their mothering roles tend to behave empathically with their children. These children, in turn, tend to develop positive self-representations and the ability to empathize. The implications of Broussard's findings are twofold: (1) Only mothers with adequate levels of self-esteem provide empathic mothering, and (2) only empathic mothering provides the type of environment in which the child can eventually become empathic.

In sum, then, the four contributions to this section provide us with a series of complementary perspectives on two signposts for the emergence of empathy in the child: (1) establishing and maintaining affective resonance with the mother and (2) transmuting this resonance into a shared language. Drawing on varied observational orientations and research strategies, they expand our appreciation of the developmental preconditions for the moving outcome of the relationship between Eliot and E.T.—the experience of being loved and understood by the object of one's own love and understanding.

15 Empathy and Affect: Reflections on Infant Experience

VIRGINIA DEMOS, Ed.D.

Empathy is considered to be an essential element in both the therapeutic and the developmental processes, and is often invoked to explain at least in part, a successful outcome. Generally, empathy has been defined as the act of putting oneself in the other's place, or entering into the other's state of mind. It is a useful term for designating a psychological stance toward the other that can be distinguished from other stances, such as confronting, advising, correcting, or teaching the other. But as an explanatory concept, empathy is often used in a global way, shedding little light on the particular aspects of the other's experience that are "entered into," on the particular processes involved in assuming an empathic stance, or on the variety of exchanges and consequences that can occur. This paper attempts to articulate at least some of the complexity of this phenomenon by viewing empathy through the lens of affect. It is argued that affect provides a useful conceptual framework for understanding infant-mother exchanges and perhaps, by extension, for understanding adult-adult exchanges as well.

This discussion departs from other approaches to empathy in several ways. First, it deals primarily with infancy, with a focus on the infant's experience of the caregiver. Second, it stresses the notion that empathy always involves making inferences about the other's inner experience from observable behaviors (including verbal statements), and describes the observational data and methods used to make such inferences about parents and infants. Third, it attempts to delineate the specific components of the infant's inner experience and the behavioral manifestations of that experience which elicit parental responses, highlighting the role of affect in this process. Fourth, it defines empathy as a data-gathering process and distinguishes it from parental action toward the infant, which may or may not be informed by the empathic data-gathering process. Fifth, it discusses the phenomenon of affective resonance and its role in the empathic process by invoking Silvan Tomkins' theory of affect. And sixth, it describes six types of exchanges comprised of combinations of parental perceptions, understandings, and actions in the context of specific affective and intentional infant behaviors.

Method

The data for the formulations presented here are derived from videotaped records of home observations during the first two years of the infants' lives. Data from two studies are utilized. The first study involved 12 infant-mother pairs, videotaped monthly over a six-month period, with four infants starting at age six months, four at age 12 months, and four at age 18 months. The second study involved two infant-mother pairs, videotaped biweekly from the infant's second week of life to two years of life. The first study contained equal numbers of male and female infants at each age level; the second study involved two female infants. In both studies filmings occurred at all times of day and captured the ongoing household activities. Every effort was made to put the families at ease.

In analyzing the videotapes, we adopted an empathic approach seeking to view the world from the infant's vantage point. As I have already indicated, in any effort to empathize with another, one is always in the position of trying to make inferences about the other's inner state from a particular set of observable behaviors. Even in seemingly straightforward verbal exchanges between adults, where words convey conventional meaning, inferences about the other's psychological state are made on the basis of the particular choice of words, their timing, the voice quality, and intensity, its pitch, gaze behavior, facial expression, and prior knowledge of the other. In other words, empathy involves going beyond the perception of behaviors produced by the other, and attaching a meaning to these behaviors that is consonant with the meaning experienced by the other. The process of empathizing with an infant is essentially the same, even though during the first two years of life the communication between the infant and the caregiver is predominantly nonverbal.

Both the observer of the infant-mother pair and the mother tending the infant must depend for the most part on the vocalizations, facial expressions, and motor behaviors that the infant produces. They may also use information that is not communicated directly by the infant, such as how long it has been since the last feeding or last nap, knowledge of what infants in general are supposed to be like, or memories of what this particular infant was like on previous occasions. But to the extent that the observer or the mother pay attention to what the infant is doing, the nonverbal cues are paramount. These cues—a combination of facial expressions, vocalizations, and body movements—convey information primarily about the infant's affective state and the infant's plans or goals in relation to that state. Indeed, before the advent of language and other symbolic forms of representation, the infant's affective expressive behaviors are probably the only reliable and valid indication of the saliency of events for the infant; they thereby constitute the primary medium of communication and meaning in the infant-mother system. Thus, assuming an empathic stance toward the infant necessarily involves making inferences about the infant's affective experience by paying attention to a variety of behaviors. What are the components of that experience and how are they manifested in behavior?

Components of Affective Experience

As I have outlined elsewhere (Demos, 1984), there are three components in all affective experience: (1) the triggering event or stimulus, (2) the affective experience per se, and (3) the response of the organism to its own affective experience, which involves the recruitment in memory of past experiences, as well as motor responses and plans. In the article cited above, I highlighted the variety of ways in which learning can occur in relation to those components; here, however, I wish to stress how each component, although conceptualized as a facet of inner experience, can nevertheless be manifested in observable behaviors that may elicit responses from others. If, for example, a pair of scissors happens to be within the visual range of a young child, and that child is observed to look at, approach, and reach for the scissors, I would argue that these behaviors indicate *simultaneously* the child's affective state of interest, the focus of that interest on the scissors, and the child's response (approaching and reaching toward the object of interest with a plan to explore the object further by handling it). All three components of the child's experience can be inferred from behavior, and any one, or all, of these components may evoke a response from the caregiver. Because the three components occur simultaneously in the child's experience, whatever the caregiver's response, it will provide the child with information about all three components.

Having just argued that the three components of the child's affective experience can be perceived and understood by observing the child's behavior, it is now necessary to acknowledge some limitations in this observational method. The components differ in the degree to which their presence may be manifested in behavior, and in the degree of specificity of the behaviors.

The first component is perhaps the most difficult to obtain certainty about through observation alone. The triggering event or stimulus is often internal—a sensation of hunger, a sequence of thoughts, a memory, or an association. Even when an external event or stimulus occurs, one cannot assume that the meaning for the child is the same as the meaning for the adult caregiver or the observer. Thus, in a number of instances it is impossible to know with certainty which stimulus or aspect of an event triggered the child's expressive and planful behaviors.

The second component, the affective experience per se, is comprised of a set of correlated vascular, autonomic, vocal, and facial responses. The vocal and facial expressions of affect are readily observable, and there are specific patterns of facial movements or vocal expressions for each discrete affect. Tomkins (1962), in describing the innate patterns of facial expression for each affect, designates nine primary affects. Listed in their mild and intense form they are: interest–excitement, enjoyment–joy, surprise–startle, fear–terror, distress– anguish, anger–rage, shame–humiliation, cotempt, and disgust. Ekman (1972, 1977) and Izard (1971) demonstrate the presence of these expressions in a variety of cultures and argue for their universality. There is less extensive work describing vocal expressive patterns for each affect. These innate patterns are subject to a variety of learned modifications, yet they are still quite discernible in the first two years of life. Thus, both the degree of behavioral manifestation and the degree of specificity of the behaviors are very high for this component of affective experience. (The amplifying function of these expressive behaviors and their potential to evoke affect in the observer are discussed in a later section.)

The third component, namely the child's response to his (or her) own affective experience, refers to what one learns to do with one's emotions. This response is twofold, involving both the recruitment in memory of past experiences and the formation of current plans and behavioral responses. Only the latter, the behavioral responses, are visible to the observer, and these behaviors are theoretically limitless in their diversity. In contrast to the highly specific facial patterns associated with the experience of each discrete affect described above, there is no such specificity associated with the responses to affect. Within some broad, general limits, one can learn to do practically anything in response to feeling angry, or sad, or excited, or happy, etc. Thus, although this third component is often manifested in behavior, the meaning of the behavior may be idiosyncratic, thereby making it difficult for an observer or caregiver to interpret.

Taken separately, then, each component of the child's affective experience differs in the degree of behavioral manifestations and in the specificity of information conveyed to an observer. Nevertheless, when the information available to the observer from each component is combined, the probability of making an accurate inference about the infant's inner experience increases markedly.

One final aspect of the components' potential for eliciting responses from the caregiver should be mentioned. Any one component can monopolize the parent's or observer's attention, often at the expense of perception of the other components which are simultaneously present. In our example of the scissors lying within reach of the child, for instance, the stimulus may monopolize the adult's attention, so that the adult responds only to the danger represented by the scissors, and ignores the affective state of interest evoked in the child, as well as the related exploratory behaviors that have been activated. Or, in terms of the affective state per se, the expressive vocalizations associated with distress may monopolize the parent's attention and activate attempts to stop the child's crying, without attention to the event or stimulus that triggered the crying, or to coping behaviors the child may be engaged in. In the same way, the behavioral responses to affect—for example, hitting, throwing, or biting in response to anger—may monopolize the parent's attention and mobilize efforts to stop the behavior, without direct attention to the triggering event or stimulus, or to the affective state per se. To anticipate my discussion somewhat, in any parent-child transaction, the parent, in an effort to empathize with the child, may focus on only one, or on two, or on all three components of the child's experience. Each of these possibilities will, I believe, produce a distinctly different experience for the child.

Parental Response as Distinct from Empathy

So far I have emphasized that empathy necessarily involves making inferences about the other's inner experience and have argued for the centrality of affect in this process, which requires one to pay attention to a variety of behaviors produced by the other and to understand their meaning in terms of all three components of the other's affective experience. In other words, empathy is essentially a method of gathering data about the other. This formulation leaves open the question of what someone then chooses to do with the information gathered through an empathic process. It assumes that the data-gathering process and the behavioral responses directed to the other are separate aspects of any transactional exchange, and that they can vary independently. A mother, for example, may perceive her child's affective state correctly, and understand its meaning for the child, yet she may act so as to invalidate the experience or block the child's plans and goals. A variety of other factors may come into play and influence the parent's response, such as ideological or familial beliefs about how children should feel or behave, or how they should be treated; temporary lapses in energy level or patience; competing affects or concerns that override the child's state or goals, etc. The empathic data-gathering process is only one among several factors that may determine a parental response, and even when it is an active factor, it may not be the dominant one (Schwaber, 1981).

If we now return to our view of the world from the child's vantage point, it becomes clear that the child is in the same situation that the adult is in—namely, the child can only get information about the parent's intentions and feelings by making inferences based on the parent's behaviors. In other words, it is only through the parent's responses to the child that the child experiences the result of the parent's empathic or nonempathic data gathering. However necessary, empathic data gathering is not sufficient to guarantee that the child will feel accepted and understood. The information gathered in this mode must also infuse the parent's responses to the child. What would characterize such responses?

In general, it might be said that the human organism strives to maximize opportunities for positive experience and to minimize opportunities for negative ones. We assume that children are continually trying to learn how to enhance or sustain their positive experiences and how to master or cope with their negative ones. Parental responses shaped by the empathic process would attempt to foster these goals. They would extend the empathic data-gathering process by communicating the message: "I know what you are experiencing; it's all right, and I'm here to help." Various terms in the literature capture this quality of responding, such as Kohut's (1971) concept of mirroring, and Stern's (1983) description of "mental state sharing." These terms are deceptively appealing, for it is easy to imagine mirroring or sharing positive experiences. But it is harder to imagine how one can constructively share or mirror negative experiences, since merely to respond to anger with anger or to distress with distress is rarely helpful. An additional assumption is needed. The caregiver must share and perhaps even absorb the child's experience while still maintaining an independent motivational stance. One might, for example, acknowledge the child's distress or anger, and offer comfort or help in coping; or join in the child's fun and excitement without intruding or dominating the play. Empathically determined responses therefore seem to have a dual quality—reflecting both where the child is at the moment (e.g., crying), and where the child would like to be in the future (e.g., mastering the situation). This formulation stresses the asymmetry of infant-adult transactions, in which the adult possesses far more capabilities than the infant for elaborating, attenuating, exaggerating, suppressing, coping with, or mastering an affective experience. It requires that the adult not only join the child by producing a response that is somewhat similar in intensity and duration to the child's response, but also lead the child on to the next step by helping the child to fashion a response to his affective experience.

To talk about sharing and absorbing the other's experience raises questions about affective resonance, by which I mean the tendency to experience the same affect that is being experienced by the other. What role does this phenomenon play in empathic data gathering and in subsequent responses? And even more basically: How do we understand the power of affect to evoke similar affect in a participant observer?

Affective Resonance

Silvan Tomkins' (1962, 1963, 1980) theory of affect is central to an understanding of the contagious quality of affect. Tomkins argues that there are a limited number of discrete affects, each with innately patterned responses and innate activators. A particular affect is activated by a variant of a general characteristic of neural stimulation, namely its density, where "density" is defined as the number of neural firings per unit time. There are three classes of variants: stimulation increases, stimulation levels, and stimulation decreases. If, for example, internal or external sources of neural firing suddenly increase, the organism will startle, become afraid, or become interested, depending on the suddenness of the increase. If sources of neural firing reach and maintain a high, nonoptimal level of stimulation, the organism will experience anger or distress, depending on the level of stimulation. And if the sources of neural firing suddenly decrease, the organism will laugh or smile with enjoyment, depending on the suddenness of the decrease. Shame is activated when positive affect (e.g., interest) is interrupted and attenuated, without being completely reduced.

The discrete affects evoked in this way act as amplifiers. They generate an analog of the stimulus' gradient and intensity by means of correlated sets of facial-muscle, blood-flow, visceral, respiratory, vocal, and skeletal response. A gun shot, for example, will evoke a startle response—a sudden, intense jerk of the body. The suddenness and intensity of the jerk are an amplified analog of the suddenness and loudness of the gun shot. That is, each affect amplifies in an analogic way the gradient or level and the intensity of its stimulus; it also imprints the immediate behavioral response with the analog. As Tomkins explains: "An excited response is accelerating in speed whether in walking or talking. An enjoyable response is decelerating in speed and relaxed as a motor or perceptual savouring response" (1981, p. 322). The biological importance of this amplification through affect is to make the organism care about quite different kinds of events in different ways. In Tomkins' words: "affect either makes good things better or bad things worse by conjointly simulating its activator in its profile of neural firing and by adding a special analogic quality that is intensely rewarding or punishing" (1980, p. 148).

By extending this model of affect, it is possible to understand affective resonance. If an affective expression is an amplified simulation of the original stimulus, then it will tend to evoke more of the same affect in a positive feedback loop, both within the person experiencing the affect and in the observer. For example, the infant's expressive pattern of distress (including facial expression, vocal cry, and bodily movements) is evoked by a nonoptimal level of stimulation; in turn it produces through amplification a nonoptimal level of stimulation that tends to evoke more distress both in the infant and in the observer. The degree of distress evoked in the observer depends on a number of factors, such as other competing affects, the context and meaning for the observer of the infant's distress, the degree of responsibility felt by the observer for doing something about the infant's distress, and the degree of defensiveness of the observer with regard to distress. Wiesenfeld, Malatesta, and DeLoach (1981) report that mothers show more automatic responsivity to their own infants' distress cries than fathers do, and more than they do to an unfamiliar infant's distress cry. Hence there is no simple, direct relationship between the intensity and kind of affect expressed by the infant and the intensity and kind of affect evoked in the observer. Nevertheless, because of the amplifying function of affect, and the relatively higher intensity and density of affect expressed by infants, it is likely that a caregiver who is engaged with the infant will experience a variant of the affect expressed by the infant.

Now let us return to the role of affective resonance in empathizing with an infant. It would seem to play a large role. When affective resonance does occur—for instance, when the infant's distress evokes distress in the caregiver—then the caregiver's ability to understand the infant's experience from the infant's point of view, and to maintain an independent motivational stance, will depend on the caregiver's response to his (or her) own affective experience at that particular moment. This response may vary in characterological ways, according to defense mechanisms or learned affective sequences (such as distress followed by anger, or excitement followed by shane). It may vary from situation to situation; for instance, what is acceptable in private may not be acceptable in public, or in front of particular people. It may vary from affect to affect, in that distress may be acceptable, but not anger, or vice versa. It may vary from moment to moment, or day to day, depending on mood, fatigue level, cumulative factors, or other competing concerns. The experience of affective resonance thus activates the caregiver's unique personal history of learning relevant to the affect. These responses evoked within the caregiver complicate the task of perceiving and understanding the infant's experience from the infant's point of view, and maintaining an independent motivational stance.

It should be clear that I am not arguing that affective resonance is a necessary element in empathy, only a prominent one. There are many situations in which the caregiver is able to anticipate the infant's needs before the infant has expressed distress or discomfort, because of their shared history together. In such cases the infant's behaviors have probably evoked in the caregiver memories of similar situations in the past that eventually led to distress. In the present situation, then, the caregiver can act to avert or prevent a problem without distress itself being evoked in either the infant or in the caregiver.

Types of Infant-Caregiver Exchanges

If we combine our model of the components of affective experience with the various aspects of an empathic data-gathering process and the subsequent response, a range of possible exchanges between the infant and the caregiver emerges. Stated in the most general terms, a mother can perceive none, some, or all three components of the infant's experience; she can understand the meaning of none, some, or all three components of the infant's experience; she can decide to respond to none, some, or all three components; and her response can take a variety of forms. Again, my assumption is that each of these possibilities represents a different kind of experience for the child.

I have selected six types of exchanges out of the range of possibilities. Briefly, the six types are: (1) The caregiver accurately perceives and understands the three components of the child's experience and acts so that the child's positive experiences are prolonged and enhanced, and the child's negative experiences are reduced or brought to an end. (2) The caregiver accurately perceives and understands the three components of the child's negative experiences and acts so that the child is helped to endure them and master them. (3) The caregiver accurately perceives and understands the three components of the child's positive experiences but acts so that the child experiences a reduction in positive affect. (4) the caregiver accurately perceives and understands the three components of the child's negative experience but acts so that the child experiences an increase in negative affect. (This may or may not be done in a hostile manner.) (5) The caregiver misperceives or misunderstands all or some of the three components of the child's experiences and acts according to this misperception or misunderstanding. And (6) the caregiver appears not to perceive the child and acts as if the child were not present.

This ordering might be seen as beginning with an ideal type of exchange and ending with an absence of an exchange. Yet such a view is only partially correct. I would not, for example, argue that type 2 is any less ideal than type 1. Nor is it clear that type 4 is experienced *by the child* as more empathic than type 5. Furthermore, it should not be assumed that these six types are pure and inviolate. A caregiver may begin by responding in a type 1 or type 2 manner and then become derailed by a shift in the child's affective state, or by a particular behavior produced by the child, and end up responding in a type 4 or 5 manner. Or a caregiver can begin with a type 4 or 5 response, and because of the child's reaction, shift into a type 1 or 2 response. In other words, these types of exchanges do not represent types of caregivers, but rather types of perceptions, inferences, and responses that any caregiver may employ. Moreover, although my primary focus is on the child, and the child's experience of these exchanges, it is not always possible to determine from observation the effect on the child of the different types of exchanges.

A final note of caution is needed: in the following discussion, although I will cite single instances for illustrative purposes, I do not assume that the empathic quality of any single exchange has a determining impact on the child. Nevertheless, each type of exchange does produce a distinctive type of experience for the child, and if such experiences become a chronic characteristic of the infant-mother system, then they will begin to shape the child's developing sense of self. (See Demos [1984] for a discussion of the relationship between affect and the maintenance of self-esteem.)

Type 1

In the ideal paradigm the mother correctly perceives and understands the stimulus, the infant's affective state, and the intention or plan represented in the infant's behaviors; she then responds in a way that communicates her empathy—facilitating or prolonging the infant's positive states of interest and enjoyment, or trying to reduce and end the infant's negative states of distress, fear, shame, or anger by comforting the infant or removing the offending stimulus. To continue with the earlier example of the interested child who is reaching toward a pair of scissors: in this ideal type of exchange the mother might distract the child from the scissors by presenting another, safer object that evokes the child's interest. She would thereby prevent possible injury, but at the same time facilitate a continuation or prolongation of the child's state of interest and the child's plan to explore an object of interest. For the child, there is the chance to discover that more than one object can be interesting, and to experience having both his state of interest and his plan to explore understood, accepted, and facilitated. Or, to take the classic example of the hungry infant experiencing distress, a mother acting in accordance with our paradigm would correctly perceive and understand the infant's state of distress and its cause, and would soothe and feed the infant. In terms of the infant's experience, a negative state of distress and hunger and the helplessness related to it have been perceived and brought to an end by the mother.

Type 2

A variant of type 1 occurs when the mother correctly perceives and understands the infant's negative affective state and the infant's intent, but her response does not prevent or end the negative experience. This may occur in several ways. First of all, there are situations in the infant's life that the mother knows are negatively experienced by the infant, but they are unavoidable—for example, an inoculation, a fever, or taking medicine. In such situations, the mother may act to help the infant endure the negative experience, and her efforts may succeed in lowering the intensity of the negative affect, without shortening its duration or removing its cause. On such occasions the infant may experience that pain or discomfort amplified by distress and/or anger is unpleasant but can be tolerated and managed without losing control, and that this negative experience can be shared and understood by an accepting and supportive other. Even when the mother cannot reduce the intensity of a particular negative experience, if, on future occasions, she continues to be there, to remain calm, and to offer support and comfort, the child may, over time, experience her empathy.

In one videotape, for example, a mother is seen bathing her nine-day-old daughter. The infant cries in an intense, angry way throughout the bath. The mother seems to perceive and understand the infant's experience correctly, for she tries to comfort her daughter with her soothing voice and gentle handling. The infant, however, stops crying only when the mother begins to dress her at the end of the bath. In this case, the intensity of the crying is a product of the particular infant's temperament (she characteristically showed high-intensity responses) and of the massive increases in stimulation resulting from being naked and thereby released from the more constant stimulation of clothing (a common source of distress in early infancy, according to Wolff [1969]). Thus, even though the mother remains calm and soothing throughout the infant's state of distress and anger, her actions are not effective in significantly reducing the density of negative affect experienced by her daughter. On this occasion, the child could not experience her mother's empathy. The immaturity of a nine-day-old infant's nervous system does not allow her to manage such an increase in stimulation, nor can she yet draw on her memory of past experiences of having been comforted or bathed that would enable her, with her mother's help, to modulate the intensity of her distress and anger. On subsequent occasions, however, the mother is able to remain calm and soothing, and as the infant's nervous system matures, and nakedness no longer results in such a massive increase in stimulation, baths do become intensely pleasurable for this child.

Another situation that is very likely to evoke unavoidable negative affect occurs when children attempt to master a task at the limits of their capabilities. At such times children tend to alternate between moments of interest and enjoyment, with the goal to master the task, and moments of distress, anger, and shame, with a wish to give up. There is a fine line between challenge and defeat. In our study, we observed that mothers who took into account all three components of the child's experience—the task, the child's alternating affects, and the related alternating goals—might do any or all of the following things. They might actively structure or redefine the task so that the child experienced just the right amount of difficulty. Or they might offer understanding during moments of distress and anger, and encouragement to continue. Or they might offer just enough help in performing the task for the child to succeed and still feel a sense of mastery.

A particularly striking example of this alternating pattern of motivation in the face of a challenge and the mother's steady support occurred with a ten-month-old infant and his mother. They were involved in a game in which he would throw his blanket over the side of the playpen, she would throw it back in or cover both their heads with it, and he would try to pull it off or pull it over his head. In one four-minute sequence, the child alternated at least 10 times between moments of intense joy and excitement when he succeeded, moments of interest as he concentrated, and moments of distress and anger when he became tangled in the blanket or could not get the blanket to go where he wanted. Over this time period, there was a gradual attenuation of the positive moments, and an increase in the intensity and duration of the negative ones. His mother shared in his enjoyment and excitement, remained intensely involved throughout, and as his distress and anger peaked, she increased her efforts to help him with the blanket and offered soothing words-"What's the matter, won't it do what you want it to?" This child's capacity to rally and to bounce back each time, after repeated experiences of distress and anger, was impressive. We assume that he, and in general any child that experiences similar exchanges, is learning that the task at hand is doable, and that distress and anger do not signal the end of the exchange or the need to give up. These states are tolerable, manageable—with renewed effort and persistence, one can master the task, and once again experience enjoyment and excitement. If such exchanges occur frequently in a child's life, a sequence of positive affect–negative affective–positive affect may become established and contribute to a general feeling of optimism and confidence in relation to approaching new tasks.

Another common situation that is likely to evoke unavoidable negative affect, particularly in the second year of life, involves the need to set limits on the child's activities, or to deny gratification of a particular wish. Often limits can be set without evoking negative affect in the child; indeed, in our study in many instances mothers were able to avoid direct confrontations with their children while still setting limits. Nevertheless, there are inevitably situations, even in the best-run households, when children force the issue, or manage to get hold of something that is either dangerous (as in the scissors example) or expensive and breakable (a stereo set, calculator, etc.). Or they express a desire for something they cannot have, such as one more cookie, a second ice cream cone, a sibling's favorite toy, or some object advertised on TV.

Such situations often entail a complex motivational experience for the child: there is the wish to please the mother as well as the wish to possess the object or engage in the activity. The ability to accept limits and to endure the disappointment derives partly from the strength of the child's positive bond to the mother and the belief that going along with mother eventually leads to something good. It helps if the mother, through the empathic data-gathering process, can appreciate the complexity of the child's situtation, and can act so as to legitimize the child's wish for the desirable object or activity, while acknowledging and sharing the child's disappointment. The child can then experience that wishing for things is all right but that not all wishes can be gratified, that disappointment can be managed and shared, and that pleasing mother can provide a different kind of gratification.

Type 3

In this type of exchange, the caregiver's perception and understanding of the three components of the child's positive experiences are accurate and therefore empathic, but the caregiver does not act to enhance or prolong these positive experiences, and thus fails to support the child's goals. Here, for the first time, the distinction between the empathic data-gathering process and parental actions becomes crucial. Let us return to our initial example of the young child looking at, approaching, and reaching for the scissors, which simultaneously indicates a state of interest focused on the scissors, the response of approaching and reaching, and the plan to explore further. A caregiver who merely removes the scissors or yells "no" has certainly perceived the child's affect and behavior, and understood the child's intentions correctly; the caregiver has acted to prevent injury as a possible consequence of the child's plan. Yet this response falls short of supporting the child's goals, because it does not go beyond concern for the child's safety to an enhancement and prolongation of the child's interest in exploring, by providing other, more appropriate objects for the child.

If the caregiver responds only with a prohibition, and offers no substitute object or activity, the message to the young child is "Stop!" But stop what? Stop being interested? Stop exploring new objects? Stop exploring scissors? The caregiver may intend to stop only the latter behavior, but the child is essentially stopped in all three components of the experience. Faced with chronic prohibition, children may learn to inhibit their interests and exploratory behaviors in a general way.

This type of exchange may also occur when the child attempts to engage the parent in play. Children use a variety of techniques to involve parents, such as bringing them objects, pulling at their legs or arms, flopping in their laps, asking them questions, or smiling. As I have reported elsewhere (Demos, 1982), even a perfunctory response from the parent is sometimes sufficient to sustain the child's interest or playfulness. But ignoring the child at such times, or reacting with irritation or prohibitions, tends to dampen or inhibit the child's capacity to sustain the interest and enjoyment on his own. Once again, there is an empathic perception and understanding of the child's positive affective state and playful intentions, but a refusal to support the child's goal by enhancing or prolonging the positive experience and joining with the child.

Undoubtedly there are a variety of reasons for the parent's behavior here—reasons ranging from temporary lapses due to fatigue or a preoccupation with other concerns, to more characterological factors. In the latter case, the parent might believe that child's play is silly; or feel embarrassed at playing on a child's level; or assume that as long as children do not cry or fuss and sound contented, a grownup need not get involved; or show an inability to value personal interests and enjoyments and the importance of sharing them.

Each of these parental stances adds its own subtle nuance to the encounter. But, to the child, all communicate the same thing—that the child's joy and interest–excitement and playful intentions have been perceived and understood, yet have not been accepted and supported. The lack of a positive response to expressions of interest–excitement and enjoyment may have all or some of the following meanings to the child: I am not interesting and enjoyable; it is not worthwhile to be interested and joyful; it is not worthwhile to be interested and joyful about this particular thing; I shouldn't bother trying to engage mommy or daddy in my interests and joys. Any one of these meanings may partially attenuate the child's positive affect and create a temporary barrier to further communication with the parent. According to Tomkin's theory of affect, such a situation will evoke shame in the child. Moreover, depending on the child's response to shame, other negative affects, such as distress or anger, are likely to be added to the sequence.

This same sequence—of a child's expressions of interest, excitement, and joy ending in shame, distress, and anger—can occur even when the adult initially responds positively and enters into the child's play. For inevitably the adult "wears out" before the child does. If the adult ends the play too abruptly or with negative and irritated comments, such as "Stop it now!" "You're getting too silly," or "I can't stand the noise any longer," the child is likely to experience shame.

The observation that grownups tire more quickly than young children of the playful antics and roughhousing typical of early childhood is a common one. And it is generally assumed that the repetitiveness of these games is a large factor in the adult's loss of interest. Our observations suggest that the high intensity of the child's excitement and joy is another factor. There is nothing inherently intolerable about intense positive affect; indeed, many children act as if they could go on forever, asking for more and more. Nevertheless, parents often appear to be uncomfortable with such prolonged intensity and try to modulate or tone down the child's exuberance. Although this can be done gently, and apologetically, it should be noted that the need for modulation is coming from the parent and the parent's own capacity to tolerate the combination of repetitiveness and intense positive affect. At such times the child does not appear to experience shame, or lack of support, but rather learns how and when to modulate his exuberance. This is an example of the subtle shaping of innate affective responses to fit a familial, social, or cultural pattern of expression that is in part determined by a mismatch between adult and child in the capacity to tolerate high-intensity repetitions.

Another variant of this third type of exchange relates to the setting of limits described earlier. Although the parent does not support the child's goal in its entirety, there is still the opportunity to enhance the positive experience of wishing for and dreaming of things just out of reach by acknowledging and accepting the legitimacy of the child's wish and the activity of wishing. When the parent fails to do this, the exchange may qualify as an example of a parent accurately perceiving and understanding the child's positive experience but acting so as not to enhance or prolong it. We observed several varieties of this type of exchange. A parent might delegitimize the wish by trying to talk the child out of it ("You already have a teddy bear"), by devaluing the object ("That's too big for you"), by ignoring the wish and distracting the child or changing the subject ("It's time for Sesame Street!"), or by simply saying "No, you can't have that," without a qualifying comment such as, "I wish you could too," or "Wouldn't it be nice if . . ." Except in the latter case, the parent's goal often seemed to be to avoid having to disappoint the child directly. But what does the child experience? Not only is the wish not gratified, but the activity of wishing and the positive affects and fantasies associated with it are not shared, accepted, and valued. For the very young child, the frustration of the wish may be the predominant experience, but as the child gets older, into the last half of the second year, the lack of support for the activity of wishing will be experienced, and may leave the child feeling vaguely discontented without understanding why.

All the examples of this type of exchange involved the experience of motivated states of interest–excitement and enjoyment–joy, with the elaboration of plans and fantasies fueled by such positive affect states. Although these states were perceived and understood by parents, they were not enhanced by them, and were sometimes discouraged and curtailed. Presenting such exchanges as a separate type lays stress on the importance of positive affect in its own right, requiring nurturance and support, as opposed to the implicit assumption in much psychiatric writing that in the absence of negative affect, positive affect will flourish unaided. One should also note that a common source of shame in childhood is the sudden attenuation of positive affect.

Type 4

In this type of exchange the caregiver again accurately perceives and understands the three components of the child's experience, but acts in a way that increases the negative aspect of the experience. This may or may not be done with a hostile intent. Earlier, in describing the second type of exchange, I pointed to several situations involving pain, mastery of a difficult task, or disappointment, where the experience of negative affect was unavoidable and the parent helped the child to tolerate and endure the experience. Type 4 differs in that in this case the parent is unable to help the child and instead heightens the intensity of the negative affect.

A type 4 exchange may arise if a mother who is affectively resonating with her child becomes distressed by her child's distress. She may then become unduly anxious, unable to remain sufficiently calm to offer any comfort or help to the child. In the early months of infancy, for instance, when the infant seems inconsolable for no apparent reason, the parents may become tense and add their own distress and anxiety to that of the infant, thus intensifying the negative experience. Such episodes may end with the exhuasted infant falling sleep, or with the intervention of a more neutral, calm third party, such as a grandparent or family friend. A similar negative spiral may occur when a child becomes seriously ill, suddenly runs a high fever, or falls out of the crib. At such times the mother's usual composure may be contaminated by a sudden increase in anxiety, which interferes with her ability to comfort and calm her child. It is assumed that the caregiver accurately perceives and understands all three components of the child's experience at such times, but that her ability to maintain an independent motivational stance is disrupted by the intensity of her own affective-cognitive response to the situation, which may entail anxiety about her competence as a mother, anxiety about the infant's survival, or anger toward the infant for evoking distress. Her response is then dominated by her own intense reactions, rather than by the empathic data-gathering process.

A type 4 exchange may also occur when the child is trying to master a difficult task. A typical sequence observed in our study involved an initial supportive exchange between the mother and the infant until, during one of the alternating periods of discouragement or frustration, the infant "acted out" the negative feelings—throwing a puzzle piece on the floor, stamping his feet, or beginning to cry. At this point the mother's response changed. Whereas at first her responses were dominated by the empathic data-gathering process and facilitated and supported the child's goals, now her responses became dominated by other factors, such as child-rearing beliefs about "good" and "bad" behaviors, anger at the child, or anxiety about the child's or her own failure. Her efforts were then directed exclusively toward controlling the child's "bad" behavior. Negative sanctions were often used, such as scolding, shaming, or withdrawing her participation and leaving the child to fend for himself. The mother's focus might be on the affect itself (e.g., crying or pouting) or on the related behaviors (e.g., the throwing or kicking), or both. For the child, the result was the same: what started as a challenging task ended in failure. The task remained undoable and the strategies and skills needed to master it remained unlearned. Moreover, it was the expression of negative feelings that signaled the end of the task, evoking more negative feelings (e.g., intensified distress, anger, and shame). If these feelings are magnified over a number of similar situations, the child may come to feel isolated and incompetent, unable to trust his ability to manage negative affect.

Another variant of this type of exchange may occur when the caregiver must set limits and disappoint the child. Once again, the parent may begin by accurately perceiving and understanding all three components of the child's experience, including the wish, the disappointment, and the effort to cope with the disappointment. But if child expresses distress or anger over the disappointment, the caregiver's response may then be dominated by an effort to "toughen up" the child (teaching the child to cope by suppressing feelings) or by a demand for unquestioning obedience. These goals often involve berating or shaming the child for any sign of weakness or softness, or punishing the child for failing to comply immediately. For the child, the distress and anger evoked by the disappointment of a wish are compounded and intensified by the shame, distress, and anger evoked by the scolding or punishment, which the child must also suppress. The child's larger goal of wanting to please the parent is achieved through suppression rather than mastery, thus leaving the child vulnerable to intrusions of unmanageable negative affect.

Parental anger or overt hostility may be added to any of the exchanges just described. When this happens, particularly when the parental anger occurs suddenly, the child is likely to experience fear as well as the other intensified negative affects. Fear will contribute its own toxic quality to the experience and increases the child's efforts to cope with the situation. In any case, for the child, the type 4 exchanges result in an experience of a positive–negative–negative affective sequence, in which the initial negative experience is intensified by the parental response. In contrast to the positive–negative–positive affective sequence discussed earlier, the effect of this intensified negative sequence is to leave the child feeling either defeated and overwhelmed, or very angry and vengeful. If such experiences are repeated often, magnified over time and in multiple contexts, the child may become increasingly compliant and pessimistic about mastering a variety of situations, thus leading to a constriction of initiative. Or the child may become increasingly defiant, adopting a reactive or oppositional stance that also severely restricts the child's initiative.

Type 5

In this type of exchange the caregiver misperceives or misunderstands all or some of the three components of the child's experience, and acts according to this misperception or midunderstanding. There are a number of possible combinations and permutations, but I shall focus on only a few that occurred with some frequency in our sample. Perhaps the most common example of this type of exchange arose when the child was engaged in play with toys designed for a particular kind of activity—stacking toys, pull toys, building blocks, balls, etc. Almost all children derive pleasure from using these toys in nonstandard ways, unanticipated by toy designers and parents alike. The child's goal at such times seems to be to explore the object, to do something interesting with it, or to practice his repertoire of skills on it without concern for proper usage. One kind of misunderstanding occurs when a parent becomes focused on doing the task properly (e.g., stacking the rings in the right order) and essentially discounts the child's goal or misjudges the child's capabilities. The parent may then begin to instruct the child in a didactic manner, ask for a level of performance beyond the child's comprehension and skill, or try to take over the activity when the child "makes a mistake" or "fumbles" in some way.

One way in which this can affect the child was illustrated by a mother and her 15-month-old daughter. Mother and daughter were outside in their yard, with the child playing in the sandbox and the mother nearby in a chair. A neighbor boy had just thrown a ball to the girl in the sandbox. She picked up the ball and "threw" it back. As often happens at this age, the ball dropped about two inches in front of her. Nevertheless, she was delighted with her efforts, smiled broadly at the boy, and clapped her hands. The mother said, "You can't clap yet; the ball didn't go out of the sandbox. Try again." The girl looked a little puzzled, but did try again, with much the same result and the same excitement and joy. The mother again insisted that the girl had not achieved "her" goal. By the third and fourth repetitions of this sequence, the child's expression had become sober; she was no longer clapping. Indeed, she soon lost all interest in throwing the ball and turned to other objects in the sandbox. From the child's point of view, joining the game of catch and "throwing" the ball back to the boy probably meant simply moving her arm and letting go of the ball, which was as close as she could come to imitating the boy's action. Her joyful, excited response clearly indicated that, by her lights, she had succeeded. The mother's refusal to accept her goal (i.e., to see her efforts as an achievement) and to share in her excitement and joy, instead holding out for a better throw, left the child feeling perplexed and unsupported. Not understanding how she had failed or how to succeed and please her mother, she gave up the task.

A similar type of exchange may occur when the child is involved in relatively unfocused play with a toy. At such times, the child may have no particular goal in mind, or may still be developing an idea about what to do with the toy. A parent, uncomfortable with the child's apparent lack of a goal, may step in prematurely with suggestions or actions, before the child has had sufficient time to mobilize his own initiative. The child then often becomes a passive observer, or wanders off to do something else. For the child, the parent has taken over the process of developing a goal or plan; thus, the child's interest is minimally engaged. This type of exchange should be clearly distinguished from an exchange in which the parent follows the child's lead and expands and enriches the child's play by demonstrating or suggesting new possibilities. The crucial difference is that in the latter case the initiative remains with the child, whereas in a type 5 exchange the parent intervenes prematurely, before the child's initiative has had an opportunity to take shape.

Another relatively frequent misunderstanding involved a variety of activities commonly engaged in by infants, such as banging, throwing, mouthing, biting, pulling, picking up, and dropping. Unless performed when the child is angry, these activities are almost always in the service of exploration and play, and they are fueled by interest and enjoyment. Nevertheless, they may result in damage, loud noise, or irritating messes. A parent may fail to perceive the child's affective state of interest and the plans related to it, and instead focus exclusively on the consequences or potential consequences of the child's behavior. From this perspective, the parent may see such behaviors as a hostile, destructive act by the child. This interpretation often leads to parental efforts to punish, scold, or restrict the child's activities. Thus, what began for the child as a relatively benign, interesting activity, ends in a negative exchange with the caregiver. Because the child may not understand what specifically has provoked the parent's response—whether it was the affective state of interest; the banging, pulling, throwing; or the result of these actions—the consequences of this type of misunderstanding may be varied. The child may reproduce the action in an effort to sort out cause-and-effect relationships. If I do this again, will I get the same rise out of mother? Or the child may gradually learn to curtail exploration and initiative because they tend to lead to negative exchanges. Or the child may begin to view himself as hostile and destructive and therefore dangerous.

In another kind of misreading, the parent misinterprets the child's affective state. For example, very young infants tend to gaze with intense interest for minutes at a time at the mother's face. One of the mothers in our sample consistently interpreted this gaze as a sign that her infant was bored. She would turn her own face away and quickly put a toy within the infant's visual range. The infant then focused on the toy, but eventually searched again for the mother's face, which for infants of one or two months of age is a far more interesting object. By the third month this infant no longer seemed to expect sustained mutual gazing from her mother, for although the infant would initiate gazing, she would also quickly look away again. This particular pair never developed the elaborate face-to-face play that is so characteristic of infant-mother interactions during the infant's second trimester of life. Such play, however, did develop between this infant and her father, and to some extent with her sibling as well. Thus, the pattern of looking away after a brief exchange was characteristic of this infant only when she interacted with her mother. This is an example of the young infant's impressive ability to discriminate between people, and to respond differentially to them. One of the things she seems to have learned from her mother's misinterpretation of her intense gazing is that mother does not like to engage in face-to-face play, but father and brother do.

Type 6

In the last type of exchange to be discussed, the caregiver does not seem to notice or respond to the child, although the child is present in the room and may be seeking a response. There are probably degrees of not noticing, with the most extreme case being a parent who looks right through a child, or walks right by, as if the child did not exist. We did not observe this extreme. In our study the most common example occurred when the mother was conversing with visitors and perhaps reached down in an absent-minded way to pat her child's head, but neither looked at nor addressed the child during a particular segment of time. It seems that during this time the caregiver does not perceive, and thus cannot understand or respond to, the three components of the child's experience. Presumably the mother has not completely tuned out the child, but has merely altered her threshold of awareness. An intense scream or cry from the child would enter her awareness and redirect her attention, whereas a low-intensity whine or ordinary contented sounds would not. For the child, however, emitting a particular set of actions and vocalizations does not result in the usual response from the mother.

The child's experience of this event, at any given moment, depends on the urgency of the child's wish, the child's expectations of the mother's responsiveness derived from their shared history, the attractiveness of alternative activities that might occupy the child until mother becomes available again, etc. The children we observed showed a variety of responses. Some children escalated their demands, becoming increasingly upset, until the mother finally responded; others, equally persistent, whined and clung to the mother, but without escalating this, until the mother responded. In both cases the children focused exclusively on their mothers; they were unable to focus on anything else during the period of her unavailability. It seemed that, for these children, the experience was overwhelming and monopolistic in the sense that it robbed them of their usual flexibility and prevented them from drawing on their repertoire of coping strategies.

Other infants, at such times, would fuss for a second or two, wait, look at mother, go back to whatever they were doing briefly, and then repeat the whole sequence two or three times until mother responded. In these cases it looked as if the child fully expected the mother to respond, even if she had to be reminded a couple of times. Either because of the strength of this expectation or because of the moderate level of their needs, these children were able to wait and to maintain a dual focus, with one eye on their own activities and the other eye on mother.

Still other children seemed to be able to make themselves a part of the situation. Although no one was interacting with them or responding to them, they would respond to the general affective quality of the exchanges in the room. They might, for example, smile and vocalize as others talked and laughed around them. Or, if the mother was describing something the child had done, the child might begin to perform the activity the mother was describing, or listen intently. One might say that these children were able to make the most of a meager situation; they derived some nutrient from the general atmosphere, but at the same time they seemed to accept their role as observers. That experience differs from participating in an interaction in which another person responds contingently to one's behaviors, in which a mutuality is established and a "conversation" develops. If a child were chronically placed in the role of observer rather than participant, it seems possible that the child would gradually come to believe that his own emotions, plans, and ideas counted for very little.

The Infant as an Accurate Observer

Before concluding, we need to consider briefly the infant's ability to accurately perceive and understand the adult's behavior. Earlier I stated that the infant is in essentially the same situation as the adult, in that the infant has to make inferences about the adult's feelings and intentions from the adult's behaviors. How good are infants at interpreting adult behavior? It is my impression that this ability is quite variable within each infant.

Generally speaking, if infants are in a playful, positive state—well-rested, well-fed, and motivated by interest and enjoyment—then they do not seem to notice the mother's "mistakes," such as bad timing, inattentiveness, rough handling, or impatience. Indeed, at such times it seems as if the mother's total gestalt is more important as a sustaining source than any particular response or behavior she may produce. (I am assuming, of course, that these off-moments occur in the context of a generally gratifying infant-mother relationship.) It is striking, also, how even overtly hostile actions by siblings, such as a hard push or throwing a ball too hard, are interpreted by the good-natured infant as vigorous, exciting play. The infant seems either not to perceive or to ignore what, to the observer, looks like a clearly hostile act by the sibling.

If, however, infants are fussy, tired, hungry, and generally irritable, then they seem to become much more discerning and demanding partners, containing their irritation only if the mother is well tuned to their state. At such times even little "mistakes" are clearly perceived by the infant, and responded to with protest behaviors.

It is worth noting that, from early on, the infant seems to be capable of resonating to the adult's affective state. But there is probably a gradual increase with age, due to cognitive, maturational, and experiential factors, in the infant's ability to perceive and derive meaning from subtle nuances in the parent's behaviors, or to achieve stable perceptions, independent from the internal state. Although we have looked at observable effects on infants of six types of parent-infant exchanges, it should be remembered that this is not a tightly coupled system. There is some leeway for misperception and slippage on both sides.

Conclusion

I have presented a conceptual framework that assigns a central position to affect. It specifies the components of both the affective experience and the empathic data-gathering process, while insisting that the parent's actual responses to the child are multiply determined and may or may not be influenced by the empathic process. In part this view represents a reaction against the overuse of the term "empathy," which, at an extreme, reduces all interactions to two broad categories—empathic or nonempathic—and blurs our understanding of the phenomenon. Yet this view also arises directly from observation of the complex transactions between parents and infants, in particular from the attempt to articulate subtle differences in the infant's experience that seemed to be present.

I have maintained that when the different combinations of parental perceptions, understandings, and actions toward the child are combined with the three components of the child's positive and negative affective states, they will produce a range of different experiential consequences for the child. On the basis of observational data, I have described the contemporaneous effects of at least six types of exchanges. Yet we need to go further. The conceptualization of affect and empathy presented here should help us to understand how a child comes to structure exchanges with the parent over time, and to begin to recognize the different types of character that may evolve out of different types of structured experiences. It should also help us to intervene more effectively with parents and children, by providing another way to understand the types of dysfunctions in the parent-child relationship.

REFERENCES

Demos, V. (1982), The role of affect in early childhood: An exploratory study. In: *Social interaction in Infancy: Affect, Cognition and Communication*, ed. E. Tronick. Baltimore: University Park Press, pp. 79–123.

———. (1984), A perspective from infant research on affect and self-esteem. In: *The Development and Sustenance of Self-Esteem*, ed. S. Ablon & J. Mack. New York: International Universities Press, pp. 45–76.

Ekman, P. (1972), Universal and cultural differences in facial expression of emotion. In: *Nebraska Symposium on Motivation*, Vol. 19, ed. J. R. Cole. Lincoln: University of Nebraska Press, pp. 207–283.

——— (1977), Biological and cultural contributions to body and facial movement. In: *Anthropology of the Body*, ed. J. Blacking. London: Academic Press, pp. 39–84.

Izard, C. E. (1971), *The Face of Emotion*. New York: Appleton-Century-Crofts.

Kohut, H. (1971), *The Analysis of Self*. New York: International Universities Press.

Schwaber, E. (1981), Empathy: A mode of analytic listening. *Psychoanalytic Inquiry*, 1:357–392.

Stern, D. (1983), The early differentiation of self and others. In: *Re-*

flections on Self Psychology, ed. J. D. Lichtenberg & S. Kaplan. Hillsdale, N.J.: Analytic Press.

Tomkins, S. (1962), *Affect, Imagery, Consciousness, Vol 1: The Positive Affects*. New York: Springer.

_____ (1963) *Affect, Imagery, Consciousness, Vol. 2: The Negative Affects*. New York: Springer.

_____ (1980), Affect as amplification: Some modifications in theory. In: *Emotion: Theory, Research, and Experience, Vol. I*, ed. R. Plutchik & H. Kellerman. New York: Academic Press, pp. 141–164.

_____ (1981), The quest for primary motives: Biography and autobiography of an idea. *J. Pers. Soc. Psychol.*, 41:306–329.

Wiesenfeld, A. R., Malatesta, C. Z., & DeLoach, L. L. (1981), Differential parental response to familiar and unfamiliar infant distress signals. *Infant Behav. Devel.*, 4:281–295.

Wolff, P. (1969), The natural history of crying and other socializations in early infancy. In: *Determinants of Infant Behaviour*, ed. B. M. Foss. London: Methuen, pp. 81–109.

16 Communication and Empathy

WILLIAM S. CONDON, Ph.D.

A GENERAL VIEW OF human existence reveals fundamental, recurrent patterns similar to those exhibited by all life forms. As infants, we are born into a given society and culture which has its own history, extending into an immense past. Many histories are intertwined. We grow, learning the language and the ways of our society, working, achieving, and surviving, as events permit, in relation to the vicissitudes faced by our society in our time. We establish a career, marry, and have children of our own. We age and die, and the pattern repeats, age after age. Societal forms emerge, involving the use of language and reason in the task of living life; sustaining traditions develop. The world and the society into which we are born existed prior to our birth and will continue to exist after our death. We are born into and take on the language of that culture and its ways—we become what it is and in turn it is expressed through us and other humans like us. We cannot exist without it, nor it without us. Our inner being reflects our experience during these processes.

Communication and empathy are fundamental to human life. As an aspect of existence, they are prior to individual interactions. Such exchange or sharing is primary. Helen Keller, lacking sight and hearing, could still learn to communicate meaningfully through touch as the vehicle of thought. We inhabit a realm of being that has communicational structure. Thinking, walking, and communicating are all real activities involving interaction in the world of time and space. They all operate in connection with the rest of things and imply linked, interpenetrating reciprocities. We are not considering an agent that communicates, we are considering a realm of being in which communication, as a basic form of actual, effective exchange, occurs. This realm of communication exists before the infant's birth and it is something within which, upon being born, the infant participates. It is as real as anything else of which the infant is a part. People are always a part of and influenced by existence, from the moment of conception till birth, and during their entire lives until death. We do not just study the messages that pass back and forth between individuals, we study the structure of a communicational field. Communication is a genuine reciprocation and force, molding both the inner and the social life of human beings. We are highly complex centers of communication—communicational beings with many forms of sharing with fellow human beings in a common world.[1]

Our relations with nature and with each other necessarily imply forms of interaction or communication. Participation and sharing in a natural order mean that vital communication is constantly transacted. And it seems essential that we share a common order, that we *are* aspects of natural structure; otherwise it would not be possible for us to eat, drink, breathe, perceive, and know. There are, then, profound, interpenetrating and structural reciprocities without which human life could not exist. These structural reciprocities of nature do not begin or end at certain levels but pervade existence at all levels at all times. Human communication involves such reciprocities: it is a multistructured realm within which we exist and of which we are composed. Many years of frame-by-frame analysis (microanalysis) of sound-films of human behavior and communication have led to the observation of precise forms of behavior within and between interactants (including the person's interaction with the surrounding world) at the microlevel, and this provides support for the view of our fundamental participation in the order of things. It reveals a connectedness and involvement with the world which challenges approaches that too sharply delineate the individual as an entity apart from other entities.

A *speaker's* speech and body motion are precisely and simultaneously synchronized across multiple levels. Further, the *listener's* body motion is precisely and almost simultaneously synchronized with the articulatory structure of the speaker's speech, and even inanimate sounds, within a latency of 42 milliseconds (msec). This interactional version of synchrony has been called *entrainment.* It occurs very rapidly, out of awareness. In entrainment, the listener's body moves in

[1] I have been deeply influenced here in my thinking by the philosopher F. J. E. Woodbridge (1940).

organizations of change which reflect the microstructure of what is being said, like a car following a curving road. Such entrainment has been observed as early as 20 minutes after birth and probably exists *in utero*. It suggests a biological-neurological connectedness between interactants (which is also simultaneously a connection between individual and nature) and appears to be a basic aspect of human communicational participation.

There is a traditional view that human beings are separate individuals and that communication occurring between them is "outside of" them. The view presented here is that communication is a form of connectedness between people, simultaneously structuring and revealing their inner life. Communication is of many different kinds and at many different levels, from very subtle interchanges between two lovers to all the complex social forms. Yet it seems to be ordered in all its manifestations. The distinction between humans *and* nature is difficult to maintain. It is similar to saying the sun *and* nature, or the sky *and* nature. When one person communicates with another person, it is also simultaneously an interaction with and within nature. We receive the same material input from other people that we receive from inanimate objects: acoustic, optical, and tactile. The input is materially the same; the objects differ and have different significances.

Infants live themselves into language and culture—into the forms that surround and support them. They do not "acquire" these as if from a separate system, existing apart. Infants are never isolated or separated from participation in the world and the realm of communication; they are constantly submerged in experiencing, just as the fish is involved with the water in which it exists. Indeed, infants entrain with the structural flow of adult speech almost as well as adults do—suggesting that infants may already be entraining with the incoming sound structure across several levels simultaneously and experiencing the integrated rhythm patterns of the language and the culture. Such entraining is thought to involve a sense of closeness so that the infant's synchronizing with the incoming sound may contribute to a basic inner feeling of contentment and security at the same time that the structure of the world and language is being experienced and learned. Our later identity as speaking and reasoning creatures appears to be strongly dependent on such very early developmental processes. It is quite possible that the mother is "aware" at some level that her baby is entraining with her speech. What is created is a precisely shared communicational dance between mother and the infant, with the infant responding in precise synchrony to the mother's speech. This early entrainment may be an aspect of the development of empathy.

Infants seem to be born with an ability to process the structure of reality (as the entrainment with sound suggests); thus they do not need to learn to create the world out of amorphous impressions. A large part of communication deals with the order and meaning that events and relationships have and how we are influenced by and react to them. The process of the acquisition of language may be importantly related to the infant's entrainment with speech. As the first words are learned, the emotional experiences surrounding the object the word refers to and the communicational atmosphere accompanying its learning become part of the meaningful resonance of that word for the person ever after. The word becomes inwardly the reality it stands for referentially, echoing the feelings surrounding the history of the experiences it signifies. Words become alive and rich with associations, with the living experiences they stand for and participate in. Much of this is out of awareness.

Part of the original purpose of the microanalysis of normal human behavior was to develop a basis for comparative analysis of dysfunctional behavior. Unless the micro-organizations of normal behavior were known, it would not be clear how dysfunctional behavior might differ from them. For example, intensive microanalyses of a variety of disorders have led to the observation of self-*a*synchrony and entrainment *a*synchrony in relation to sound, suggesting a general and characteristic dysfunctional version of normal entrainment to sound when there is brain dysfunction.

Let us turn now to some observations on normal and dysfunctional behavior and communication at the microlevel which illustrate the connectedness of human beings with each other and with nature. We will then look at macrolevels of communication and explore the relation of the micro- and macrodimensions. *Sharing of form* appears to be the fundamental communicational principle running through all levels of behavior.

Microsharing

The focus here is primarily on the microdimensions of human communication. However brief, these complexly organized events are important communicationally. In dealing with behavior, we are concerned with multiple, ongoing events and their interlocking relationships. The major difficulty facing the investigator, especially at the microlevel, is that of determining the nature of the units of behavior on which communication is based. Human communicational behavior is very complex, with many things happening at the same time. This has been stated before, but it needs to be reemphasized. When a speaker speaks, for example, he (or she) usually moves several body parts at the same time. There are many co-occurring and overlapping movements, with constant, ongoing changes. What are the units within these ongoing body motion processes and what, if any, relationship do they bear to the emergent flow of speech?

Initially, then, the determination of units was the critical problem in the study of human communication. Sound-films of naturalistic human interaction, which stored the behavior, were studied over and over, using special analyzing equipment. This permitted a frame-by-frame analysis of speech and body motion at a very minute level. The method was primarily naturalistic, for little was known about behavior at that level. The initial task was not to control the variables so much as to discover what the variables were in the first place so that they could be controlled.

Body Motion Units

A basic and continuous form of order in the body's motion was observed and was interpreted to constitute units. Although several body parts might be moving at the same time, they did so in a synchronous fashion, forming configurations or organizations of change (quanta) that were isomorphic with the articulatory structure of speech. Units are forms of behavior, not discrete items that make up behavior. Thus, forms of *organization* flowing through behavior defined body motion units. The body parts as independent items do not constitute the units of behavior, although behavior could not exist without them. Unit status is determined by the organizations of change of the body parts: the ordered forms of change they sustain with respect to each other in an ongoing fashion.

The different body parts moving at the same time may be moving in different directions and at different speeds, but they will sustain a relationship together for a brief duration, usually lasting two or three frames using 24 frames-per-second (fps) film. This sustaining of a relationship together for a brief duration seems more than a coincidental happening. There is an inner unity and integrity to the sustained relationship, as if the body parts were obeying a pulse or wave train which organized them together during that and subsequent moments of time. Body motion appears to be an emergent, continuous series of such pulselike, organized forms. It does not seem to matter which parts of the body are moving. They will, in normal people, all be synchronized together for a brief duration to transform into another similarly sustained form and so on continuously.

These body motion bundles or quanta are, to reiterate, synchronous with the articulatory structure of the speaker's speech across multiple levels. They have been called "process units" to emphasize their organizational nature. The speaker's body motion parallels his speech across multiple levels simultaneously. Metaphorically, it is as if body motion and speech were being organized across several levels of integrated wave trains as the behavior emerged. This organized, multilevel parallelism of speech and body motion illustrates the nature of organization *as* organization at the microlevel. It may be a characteristic of all organization. Although different cultures exhibit different microrhythm forms, they all follow the same principles of organization.

Self-Synchrony

Running through behavior and constituting its structure are *forms of organization*. Using frame-numbered sound-film, it is possible to describe the points of change of movement of the body parts, with the joints as the descriptive points of change. The frame-numbered sound-film also functions as a clock. The subjects are embedded in a clock. A 24 fps film has 24 still pictures taken serially, with each lasting 41.65 msec. If one uses a 96 fps camera, each frame lasts 10.42 msec. The time at which an arm begins to extend and how long it extends before flexing can be compared to when the head begins to turn and how long this goes on before it changes direction. These observations can in turn be compared to when the eyes and any other body parts move and for how long.

A variety of movements often occur during speaking, in both the speaker and the listener. It is, then, possible to compare the organization of the speaker's body motion with the articulatory structure of his own speech and the organization of the listener's body motion with the articulatory structure of the speaker's speech. The organizing factor in these synchronous change patterns does not reside in the body parts as separate, but in the ordered relationships they sustain with each other. The units are not put together to form the behavior, since the behavior emerges at multiple levels simultaneously. The same organizing factor (ostensibly the central nervous system) also appears to be regulating the emergence of speech, such that the speech and body motion of the speaker are precisely and intricately organized together across multiple levels. This has been called *self-synchrony*. It is disrupted in many disorders, appearing as behavioral asynchrony.

Once again, the nature of behavior, both speech and body motion, is that of an organized process, not of discrete, isolated items which are combined to suddenly create organization at some point. Dealing with behavior as organization results in a new conceptualization of the nature of the "units" composing behavior and their manner of connection. The synchronization or timing of changes in relation to each other and across multiple levels of change becomes critical. Such organization also characterizes the realm of communication, including empathy, across many dimensions. Dysfunctional behavior is also organized, but in ways that differ from the normal, reflecting the normal in distorted ways. This, too, occurs across many dimensions.

Figure 16.1 illustrates the nature of the process units and the emergence of several levels simultaneously. A young woman is talking to a young man. They are seated side by side. The film was taken at 96 fps, which is four times faster than a film seen at the local cinema. The woman says, "an' so I'd get put back in that way." There is silence preceding and following this utterance. The nine-word sequence lasts for 95 frames, or almost exactly one second. Her hands are resting in her lap. At the onset of the first word "an'" her right hand and arm begin to lift off her lap. There is a movement up and to the right across the first four words "an' so I'd get." The arm then sweeps left across the front of her body during "put back" and then goes back down to her lap across "in that way." Thus, the total utterance is accompanied by the hand and arm leaving the lap and coming up to the right, then moving across the body, and finally coming down to the lap just as the utterance ends. This is in turn divided into the three subaspects at the same time: arm up and to the right, across the body, then down to the lap. These are themselves composed of separate words, which are in turn composed of sound types (the phones). The body accompanies all these levels with simultaneously emerging, parallel and synchronous forms of organization. All are hierarchically integrated as they emerge together. This precision of organization of behavior at the microlevel is impressive. For example, a partial eye blink–eye movement occurs in precise synchrony with the word "so." The eyes move left and the lids come down precisely across the /s/ and then the eyes move right and the lids come up across the /o/. Sound-film microanalysis indicates that eye blinks (and apparently eye movements as well) do not occur randomly but at characteristic points during speech.

The speech and body motion shown in Figure 16.1 also illustrate the hierarchic nature of behavioral organization. The several levels emerge simultaneously. That is, one level does not compose another as parts put together to form larger parts. Analysis reveals forms of

FIG. 16.1. Sound-film microanalysis of a young woman's speech and body motion. The film was made at 96 fps.

organization within wider forms of organization. The lower forms of organization are detected in terms of their ordered patterns in contrast to other forms of organization, all of which are functioning simultaneously. By focusing on or discriminating one item of behavior, we do not thereby remove it from its functional participation in the total ongoing organization. While we are attending to that discriminated item, all the other aspects of the behavior are still there and sustaining behavior, even though we are not focusing on them and may never focus on them. By such "focusing on" an aspect of the ongoing behavior, we do not discover a part or piece out of which the behavior was originally composed. We discover an *aspect* of the organization, which does not exist independently of the totally organized behavior. The arm gesture that co-occurred with the utterance of the entire phrase began at the same time that the micro-organization covering the first word "an'" began. The subsequent series of words and accompanying behaviors are not, strictly speaking, put together to form the higher units. To repeat, organization occurs at multiple levels simultaneously and cannot be analyzed into parts which are put together to give rise to organization at some point. Simultaneous multiple-level occurrence appears to be a basic characteristic of organization *as* organization. If the higher-level form begins at the same time that a lower-order form begins, then there is no second lower-order form added to that first one which can go back in time to create the beginning of the higher-order form. The higher and the lower emerge *together* and are discovered *through* the analysis of behavior. The nature of behavioral organization, then, is a fundamental issue and must be dealt with by any investigator purporting to analyze human behavior and communication at the microlevel.

There is an interesting similarity between the units of behavior and the brain waves. The multilevel organized speech and body motion of normal speaker self-synchrony can be interpreted as wavelike processes having characteristic periodicities (the pulses or waves coursing through behavior). These are similar in periodicity to the Delta, Theta, Alpha, and Beta (DTAB) waves of the brain revealed by EEG analyses. This similarity might just be an interesting coincidence, but overt behavior and brain behavior are not separate. The task is one of determining the nature of this organizational integration. There is an integrity or unity of operation to which the distinction "inside of" and "outside of" the body is not relevant. Behavior is not outside of the body; it is what the body does.

Delta, Theta, Alpha, and Beta waves all occur together at the same time in the brain (F. Duffy, personal communication, 1981). The brain waves occur in sequential periodicities. There are no gaps from the fast Beta, at 32 or more per second, up to and including the slow Delta, which last one second or longer. They are all there at the same time. The "behavioral waves" exhibit the same characteristics as the brain waves: they have the same periodicities and they are all there at the same time. The body motion organization accompanies the phone types *while* it accompanies the words, *while* it accompanies the phrases, *while* it accompanies the sentences. All these "whiles" bracketed in an emergent unity is behavior.

The DTAB, if synchronized together, could be considered as fulfilling the requirements of organization by exhibiting multilevels simultaneously. They are always there and available to mediate multilevel behavior. It is the periodic and organized forms of order in the behavioral waves that seem to be organizationally similar to the order of the brain waves. Thought as well as speech, which is thought expressed, would seem to require a wave-form hierarchy like this, which permits the seemingly discrete and the continuous to occur and to function together without contradiction. The sentence is emerging as a total unity at the same time that the separate words making it up are emerging. Figure 16.2 presents a schematic comparison of behavioral wave periodicities and brain wave periodicities. A variety of careful sound-film microanalyses have led to the determination of the behavioral wave periodicities.

The point about discussing the similarity between behavioral waves and brain waves is, again, to emphasize the connectedness of behavioral processes. It appears that whatever generates the units of body motion simultaneously generates the units of speech, synchronizing them across multiple levels. In this respect, behavior may not be able to violate the hierarchic organizational rhythms of the brain, which may mediate its expression. Speech and body motion may occur in terms of the basic organization of brain processes and thus necessarily be synchronized together across multiple dimensions. For example, eye blinks do not seem to occur randomly in relation to speech (i.e., interstitially to the speech-unit behavioral waves), but only at wave boundaries. This may be related to the DTAB periodicities.

There appear to be different rhythm-hierarchy suborganizations in different cultures. Each language-culture group will probably manifest its own particular style of speech and body motion rhythms. These cultural rhythms are formed in intricate patterns, which involve an orchestrated timing of change and speed of movement of the body parts in relation to each other and to speech, particularly the prosodic pattern of the language. For example, American black speaker move-

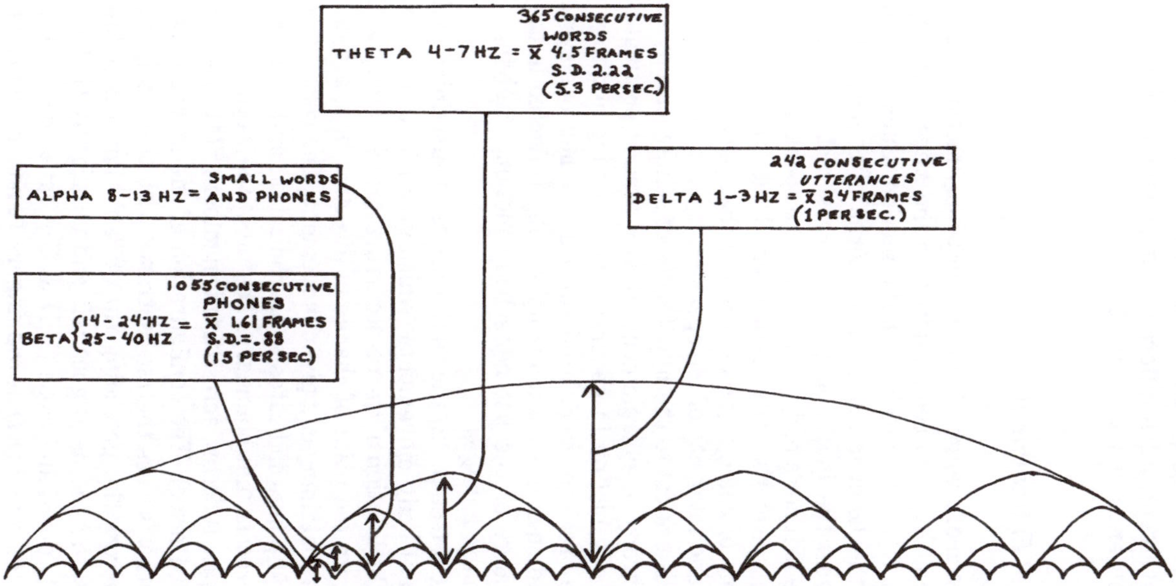

FIG. 16.2. Schematized relationship between behavioral wave and brain wave periodicities. The behavioral waves emerge simultaneously across multiple levels and are hierarchically integrated.

ment exhibits a syncopated rhythm, in contrast to American white speaker movement. Such differences may subtly affect the quality of interracial interactions and empathy.

Interactional Entrainment

The pattern of change of the listener's body motion while the speaker is speaking has also been studied, in the same detailed, frame-by-frame fashion as the speaker's body motion. Such microanalysis reveals that the listener moves in patterns of change which are synchronous with the incoming articulatory structure of the speaker's speech. The listener's body moves with the speaker's speech almost as well as the speaker's body itself does. Thus, the listener moves in organizations of change (process units) that parallel the articulatory patterning and intensity of the speaker's speech. The concept of "process units" is critical to the hypotheses of self-synchrony and interactional synchrony or entrainment. It is a central postulate about the nature of body motion in general. The incoming auditory signal appears to be precisely modulated early in the nervous system for the listener, and such modulation is holistically reflected in the organizations of change of the listener's body motion, implying subcortical auditory-motor linkages.

Figure 16.1 (see p. 42) shows the points of sustaining and changing of direction of body movements (which give rise to the basic process units) and the location of the co-occurring speech elements. The arrow points indicate the point of change of direction or speed and the lines indicate the sustaining of a given movement. The vertical co-occurring of the arrow points indicates synchronization and defines the occurrence of a process unit boundary. The /s/ of the word "so" will be used as an example. It occurs across frame numbers 5741–5745 or 10/96th of a second (104 msec). The configuration of the movements being sustained together across the /s/ contrasts with the configuration being sustained across the preceding /n/ of "an'" and the following /o/ of "so." Across /s/ the head goes left and up slightly (L,Us), *while* the eyes go left, down and close (L,D & C), *while* the right thumb continues extending fast (Ef), *while* fingers 1 and 2 of the right hand stop moving (H or hold), *while* the right wrist moves slightly in the direction of the thumb (♉), *while* the right elbow flexes fast (Ff), *while* the right shoulder rotates out and adducts (RO, AD). These movements sustain their directions and speeds together; they durate together, creating a unitary pulse or wave which occurs isomorphically with the emission of /s/. This contrasts with the similarly "sustained durating together" of the movements across /n/ and /o/. Such is the nature of the continuously ongoing motion at the microlevel. There are no stops and starts, but rather continuous transformations of one configuration into another.

The word "so" is also hierarchically synchronized. The /s/ and the /o/ each have process units co-occurring with them. At the same time the word as a totality is also accompanied by body motion forms. Fingers 1 and 2 of the right hand extended across the /n/ of "an'." They hold still across "so" and then begin to flex across "I'd." They thus sustain a form isomorphically with the occurrence of "so" as a totality. This principle characterizes speaker behavior in different cultures and may be pan-human.

There is a physical continuity in the flow of sound between interactants. The listener, to repeat, appears to precisely modulate the incoming auditory signal in an ongoing fashion, with this modulation holistically reflected in the organizations of change of his body motion. The modulation occurs very rapidly, within a latency of 42 msec. Communication thus involves a linkage between communicators. The speaker encodes his thoughts into physical vibrations of his vocal cords, which are propagated through the air in waves to the eardrum of the listener. These are in turn converted into electrical forms, which become ideas in the mind of the listener. There is never an absence of structure. When we speak of communication occurring "between" people, we sometimes overlook the fact that this distinction does not create a vacuum in the intervening space between them. The media may differ: the brain, vocal cords, and mouth of the speaker—the compression and rarefaction of the intervening air—the auditory receptive system of the listener. But that which flows through the different modes is a similarity of *order*, so that what is sent and what is received are understood and shared by both speaker and listener. This is the realm of communication. What all aspects of this process have in common is the propagation and reception of order. There is no "between" in that continuum of order. Nature's order can be accurately formulated through the neurological-verbal order and can be shared and passed on from generation to generation. This is a communicational participation in the order of nature. The order of the mind reflects the order of nature: without the order of nature, there would be no ordered mind or any language to say what the order of nature or anything else was. Such ordered translation or communication is a genuine aspect of existence—perhaps one of the most impressive for humans.

That a continuous and constantly varying stream of speech from the speaker is being almost simultaneously and organizationally tracked is expressed in the parallel body motion changes of the listener. The body of a normal listener moves in organized bundles of change, process units, which are precisely synchronous (entrain) with the emergent structure of the speaker's speech. The precision and speed with which the listener's body moves in synchronized organization with the speaker's speech have led to the postulation of a basic, short-latency entraining process, probably occurring in the brainstem (Condon, 1977). Entrainment often occurs in relation to inanimate sounds; it is not just limited to speech sounds. Thus, the term "entrainment" may be more precise than "interactional synchrony." We are organizationally linked with and part of the universe in which we evolved; the organizations of change of the listener's body in relation to sound reflect that profound participation.

Dysfunctional Asynchrony

Normal communication manifests regularities which can be observed in the timing of eye movements, the turn of the head, verbal acknowledgments, and the motion rhythm of the listener's body in relation to the speaker's speech. Again, the organizations of change of the listener's body move in time and intensity with the speaker's speech. Many degrees of empathy, of closeness and distance, are conveyed by the degrees of sharing expressed through these changes and their intricate timings. One of the general hypotheses emerging in the study of human communication is that the more one shares posture and/or movement with another, the greater the degree of rapport (Charny, 1966; Condon, 1968; Scheflen, 1974). Thus, the listener provides the speaker with continuous feedback that he is attending, as well as indicating the quality of that attending.

Interactants participate across many levels at the same time in all the subtle variations, complexities, and reciprocities of this ongoing and changing process. We are also involved in an interactional reciprocity with nature, which surrounds us and runs through us, translating the natural order into mental order. When there is damage or dysfunction of the brain, this reciprocity may be impaired in subtle or severe ways. Sound-film microanalyses of several forms of dysfunctional behavior have revealed a response to sound that differs from that of normal subjects. A recent study of six dyslexic and six autisticlike children, for instance, revealed an asynchronous response to sound (Condon, 1981). The dyslexic children tended to exhibit an entrainment on the right side within 42 msec (like normal subjects), but there was a delayed entrainment on the left side, as if one half of the body were entraining out-of-phase with the other half. The reverse was the case with the autisticlike children. Their left side would entrain within 42 msec (i.e., on the next frame after sound onset) and the right side would entrain after a delay.

All 12 children exhibited four patterned entrainments within the first two-thirds of a second following most sounds.[2]

These children seem to entrain to one sound as if that sound were echoing or reverberating. They exhibit jumps and jerks at various latencies following a sound. It is as if the short-latency entrainment phase, instead of occurring just once as in normal behavior, repeated several times, at specific delay intervals. The first delayed asynchronous entrainment may vary in latency from 100 to 250 msec. Yet if, for example, a given child has a delay of 150 msec, this delay remains the same for that child in response to most of the sounds occurring around him.

The dyslexic children did not hear sound multiple times, but there was evidence that some of the autisticlike children may have actually heard sound echoing. Severely autistic children display a *multiple orienting* to sound as well as a multiple entrainment (the jumps and jerks in the body). They *look around* several times after a sound, as if the sound were coming from several different directions, one after the other. A well-functioning 32-year-old autistic man said he heard echoing as a child up until the age of 24. He also said he experienced visual echoing or a form of double vision until he was nine years old. He still experiences both phenomena occasionally. (This information was offered voluntarily without prompting.) His self-report plus evidence from sound-film microanalysis suggests that autistic persons may suffer from perceptual distortions. Many seem to be overwhelmed and tormented by this auditory input, which they cannot shut off. Another autistic adult also reported hearing some echoing until he was 15. The sounds constantly echoed six or seven times. He said he was in a fog and would stand in his lonesome, handicapped corner because of fear of people.

---

[2] As asynchronous, multiple entrainment to sound has also been observed in a variety of other disorders—schizophrenia, cerebral palsy, fetal alcohol syndrome, hyperactivity, and Huntington's disease (HD). It is strongly suspected in some forms of stuttering as well. The two HD patients studied so far exhibited a multiple entrainment to sound very similar to that observed in autistic subjects, with the initial entrainment on the left and a delayed entrainment on the right.

One gets the impression that some, perhaps many, autistic persons have normal intelligence, but are living in a partially distorted world. This seems to range in degree of severity. The multiple entrainment to sound appears to control the orienting response in many severely autistic persons, so that they look around many times in different directions in response to the same sound. They may not know which is the real sound. In this sense there may be a dissociation between sound and vision and the real world. Because the delayed entrainment is on the right side of the body in autism, it may implicate the left side of the brain. Hauser et al. (1975), using pneumoncephalographic (PEG) techniques, report evidence of possible damage to the left temporal lobe of autistic subjects. In this regard, one should note that some autistic subjects appear to have major semantic problems, especially in attaching the correct meaning or signification to words.

When the organization of our perceptual and intellectual processing of the world is defective, that world may become distorted and we may no longer be able to function adequately. Actually, entrainment to sound is seen much more dramatically in dysfunctional behavior than in normal behavior. This may be due to the asynchrony, in which one side moves or responds to sound more vigorously, as if released from a balancing inhibition from the other side. In the study involving the six dyslexic and six autisticlike children, there was a *marked* jerk in the body in the frame immediately following the onset of sounds, i.e., within 42 msec. Although dysfunctional behavior reveals the same fundamental linkage with nature as normal behavior, it is in an out-of-phase form.

Entrainment in Infancy

The short-latency entrainment to sound begins very early in human life, as was observed in sound-films taken of 16 normal neonates, one to four days old. Audiotape recordings of human voices (including spoken Chinese from learning tapes) and live human voices were presented during the filming. All of the infants exhibited a marked synchronization of body movement with both tape-recorded and live human voices (Condon and Sander, 1974). Such precise entrainment, with the body moving in synchrony with the articulatory structure of speech, has been observed in a sound-film of an infant as early as 20 minutes after birth. This observation supports the possibility that such entrainment exists *in utero*. It may occur there at least two months before birth. If this is the case, the infant is exquisitely prepared for participation in human language. The ability to entrain with human speech *in utero* would be an advantage to a creature whose adult task

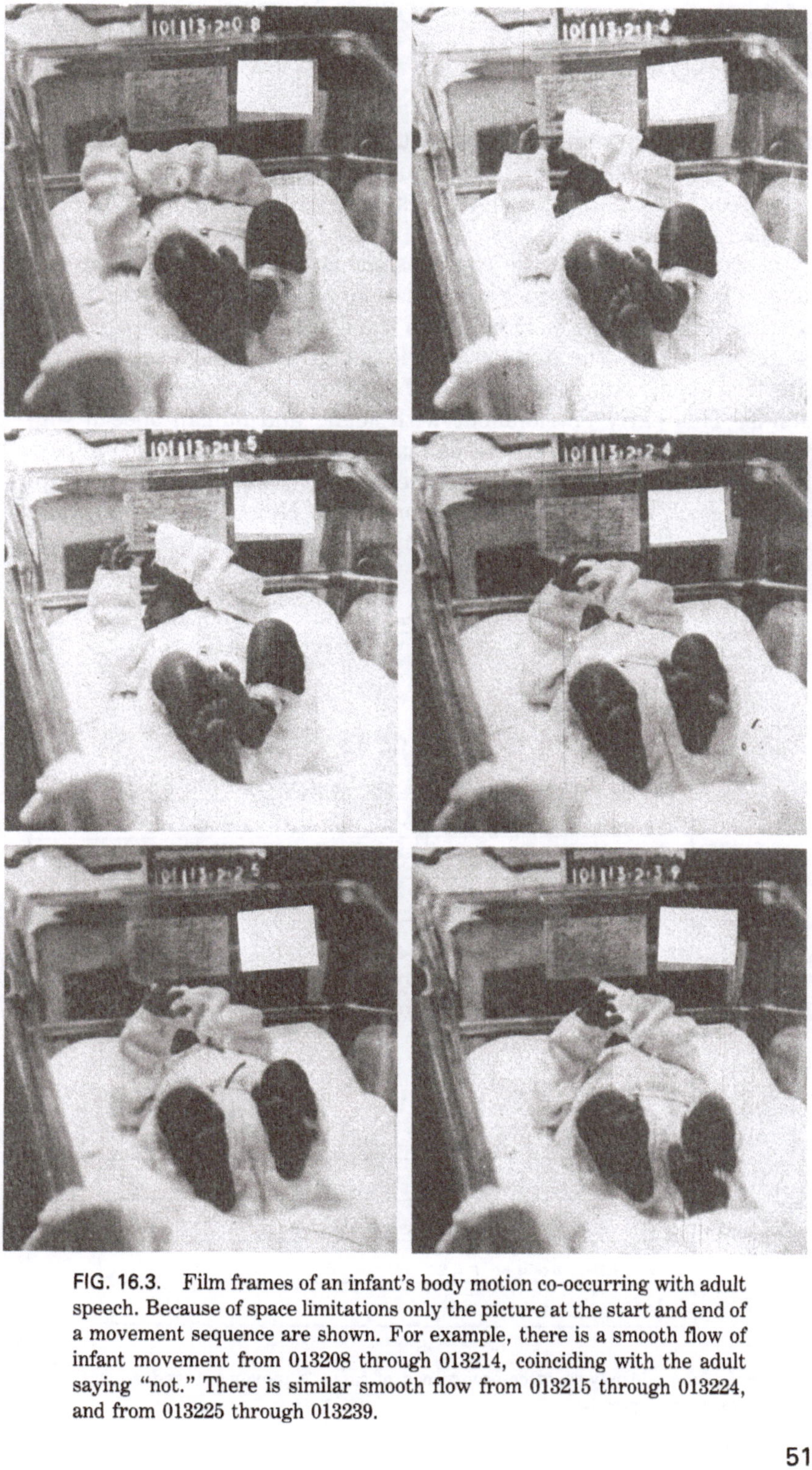

FIG. 16.3. Film frames of an infant's body motion co-occurring with adult speech. Because of space limitations only the picture at the start and end of a movement sequence are shown. For example, there is a smooth flow of infant movement from 013208 through 013214, coinciding with the adult saying "not." There is similar smooth flow from 013215 through 013224, and from 013225 through 013239.

is to use speech in communicating. Such synchronization may also play a role in the development of consciousness and the formation of ego processes. If this is true, it may necessitate a reexamination of psychodynamic formulations.

Infants do not recognize the consonants and vowels of their language system, yet they move in almost precise synchrony with them. In other words, infants entrain with the *sound structure* of their language long before the units of that language are recognized as such. Affective aspects may also begin to be tied in, with feelings related to sounds. This early entrainment with sound and human speech suggests that the auditory processes may play an important role in psychodynamic development. The process of discriminating a world appears to start very early and very precisely. Newborns are naturally receptive to the structure of the universe into which they are born.

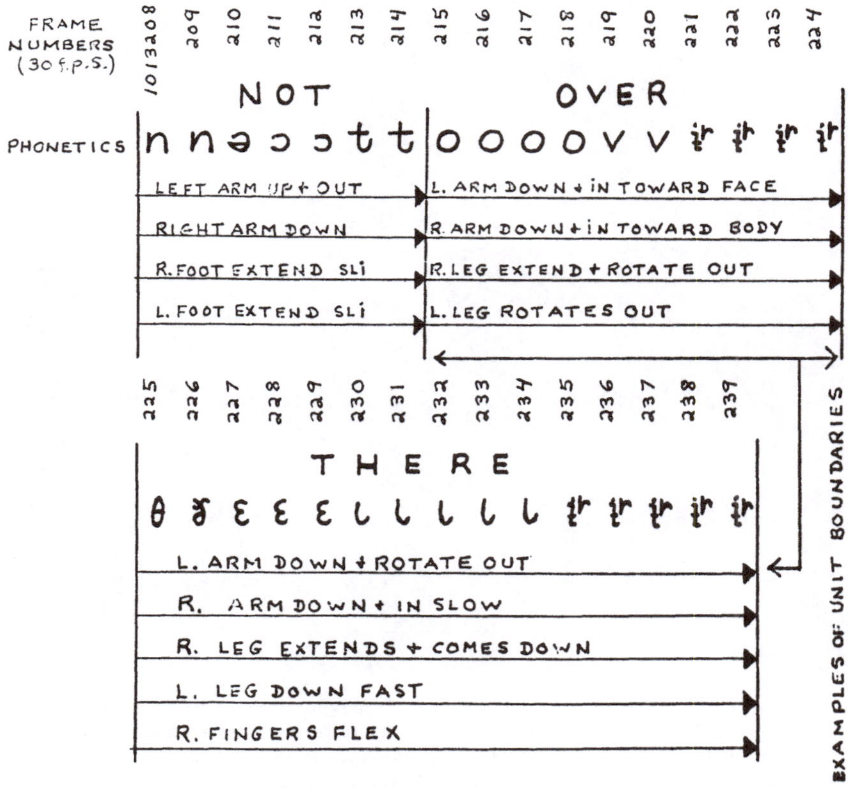

FIG. 16.4. Analysis of co-occurrence of infant's movement and adult's speech in Figure 3.

Infant entrainment to adult speech can be seen in Figure 16.3, which shows a series of still pictures taken from a 16 mm film. This two-day-old infant is awake/alert and looking away from the adult speaking. An analysis of the film frames (Figure 16.4) reveals the relation of shifts in the infant's body motion to changes in the adult's speech sounds. Across the word "not" the infant's left arm moves rapidly up and out. Across "over" the left arm comes down and in over the face, the right arm comes down and in toward the body, and the left leg rotates rapidly outward. Across "there" the left arm flexes at the elbow and rotates out. This can be seen against the card at the back of the crib. The left leg comes down rapidly toward the mattress and the right fingers flex. These three bundles of movement also illustrate process units. This is not a unique sample of infant entrainment; it occurs in all normal infants studied.

Macrosharing

Again, we exist within and participate in a realm of communication. Distinguishing us from the world in which we exist does not separate us from that world. The order and structure that run through nature also run through us; there are not two separate forms of order. As we have just seen, the infant has an organized auditory system, which appears to be directly linked to motor processes in such a way that the structure of incoming speech is rapidly and isomorphically reflected in the organization of change of the infant's movements. This integrated reciprocity between infants as listening organisms and the sounds they listen to and later use constitutes, to repeat, a realm of communication. There appears to be a somewhat similar reciprocity in the more macro domain of human communication.

The realm of communication includes human beings and the media by which we communicate; we see and talk with each other and react to the messages interpreted in such seeing and talking. The way infants experience their world and significant caretakers molds their inner life as well as their ability to speak. Experience does not occur in a vacuum but is mediated through communicational interactions. The study of communication is thus directly relevant to psychodynamic structuring and the shaping of inner life.

Sharing of form (similar order), whether a perceptual reflection of nature's structure, a rhythmic synchronization with speech at the microlevel, or posture sharing at the macrolevel, appears to be one of the major characteristics of the realm of communication. Forms can be shared in many subtle ways between interactants. Sharing thus characterizes both micro- and macrolevels of communication. Such sharing of similar forms—for instance, both interactants having their hands on their chins—may contribute to an inner sense of belonging and well-being, out of awareness. Dance may be a social celebration of such sharing.

MacLean (1973), in studying species-specific behaviors in monkeys, found that many of these behaviors appear to be mediated by subcortical structures. Specifically, he reported: "I have since found that bilateral lesions of the striatopallidal complex abolish the innate display behavior of squirrel monkeys. . . . Because of the traditional clinical view that the striatopallidal complex subserves purely motor functions, it should be emphasized that large lesions of the complex may result in no apparent motor incapacity if there is no injury to the internal capsule. These findings . . . suggest that the striatopallidal complex is fundamentally involved in species-specific and imitative forms of behavior" (p. 50). Entrainment to sound, especially speech, also appears to be a subcortical process and may be an important species-specific behavior intimately related to human enculturation and communication.

In 1956, at the Institute for Advanced Studies in the Behavioral Sciences at Palo Alto, Frieda Fromm-Reichmann stimulated an interdisciplinary effort to study human behavior and communication which would deal with the subtleties of interaction in the everyday life of people within a given society (Bateson, 1958). She was deeply interested in intuition, in how one picks up subtle cues in the behavior of others which reveals their inner state to some extent and their reactions in a given situation. Thus, an interdisciplinary study of human interaction began and led to the writing of a book—*The Natural History of an Interview*, edited by Norman McQuown (1960)—although, unfortunately, this book was never published. Gregory Bateson, who wrote the introductory chapter, saw the book as an attempt at synthesis, starting with a sound-film as the observational basis. It was called "natural history" because a minimum of theory guided the collection of data, although the influence of Freudian and Gestalt psychology can be seen in the choice of a basic perspective.

Bateson states: "any analysis of communicational data is shaped by premises which define the units into which the stream of data is to be divided." Here he is seeking to articulate some of the problems that have to be dealt with in analyzing behavior and communication as organized processes. In his view, it is essential for humans to develop ways to "talk" about the rules of communication. The patterns of self-perception, the rules governing the formation of a self-image, are modified by the way in which others receive our message and we interpret theirs. According to Bateson:

> To build a bridge between the study of psychiatric functional pathology and the pathologies of communication, it is necessary to insist upon the existence of the facts of learning and conditioning. Two considerations become especially relevant. First, every failure of communication is painful. Second, the learning organism always generalizes from experience. Further, the business of communication is a continuous learning to communicate. Codes and language are not static systems which can be learned once and for all. They are, rather, shifting systems of facts and premises which govern how messages are to be made and interpreted. Every signal which establishes a new premise or pact bringing the persons closer together or giving them greater freedom may be a source of joy. But every signal which falls by the wayside is in some degree a source of pain to both. The ongoing stream of communication is thus, for each individual, a continuous chain of contexts of learning, and, specifically, learning about premises of communication.

There are thus no preordained commands legislating human communication or human lifestyles. Existence offers a profound opportunity for communicational creativity and the development of cultural styles in which our inner life can find fulfillment.

Bateson and others, particularly Henry Brosin, Ray Birdwhistell, Charles Hockett, Norman McQuown, and Al Scheflen were deeply interested in the careful analysis of human interaction in various settings. The initial efforts in sound-film microanalysis were directed at detecting and describing such out-of-awareness forms of order regulating and influencing human interaction. As Bateson puts it:

"A major function of the techniques of microanalysis is, therefore, to obtain from small quantities of data, accurately and completely recorded, insights into human relationships which could otherwise only be obtained either by long-time observations or from the notoriously unreliable data of anamnestic reconstruction."

Again, there is no decreed "kind" of communication or goal which is the norm. Human interactions are complex contexts of learning, with many levels occurring together simultaneously. All the daily ministrations and involvements of the mother in relation to the infant, for instance, are fundamentally communicational in nature. The mother's feelings and attitudes toward the child, which are affected by many factors in her life, are constantly conveyed in many subtle ways, to become a basic part of the inner being of that child. In other words, even our inner being is part of the communicational realm. It is not separate from all the experiences in which, by its very nature, it is constrained to experience. An individual's form of relating to others is crucially determined by these early experiences. (Much of this occurs out of awareness and has not really been studied adequately.)

Many things are happening simultaneously in subtle ways during an interaction. There is a constant waxing and waning with approaches and retreats, dominance and submission, closeness and distance, superiority and inferiority, and all the subtle explicit and implicit evaluations contained in fleeting facial expressions and changes in the voice. The inner life has its ordered molding forces, and as the nature and effect of these forces become more fully understood, it may be possible to transform the inner life. The inner life is ultimately the great frontier, not outer space, or the depths of the oceans, or the amassing of wealth and power. Communication is an existential realm, as real as anything else, having real consequences. It therefore has ethical dimensions which need to be made explicit. The following examples illustrate a variety of such communicational events.

The first example is from a 16 mm sound-film of a mother being interviewed. The interviewer is sitting on the couch beside her while her four-year-old son is playing on the floor in front of her. A variety of out-of-awareness behaviors occur as she talks about her son. She sees him as being a constant sleeping problem and always whining. When she refers to him, she often makes a marked grimace. This occurs rapidly, within one-fourth of a second, and it is difficult to detect. At other times there is a rasping clearing of her throat when she refers to him. At one point when she says, "He was a physical feeding problem early," she pulls far away from him, clearing her throat and grimacing at the same time. On the word "feeding," he bows his head and drops the toy he is playing with. She continues talking and in a squeezed and breaking voice says, "I tried to nurse him and couldn't." Exactly on the word "him," she flicks the ashes off her cigarette. In another film of her with her therapist, she also complains bitterly about his whining and not sleeping at night. She cannot willingly and lovingly give to him, seeing him as burden and an intrusion in her life. This attitude is constantly conveyed to him in subtle and not so subtle verbal and nonverbal ways. These are not just interesting behaviors with no effect. They become part of the inner being of the child, forming a core of dark self-judgment and despair. The term "existential" is not limited to a school of philosophy—such communications exert an existential force on the inner life. The child is already "sick" at four years of age. After his mother says, "He was a physical feeding problem," he gets up and brings her a pillow and then turns away. She takes the pillow and glares at his retreating back, her eyes furrowed malevolently. At four years of age, this boy has, as a result of these constant "communications" (which were probably there as soon as he was born), become estranged from himself, judging himself as bad and ugly. He does not have the love of this important parent, and he assumes it must be because of his own unworthiness, not from any lack in her.

In another family with lovely, teen-aged twin daughters, one daughter was diagnosed as schizophrenic. A sound-film was made of the mother and the twins talking to a psychiatric resident. In the film the mother shared posture or moved in heightened synchrony with the "well" twin most of the time. The "sick" twin seemed to be systematically excluded, although this was nonverbal and out of awareness. The mother would only briefly share posture or movement with her. There was a poignant aspect to some of the hidden features in this out-of-awareness interactional process. The mother, for example, might be sitting with her right hand on her chin. The sick twin would change posture, bringing her right hand up to her own chin. A fraction of a second after the twin's hand reached her chin, the mother brought her own hand down to her lap. This happened over and over in subtle ways. One of the complaints of the sick twin was that her mother loved her sister more than her, which the mother denied.

One day while shopping I observed the following episode. A black mother and her children were slowly moving down the department store aisle from table to table, examining clothing. A white mother and her children were doing the same from the opposite direction, on the other side of the aisle. As the two groups passed, a girl from the black family smiled in a friendly way at a girl about the same age in the white family. The white girl grimaced. The black girl walked a short distance away and turned, glancing back with a sad hurt look on her face. This exchange lasted just a moment. The meeting glances and the timing of the smile and responding grimace are not just indifferent features of the structure of a brief passing; they can have a lasting effect on the inner life. Erikson (1958) has the following to say: "But the center of the problem is simply this: in truly significant matters people, and especially children, have a devastatingly clear if mostly unconscious perception of what other people really mean, and sooner or later royally reward real love or take well-aimed revenge for implicit hate. Families in which each member is separated from the others by asbestos walls of verbal propriety, overt sweetness, cheap frankness, and rectitude tell one another off and talk back to each other with minute and unconscious displays of affect—not to mention physical complaints and bodily ailments—with which they worry, accuse, undermine, and murder one another" (p. 210).

Communication is not just a process of "bits" of information traveling between people; it is also a domain of trust and distrust, of the multitudinous and subtle ways people love and hate, praise and blame, accept and reject—themselves as well as others. Communication affects the inner being of others, aiding or hindering, with greater or lesser consequences on that inner life. Our lives become ordered in terms of the experiences that we undergo. Freud was well aware of subtle communicational features revealing psychodynamic processes. The study of human communication can provide an additional avenue for psychoanalytic inquiry.

REFERENCES

Bateson, G. (1958), Language and psychotherapy: Frieda Fromm-Reichmann's last project. *Psychiatry*, 21:96–100.

Charny, E. J. (1966), Psychosomatic manifestations of rapport in psychotherapy. *Psychosom. Med.*, 28:305–315.

Condon, W. (1968), Linguistic-kinesic research and dance therapy. *Amer. Dance Ther. Assn. Proceed., 3rd Ann. Conf.*, pp. 21–44.

______. (1977), A primary phase in the organization of infant responding behavior. In: *Studies in Mother-Infant Interaction*, ed. H. R. Schaffer. New York: Academic Press, pp. 153–175.

______ (1981), Sound-film microanalysis: A means for correlating brain and behavior. Presented at Institute for Child Development Research symposium, Philadelphia, May 22.

______ & Sander, L. (1974), Neonate movement is synchronized with adult speech: Interactional participation and language acquisition. *Science*, 183:99–101.

Erikson, E. (1958), *Young Man Luther*. New York: Norton.

Hauser, S., Delong, R., & Rosman, N. P. (1975), Pneumographic findings in the infantile autism syndrome. *Brain*, 98:667–688.

MacLean, P. (1973), *A Triune Concept of the Brain and Behavior*. Toronto: University of Toronto Press.

McQuown, N., Ed. (1960), *The Natural History of an Interview*. Microfilm: Collection of Manuscripts on Cultural Anthropology, 15.

Scheflen, A. E. (1974), *How Behavior Means*. Garden City, N.Y.: Anchor Books.

Woodbridge, F. J. E. (1940), *An Essay on Human Nature*. New York: Columbia University Press.

17 Thoughts about Stages on the Way to Empathy and the Capacity for Concern

ANNI BERGMAN, Ph.D., and ARNOLD WILSON, Ph.D.

THE CONCEPT OF EMPATHY is one that has been receiving an increasing amount of attention in recent psychoanalytic literature. A great deal of attention has been paid to the developmental antecedents of how one adult comes to "know" another's emotional state. The capacity for empathy has been reconstructively traced to various points in human ontogeny. In this way, different understandings of empathy have emerged, shaped by views on the developmental period in which it is thought to originate. Some investigators, for instance, conceive of empathy as a special ability to merge with another and assert that its genesis lies in certain optimal conditions during the symbiotic phase (Olden, 1958; Greenson, 1960; Schafer, 1968). Others view the capacity for empathy as a form of identification and locate its point of origin at a more advanced developmental stage, when self and object are more differentiated (Fliess, 1942; Beres, 1968; Beres and Arlow, 1974; Bachrach, 1976). These investigators follow Freud (1921), who noted that "a path leads from identification by way of imitation to empathy, that is, to the comprehension of the mechanism by means of which we are enabled to take up any attitude at all towards another mental life" (p. 110).

The problem of reconciling these two perspectives within a developmental framework has been addressed by several authors. Schafer (1959, 1968) asserts that merging is present in all empathy, but that the most mature form of empathy, which he terms "generative," is characterized by the simultaneous appearance of merging and an "identification which remains segregated within the ego." Here the empathizer merges while simultaneously maintaining a separate and individual perspective.[1]

Shapiro (1974) examines empathy within classical developmental framework. At times, he proposes, empathy may serve a defensive function, for "in the case of empathy . . . the denial of the wish or emotion toward the object is absent and a feeling of unity is substituted" (p. 12). In this view, some of the earliest forms of empathy emerge from an infantile matrix of nondifferentiation in which projection and identification are not yet discrete ego functions. Shapiro's formulation is that instead of a shift from "I feel angry" to "I don't feel angry" (denial), the move is to "I feel angry in the same way he (or she) does" (defensive empathy). Later regressions are likely to elicit a mixed deployment of the nondifferentiated identification-projection mechanism, leading to adult distortions in empathy.

Buie (1981) asserts that neither merging nor identification is the necessary forerunner of empathy. He states that merging is not a mechanism of empathy because true object-oriented empathy depends on the development of an inner world of object and self-representations as well as introjects, and this commences only at about 18 months of age. Egocentrically oriented forms of empathy may commence during the symbiotic period, but even these do not depend on merging for their development. Nor, in his view, does the notion of identification as a necessary component of empathy hold up theoretically. Citing Meissner (1970, 1971, 1972), Buie notes that identification is a process that affects the ego by adding new structures. Yet authors who assert that identification is the necessary ingredient for empathy think of it as a process involving already-existing psychic structures, without requiring additional structuralization. Buie concludes that "they are either referring to some other phenomenon which is theoretically unspecified . . . or they are simply employing the term identification in a non-technical, descriptive sense" (p. 291).

---

[1]Maternal "generative empathy" may well facilitate the developmental unfolding of the capacity for empathy. Sander (1976) describes what he believes is required of the mother, during the first phase of the infant's life (birth to two and one-half months), as the capacity to maintain a balance between her intuitive sensing of what the child needs and her objective view of the child. This "generative empathy" on the part of the mother with her newborn may well set the stage for the reciprocity between mother and child characteristic of the symbiotic phase, during which the infant's capacity for empathy begins to develop.

A question that arises with all these views is: What constitutes appropriate psychoanalytic data for the validation of a developmental hypothesis about empathy? Many of the published reports rely on transference manifestations and reconstructions, so that inferences about the early developmental components of empathy are made from verbal reports of adult patients. The reactivation of phenomena related to empathy in the transference has also been a primary source of data on empathy in the clinical psychoanalytic literature. Data from direct child observation, however, seem to have had little impact in this area. Recently, infancy researchers and developmental psychologists have directed their attention to such related phenomena as early role-talking, social cognition, and similar cognitive and behavioral advances. If analysts are willing to accept direct child observation as a valid psychoanalytic source of data, the results of these studies may prove helpful when interpreted in conjunction with analytic understanding.

None of this denies the role of construction, reconstruction, and transference reactivation as essential sources of psychoanalytic data. Yet our understanding may be enlarged by integrating direct child observation with data from the psychoanalytic situation. Along these lines, we have chosen to use direct observation of children during the preoedipal period to understand the antecedents of the capacity for empathy. Our observations and inferences are informed by psychoanalytic theory and view children through "the psychoanalytic eye" (Mahler, Pine, and Bergman, 1975).

In examining the development of empathy and the capacity for concern, we use the perspective of separation-individuation. As indicated, many investigators hold that identification, merging, or some state of fusion is the intrapsychic basis for the genesis of empathy. In our view, it is the pathway of separation-individuation itself that shapes the developing capacity for empathy in accordance with the dynamics of each subphase. From this point of reference, we intend to look at how the infant comes to understand, anticipate, and respond to the conscious and unconscious wishes and needs of another person, in particular the mother. Many psychoanalytic theorists hold that the development of empathy should be studied in the context of the unfolding mother-child relationship. So, too, have many infancy researchers concluded that the milieu for the proper development of empathy is the mother-child relationship rather than the peer-peer relationship (Bowlby, 1961; Harlow and Harlow, 1965; Lewis and Rosenblum, 1974; Hoffman, 1978).

Developmental Considerations

In an earlier paper (Bergman, 1981), it was shown how a sense of mine and yours, which emerges during the second year of life, is a prerequisite for sharing on a more mature level. This capacity to share on a mature level has earlier sources during the separation-individuation process, in particular during the symbiotic phase and again during the subphase of early rapprochement. It was hypothesized that the mature capacity to share is most pleasurable when the earlier symbiotic pleasure of relatedness with mother is revived. Similarly, it is our contention here that the capacity for mature empathy receives an important increment from the periods of symbiosis and early rapprochement—the periods of greatest intimacy and mutuality between the infant and the mother.

Brazelton, Koslowski, and Main (1974), Stern (1971), Sander (1977), Emde, Gaensbauer, and Harmon (1976), and others have described in rich detail the fine tuning of early interaction between the infant and the caregiver. A significant contribution of this research has been to revise the notion of the infant as a passive recipient of the mother's care. Instead, the infant, from the beginning, is seen as an active elicitor of care. This discovery has important implications for ideas about early building blocks for empathy, or what will eventually evolve into empathy.

The Symbiotic Phase

The mother's empathic understanding of her infant's needs and states during the symbiotic phase is counterbalanced by the infant's early capacity to evoke responsiveness from the mother. By the time the symbiotic phase is reached (two months), both infant and mother have become fairly adept in eliciting each other's responsiveness and, more and more, this is accompanied by mutual pleasure. Affect contagion is reciprocal. Mother's pleasure in her infant is immensely enhanced by the infant's smiling, and the infant's smile blossoms forth into more sustained pleasurable expressions, which gradually include a large repertoire of increasingly differentiated and integrated functions (vision, language, motor responses). As Brazelton (1981) notes, the mother learns the infant's "capacity for attention-nonattention early in order to maintain his attention to her. Within this rhythmic coherent configuration she *and* he can introduce the mutable elements of communication. Smiles, vocalizations, postures, tactile signals, all are such elements" (p. 18). Mahler (1942) may have had something similar in mind when she said: "Between child and mother there exists from the beginning a close phylogenetic bond which is unique and much more exclusive than communication by words and thoughts; it is an interrelationship through the medium of affective expressions" (p. 4).

From the beginning, then, mother and infant mutually respond to each other. Mutual gazing, gaze aversion, mutual smiling, cooing, infant and mother play—these are all important ingredients in the dialogue during the symbiotic phase. Other writers have emphasized the importance of the early mother-child symbiotic relationship to the later development of empathy (Olden, 1958; Greenson, 1960; Ferreira, 1961; Schafer, 1968). Most of them, however, see it as contributing to a merging form of empathy. In contrast, we believe that during this early phase, even though self-object differentiation is not fully established, there is a certain amount of differentiation, allowing for the mutual responsiveness. What is unique to the mother-infant interaction during the symbiotic phase is the intensity of pleasure and mutual attunement. *We believe that for mature empathy to fully develop at a later stage, this early pleasurable interaction must have taken place.*

Winnicott (1953) places great emphasis on the phenomenon of mirroring during this phase—to see oneself reflected in the other. He suggests that this mirroring is an important protection for the infant from seeing the other as separate from the self at too early a time. The mirroring function also brings a sense of how one appears to the other, an incipient sense of being perceived by another, and this may be another building block during symbiosis, which complements learning how to elicit a wished-for response from the other. In agreement with Buie (1981), we contend that the concept of merging has been used to subsume *many* phenomena occurring during this phase, which can now be pinpointed more precisely and vividly. Pine (1981), for instance, describes merging as occurring only during certain moments of heightened drive arousal during the symbiotic phase, rather than as a constant prevailing state.

All these recent findings suggest the need to reformulate the notion of the origins of empathy during the symbiotic phase. Instead of empathy based on merging, we prefer to refer to empathy based on "mutual attunement," which would include a more clearly defined scope of interactions between infants and their caregivers. Winnicott's (1953) notion of transitional experience seems relevant here, in the sense that it is these early interactions of mutuality, attunement, or communion between mother and infant that are revived throughout the lifespan and become a reservoir of creative experience.

Stern (1983) distinguishes several modes for mother and infant "to be" with each other. In particular, he distinguishes between state sharing and state complementing. Here, it would seem, lies the root to two paths toward empathy: one based on feeling the same as another person (state sharing), the other based on responding in one's unique way to the stimulus coming from the other person (state complementing). State complementing, the earliest nonmerger road toward empathy, develops into mutual cueing. Selective cueing has been described by Mahler and Furer (1963) as the way in which an infant learns to preferentially send those cues to which the mother has responded. This presumes an early form of empathy on the part of the infant, an anticipatory sense of response of the other to the self, concomitant with an accommodation of the self to the other.

Differentiation

The differentiation subphase begins during the height of symbiosis, at about five months of age. Presumably, the mother is now thoroughly and specifically known through all the child's sensory modalities, as is heralded by the specific smiling response, unmistakably directed toward her. A unique attachment has been formed. Although mother and infant are intensely at one with each other, the infant now begins actively to take in more and more of the nonmother environment.

It is no longer necessary or possible for the mother to be so perfectly attuned to her growing infant. Indeed, that she is not promotes both the creation of the transitional object and the sending out of more specific signals for her to provide for the satisfaction of the infant's needs. The infant, in signaling these needs to the mother, is now also more able to take into account the mother's capacity to respond to his demands.

To illustrate this point, we cite the observation of an eight-month-old boy and his mother:

> C.'s vocalizations have become more specific. He now seems to be mouthing sounds that appear more like words. For instance, at one point his mother asked him if he wanted a cracker, and he seemed to be

> repeating that sound. C.'s mother was a mother who responded exquisitely to her child's signals that indicated those capacities which lead to increasing individuation. She was much less able to respond to signals which indicated her child's needs for physical closeness.[2]

Here we see an eight-month-old's preference for giving those signals to which his mother can best respond. This we would characterize as an example of empathy that has its source in the differentiation subphase.

At this stage, infants more clearly distinguish mother, father, siblings, strangers. By learning that different people react in unique ways, through "customs inspections" and other means of recognizing and assessing people, children widen their repertoire of interactions and signals that elicit responses from the other. During this period, in which stranger anxiety appears, children often mysteriously take to certain people immediately and recoil from others. It seems, then, that they "read" the stranger in some way that must relate to the intimacy and familiarity they have established with their mothers. There exists an awareness of sameness and difference, based on the cognitive coordinations that develop during the last quarter of the first year.

Experiences pertaining to empathy become more varied and complex as the child's world widens and the world beyond the family is cathected. Children learn about other people's different ways of responding, and are often fascinated and sometimes frightened by strangers. They experiment with their newly acquired ability to signal and may try in this way to gain the attention of strangers. A little boy, observed at eight months, used a kind of shout to elicit a response from strangers. Once he succeeded, he excitedly initiated a smiling interaction with the stranger. He had learned that he needed to approach strangers differently from his family in order to gain their attention. He had also, through his family interactions, acquired the "confident expectation" (Benedek, 1938) that he could initiate pleasurable interactions.

---

[2]This mother-infant pair was observed in the separation-individuation study of normal infants conducted by Margaret Mahler and her associates at the Masters Children Center (See Mahler et al., 1975). This research is supported by NIMH Grant MH-08238, U.S. Public Health Service, Bethesda, Maryland, and FFRP Grant 069-458, Foundation Fund for Research in Psychiatry, New Haven, Connecticut, with Margaret S. Mahler, Principal Investigator, and John B. McDevitt, Co-Principal Investigator.

Practicing

The practicing subphase, which begins at about nine months, is ushered in by the infant's capacity for independent locomotion. During this period infants turn to the outside world with much greater energy and enthusiasm through their ability to move away from mother independently, first by paddling and crawling, and finally by independent upright locomotion. They seem relatively oblivious of mother as long as she remains peripherally available—in part because mother is still taken for granted. We hypothezise that the infant's omnipotence has not yet been disturbed so that the infant experiences mother as his extension. An invisible bond connects the infant with the mother, who is assumed and expected to be empathic to the infant's alternating needs for freedom to explore and to return for emotional refueling. The mother who is empathically available does not intrude, nor does she prematurely remove herself at this time. In this way the infant can put interactions with her temporarily into the background, gaining the freedom to put his energies into exploration and mastery. It is as if the infant had called a temporary halt to interactions with mother to allow for the push in autonomous and conflict-free functioning characteristic of this period. In other words, we hypothesize something akin to a "moratorium" on empathy in the service of individuation. It may be that too much attention to the mother would counteract the omnipotent belief in her presence and availability.

It is important that it is during this period of growing ability to be at a distance from mother that the beginning capacities for imitation and mental imagery appear. Imitation games previously initiated by the mother now begin to be initiated by the child. Imitation is an early attempt at being like the other, an essential intrapsychic process for the later maturation of empathic ability. As Gaddini (1969) notes: "The psychic protomodel of imitation—'imitating in order to be'— . . . installs itself not in the presence of the object but in its absence, and . . . precisely because of this, its aim seems to be that of reestablishing in a magical and omnipotent way the fusion of the self and the object" (p. 477).

Eventually the practicing toddler cannot help but experience limits to his elated exploration of the world. This brings about a deflation of mood and a painfully growing awareness of separateness, in turn making the toddler more aware of his need for the mother. Along with this greater awareness of his own needs, the toddler develops a greater sensitivity to the feelings of others. The following observations of a 16-month-old boy, Peter, illustrate the developing connection between the awareness of self and other (empathy).

Peter was observed at weekly intervals during his practicing subphase. Around the age of 16 months, a change in his mood was noticed. Only a week earlier this little boy had marched about the world as if he owned it, fearless and intrepid. Suddenly he seemed sober and clearly asked for more attention from and contact with his mother. When an observer mentioned this change to the mother, she agreed and connected it with an experience the day before. The beloved family dog had been taken to the vet and had to be left there overnight. Peter appeared to be very upset for many hours and was comforted by his mother. He was distressed by the possibility of absence of anyone in the family. We assume that the dog was an object upon which Peter displaced as well as projected his concerns. Saying this does not exclude the fact that Peter also missed the dog. When the dog returned, Peter was overjoyed and showered the dog with love and attention.

Peter himself had never been separated from his family for more than a few hours. Nevertheless, he seemed to empathize with his beloved dog, his constant playmate. Peter's behavior at the return of the dog suggests a shift from the height of omnipotence to a growing painful awareness of separateness. We hypothesize that he could no longer take his mother completely for granted and assume that she would always be available to him. His reaction to the dog's absence and return shows a double identification—the dog represented both the mother who could leave and a child who could be left. Peter identified with the comforting mother by comforting the dog, but he also identified with the abandoned dog by imagining the dog's pain.

Peter's reaction calls to mind a point made by Furer (1967), who connects the child's earliest ability to show empathy for another with the sense of loss caused by separation from mother. This sense of loss initiates a wish for incorporation in order to reunite with a loved subject. The reunion is accomplished through temporary and partial identification with the other's affective states. Furer names this phenomenon "identification with the consoler or the comforter."

The vignette of Peter suggests a similar process. Peter became very upset when separated from his dog and was comforted by his mother. Then, when the dog returned, he himself became loving and comforting with the dog. Furthermore, on the subsequent day he became especially attuned to his mother. When another person particularly close to Peter came to visit that day, Peter repeatedly came over to her, trying to feed her and showing affectionate concern by stroking and patting her back. We believe he was reenacting the "loss of dog" episode, which contained an empathic moment of comforting. He showed that the experience of being a comforter had become part of his behavioral repertoire—an early form of internalizing an interactive process (Loewald, 1978).

A week before the dog incident, Peter was observed watching his mother tend the garden. His mother was particularly pleased with a bed of red tulips. Peter, an active and curious little boy, did not touch the tulips. When the observer commented on this, the mother noted that when the tulips had first begun to bloom, Peter had touched them and tried to pick them, but then she had said, "Please don't do that. I like them so much. They are so beautiful." Peter apparently responded to the way in which his mother made this request, for on other occasions, when he was asked not to do something because it concerned his safety, he did not necessarily comply. That he did comply with the mother's request not to pick the flowers speaks to the possibility that he empathically understood her affect.

Rapprochement

During early rapprochement there is a renewal of the emphasis on state-sharing functions. (During differentiation and practicing there is more emphasis on state-complementing functions, such as signaling.) In the transition between practicing and rapprochement, children begin to be able to modulate their impulses and to relinquish a phase-specific activity (exploration) in the interests of joining in mother's pleasure. This step may be similar to what Furer (1967) refers to as the beginning ability to neutralize aggression.

The period of early rapprochement, from 15 to 18 months, is one that seems of special importance for the further development of empathy. This is the time at which most writers concerned with developmental issues place the beginning of true empathy (Schafer, 1959; Furer, 1967; Hoffman, 1978; Buie, 1981; McDevitt, 1981).

The early rapprochement subphase brings a major spurt in individuation which makes possible the developments leading toward more mature empathy. More and more, the child is forced to recognize that he and mother are separate, and at times reacts by wanting to again experience symbiotic bliss. This regressive pull toward a state entailing less awareness of separateness coincides with an upsurge in the development of empathy. In other words, although there is a regressive component to this period, there is also a progressive component in the child's newly enriched ability for empathic communication. Indeed, the unfolding of empathic ability has an ebb-and-flow quality.

Throughout separation-individuation there is a constant alternation between the development of capacities pertaining to object relating (such as empathy) and those that are more narcissistically invested, such as those found during the practicing period. One should also note that activities deriving from what Stern (1983) calls state complementing enter more prominently into empathy as children come to understand a higher level of sharing, in which their actions may complement those of the other, rather than simply imitating or joining with the other's wishes and needs.

Earlier, we referred to Furer's concept of identification with the comforter. The following vignette of a 17-month-old, Paula, illustrates a different aspect of this identification. Rather than identification with the comforter per se, it reveals something we might call identification with the pleasure-giver. Wishing to give and share is characteristic of the child during early rapprochement, and this may also be seen as an identification with the mother who has been giving to the child.

Paula was taken to the playground by her mother on an early spring day. Her mother had not brought along toys, but many children there had toys that Paula desired. In a way typical of a toddler of her age, she wandered around, picking up toys of the other children. The mother suddenly had the feeling that Paula needed a toy of her own. She picked her up and walked with her to a nearby store to buy a toy. Paula had just learned to kiss, an act which delighted her mother. On the way to the toy store, mother asked Paula for a kiss, but Paula refused. Mother found a ball at the store, which she bought for Paula. Together, with Paula holding the ball, they walked back to the playground. On the way back to the playground, Paula spontaneously hugged and kissed her mother.

To understand this vignette in terms of empathy, it is necessary to assume that Paula understood her mother's concern and wish to make her feel happy. She then identified with the mother and in turn did something she knew would make her mother happy. In this vignette we see both state sharing and state complementing. Paula and her mother shared the happy mood, but the happy mood was brought about by each giving to the other what she empathically understood the other to want.

The wish for symbiotic pleasure and the wish to be separate and autonomous constitute a conflict, which becomes more acute and internalized during the second part of the second year, as the child reaches the rapprochement crisis. Along with a relative sense of helplessness, a depressive mood often occurs as the mother can no longer consistently relieve the child's sense of aloneness. Thus, there is an unavoidable break in the mother's empathy with her child.

Splitting is a characteristic phenomenon during the rapprochement subphase. We observe something akin to a split in the capacity for empathy, for the memory of the good mother is different from the actually experienced mother. The mother can no longer counteract the developmentally necessary waning of omnipotence. At times when she is seen as bad, a phenomenon occurs which we might call negative empathy (M. S. Mahler, personal communication). The concept of negative empathy suggests that at particular moments of acute conflict or frustration, the child can only empathize with the "bad mother" or, as Mahler (1971) has called her, the mother of separation.

Examples of such negative empathy may be found in the toddler's new suspiciousness of mother and her intentions. Toddlers at this time often display sudden, extreme fussiness in relation to the food mother provides. Also particularly characteristic of this period are fights about getting dressed. One child who was observed during the rapprochement period had had a particularly good early relationship with his parents, but now often acted as if mother were about to inflict terrible pain upon him when it was time to get dressed. He fought and struggled, and sometimes it would take hours before he agreed to get dressed. A particular aspect of this struggle over dressing seemed to be that the child did not want to give up the clothes he was wearing, sometimes clinging to his pajamas while getting dressed for the day, or, the other way around, holding onto his daytime clothes when it was time to go to bed. The seeming fear was probably overdetermined. In part, it may have been due to projection of his own aggressive impulses. Yet it may also have been due to fear of reengulfment and intrusion on his burgeoning autonomy, which had to be defended against to the hilt. Further, clinging to the clothes he was supposed to take off may have been connected with wanting to cling to the old all-good mother, who was not contaminated by frustration and badness.

Characteristically, in this time of struggle, the mother is not treated as the person the child has formerly known her to be. Instead, she seems to become the person to be fought with or clung to—the person who is the frustrator or the giver of pleasure. During practicing the real mother is temporarily ignored or treated as an object of convenience in order to allow for the spurt in individuation; somewhat differently, during rapprochement the real mother may sometimes not be perceived because of the child's tendency to see the mother as all-bad if she cannot be all-good.

As long as the mother is perceived as "good," state sharing is pleasurable. But when the mother is no longer perceived as all-good, state sharing becomes contaminated by her badness. By the time of the rapprochement struggle, then, identifying with the mother is no longer as pleasurable because of how she is perceived; on the other hand, if the child can no longer identify with mother, feelings of loneliness and abandonment may occur. At times the child may seek to reunite with mother by clinging. Clinging, however, does not take into account the feelings of the other; it does not contribute to the development of empathy.

During early rapprochement we saw the beginnings of indentification with the good, providing mother. During the rapprochement crisis we see a similar phenomenon in regard to the bad, frustrating aspects of mother. In other words, we see two strands of empathy—empathy with the good, providing mother and empathy with the bad, frustrating mother. In our opinion, these two strands—positive and negative empathy—must become integrated for mature empathy and the capacity for concern to come about. One might relate this to the idealization and devaluation processes regularly seen in narcissistic and borderline patients, whose ability to empathize with the other remains in its primitive mode, split between positive and negative empathy.

It is not unusual for mothers to ask for consultations because their rapprochement toddlers have inexplicably turned into little tyrants. One mother came in for such a consultation because her usually bright, charming 20-month-old daughter had recently developed intense hostility toward her. Observed in a play session, the mother seemed quite patient and understanding, eager to please her willful and disgruntled child. The little girl began to feed and put some dolls to bed. In between taking care of the dolls, attempting to be loving, she would stamp around the room and mutter, "Look at the mess, look at all this work I have to do." Mother looked shocked because she knew that this was how she herself often felt during this difficult period. She had not at all realized that this was how her daughter perceived her. All her goodness, self-sacrifice, and concern seemed to go unperceived by the little girl at this time.

Eventually, toddlers have to resolve the rapprochement conflicts. Partial resolution of the ambivalence characteristic of the rapprochement crisis takes place by way of selective identification, which brings about primarily libidinal cathexis of the maternal representation—one of the essential determinants of object constancy. As McDevitt (1981) describes it: "In [the] fourth subphase the senior toddler's more complex fantasy, more friendly and cooperative behavior, more mature ego-determined object relations, and increased regard for others, all suggest that his identifications have moved from the previous, primitive imitations to more selective ego identification" (p. 140).

To take this step, toddlers may have to develop some recognition of their capacity to inflict pain as well as to experience pain. At the end of the rapprochement subphase, one toddler we observed showed a tendency to identify with the victims of his aggression. It is by way of "identification with the victim" that an incipient stage of compassion may be experienced. One must know how it feels to be hurt before one can realize that one is capable of hurting another person. This is a selective identification, in which the child does not become the other, but imagines the pain of the other by imagining the other's experience. The toddler we observed had a history of attacking other infants when they interfered with him. At a certain point, he became preoccupied with talking about his own pain, real or imagined. We hypothesize that this preoccupation was a precursor to the ability to develop concern for the other.

Similarly, the same little boy often played a game in which he ordered his mother to cry as he was saying goodbye, leaving the room. In play, he inflicted pain on her that he felt when she left him. How would one analyze this play from the point of view of developing empathy? The boy seemed to be telling his mother how he felt by asking her to have the same experience. He clearly derived satisfaction when he could become the comforter and stop her crying on his return. From the point of view of drive-defense interpretations, we would see this play as identification with the aggressor, as well as an attempt at mastery by rendering active what was passively experienced. Looking at this play from the perspective of empathic development, we would point to the wish to share important feelings—namely, sadness over separation and joy over reunion.

Beginning Object Constancy

Good and bad self- and object representations become integrated into a whole-object representation when the subphase of beginning object constancy is reached. There is a dramatic difference between a toddler caught up in rapprochement struggles and a toddler who has reached a degree of object constancy. With regard to the development of empathy, an important change occurs in the child's capacity to show concern for the welfare of others.

In normal development, the good mother manages to survive the rapprochement storms without becoming unavailable to the child. The mother who remains available and nonretaliatory promotes the representation of herself as constant and "indestructible."[3] Once on the way to object constancy, the child can develop the capacity for selective and "trial" identifications (Fliess, 1942) necessary for mature empathy. The child must learn to tolerate separateness, without overwhelming fear of abandonment, to obtain positive, internal, libidinally cathected self- and object representations, which allow for the trial identifications.

Children who develop object constancy can maintain a balance between narcissistic needs of the self and object-relational needs pertaining to others. They do not need to be overly sacrificial in order to please another: they do not have to please another at all costs, nor do they need to fight their wishes to please mother for fear of being overwhelmed. Thus, the road of state sharing and state complementing leads to relaxed give-and-take abilities and skills.

A child of two and a half years was at the beach with his parents and friends. While they were taking a walk, they were attacked by a swarm of mosquitoes. They all ran to the car to drive back to the house in which they were staying. When they arrived at the house, the little boy rushed to the house and called to the person who had been most severely attacked, "Come here, come here." He then rushed to the shower to show her where she could shower off the mosquitoes. He had perceived her discomfort and was concerned with showing her where the shower was.

The capacity for concern and mature empathy is possible only when self and other have been sufficiently separated for the self to be concerned with the other. This advance coincides with the capacity for higher forms of symbolization. It is through symbolization that issues relating to self-other interactions can be played out and experimented with. Children's play and role-taking is a constant way in which these issues are practiced. Although regressions occur, there is nevertheless a qualitative change that seems to take place once the fourth subphase of separation-individuation is reached. This qualitative change endures through regressive episodes and upheavals.

---

[3]Winnicott (1963) describes these as necessary qualities in analysts treating patients who maintain what we are calling a perspective of negative empathy. In his terms, analysts must let themselves be used and destroyed by these patients and yet remain indestructible and nonretaliatory.

Clinical Considerations

In tracing its development, we saw that the capacity for empathy does not unfold in an uninterrupted linear fashion. There is an ebb and flow of empathic ability, which can be explained by the back and forth flow of the child's developmental momentum toward subphase resolution. At times the attainment of certain subphase functions, which must eventually be integrated within the child's psychic economy, may result in the temporary suppression of competing functions or a slowdown in the unfolding of other, as yet undifferentiated functions. Pine (1971) has alluded to this in relation to locomotion and separation anxiety. The same seems to hold with empathy.

As with other developmental lines (A. Freud, 1963), there may be developmental impasses and fixations that lead to impaired empathic functioning. Observations of impaired empathic ability in adult and child patients provide additional insights into the nature of early object relations. Two adult patients—Miss A. and Miss B.—illustrate how a severely disturbed mother-child relationship during symbiosis and separation-individuation may have an effect on the capacity for empathy.

Miss A., a woman in her twenties, of exceptional intelligence and artistic ability, concealed her sensitivity behind a belief that she should interact with others in a mechanical, almost robotlike fashion. She was severely frightened by any deviation from her rigid expectations. She did not complain that she found it difficult to interpret the reactions of others to her; she always felt that she knew they hated her because she was bad. She thus felt there was no use in trying to reach out to others; she already knew what the outcome of the relationship would be.

Although Miss A. was capable of being caring and empathic with plants, animals, and people in need, she tended to project onto these objects her own intense and unmet needs for nurturance. If a plant in the analyst's office was not healthy, she interpreted it as a sign that the analyst was cruel and uncaring toward her. If even a book was leaning or out of place, she expressed pity, concern for the uncared-for object, and anger at the uncaring analyst. A sense of frustration and anger was readily invoked by and in others. With the analyst, for instance, it often seemed as if Miss A. were simply refusing the good nurturance of interpretation and insight. Her omnipotent demands, coupled with helpless clinging, made the analyst feel somewhat like the mother of the rapprochement child, who is expected to do the impossible. The collaborative therapeutic alliance was extremely fragile and easily disrupted.

Growing up with a depressed mother and a sadistic father, Miss A. had lacked the opportunity for rich emotional interactions. Her mother had been physically ill, depressed, and depleted, receiving little or no emotional supplies through her marriage. Thus, during those periods in which development is propelled by closeness and psychological proximity, Miss A. was instead reprimanded for her striving for attachment; she was expected to be self-sufficient and nondemanding at all times. Being well-endowed, she eventually gained some satisfactions from autonomous endeavors, which brought little shreds of recognition from her parents. We hypothesize that she never experienced empathic understanding and withdrew into a world in which she might experience a measure of predictability—the world of inanimate objects, which she endowed with animate qualities. In her adult life, she lived out her infantile destiny, in that she could never find anyone who responded to her emotional or physical needs. She constantly found subtle ways to defy and render ineffective the attempts of others to respond empathically to her.

In sum, Miss A.'s difficulties with empathy made it almost impossible for her to build satisfying relationships. She was lonely, longed for closeness, but was unable to find it. In the transference she had a tendency to attune herself to negativity and could not focus on issues involving the analyst's warmth or concern. The developmental line of empathy seemed to be disturbed in all its phases. There was none of the mutuality of the symbiotic phase. She was not able to take anyone, including the analyst, for granted—a practicing subphase element of empathic ability. Negative empathy, originating during rapprochement, was present in full force. Thus, her capacity for object constancy as well as mature empathy was impaired.

Miss B., a woman in her early thirties, had a tendency toward severe depression, which originated in her disturbed relationship with a severely narcissistic mother. Her father, although a kind man, had been withdrawn, unavailable, and unable to fully counterbalance the mother's sadism and her constant tendency to abandon her child. The mother took pleasure in interacting with her daughter only as long as the child was obedient and subservient to her wishes. The sweet little lap baby of symbiosis, the early rapprochement toddler wishing to please the mother—these phases of the child's development were probably enjoyed by the mother. In the practicing subphase, however, Miss B. was most likely deprived of emotional supplies, thus undermining her autonomy and the formation of an integrated self, at a distance from the mother. The cranky, demanding child of the rapprochement crisis was intolerable for this mother. As a result, during her childhood, Miss B. struggled to appease her mother and extract emotional supplies. This tendency to persevere remained a characteristic feature of her object relating, along with a propensity for a "false self." Although she strove for authenticity in her relationships, she was paralyzed by fear of disapproval and the potential loss of relationships. Miss B. was well aware of her tendency to try to elicit emotional supplies from others, but despised herself for it. Thus, she was overconcerned with fairness and evenness in all her relationships.

Tortured by her need always to know what others were thinking of her, Miss B. often imagined the analyst to be critical. She would then become suffused with depressive feelings of badness and worthlessness. Frequently, she became distressed after personal encounters with friends. She always thought she had antagonized the other person by doing something wrong. The childhood situation with her unpredictable mother was replayed over and over, interfering with her ability to find what she most desperately wanted—companionship, understanding, and warmth. On those occasions when these were available, she felt truly happy.

Miss B. had a genuine capacity for empathy, but it was interfered with by her tendency to overidentify or be overconcerned with the internal states of others. Unlike Miss A., however, Miss B. was able to distance herself and observe angry and violent feelings as they emerged in the transference. Her lack of empathy was almost a symptom from which she suffered, one which she aimed to resolve. She wished not just to be understood, but also to be understanding. This meant that narcissistic hurts and misunderstandings could be cleared up. Although object relating was painful to her, she never doubted its ultimate value. As a small child, Miss B. had known that it was possible for her to please her mother, although eventually her mother's narcissistic character structure rendered the cost too great. Moreover, her father, though emotionally unavailable, had been a benign rather than a cruel force.

Looking at Miss B. from the perspective of developmental stages toward the capacity for concern, we surmise that her difficulties began very early. Yet she must have experienced moments of symbiotic attunement, because of her wish to elicit responsiveness from others. Her difficulties may have begun during the differentiation subphase, for what seemed most disturbed was the ability to read others' cues. This hypothesis fits the picture Miss B. painted of her mother's inability to tolerate independence in her child. During the practicing period Miss B. was not allowed to develop her individuality while taking mother for granted. Thus, she was constantly afraid of losing the other's love if she pursued her own autonomous interests, which she was quite determined to do. From these difficulties, it follows that all subsequent stages of empathy would be disturbed.

Contrasting these two cases, we hypothesize that the rapprochement crisis was less severe and destructive for Miss B. than for Miss A. because, during the symbiotic phase and early rapprochement, there was an increased potential for positive affective contacts between mother and child. Further, during rapprochement Miss B.'s father was present as a noncontaminated other, possibly offering some refuge and consolation. In both cases, however, we see a complex interaction between the mother's character structure, her incapacities and capacities for empathy with her growing child, and the child's internalizations, which were eventually amalgamated in a self lacking in certain abilities for understanding the other's internal states and expressing concern.

Conclusion

In examining empathy from the perspective of separation-individuation, we have noted that the symbiotic phase and the period of early rapprochement are the periods in which the forerunners of empathy are most clearly discernible. By contrast, the practicing subphase, with its empahasis on mastery, autonomy, and narcissistic enhancement of the self, is a time at which there is a moratorium on the unfolding of the capacity for concern. The periods of differentiation and the rapprochement crisis are times of tension or unbalance between active and autonomous exploration of the world away from mother and closeness to the mother. Optimally, when this conflict is resolved during the period of differentiation, the path to a full blossoming of the practicing period opens. Similarly, when the rapprochement crisis moves toward resolution, the way is open for the emergence of self- and object constancy and the attainment of a true capacity for concern.

With the two adult patients we described, we attempted to apply our understanding of early empathic development to the clinical analytic situation. We hope we have avoided the oft-described pitfall of oversimplification in presenting these cases and drawing comparisons between infantile events and adult personality outcomes. In both cases, we believe the parents' character structures interacted with the child's patterns as they emerged during the separation-individuation subphases and influenced developing psychic structures which determined subsequent object relations. For both Miss A. and Miss B., it must be noted, the difficulties in the capacity for empathy were only one aspect of a very complicated clinical picture. Subsequent experience which overlays a particular infantile psychic resolution will always alter the nature of the psychic structure. Nevertheless, the original resolution is significant. Although the correspondence with adult structure is not exact, we think it is important enough to merit a return to a consideration of the formative stages of psychic structuralization.

REFERENCES

Bachrach, H. M. (1976), Empathy. *Arch. Gen. Psychiat.*, 33:35–48.

Benedek, T. (1938), Adaptation to reality in early infancy. *Psychoanal. Quart.*, 7:200–214.

Beres, D. (1968), The role of empathy in psychotherapy and psychoanalysis. *J. Hillside Hosp.*, 17:362–369.

_____ & Arlow, J. (1974), Fantasy and identification in empathy. *Psychoanal. Quart.*, 43:26–50.

Bergman, A. (1981), Ours, yours, mine. In: *Rapprochement: The Critical Subphase of Separation-Individuation*, ed. R. F. Lax, S. Bach, & J. A. Burland. New York: Aronson, pp. 199–216.

Bowlby, J. (1961), Separation anxiety: A critical review of the literature. *J. Child Psychol. Psychiat.* 1:251–269.

Brazelton, T. B. (1981), Neonatal assessment. In: *The Course of Life: Psychoanalytic Contributions toward Understanding Human Development*, Vol. 1, ed. S. I. Greenspan & G. H. Pollock. Washington, D.C.: U.S. Government Printing Office, pp. 203–233.

_____ Koslowski, B., & Main, M. (1974), The origins of reciprocity: The early mother-infant interaction. In: *The Effect of the Infant on Its Caregiver*, ed. M. Lewis & L. Rosenblum. New York: Wiley, pp. 49–76.

Buie, D. (1981), Empathy: Its nature and limitations. *J. Amer. Psychoanal. Assn.*, 29:281–307.

Emde, R., Gaensbauer, T., & Harmon, R. (1976), *Emotional Expression in Infancy: A Biobehavioral Study* [*Psychol. Issues, Monogr.* 37]. New York: International Universities Press.

Ferreira, A. J. (1961), Empathy and the bridge function of the ego. *J. Amer. Psychoanal. Ass.*, 9:91–105.

Fliess, R. (1942), The metapsychology of the analyst. *Psychoanal. Quart.*, 11:211–227.

Freud, A. (1963), The concept of developmental lines. *The Psychoanalytic Study of the Child,* 18:245–266. New York: International Universities Press.

Freud, S. (1921), Group psychology and the analysis of the ego. *Standard Edition,* 18:69–143. London: Hogarth Press, 1955.

Furer, M. (1967), Some developmental aspects of the superego. *Int. J. Psycho-Anal.* 48:277–280.

Gaddini, E. (1969), On imitation. *Int. J. Psycho-Anal.*, 50:475–484.

Greenson, R. R. (1960), Empathy and its vicissitudes. *Int. J. Psycho-Anal.* 41:418–424.

Harlow, H. F. & Harlow, M. K. (1965), The affectional systems. In: *Behavior of Nonhuman Primates,* Vol. 2, ed. A. M. Schrier, H. F. Harlow, & F. Stollnitz. New York: Academic Press.

Hoffman, M. L. (1978), Toward a theory of empathic arousal and development. In: *The Development of Affect,* ed. M. Lewis & L. A. Rosenblum. New York: Plenum, pp. 227–256.

Lewis, M. & Rosenblum, L. A., Eds. (1974), *The Effect of the Infant on Its Caregiver.* New York: Wiley.

Loewald, H. (1978), Instinct theory, object relations, and psychic-structure formation. *J. Amer. Psychoanal. Assn.*, 26:463–506.

Mahler, M. S. (1942), Pseudoimbecility: A magic cap of invisibility. In: *Selected Papers,* Vol. 1. New York: Aronson, 1980, pp. 3–16.

_____ (1971), A study of the separation-individuation process and its possible application to borderline phenomena in the psychoanalytic situation. *The Psychoanalytic Study of the Child,* 26:403–424. New York: Quadrangle.

_____ & Furer, M. (1963), Certain aspects of the separation-individuation phase. *Psychoanal. Quart.*, 32:1–14.

_____, Pine, F., & Bergman, A. (1975), *The Psychological Birth of the Human Infant.* New York: Basic Books.

McDevitt, J. B. (1981), The role of internalization in the development of object relations during the separation-individuation phase. In: *Rapprochement: The critical subphase of Separation-Individuation,* ed. R. L. Lax, S. Bach, & J. A. Burland. New York: Aronson, pp. 135–149.

Meissner, W. W. (1970), Notes on identification, I: Origins in Freud. *Psychoanal. Quart.*, 39: 563–589.

_____. (1971), Notes on Identification, II: Clarification of related concepts. *Psychoanal. Quart.*, 40:277–302.

_____(1972), Notes on identifications, III: The concept of identification. *Psychoanal. Quart.*, 41:224–260.

Olden, C. (1958), Notes on the development of empathy. *The Psychoanalytic Study of the Child,* 13:505–518. New York: International Universities Press.

Pine, F. (1971), On the separation process: Universal trends and individual differences. In: *Separation-Individuation: Essays in Honor of Margaret S. Mahler,* ed. J. B. McDevitt & C. F. Settlage. New York: International Universities Press, pp. 113–130.

_____ (1981), In the beginning: Contributions to a psychoanalytic developmental psychology. *Int. Rev. Psycho-Anal.,* 8:15–33.

Sander, L. W. (1976), Issues in early mother-child interactions. In: *Infant Psychiatry: A New Synthesis,* ed. E. M. Rexford, L. W. Sander, & T. Shapiro. New Haven: Yale University Press.

_____ (1977), Regulation of exchange in the infant-caretaker system: A viewpoint on the ontogeny of "structures." In: *Communicative Structures and Psychic Structures,* ed. N. Freedman & S. Grand. New York: Plenum Press.

Schafer, R. (1959). Generative empathy in the treatment situation. *Psychoanal. Quart.* 28:342–373.

_____ (1968), *Aspects of Internalization.* New York: International Universities Press.

Shapiro, T. (1974), The development and distortions of empathy. *Psychoanal. Quart.,* 43:4–25.

Stern, D. (1971). A micro-analysis of mother-infant interaction. *J. Amer. Acad. Child Psychiat.,* 10:501–517.

_____ (1983), The early differentiation of self and other. In: *Reflections on Self Psychology,* ed. S. Kaplan & J. D. Lichtenberg. Hillsdale, N.J.: Analytic Press.

Winnicott, D. W. (1953), Transitional objects and transitional phenomena: A study of the first not-me possession. *Int. J. Psycho-Anal.,* 34:89–97.

_____ (1963), The development of the capacity for concern. In: *The Maturational Processes and the Facilitating Environment.* New York: International Universities Press, 1965, pp. 73–82.

18 Maternal Empathy: Its Relation to Emerging Self-Representations and Empathy in Infants

ELSIE R. BROUSSARD, M.D., Dr. P.H.

Helen Ross has said: "Having empathy with a child requires the ability to jump into the skin of the little child long enough to know what the child is feeling *and* the ability to jump out quickly enough so as not to be trapped there" (personal communication, 1974). This operational definition implies that empathy is a special mode of perceiving what the child feels that requires the observer to maintain an awareness of differentiation from the child.

Much remains to be learned about how an individual acquires the capacity to be empathic and the factors that enhance or impede the development of that capacity. I am in agreement with Buie (1981), who takes issue with the idea that "merging" is the origin and basic component of empathy. Rather, he posits a theory of empathy as a "capacity that evolves with neuropsychological maturation and interpersonal interactions in the course of individual development" (p. 305). He considers empathy to depend on the observer's sensory perception of behavioral cues that the other person provides about his (or her) inner state. These cues are compared with referents in the observer's mind for similar behavioral expressions. This observation then leads to an in-

---

This research has been supported by the Amelia Miles Foundation, Benedum Foundation, Buhl Foundation, Pittsburgh Foundation, Staunton Farm Foundation, private donations, and NIH General Research Support Grant No. FR 5451.

I wish to express sincere appreciation to Dr. Margaret B. McFarland for her careful review of the two cases presented in this paper.

ference that the other person's inner experience qualitatively matches that associated with the observer's referent.

The mother's capacities to read the infant's cues and facilitate the infant's emergent sense of potency—of being able to have an impact on the environment—have long been considered essential ingredients in fostering optimal development (Winnicott, 1958, 1960); Burlingham, 1967; Basch, 1975; Sander, 1975). Communicating to infants that they are understood, that their messages do count, may take a variety of forms, as adults provide infants with experiences designed to maintain internal and external stimuli at an optimal level. When infant's communications are responded to in a facilitative fashion, they learn that they are valued and that the world can be a pleasurable place.

A number of authors view a failure in communication and the subsequent recovery between mother and child as providing a basis for the formation of new associations, which are then utilized in fostering the child's maturation (Kohut, 1971; Basch, 1975). As organization is repeatedly restored, a brain pattern of expectation is laid down—the anticipation that restitution will follow disorganization later becomes "hope." Conversely, if failure in restoration of organization predominates, an encoded experience of mounting disorganization for which no help is forthcoming is presumed to occur. The likely outcome is escape into isolation, regression, apathy. An infant's experience of maternal failure to provide a predictable, rhythmic environment, which supports the brain's need for active creation and ordering of patterns, may later become associated with lowered self-esteem and ambivalence toward narcissistically significant objects (Basch, 1975). When the mother evidences an affective and perceptual failure, so that the infant's messages are not heard, received, and implemented in a facilitative fashion, we observe a mother-infant system in distress (Broussard and Cornes, 1981).

Some Longitudinal Studies

Within the Pittsburgh First-Born Program, we have conducted prospective longitudinal studies of healthy, full-term, first-born infants. The studies of a cohort born in 1963 demonstrated the relationship between the mother's perception of her neonate and the child's subsequent psychosocial development (Broussard, 1976, 1979, 1982). The Broussard Neonatal Perception Inventories (NPI) were used to measure the mother's perception of her newborn compared with her concept of the average infant. They provide a measure of the adaptive potential of the mother-infant system during the first month of life. With the NPI, which may be viewed as a projective measure, the mother is presented with a set of ambiguous stimuli—the Average Baby and Your Baby—onto which she projects her concept of what little babies are like and her perception of her newborn. When a mother does *not* perceive her one-month-old as better than average (negative perception), the infant is considered to be at high risk for subsequent psychosocial disorder. Those infants viewed as better than average (positive perception) were considered to be at low risk.

Subsequent evaluations, conducted by psychiatrists who did not know the one-month risk ratings of the first-borns, established the predictive validity of the NPI. There was a statistically significant correlation between prediction and outcome. At each age (4½, 10½, and 15), more children rated at high risk at one month were found to have psychosocial disorder than those who were rated at low risk. At age 15, the odds ratio was 5.5 to 1. In other words, a one-month-old who had been viewed negatively by the mother was 5.5 times more likely to have a psychosocial disorder at age 15 than an infant who had been viewed positively.[1]

Longitudinal studies were begun in 1973 of a second cohort of healthy, full-term, first-born neonates (Broussard, 1977, 1978, 1979; Broussard and Cornes, 1981).[2]

Our observations revealed differences in the maternal characteristics between mothers of high- and low-risk infants. The mother's perception of her neonate seems to tap her own self-esteem. In contrast to mothers of infants at low risk, mothers of infants at high risk were noted to: (1) have negative self-images, lack confidence in themselves as mothers, and be dependent on the external world, although often not able to use available help; (2) distrust the available environmental

---

[1]The presence of a positive maternal perception during the neonatal period does not guarantee that there will be no difficulties in the child's subsequent development. Many intervening life variables may impinge and interfere with development. However, successful negotiation of early developmental tasks prepares the infant-mother system to face the tasks yet to come.

[2]Observations were made during mother-infant group meetings and home visits. Each group, consisting of seven or eight mothers and their first-born infants, met every other week for one and one-half hours. When the children were two years old, they remained in the familiar room while their mothers met in an adjacent room for one hour. During each meeting, observers recorded sequential notes on each infant, mother, and mother-infant interaction from behind a one-way-vision mirror. The majority of the meetings were also videotaped. Home visits provided another source of data.

support systems; (3) have difficulty recognizing and responding to their infant's cues; and (4) often seem depressed and anxious.[3] We found that mothers who have a positive perception of their infants tend to have "optimal" empathy—i.e., they can recognize the infant's cues, are aware of the infant's state, and use a flexible range of modalities to respond to the infant's needs. Their self-images are predominantly positive; they are optimistic, showing pride and pleasure in their infants and pleasure in motherhood.

What, then, is the relationship between maternal empathy and the development of the infant's emergent self-representations and empathy? To illustrate this relationship, I have chosen longitudinal observational data for two infants. My premise is that a generational transmission of patterned communicational behavior serves as a precursor for the variations in self-representations and empathy.

Bobby

Bobby, product of an uncomplicated pregnancy and delivery, was the normal, healthy, eight-pound first-born of white, married, 24-year-old parents. The pregnancy was unplanned, a "shock," interrupting the parents' lifestyle. Both parents expected a girl. Mrs. X. said Bobby's kicking *in utero* was "his way of getting back at me." She described her delivery as horrible and viewed Bobby as a destructive male child. "He was crying before he was fully born," she complained, adding, "My mother had a very hard time delivering her boy baby."[4]

Both parents said the first postpartum month was "frantic." As Mrs. X. put it: "All the time is his; what's left over is mine." Unable to read his needs, she felt helpless: "I wish I knew when a problem was a problem." Bobby's difficulties in sleeping and feeding and his excessive crying attested to his mother's inability to regulate his life functions. Lacking the maternal basis for stability, Bobby had little opportunity to develop confidence in a need-meeting mother.

---

[3]Our observations of mother-infant pairs do not substantiate Greenson's (1960) contention that depressed individuals tend to be more empathic.

[4]Mrs. X. was the fifth girl born before the birth of her only brother. Her earliest memory was of his birth when she was two years old. She claimed that as a child she often feared her parents. Cumulative observations suggested that she projected her angry, aggressive feelings onto the infant brother, who had displaced her and identified with her parents, whom she experienced as harsh and punitive.

Mr. and Mrs. X. were committed to being good parents and providing for their infant's needs, although their opinions differed. Mother bought Bobby a doll because she wanted him to develop feelings of tenderness. Father wanted him to have only boy-type things. He said, "He'll have to decide to be a boy some day."

When Bobby was three and a half months old, Mrs. X. brought him to a mother-infant group meeting. Although he was able to turn over, she placed him supine on a high table and sat outside of his visual range. For 30 minutes she left him on the table in this location, which did not facilitate his engagement with the world of others. He brought two hands to midline, mouthed his fingers, and babbled. When his hand touched a nearby blanket, he covered and uncovered his face with it several times. When he kicked his legs, Mrs. X. asked if he were hyperactive. She unduly delayed responding to his cues of fatigue until he cried loudly. Then she stood and held him tightly against her chest while swaying to and fro. "The only way I can get him to sleep is to hold him very firmly," she explained. An observer noted that she seemed locked in a stranglehold with the infant. Moreover, she appeared anxious and depressed. Although Bobby was a handsome, vigorous infant, she showed no pride. There was an absence of joy in mother and infant.

Mrs. X. complained that breast-feeding lasted an hour and usually had to be terminated by her. She asked other group members how to teach a child not to bite and how to discipline him so he would not hurt others. She feared Bobby was getting spoiled and said she was reluctant to pick him up too quickly, lest he become too demanding. When Bobby continued to fuss, mother was reluctant to breast-feed. She made several "false" starts—picking him up, undoing her bra, then returning him to the floor, then lifting and holding him, etc. When she did give him the breast, Bobby gulped vigorously and mother seemed uncomfortable. She held him very tightly with his right arm around her back. Consistently, she inhibited his touch, removing his free hand from her face, hair, or clothing. This pattern of repeatedly restricting Bobby's exploratory contacts with her body was also typical of other interactions with him. Her behavior suggested that she considered his behavior to be aggression against her, rather than natural exploration.

With the appearance of Bobby's first two teeth at five months, 15 days, Mrs. X. expressed many concerns: Were the teeth straight? Could he damage them by his grinding? She brought a toy to the group that other mothers thought dangerous. Mrs. X. mirrored to Bobby her fear of the devouring male, her hostile wish to be free of him, as well as fleeting moments of loving tenderness (the latent positive end of her ambivalence). Guilt feelings about her wishes to be free of Bobby made her perpetually anxious. Bobby was an object for her projection and was viewed as bad and aggressive. Thus, with her infant son, Mrs. X. seemed to repeat her perception at age two of the aggressive mother and the bad, demanding male infant, that is, of her own mother and baby brother.

By six months Bobby had achieved integration of eye-hand-mouth-autonomous sit coordination (Resch, 1979). He was an alert, vocal, handsome, active infant, interested in the other infants and his surround. As he began to creep, Mrs. X. was repeatedly unavailable to him—out of his perceptual range. Often he approached her, only to find her unresponsive to his presence. His expression at these times was forlorn.

Abruptly, Mrs. X. weaned Bobby from the breast at six months, 20 days. She still held him very tightly for bottle-feeding at seven months, 15 days. Once, when he tried to terminate the feeding, she re-presented the bottle four times before responding to his struggles to end. She called him "a louse," complained about his irregular sleeping and feeding, and said she wished for a two- to three-month period of relief from childcare.

There was an increase of aggression in both mother and child. At eight months, 20 days, Bobby sat on his mother's lap. When he touched her scarf, Mrs. X. immediately put him down. He grabbed at the hair of another infant, Jay, and mother slapped his hand, saying "No." He persisted in pursuing Jay and mother repeatedly slapped his hand, saying, "No, bad." Bobby did not sustain interest in toys. His darting, restless activity had a driven quality, and he often bit or pinched other infants.

There was evidence of an attempt at early reaction formation in Bobby's handling of oral aggression. At nine months mother said she could now distinguish between his biting mouth and kissing mouth. Crawling and darting everywhere, he roughly explored and attempted to "kiss" other babies. Mrs. X. hovered, waiting for him to aggress; then she would counteraggress, slapping and scolding.

Mrs. X. had difficulty in functioning simultaneously within and without the mother-infant dyad. When talking to another adult or child, she seemed unable to disengage from that relationship to focus on Bobby. Often she lost him from her perceptual field, oblivious to impending dangers and unaware of his cues to her. When he was 10 months, 20 days, mother was unaware of Bobby's attempt to crawl into a trashbasket. Another mother moved quickly to protect him. Hence Bobby's "practicing" served to confirm his identity as the oral-aggressive baby of this particular mother. But Bobby's moving away from his mother was more frightening than pleasurable because she did not remain visually and emotionally available or protective.

There were many instances when Bobby approached mother only to experience rejection. For example, at 14 months he climbed into mother's vacated chair. Sternly she said, "You took my chair; I suppose now you will want my drink too. Get down." Mrs. X. viewed him as continually taking from her. She showed little evidence of gratification in giving to him or in receiving from him.

At 15 months, Bobby's outwardly directed aggression toward the other children dramatically decreased in the group setting. Even the "kissing" disappeared. But it was replaced by an abundance of self-directed aggression—biting of the tongue or mouth, accidents, pinching his own abdomen, etc. At home his acts of aggression continued; these included head-banging, hurling objects, and attacking his mother. When he hit her, her response was: "No! Nice Mommy. Mommy nice." Then Bobby hit himself. Seldom did Mrs. X. help him to modulate his aggression. She continued to aggress on him—spanking, slapping, and speaking harshly.

During the ensuing months, Mrs. X. repeatedly struggled to contain her aggressive feelings. She talked in a soft, sweet voice to Bobby, and postponed appropriate action when he needed redirection. Finally, unable to contain her anger, she lashed out furiously. Her chief mode of dealing with aggression was containment; when this ultimately failed, she turned her aggression on Bobby.

At age 17 months, 28 days, Bobby had a large bruise on his forehead. Mother said, "He falls so much; I can't get a picture of him without a bruise on his forehead." On this day Mrs. X. held him on her lap, feeding him cake from her plate. As though approving of his passivity, she gently stroked his head, saying, "He's gotten to be a better boy." His interactions with the staff and other children lacked spontaneity. He withdrew to isolation under a desk and intentionally banged his head against the desk. Mother took no action and a staff member intervened.

Bobby (19 months, 11 days) arrived at group with several sutures across his nose. He clung to mother as she told how he fell when he "went where he was not supposed to go." Mrs. X. cuddled Mrs. K.'s two-month-old son, Jon, and told Bobby, "I'd like to take Jon home." Hastily she added, "Oh, I shouldn't tease you. We can't do that." Bobby wooed his mother, bringing toys and a cookie. When this failed to divert her attention from Jon, his behavior deteriorated. He ran, not looking at what he was doing or where he was going, bumped into another child, knocked her down and walked on her, as though not recognizing her presence.

There was evidence of a generational transmission of the patterned behavior used in communication. Just as Mrs. X. lacked empathy for Bobby in his needful states, Bobby was hampered in his ability to invest in caring for his own body and to refrain from harming others. Neither parent seemed alert to potential dangers or to take adequate precautions to prevent Bobby's frequent accidents. Mrs. X. said her husband often spanked Bobby. When attending a group picnic, Mr. X. joked, "If I put Bobby [23 months] in that trashcan, I could relax." Father sat him on a small scooter and pushed him, unprotected, down a small hill. Mr. X. seemed unaware of the potential danger or Bobby's panic as he looked wide-eyed and unsmiling at his father. The scooter toppled over and Bobby fell off. Father put him back on and pushed him further downhill.

Mrs. X. was briefly able to modify her behavior toward Bobby after she received support from the research staff. There were recurrent, though inconsistent, breakthroughs of tender responsiveness toward Bobby. Bobby was able to reciprocate. For example, Bobby (24 months, 12 days) was relatively calm in group. None of the tiny second-born infants were present. Mrs. X. was more available to Bobby. When he asked for grapes, she prepared them and gave them to him on a plate. He smiled broadly and seemed pleased. After finishing this refreshment, Bobby played with a puzzle with the assistance of a staff member. He then crawled into one of the doll beds, holding a tiny toy bottle, and lay quietly. A staff member covered him with a small blanket. He closed his eyes and pretended to sleep and then crawled out of the box and went to his mother, who affectionately embraced him. Bobby then joined the other first-borns and with quiet enthusiasm became involved with play dough.

When Bobby was two years old, the mothers and infants in the study were separated into discrete groups. The mothers went to an adjoining room for a one-hour meeting and the children remained with staff in the familiar playroom. During these times of separation, Bobby had difficulty. When mother left the room, he seemed "lost," unable to gain comfort in play with toys or find pleasure in the one-to-one contact offered by familiar staff. Bobby had not acquired a sense of confident expectation that gratification would be forthcoming. He lacked the capacity to invest in the nonmother, available staff and was rarely able to sustain play. At times he sobbed, "Mommy, mommy," and was only comforted by mother's return.

At 26 months Bobby clung to Mrs. X. when she left. Then he sat immobile at the play table, staring with a blank expression for 10 minutes. Slowly he slid off the chair and began to push a large wooden car across the floor in an inhibited fashion. Suddenly Bobby ran and crashed it into the wall with tremendous force. He looked at the staff terrified, then seemed relieved that he had survived the experience.

Mrs. X. said Bobby had tantrums when she tried toilet training and refused to wear training pants. She added, "He runs to hide, has a BM in his diaper, then asks to be changed."

Bobby (30 months, 23 days) greeted the home visitor with an anxious facial expression and said, "I'm stinky," in a loud voice.[5] Mrs. X. commented in a sweet, quiet voice, "He's telling you he needs his diaper changed." After the diaper change, he played briefly but soon became aggressive. After several angry confrontations with Bobby, mother cried quietly and told the visitor, "There are days when I don't want to be here and wish I were not a mother." She spoke of her guilt about her aggressive feelings toward Bobby, her attempts to disguise them, her inconsistency, and her excessive punitiveness. Mrs. X. said Bobby was exceedingly stubborn, especially about potty training, and spoke of her younger brother having had some type of toilet-training problem. The visitor was uncertain to what extent Mrs. X. related her feelings about her brother to her feelings about Bobby.

Bobby (33 months) cried when he bumped his head at home. Mother picked him up and lay on the couch, holding him on her chest with his legs between her thighs. He quieted, closed his eyes, and lay on top of her. For some time Mrs. X. stroked his face gently and spoke soothingly. They seemed unaware of the home visitor's presence. When the visitor announced it was time for her to go, neither one moved or seemed to hear her. When the visitor again said she was leaving, mother asked Bobby if he wanted to walk to the car to say goodbye as he usually did. He briefly shook his head negatively, then lay back against mother. Mother remained in her reclining position and said goodbye. The visitor paused at the door to wave. In contrast to all previous visits, neither was watching her departure. They seemed lost in union. Following this visit, Mrs. X. seemed somewhat warmer in her behavior toward Bobby and more aware of his feelings. Bobby's crying during mother's absence in group ceased. Nevertheless, he required the one-to-one interchange of quietly being with an adult staff

---

[5]Mr. X. often called Bobby "Stinky"—calling out "Hi, Stinky," or "watch what you're doing, Stinky."

member, maintaining close bodily contact, and he frequently asked for mother.

Mrs. X. said Bobby (34 months) was pleased when she told him she was pregnant (three months' gestation). But his concern about being displaced was evident. He asked if the sitter was "going to be my new mommy."

At 36 months Bobby's self-directed aggression increased. Standing in his yard, he deliberately pushed a swing forward and stood in its path, smiling until it hit his head. The home visitor picked him up, saying she did not want him to be hurt. Bobby replied, "But I like it." He then hung upside down from a bar and let go so as to fall on his head. The visitor caught him mid-air, repeating that she did not want him to hurt himself. Again he insisted, "I want to." He began to swing forcefully, holding his head at an angle as if deliberately trying to hit one of the main steel posts. Gently the visitor moved his head from danger, urging him to be careful. Quickly he thrust his head out and hit it on the bar while looking at the bar. The visitor took him off the swing, once again repeating that she did not want him to hurt himself. Smiling, he protested, "But I like it." Mother shrugged her shoulders and said, "He likes being hurt; he aimed at the bar with his head."

In group Bobby usually required constant supervision from staff. With their consistent availability, Bobby was able to be less impulsive and channel aggression by pounding on a workbench, building with blocks or playing with race cars.

The last group meeting occurred when Bobby was 41 months, five days old. The other mothers and children hovered around Mrs. X. and Bobby's three-week-old baby sister, Peg. Bobby sat next to his mother, staring ahead with a look of panic on his face. He accepted juice from a staff member but could not invest in interaction or play. When Mrs. X. and Peg left, he looked forlorn but did not cry. He whispered, "My mommy said I should be good today." For a short time he pushed a large toy truck, his face impassive. He remained on periphery of the group of children, watching intently. When staff members initiated interaction, he seemed compliant but not enthusiastic. When Mrs. X. and Peg returned, Bobby became agitated, crashing the large truck wildly, requiring the staff to intervene.

At four years, 10 months, 24 days, Bobby was evaluated at the research office by an interviewer with no prior knowledge of the family.[6] He did not play at all but cried and clung to his mother. Mrs. X.

---

[6]Behavioral observations were made directly with the interviewer in the room. The situation was relatively unstructured, with 25 minutes of free play

took him in her lap, saying in a calm, angry voice that he was too big to cry. She then put him down and threatened to leave if he did not play. However, he stayed close, almost melting into her, whispering, "Mommy, mommy," and crying. Mother focused on completing a questionnaire while he leaned against her. There was tension between them and hostility in mother's voice as she enjoined, "Don't expect to be treated like a big boy if you can't act like one!"

When the examiner initiated the semistructured interview, Bobby seemed somewhat relieved. He accepted a glass of juice and began to answer questions. At first he stayed close to mother and visibly masturbated. As the interview progressed, however, he became more animated, obviously enjoying the process. He confided that he wanted to be a fireman when he grew up and keep houses from burning. Bobby seemed to transfer his intense attachment from Mrs. X. to the examiner and tried to delay her departure by asking, "Don't you have any more questions?" At the end of the evaluation, the examiner concluded:

> There was a dramatic shift from this little boy's behavior with his mother, clinging and melting into her, unable to play independently, to his very involved responsiveness with me. Perhaps one reason he could make such a shift was that I became the substitute object of attachment, and offered him the same kind of intensity, but with reciprocity which he earlier looked for and had not received. He would be classified as having a psychoneurotic disorder, anxiety type (possibly depressive as well).

In response to the request to "Please describe any special worries or concerns you have about your child," Mrs. X. wrote: "His actions seem to be totally unpredictable and I have difficulty relating them to anything in the environment. It is therefore very difficult to control his behavior. He is often deliberately very good or deliberately very bad without any obvious reason."

---

followed by a 25-minute, semistructured interview with the child. To keep the mother occupied, yet accessible to the child, she was seated at a table and asked to complete behavioral data forms. During the free-play period the child was given permission to play with toys in a play area eight to 10 feet distant from mother. During the semistructured interview the child was asked to choose a crayon and draw a person. The Complete-a-Man (Binet) and the Information Subtest of the Wechsler Preschool and Primary Scale of Intelligence were also administered. Subsequently, the examiner dictated sequential detailed notes on the interview, including diagnostic impressions. Each evaluation was videotaped from behind a one-way-vision mirror.

Bobby was next seen during a home visit, when he was five years, four months, seven days. His behavior was a study in contrasts. Initially he held his one-month-old brother, Matt, in his lap, tenderly kissing him. Later he hit his two-year-old sister, Peg, quite hard. Mother admonished him: "You know that's wrong. She's too little." Bobby smiled in response. Bobby repeatedly threw a sharp trowel into the sandbox, dangerously near Peg. Although Mrs. X. told him to stop after each episode, she did not take the trowel away until he ignored her injunction nine times. Throughout this hour and a half visit, Bobby stayed close to his mother, clamoring for her attention. Mrs. X. reported that the school officials had advised against sending Bobby to kindergarten because he was too dependent and needed a one-to-one relationship.

What stood out in all the observations was how Bobby was an object for the mother's projection. A drama unfolded as mother played out with her baby what had been done to her, while at the same time desperately trying not to do so. Their early interactions were records of inadequate communication and faulty stimulation. Bobby's later attempts at symbolic control over these patterns generated pain and avoidance reactions, leading to development of psychic conflict.

How did these patterns of communication originate? Did these begin with mother's fantasies of Bobby *in utero* as retaliatory and destructive? Recall her phrase: "When he kicked, I thought it was his way of getting *back* at me." Did Mrs. X.'s image of Bobby *in utero* reflect her self-perception? Did she condemn in the child the bad part of herself and then bring her own unique "narcissistic set" into the mother-infant relationship? Did she convey to him that he was to fulfill her own unacceptable self-destructive wishes? Did these wishes have an erotic component?

Neither mother nor child seemed comfortable with closeness or distance, and there was rarely evidence of sustained pleasurable interaction. For the most part Bobby either contained his aggression (as mother contained hers) or directed it violently against himself or others, as if appealing for it to be contained.

Mary

Mary's developmental achievements stood in marked contrast to Bobby's. A normal, healthy, full-term baby (seven pounds, four ounces) she was the first-born of white, married parents (the mother was 23, the father 26). Mr. and Mrs. J. had been saddened by a miscarriage two months before Mary's conception and were thrilled with this pregnancy. They said they wanted a healthy baby and had no sex preference. At three months' gestation, Mrs. J. bled for a week and feared another miscarriage.

Describing her labor, Mrs. J. remarked, "My labor was long, 36 hours, but it wasn't all that bad; I've forgotten all about it." When asked who Mary reminded her of, Mrs. J. said, "Herself . . . when she was first born she reminded me a little of my sister, now she just looks like herself."[7] She went on to describe Mary as a very pleasant baby, who rarely cried during the first few weeks. Mother credited Mary with competence, saying, "She knew how to nurse from the very start. I've never had any problems."

At three months, 25 days, Mary came with her mother to a mother-infant group meeting. Mrs. J. said Mary slept all night and was generally happy. Mother held Mary in her lap, facing away, and supported her by holding both hands. Mary looked with interest at another mother and at an infant (Ray) on the floor. She followed the sound of the conversation, orienting to it, and then made a slight sound and put her right hand in her mouth. Mrs. J. released Mary's right hand and gently stroked her head. Mary turned to her mother in response and they smiled. Again, Mary looked at Ray, she leaned forward and slightly fussed. When mother offered her a small, soft doll, Mary quieted and looked intently at the doll's prominent eyes. "She's fascinated with eyes," Mrs. J. commented, "it's like she knows they're important." Mother put Mary facing her, prone on the floor, amidst several other babies. Mrs. J. was friendly and interested in the other mothers and infants while simultaneously aware of and available to her own infant. In contrast to Bobby's mother, she facilitated Mary's engagement with the world of others while maintaining a protective role.

Mother breast-fed Mary, providing good support for Mary's body and head and frequently gazing at her. Both mother and child appeared relaxed and comfortable. Mary explored her mother's fingers and breasts—her eyes sometimes closed and sometimes open, looking at her mother. During the feeding, mother patted Mary's buttocks

---

[7]Mrs. J. was four years old when her sister was born. It is likely that her beginning fantasies of motherhood evolved in the context of her mother's tenderly caring for her baby sister. In the development of her positive motherliness, as she began to perceive herself as a mother, she may have viewed Mary as similar to the baby sister already woven into her fantasies of motherhood. Mrs. J. was closely attached both to her mother and grandmother; in this family the transfer of motherliness from one generation to another seemed related to positive identifications.

with rhythmic audible pats on the well-padded diaper area.[8] When another mother commented on the sound, Mrs. J. replied, "She seems to like it." Mrs. J.'s tactile contact with all other areas of Mary's body was very gentle. Indeed, Mary seemed to thrive on mother's care, which, during subsequent observations, was judged exceptionally in tune and well timed.

Mrs. J. sat behind Mary (five months, 20 days), who was prone on the floor of the group room. Mary held a toy with both hands and intermittently mouthed the toy, pausing frequently to watch the other infants intently. Mother gently stroked Mary's back and Mary looked at her, smiled, and moved her arms and legs in an excited manner. When Mary played with a small mirror rattle, Mrs. J. asked her affectionately, "Who's that pretty girl in the mirror?" This comment reflected her pride and approval, as well as her ability to identify Mary's femininity.

Eight-month-old Mary walked with support. Mrs. J. walked behind her, patiently providing her fingers for Mary to hold. Mary was faced "toward the world" and set the pace for movement. She smiled with delight as she practiced her new skill. Mother reported that Mary had completed a gradual weaning from the breast to the cup. She kissed Mary and said, "My little girl is growing up. I miss the close contact of breast-feeding, but I'll find other ways to enjoy her." Mrs. J. accepted points of developmental change as a challenge, consistently showing confidence in her ability to meet Mary's needs to be loved and loving.

No mother is 100% available and responsive. Mary (11 months) crawled toward mother as though wanting a sip of her tea. Mrs. J. rose abruptly, without speaking to Mary, and went to get her some juice. Mary cried and watched mother but quieted when offered her own cup of juice in a training cup which had a lid. Indeed, had there been an oversynchronization so that Mary became locked in tandem with mother, it is unlikely that either member of the dyad would have had any freedom for progressive development. Mrs. J. seemed confident that Mary had resources to cope with moderate frustration. For example, when Mary dropped the cup and fussed as it rolled away, Mrs. J. responded, "What?" Mary looked at the cup and "complained." Mrs. J.

---

[8]Mrs. J. continued to pat Mary on the well-padded diaper area during breast-feeding until weaning was accomplished. A male sibling was born when Mary was two and a half, and mother repeated the forceful patting on his buttocks when breast-feeding him. We wondered if this style of mothering reflected "fusion" of aggressive and libidinal behavior.

encouraged her independence, saying, "Pick it up; you can get it." And indeed Mary did.

Mrs. J. brought her mother, Mrs. R., to group, explaining, "I thought she would enjoy it." Like her daughter, Mrs. R. was friendly and interested in the other mothers and infants and did seem to enjoy being there. Mrs. J. showed her mother a research toy. Mrs. R. examined it with careful interest, as though attaching similar importance to the children's play things as her daughter. Mary (12 months, 10 days) held another child's toy. He snatched it away and she looked perplexed and disappointed. Mother and grandmother simultaneously sighed, "Ahh," with soft empathy. Then Mrs. J. handed Mary one of her own toys in replacement. This mother consistently invested in toys and showed them to Mary—thus toys became actively cathected by Mary as an extension of mother's body. The maternal grandmother-mother-daughter interactions suggested that we were observing the third generation in which the developmental line from the mother's body to the toy and from play to work (A. Freud, 1965) was being traversed smoothly.

Mary (13 months) stood exploring with interest a picture on the wall when Meg fell. Mary startled, looked intently at Meg, then slowly walked to her mother.[9] Mrs. J. lifted her to snuggle closely. Still holding Mary, she knelt down, showing her a small toy before setting her free on the floor. Mary smiled, took the toy, and approached the other children in the rocking boat.

With determination Mary (14 months, 15 days) tried to get out of the rocking boat by thrusting one arm and one leg over the side. Failing, she sat down briefly. Then she went to the opposide side of the boat, where a staff member stood, and again tried to get out. However, instead of moving her limbs so purposefully, she squealed in appeal to the adult, who facilitated her exit. Mary could solicit essential support from an available adult in contrast to Bobby, who did not turn to adults for help. Progressively, Mary displayed responsibility for her body management. In her walking, she carefully stepped over toys on the floor and did not have repeated falls and accidents.

Mrs. J. brought me a picture of Mary (15 months) surrounded by her mother, maternal grandmother, great-grandmother, and great-great-grandmother. She said proudly, "I thought you'd like to have

---

[9]Did Meg's fall evoke in Mary a memory of having herself been comforted by mother in similar situations? Was this the stimulus to return to mother? Did mother's response then enable Mary to return to play?

this—it's five generations of girls." Her predominantly positive perception of family included her husband, parents, in-laws, and her younger sister. The relationships were not without ambivalence, however. Mrs. J. spoke of being free to express a dissenting point of view in her family without jeopardizing the affectionate ties.

Mrs. J. held Mrs. K.'s one-month-old son, Jon, cradled in her left arm and patted his diaper area briskly with her right hand. Mary (15 months, 24 days) approached her mother and reached up to touch Jon, making direct eye contact with mother as she did so. Mother spoke to her, saying, "It's a nice baby." Mary repeated "baby" and then joined the other toddlers at the snack table. She sat facing mother as she ate a cookie and several times said "baby." Although interested in Jon she did not seem unduly concerned at her mother's attention to him and engaged with the staff in many pleasant and charming ways. When Jon's mother held him, Mary came near and said "baby" in a wondering tone of voice. Then she lifted a doll and sat down to hold it cradled in her arms.

Mother set appropriate limits without apparent anxiety about frustrating her daughter. Mary (16 months, eight days) walked around the room exploring projections on the furniture. When she moved toward an electrical outlet, Mrs. J. sternly called once, "No!" Mary responded by moving to the center of the room. Mrs. J. leaned forward in her chair and cheerfully talked to Mary, pointing toward some toys. Mother could be firm yet maintain a positive affective relationship with Mary. Thus, Mary did not experience the disorganization and resultant anxiety and depression that Bobby did.

Upon entering the playroom, Mary (19 months, 28 days) seemed to be in a happy mood, but stayed closer to her mother than usual. Mr. J. had expressed a desire for another baby, and Mrs. J. said she was thinking about it. Mary spent much of her time with the toy bottles, alternating between feeding the dolls and putting them in her own mouth. When Mrs. A. arrived with two-month-old Sue, Mary abandoned the pretend dolls for the real baby. Dancing with excitement, she touched Sue's toes very gently. On this day each time Mary played with a new item, she either returned to show her mother what she was doing or shared her experience with mother by making visual contact while she was playing.

When Mary was 20 months, 12 days old, Mrs. J. spent some time holding Jon, obviously enjoying the closeness of a tiny baby. In contrast to earlier times when mother held one of the babies, Mary seemed subdued. Several times she approached her mother, put her head in mother's lap, and sucked her thumb. Mrs. J. was involved with Jon and less available than usual to Mary. On one occasion Mary placed a doll in the lap of a staff member (CT) and covered it with a blanket. She then hugged the doll, placed her head in CT's lap, and sucked her thumb, seeming to re-create the situation when Mrs. J. was holding the baby and Mary put her head in mother's lap.

At 21 months, nine days, Mary leaned against Mrs. J. and gazed intently around the room, as though searching for someone. Mrs. J. said Mary had asked if Jon would be there. Mother fondled Mary's hair and seemed accepting of Mary's need to be in close contact. Soon Mary moved to play with a shopping cart containing play food. Vivaciously she inspected and identified the items by naming. When Mrs. K. and Jon arrived, Mary looked at them and ran to her mother, pointing to mother's lap. Both mothers laughed, commenting that this gesture meant Mary expected her mother to hold Jon, as she had in the past. However, Mrs. K. began to nurse Jon and Mrs. J. did not hold him. Mary retained her interest in Jon, often going to peer at him; she was particularly attentive when he fussed. Throughout the hour and a half meeting she initiated a variety of play activity with enjoyment and did not require continual involvement of an adult on a one-to-one basis.

Mary was 21 months, 23 days old when the mothers began to meet for one hour apart from the toddlers. When Mrs. J. left, Mary was not overtly distressed but joined a staff member (CT), who was reading to another child. Mary had the capacity to invest in adults (staff) other than mother, as though confident they would afford pleasure and find her pleasurable. She maintained her ability to sustain interest in play and frequently "shared" with other toddlers. Although she tolerated the separations well, she was always delighted at reunion with mother.

Initially Mrs. J. had cried upon learning she was eight weeks pregnant, thinking that Mary (23 months, 15 days) was too young to be a sister. Now, however, she said that she looked forward to having a new baby. She also commented, "I tried toilet training Mary for a few weeks but I got so irritated when she wouldn't go, I decided to stop for a while rather than be so cross with her."

Dr. C. entered the playroom and smiled at Mary (27 months, 20 days). Responding with a smile, Mary said with a tone of pride, "Want to see what I made? Turn around." She pointed to her art work with confidence that he would like her product. Mary's toilet training had been unhurried, and she had been permitted a time of refusal to use the pot her mother provided. This refusal was followed by Mary's voluntary use of the potty, interspersed with self-assertive episodes of wetting and soiling. Now she reliably used her potty chair, needing little help from mother.

Just as Mrs. J. earlier spoke of her chagrin at Mary's refusal of the potty, now she spoke with pride in Mary's competence. She chuckled and related that Mary asked if Mr. Rogers (of television fame) also used the potty—"I told her, 'Yes, Mr. Rogers uses the potty; daddy and mommy use the potty, too. Now she does very well."

Mary's approach to the other children was usually friendly. She participated in the snatching back and forth of small toys but did not seem angry. She was not easily frustrated and seemed relatively satisfied when a substitute item was offered for the one taken away. This is not to say that she did not protest or show selectivity in her choice of toys. We often observed her immediately reclaiming a preferred doll when a larger, more aggressive child had lost interest in it.

As Mrs. J.'s pregnancy advanced, Mary's anticipation of the birth of a sibling was evidenced by her interest in the second-borns, Jon and Sue, and in her play interests. Frequently she lay in a child-size bed, covered herself, and pretended to rest for prolonged periods. Her usually clear speech often deteriorated into baby talk. Her behavior became more aggressive, her attention span decreased, and her play was more fragmented and disorganized. Mrs. J., aware of Mary's distress, was very empathic in trying to meet Mary's needs. She said, "She wants an extra hug at bedtime. It's like she knows trouble is coming."

Mary was 30 months old when her brother, Ronnie, was born. Mother said that when Mary first saw her nursing Ronnie, she ran over, lifted her dress, and wanted to "feed the baby." Mother chuckled, "It was so funny to see her lift her dress and want to feed the baby with those tiny 'boobs.' I told her she couldn't and told her to feed her doll. She does that now."

Attending the toddler group for the first time after Ronnie's birth, Mary (31 months) was low-keyed. After Mrs. J. left the room, she asked, "Where's mommy?" She was told that mommy was across the hall drinking coffee with the other mothers. With support from the staff, she was able to resume play, showing an ability to cope with her distress at the separation as well as the knowledge that Ronnie was with her mother.

A home visitor observed Mary (31 months, 15 days) feeding her doll and commented, "You're a good mommy." Mary quickly responded, "I'm not a mommy! I'm a big sister!"—a clear statement of her emergent self-representations.

At 32 months Mary alternated between feeding a doll and feeding herself with the toy bottle—an instance of her ability to take on the roles of both feeding mother and receiving child. Mrs. J. commented that at home Mary usually gave her dolls the bottle but occasionally held them to breast.

Mary's emerging identification with her mother was evident and seemed based on a wish *to be like* her own loved mother. At 32 months, 15 days, Mary was quite selective in her dress-up play. She adorned herself with bracelets and a purse but rejected the offer of a hat (mother never wore a hat). Thus attired, she took a doll for a ride in the stroller. During the ensuing months, both parents were sensitive to Mary's attempts to cope with Ronnie's entrance into the family. Their consistent availability and appreciation of Mary facilitated her developmental progress.

At the last group meeting Mary (38 months) played with play-dough companionably with the other first-borns and cheerily announced, "I'm making a cherry pie for dinner." She practiced her culinary skills with sustained interest after the other first-borns began water play. When the pie was completed to her satisfaction, she requested a basin of water and allowed Jon, now 23 months old, to join her. When he poured water onto the table, Mary calmly called a staff member to help him and continued her careful pouring of "soup" into a cup.

On that day another mother asked Mrs. J. if she had problems with Mary. Mrs. J. replied, "No. For a while, she was flighty but now she can settle down and play longer." Reflecting appreciation of Mary's autonomous strivings, she added, "She just has a normal amount of wanting to do things her own way."

At four years, six months, 23 days, Mary was evaluated in our research office by the same examiner who evaluated Bobby. Mary's mood was cheerful and she was invested in her play. Adorning herself with play jewelry, she looked in the mirror, brushed her hair with a toy brush, and smiled approvingly at her mirror image. Mary used miniature toys to construct her own family configuration, placing dolls in a car with the father and the mother in the front seat, a girl and a boy in the back seat, and a tiny baby in the trunk. (Mrs. J. was near term with her third child.) Her play themes also included cooking and building a complex structure with Lincoln logs.[10]

---

[10]During Mrs. J.'s second pregnancy, Mr. J. remodeled and enlarged the house. Mary was actively involved in this process—following father, carrying tools, and painting. At that time we wondered if following father and playing

When asked by the examiner to draw a person, Mary did so, showing her pleasure in mastery of the task. Beaming, she called to her mother, "Look what I did!" Mrs. J. responded approvingly. The examiner also asked Mary what she wanted to be when she grew up. Without hesitation, Mary grinned and replied, "A mother."

At the end of the evaluation the examiner concluded: "This little girl is quite sure of her femininity, eager to relate and both comfortable and spontaneous in doing so. She is making healthy developmental progress." When asked to "describe any worries or concerns you have about your child," Mrs. J. had none.

Mary (four years, 11 months, 20 days) began kindergarten. A home visit coincided with her return from school on that first day. She bounced off the school bus and joyously greeted her mother. Mrs. J. inquired about school and held Mary in her lap for a few moments. Mary snuggled close and mother asked if she was tired. Mary nodded and briefly sucked her thumb before getting off Mrs. J.'s lap to chat with the visitor.

Mrs. J. had baked a special cake decorated with a school bus, a little girl, and the words "Mary's First Day." While mother breast-fed her one month-old-son, Mark, Mary admired the cake. Ronnie (now 29 months old) poked his finger in the icing. Mary said, "Mommy, Ronnie put his finger in my cake!" Mrs. J. looked over and pleasantly said, "That's OK, we'll give him that piece." in that succinct statement was a clear message—that although it was Mary's special cake, there was no doubt that it was to be shared and there was enough for all. Mrs. J.'s ability to handle the expectable rivalries between her children, yet enable each to feel valued, was impressive. Mary accepted her mother's statement and maintained her cheerfulness and spontaneity.

Helene Deutsch (1945) has written that a mother must not strive to achieve any other goals through her child but those of the child's existence, otherwise she runs the risk of failing in her purpose and of being cheated of the experience of motherhood. Mrs. J.'s behavior reflected her ability to permit Mary to "exist," separate and individual, while continuing to be the cherished child of a cherished mother. Mary's awareness that she was "cherished" seemed intimately con-

---

with tools was Mary's way of being involved with father. Did she recognize the biological difference from mother and her own inability to please him in the way mother could? Did she imitate some of father's behavior while striving to be a pretty feminine little child and thus maintain an affiliation with both parents?

nected to her ability to be considerate of others, to care for herself, and to acquire predominantly positive self-images.

Discussion

At the time of transition from pregnancy to motherhood, Mrs. J. had a positive perception of Mary and experienced Mary as the gratifying child of a mother who could gratify. She had predominantly positive self-images of herself as a woman, a wife, and a mother and viewed her daughter as the attractive feminine child of the attractive feminine self. Mrs. J.'s empathy and consistent availability provided Mary with prolonged periods of tranquillity, during which she was able to explore and gain understanding of both the human and inanimate world. Mary had achieved a "recognition of self-as-having-option-to-initiate" (Sander, 1975) and had acquired a relatively secure sense of being able to have an impact on her environment.

One could say that Mary's representations were becoming more sharply defined and that her behavior indicated that these differentiated representations were being organized into groupings endowed with increasing stability of organization and content. She seemed to predominantly consider her self-representations lovingly, happily, confidently, competently, and considerately—as a child of her parents, a "big sister," and an individual "I." Adults in the environment were predominantly viewed considerately, lovingly, confidently, yet at times angrily. Within her peer group, Mary's behavior indicated that she considered the children differently—pleasurably, competitively, lovingly, or angrily. For the most part, Mary was considerate of others, respecting them as other humans with feelings. Her modal behavior was not characterized by actions intended to inflict pain upon them.

In contrast to Mrs. J., Mrs. X. had persisting narcissistic injuries. These were reflected in negative self-images, evidenced in her statement that the child whom she produced was "a louse." The disturbance in her self-esteem was reflected in her negative perceptions of Bobby, and she was hampered in her ability to cathect her infant son with optimal love and concern. Mrs. X. did not perceive a potential within Bobby for healthy developmental progress, nor within herself for "competent mothering."

Mrs. X. seemed aware of her hostile feelings and struggled endlessly with her need to contain these impulses. After delivery, instead of normal feminine masochism, there was evidence of "moral masochism" as she "patiently and silently" suffered until her counteraggression broke through and the cycle repeated itself (Deutsch, 1945).

Mrs. X. had difficulty in providing the "holding environment" Bobby needed for establishment of an optimal psychophysiological equilibrium. Thus, he was deprived of a "tranquil space" in which to explore his world. His early experiences did not enable him to acquire a sense of having impact on determining aspects of his own regulation. His anxiety was manifested in behavioral disorganization and a paucity of pleasurable goal-directed activity.

Bobby's behavior indicated that he endowed his emergent self-representations with hostility—that is, if his aggression were expressed, he might destroy the world and, in turn, he would be destroyed or abandoned. There were themes of continuity, suggesting that his predominantly negative self-representations were emerging in response to his mother's need for him to become *an aggressor who must be contained*. Bobby's awareness of being "stinky" and a "louse" interfered with his ability to care for himself and to view others considerately.

The longitudinal studies of these two infants in their respective environments illustrate the relation between maternal empathy and the nature of the infant's emergent self-representations and empathy. Mrs. J. provided messages to Mary that facilitated her development in an optimal fashion. Mary in turn was acquiring an appreciation of her self-representations and a respect for the feelings of others. Mrs. X., however, through her choice of patterns of behavior, communicated messages to Bobby that fostered his development of negative self-images, lack of concern for his body, and lack of empathy for others.

REFERENCES

Basch, M. F. (1975), Toward a theory of depression. In: *Depression and Human Existence*, ed. E. J. Anthony & T. Benedek. Boston: Little, Brown, pp. 485–534.

Broussard, E. R. (1976), Neonatal prediction and outcome at 10–11 years. *Child Psychiat. & Human Devel.*, 7(2):85–93.

——— (1977), Primary prevention program for newborn infants at high risk for emotional disorder. In: *Primary Prevention: An Idea Whose Time Has Come*, ed. D. Klein & S. Goldston. Washington, D.C.: U.S. Government Printing Office, pp. 63–68.

——— (1978), Psychosocial disorders in children: Early assessment of infants at risk. *Continuing Ed. for Family Physician*, 8(2):44–57.

——— (1979), Assessment of the adaptive potential of the mother-infant system: The Neonatal Perception Inventories. *Seminars in Perinatol.*, 3(1):91–100.

_____ (1982), Primary prevention of psychosocial disorders: Assessment of outcome. In: *Primary Prevention of Psychopathology, Vol. 6: Facilitating Infant and Early Childhood Development*, ed. L. A. Bond & J. M. Joffee. Hanover, N.H.: University Press of New England, pp. 180–196.

_____ & Cornes, C. C. (1981), Early identification of mother-infant systems in distress: What can we do? *J. Preventive Psychiat.*, 1(1):119–132.

Buie, D. H. (1981),. Empathy: Its nature and limitations. *J. Amer. Psychoanal. Ass.*, 29:281–307.

Burlingham, D. (1967), Empathy between infant and mother. *J. Amer. Psychoanal. Ass.*, 15:764– 780.

Deutsch, H. (1945), *The Psychology of Women, Vol. 2-Motherhood.* New York: Bantam Books, 1973.

Freud, A. (1965), *Normality and Pathology in Childhood.* New York: International Universities Press.

Greenson, R. R. (1960). Empathy and its vicissitudes. *Int. J. of Psycho-Analy.*, 41:418–424.

Kohut, H. (1971), *The analysis of the self.* New York: International Universities Press.

Resch, R. C. (1979), Hatching in the human infant as the beginning of separation-individuation. *The Psychoanalytic Study of the Child*, 34:421–441. New Haven: Yale University Press.

Sander, L. W. (1975), Infant and caretaking environment. In: *Explorations in Child Psychiatry*, ed. E. J. Anthony. New York: Plenum Press, pp. 129–166.

Winnicott, D. W. (1958), *Collected Papers: Through Pediatrics to Psychoanalysis.* New York: Basic Books.

_____ (1960), The theory of the parent-infant relationship. *Int. J. Psycho-Anal.*, 41:585–595.

V

EMPATHY IN PSYCHOANALYTIC WORK

•

Introductory Remarks

MELVIN BORNSTEIN, M.D.

Although Freud (1921) said that empathy was indispensable when it comes to taking a position regarding another person's mental life, that it plays the largest part in our understanding of what is inherently foreign to our ego in other people, the term has not received widespread attention until recently. The papers in this section add to a clarification of the multiple facets that make up empathy in psychoanalytic work. For analysts to act empathically and foster an empathic process in psychoanalytic work, they must be able to come to know the entire experience of the analysand within the psychoanalytic interaction. They must be able to put themselves into the shoes of the analysand.

Basch (1983), in discussing the etymology of "empathy" points to its origins in the German *Einfühlung*, which refers to feeling into, finding or searching one's way into, the experience of another without specifying or limiting the means by which this occurs. Thus, for an analyst, to put himself (or herself) into an analysand's shoes is not simply to share a feeling or a fantasy, but to know the full experience of the analysand, including the emotional, affective, cognitive, integrative, motivational, interactional, and even, for some, the telepathic. Furthermore, the analyst must take into account the genetic, transference, and actual reality components of the analysand's experience.

Focusing on the use of empathy in psychoanalytic work, the papers in this section complement the theoretical considerations raised in Part II of this book, on "Empathy as a Perspective in Psychoanalysis." Six of the papers first appeared in *Psychoanalytic Inquiry's* issue "On

Empathy" (those by Joseph D. Lichtenberg, Evelyne Schwaber, Herbert J. Schlesinger, N. Gregory Hamilton, René Major and Patrick Miller, and Bennett Simon). For this book, a discussion has been added to each paper (by John E. Gedo for Lichtenberg, Merton M. Gill for Schwaber, Alan Z. Skolnikoff and Mardi J. Horowitz for Schlesinger, John J. Hartman for Hamilton, Stanley A. Leavy for Major and Miller, and James C. Skinner for Simon). Also included are three new papers: James H. Spencer, Jr., and Leon Balter discuss the special place of empathy in the psychoanalytic process through a consideration of the "analyzing instrument;" Ping-Nie Pao reflects on the use of empathy in the treatment of schizophrenic patients; and Bernard Brandchaft and Robert D. Stolorow reconsider the borderline concept in the light of possible empathic failures in work with these patients (their ideas are then discussed by Gerald Adler).

Defining empathy as a general process by which one individual is able to be in touch with another's affective and cognitive experiential state, Joseph Lichtenberg delineates "The Empathic Mode of Perception and Alternative Vantage Points for Psychoanalytic Work." For him, the psychoanalytic use of empathy is a highly specialized mode of perception by which an analyst gains information about the analysand's state of mind. This is done by the analyst's systematic attempt to orient his listening stance to be within the mental state of the patient. Lichtenberg contrasts the advantages and disadvantages of the empathic mode of perception with other modes and describes how the analyst may employ these other vantage points as auxiliary modes, while retaining the empathic mode as primary. According to John Gedo, the value of Lichtenberg's paper lies in his refusal to abandon the alternatives to the empathic vantage point in the psychoanalytic situation. Gedo is critical of the emphasis Kohut and his students place on the empathic vantage point as the only mode for an analyst to understand an analysand. He believes this exclusiveness narrows the observational field and eliminates consideration of presymbiotic, biopsychological data.

Evelyne Schwaber's paper on "Empathy: A Mode of Analytic Listening" adds to her many contributions related to empathy. Like Lichtenberg, she sees empathy as the predominant mode of analytic listening. It is a listening that seeks to elucidate and explore the analysand's perception of reality. In this mode analysts are less likely to approach their parients from the standpoint of an external or "objective" reality assessment. They thus shift their emphasis away from viewing transference simply as a distortion to be modified. Instead, seen from within the patient's psychic reality, transference reveals an emerging intrapsychic experience that permits analytic understanding and articulation. With rich, sensitive clinical vignettes, Schwaber illustrates how this view increases the analyst's awareness of the analysand's present and past experiential world. From a slightly different perspective, Merton Gill, in his discussion, also emphasizes that to grasp the patient's subjective reality, it is not sufficient to trace the patient's experience to its genetic roots. Rather, it is essential to explore the meaning within the immediate interaction with the analyst. He then contrasts Schwaber's conceptualization of empathy with Kohut's.

Focusing on "The Process of Empathic Response," Herbert Schlesinger describes empathy as a process of interaction with the multiple object relations expressed in the transference. Empathy allows the analyst to enter into several actual and potential aspects of the patient's experience while acting as the patient's ally therapeutically. Within an empathic process, Schlesinger contends, the analyst assumes a position of looking over the analysand's shoulder at the transference figures yet sharing the emotions expressed. During periods of empathic failure, Schlesinger warns, a disruption of the therapeutic split occurs: the analyst overidentifies with the patient or becomes alienated from the needed degree of sensitivity to him. Alan Skolnikoff and Mardi Horowitz expand on Schlesinger's concepts by emphasizing the importance of the affective component, which is often unconscious and frequently is not integrated into a cognitive and conceptual understanding of the interaction with the patient.

In a charming clinical vignette that complements the three preceding papers, N. Gregory Hamilton describes the use of empathy as a mode of perception. He suggests that his empathic response to a severely regressed patient was determined by a combination of cognitive and emotional factors. In attempting to understand his bewildering experience, he describes the impact of a direct observation of his child augmented by a subjective experience. Finally, he points to his attempt to conceptualize and communicate what had occurred. To this, John Hartman adds a note of caution. Viewing empathy as an unconscious affective mode of understanding, he warns against an overemphasis on empathy over cognitive modes of understanding.

The next two papers describe and discuss occasions of unexpected communications between analyst and patient that may be regarded as special instances of deep empathy. Some (e.g., Major and Miller) believe such instances represent a form of thought transference, whereas others (e.g., Simon) do not.

In "Empathy, Antipathy, and Telepathy in the Analytic Process," René Major Patrick Miller postulate that the kernel of the empathic experience is of a telepathic nature. Major and Miller exemplify the concerns of many French analysts with the means by which the unconscious of the other informs and gives shape to the unconscious of the subject. They write in a style that may be unfamiliar to Americans not acquainted with French psychoanalytic literature: they use metaphor and word puns to activate associations aimed to evoke the reader's unconscious and increase his capacity to apprehend the meaning of the author. In an effort to understand the premises of this paper, then, the reader may wish to refer to Major's earlier work or the work of other French analytic writers.

In the experiences Major and Miller write about, information about the analyst or analysand is communicated to the other, not by the usual means of transference, but by a direct (telepathic) communication operating at a psychic depth. Direct communication or thought transference occurs when empathy is blocked by antipathy, an "empty space" develops, and information passes directly from one unconscious system to another. According to Major and Miller, this represents a reversal of the jamming of direct thought transference possible in infancy. They review examples from Freud's studies of telepathy and add others of their own. Stanley Leavy then raises the intriguing consideration that an empirical explanation of a communication of thought and affect, which he describes in a clinical vignette, is no purer than Major and Miller's explanation of a physical transmission of ideas at a distance. His suggestion is that telepathic communication, if it exists, should be studied outside of psychoanalysis. A reply by Major and Miller follows.

In his paper "Confluence of Visual Image Between Patient and Analyst: Communication of Failed Communication," Bennett Simon describes an unusual image that came to his mind during an analytic session. A few minutes later his patient described a strikingly similar image. Simon demonstrates that, rather than representing a complete empathic resonance that furthered the analytic process, this apparent congruence of the analyst's and analysand's visual images, upon further analysis, revealed a state of isolation and misunderstanding within and between them. Simon then discusses such communications from the point of view of telepathic phenomena, similar to extrasensory perception. He suggests that these phenomena are in part determined by an important unresolved communicative issue which is not being apprehended by ordinary means. Elaborating on Simon's theme, James Skinner offers several clinical examples of confluent and parallel communication between the patient and the analyst. He suggests several conditions within the patient and analyst under which coincident or increasingly parallel streams of thought induced by subliminal cues occur and argues that these processes have not been sufficiently explained.

In "Empathy and the Analyzing Instrument," James Spencer, Jr., and Leon Balter elaborate on the special use of empathy in the psychoanalytic situation because of the analyzing instrument. As they describe it, the analyzing instrument is a complementary intrapsychic process of the analyst and analysand that forms a circuit within the psychoanalytic relationship. Thus, empathy is focused on the assimilation of manifest and secondary process with latent and primary process in a continual interactional process.

In a posthumously published paper, "Therapeutic Empathy and the Treatment of Schizophrenics," Ping-Nie Pao applies his sensitivity, gentleness, and respect for human individuals suffering from schizophrenia to enhance our understanding of empathy. Pao presents three cases of schizophrenic patients with difficulties in communication. Through these examples, he demonstrates that empathy is a process requiring two participants, one who actively desires to understand and another who actively desires to be understood. Pao calls attention to the patience required to establish this delicate interaction and to maintain it, for it is quickly disrupted if either participant does anything to block the communicative process.

In "The Borderline Concept: Pathological Character or Iatrogenic Myth?" Bernard Brandchaft and Robert Stolorow underline the centrality of empathy in the conceptualization and treatment of the borderline condition. They suggest that the so-called borderline condition is based on a deficiency of self-organization that has evolved from pathological interactional experience. Furthermore, they see the expression of primitive aggression, splitting, and projective identification as secondary to empathic failure within the intersubjective field, and not as defenses against aggression. If this is not understood by the analyst, further empathic failure will occur, leading to an iatrogenic aggravation of the borderline state. Gerald Adler takes issue with this empahsis on the centrality of empathic failure, leading Brandchaft and Stolorow to clarify their position in a reply.

Clearly, a variety of issues are raised by the papers in this section. On the one hand, there is the question of empathy as a general process and a mode of analytic listening: Is empathy at the core of psychoanalytic perception? Should the emphasis in clinical work be on insight and rational understanding, or on emotionality and sympathic affective attunement, or somewhere in between? From a different angle, there is the question of empathy as a special mode of affective communication and its relation to extrasensory perception: What allows us to touch the deepest levels of apprehending another individual's state of mind? And when have we ventured beyond psychoanalytic understanding into the realm of mysticism and the occult? The scope of the issues touched upon indicates that there may be, as Simon suggests, an "anatomy of empathy" we are only beginning to explore. The definitions and delineations suggested by some of the contributors seem clear in themselves and directly applicable to clinical psychoanalytic practice. Still, the state of our knowledge about empathy requires further investigation and study.

REFERENCES

Basch, M. F. (1983), Empathic understanding: A review of the concept and some theoretic considerations. *J. Amer. Psychoanal. Assn.*, 31:101–126.

Freud, S. (1921), Group psychology and the analysis of the ego. *Standard Edition*, 18:69–143. London: Hogarth Press, 1955.

19 The Empathic Mode of Perception and Alternative Vantage Points for Psychoanalytic Work

JOSEPH D. LICHTENBERG, M.D.

FROM ITS INCEPTION, psychoanalysis has indicated that the ideal for analytic listening and analytic interpretation is to be without bias. The goal of an unbiased approach has been evident in the key words, phrases, and sentences of Freud and leading analysts since then. The analyst's position is one of neutrality; he listens with "evenly suspended attention" (Freud, 1912, p. 111). He suspends prior judgments and gives "empathic attention to everything that there is to observe" (Freud, 1909, p. 23). Modeling himself on the surgeon, he "puts aside all his feelings" (Freud, 1912, p. 115) and concentrates all his mental forces on the aim of skillfully carrying out his function. Like a "mirror" he shows the patient "nothing but what is shown to him" (1912, p. 118). Anna Freud noted that the analyst "takes his stand at a point equidistant from the id, the ego and the superego" (1936, p. 30). He steers a course between Fenichel's Scylla of failing to give himself the fullest opportunity to *experience* the patient's communication" and the Charybdis of unsystematic "free floating' that . . . is not comprehended by a reasoning power that keeps ultimate aims in view" (1941, p. 6).

As would be expected in a growing, changing therapeutic discipline, analysis has not followed the ideal course prescribed in these dictums.

Reprinted from *Psychoanalytic Inquiry*, 1:329–355 (1981).

I greatly appreciate the helpful suggestions received from Drs. Evelyne Schwaber, George Klumpner, and Ping-Nie Pao, and from Charlotte Lichtenberg, M.L.A., in the preparation of this paper.

Fenichel (1941) states: "In the history of psychoanalysis Scylla periods (overemphasis on intellectualization) and Charybdis periods (overemphasis on emotionality) alternated . . . it must have been very difficult to pass evenly between the opposite dangers" (p. 100). Since our clinical theory is interrelated with our general theory, it is inevitable that different techniques would be followed as causal and curative factors are perceived and formulated differently. Thus one technique was followed when revelation of the existence of pathogenic unconscious complexes was considered curative, and another technique when recognition and interpretation of resistances (defensive operations) were pursued systematically.

Consequently, a new theoretical proposal such as Kohut's orientation of a psychology of the self (1971, 1977) perforce shifts the vantage point from which analytic listening and analytic interpretation takes place. In fact, Kohut's work began with an explicit focusing of the vantage point for psychoanalysis on empathy and introspection (1959) and developed its theoretical assumptions as an outgrowth. Because of its espousal of an empathic (vicarious introspective) vantage point, Kohut's self psychology has been criticized as tilting "toward affect and experientialism rather than interpretation (in the discrete secondary process, articulated sense) and insight. The enthusiasm for cure embraces the notion of an intensified and interpersonalized transference mutualization" (Valenstein, 1978).

In this presentation, I shall discuss this critical evaluation of Kohut's theoretical and therapeutic proposals. I shall endeavor to indicate that: (1) there is a clarifying distinction to be made between empathy as a process and the empathic vantage point in analytic listening; (2) the empathic vantage point as proposed by the psychology of the self includes the theoretical base for interpretation in the discrete secondary process sense by providing new insights into psychopathology; and (3) the empathic vantage point can be compared to other vantage points as to the advantages and disadvantages of each.

Empathy as a Process and the Empathic Vantage Point

According to *A Glossary of Psychoanalytic Terms and Concepts*, empathy is "a special mode of perceiving the psychological state or experiences of another person. It is an 'emotional knowing' . . . rather than intellectual understanding. To empathize means temporarily to share, to experience, the feelings of the other person. . . . Empathy establishes close contact in terms of emotions and impulses; intuition does the same in the realm of ideas" (Moore and Fine, 1967, p. 38). The key issue here is the defining of empathy as a process for obtaining quick deep understanding of another's "emotions and impulses." Hypothetically this places analyst and analysand in a communicative affective "transference mutualization" in Valenstein's words, and leaves both devoid of contact "in the discrete secondary-process, articulated sense." I disagree with Kohut's (1971, pp. 300–305) phrasing in which he essentially follows the *Glossary's* definition of the empathic process and explicitly excludes intuition as a prime method of perception by the analyst.

My view disagrees with a conception of the empathic process that would limit it to an understanding of emotions. Greenson (1967) has offered what I believe to be a clear detailed description of an appropriately broad conception of the empathic process as an analyst uses it in the clinical situation:

> I change the way I am listening to her. I shift from listening from the outside to listening from the inside. I have to let a part of me become the patient, and I have to go through her experiences as if I were the patient and to introspect what is going on in me as they occur . . . I let myself experience the analytic hour, her associations, and her affects as she seems to have gone through them in the hour. I go back over the patient's utterances and transform her words into pictures and feelings in accordance with her personality. I let myself associate to these pictures with *her* life experiences, *her* memories, *her* fantasies. As I have worked with this patient over the years I have built up a working model of the patient consisting of her physical appearance, her behavior, her ways of moving, her desires, feelings, defenses, values, attitudes, etc. It is this working model of the patient that I shift into the foreground as I try to capture what she was experiencing. The rest of me is de-emphasized and isolated for the time being [pp. 367–368].

Other authors have used the concept of a trial or transient identification to describe the empathic process (Beres and Arlow, 1974). Thus an extensive literature defines and depicts empathy as a general process used within and outside of the therapeutic situation. The empathic vantage point of analytic work constitutes a particular highly specialized usage of the empathic process.

I know of no formal definition of the empathic vantage point for analytic listening, so I shall offer one based largely on the suggestions of Schwaber (1978). The empathic vantage point in psychoanalysis is a means employed by the analyst to gain information in which he orients his listening stance to be from within the perspective, the state of mind of the analysand. As Greenson (1967) has described, a listening stance oriented within the state of mind of the analysand means far more than the patient's emotional state, although I place a very high priority on sensing the patient's emotional leanings. Listening from within the analysand's perspective means perceiving and conceptualizing the whole context of how the analysand is sensing himself, how he is sensing others, how he senses the source of his affective-cognitive state, and what he feels is the range of his active and passive potential responses to this state. Thus, when in a shorthand way we say we have made a successful interpretation based on our use of empathic perception, and the patient has responded with convincing, affirming, and confirming associations, we mean more than being in touch with his feelings—his affective experiential state. We mean that we have been in touch with his whole experiential state in an articulated sense, having coordinates of self and object (separate or selfobject), temporal linkages, causal explanations, affective ranges, and conscious, preconscious, and often unconscious associative threads. We could say that in taking an empathic vantage point (orienting listening to be from within the patient's state of mind) the analyst employs: (1) his empathy, (2) his intuition, and (3) his more "labored" cognitive reasoning. The statement of the means employed in using the empathic vantage point retains the traditional distinction between empathy, intuition (preconscious automatized, learned cognitive sharing), and conscious rational cognition. This would semantically remove the empathic vantage point from the accusation of placing an overemphasis on emotionality and underemphasis on cognitive insight.

I believe, however, there is evidence to support Kohut's (1971) insistence on defining empathy as "a mode of *cognition* which is specifically attuned to the perception of complex psychological configurations," the means of observation to be employed in order to gather data on "the inner life of men" (p. 300) (italics mine). The overwhelming weight of evidence from infant research indicates that the neonate begins life in an interactive dialogue with his mother. From the beginning, for both partners, this dialogue has modes of perceptual organization that activate the responsiveness of the other. Within this dyadic communicative exchange there is no distinction between affect response and perceptual-cognitive ordering. Condon (1977) states, "The central hypothesis emerging is that interactional synchrony may be an indication of a primary phase of the responding process and that this phase is simultaneously the beginning of a discriminating function, laying an essential organized groundwork for later operations. This would also apply to the adult responding process as well. A different way of stating it may be that interactional synchrony is an early stage in the discrimination/cognition process" (pp. 168–169).

Of course, the simultaneous affective responsiveness and discriminating function of the infant and the adult are not the same. Experientially, affective-cognitive integration is gradually partially abandoned in order to free thinking from an overbias by emotionality (Freud, 1926), or the bias of emotionality is employed to override reason or doubt, as in infatuation. The cognitive component of the neonate responsiveness is, of course, preverbal and preinternalization of symbols.[1] Experimental evidence indicates that the infant begins life in a communicative responsiveness in which affect and cognition rapidly become strongly interlinked, and that the regression of the analysand in the psychoanalytic process puts us closer to this early achieved unity of cognition and affect as it is perceived through the empathic mode of observation.

To summarize the issue of definition—the term empathy is often used in three interrelated but confusing ways: (1) to convey a process or mode of perception in which an analyst orients his listening stance to be *within* the perspective of the analysand in order to gather information about the analysand's state of mind (the use I follow in defining an empathic vantage point for psychoanalytic work); (2) to refer to the special bond of intercommunicatedness between caretaker and infant (this genetic occurrence is, of course, the necessary naturalistic developmental precursor for the refined process that is utilized purposefully by the analyst); and (3) to refer to a traditional therapeutic approach in psychoanalysis—making an empathic interpretation. This usage is, I believe, less precise. It refers at times to the conceptual stance used to form an interpretation from within the empathic vantage point. At other times, it describes the information conveyed, i.e., that the analyst informed the analysand that he understood the patient's mental state. In addition, it is used to refer to the way an interpretation is phrased and spoken—that the analyst is tactful, sensitive and sympathetic in words and tone.

---

[1]"Language is not the basis of thought. If anything, it eventually describes thoughts in a discursive manner. As the [infant] experiments indicate, the organization of experience into sensorimotor action patterns and even possibly into 'hypotheses' proceeds in the preverbal stage as does the formation of analogy and metaphor through symbolism in what Piaget calls the presentational phase of development" (Basch, 1977, p. 250).

The Empathic Vantage Point and New Interpretative Insights

An important source of the criticism that Kohut's psychology of the self tilts toward an "intensified and interpersonalized transference mutualization" lies in the failure to understand and/or accept the specific findings, the "insights," that, indeed, are interpreted "in the secondary process, articulated sense." Kohut's systematic adherence to experiencing from *within* the patient has led to the discovery that for those with serious problems in narcissistic development, the sense of an empathic synchrony with the analyst constitutes a major resource for self-regulation. Small disturbances in these patients' sense of the analyst's empathic synchrony lead to disturbances in the regulation of their self-state, ranging from overexcitement and grandiose feelings to enfeeblement and deflation. The analysand's requirement (wish) of the analyst as selfobject can then be deduced and shared with the analysand, and the wish can be interpreted in terms of what is transpiring, and what associations can be made to the past. This constitutes, I believe, interpretation in the secondary-process, articulated sense, but it is insight and systematic interpretation of an area of psychopathology different from the areas previously focused on. Goldberg (1978) eloquently states his interpretive approach:

> The analyst does not actively soothe; he interprets the analysand's yearning to be soothed, the analyst does not actively mirror; he interprets the need for confirming responses. The analyst does not actively admire or approve grandiose expectations, he explains their role in the psychic economy. The analyst does not fall into passive silence; he explains why his interventions are felt to be intrusive. Of course, the analyst's mere presence, or the fact that he talks, or, especially, the fact that he understands, all have soothing and self-confirming effects on the patient, *and they are so interpreted* [italics original]. Thus the analytic ambiance that makes analytic work possible becomes itself an object for analytic interpretation [pp. 447–448].

The case presentations of Kohut (1971, 1977) and of the self psychology *Casebook* (Goldberg, 1978) amply illustrate the vicissitudes of depletion and enfeeblement of the sense of self, exhibitionistic overexcitement, omnipotent self-aggrandizing, erotized restorative efforts, the rise and fall of idealizing efforts, and the expectations for responses from the analyst as self-object.

In some of the writings aimed to explicate the new insights and the technique for their interpretation, a distorted picture may have emerged. While it is clearly stated that working with defenses and making genetic reconstructions are a regular part of the analytic work, they are infrequently illustrated. Dreams are often presented without associations, and interpretations offered the reader without reference to the dreamwork and its disguising function. Genetic references are sometimes subsumed under the generalization of unempathic parenting without specifying the particular instances, times and situations of the empathic failure. Similar interpretations restricted to narrow aspects of self-selfobject regulation are repetitiously presented. This, I believe, contributes to the suspicion of an unbalanced emphasis away from a broad, rational, interpretative approach.

A more fundamental source for the claim that Kohut's self psychology leans toward an overemphasis on emotionality and involves transference mutualization originates in the emphasis placed on regulations rather than intrapsychic conflict. For patients with problems with self-state regulation, the empathic vantage point from within the analysand's experience puts a spotlight on his wish for soothing, mirroring, affirming, confirming, and supportive idealization from a selfobject. The experience of tempered excitement vs. overstimulation, pride vs. humiliation, comfortable self-display vs. exhibitionistic tension or shy avoidance, spirited assertiveness vs. shame-ridden aggression, and general vitality vs. deflation or enfeeblement all reflect the regulatory effect of past empathic reponsiveness by the caretaking selfobject vs. empathic failures. As these are reflected in the transference, they provide data that is best perceived by the empathic vantage point. Schwaber (1980) suggests that the "concept 'selfobject' will determine a way of listening and organizing clinical data in which the analyst's contribution, silent or stated, is seen as meaningfully influencing and ordering the nature of the patient's response—of transference, of memory, and essentially of *ongoing* [italics original] regulation within a system" (p. 216). This data delineating the analysand's disturbed experience in self-regard and idealization may then be interpreted to him. To repeat the technical precept quoted above: "the analytic ambiance that makes analytic work possible becomes itself an object for analytic interpretation" (Goldberg, 1978, p. 448).

Let us contrast this precept with the following more traditional descriptions of the analyst's interpretative stance. First, "We try . . . to understand the patient's inner *conflicts* [italics original]. We try to make clear to each patient both the antiinstinctual and the instinctual aspects of his conflicts and to trace the history of both back to the experiences and events of childhood . . . " (Arlow and Brenner, 1964, p. 141). Second, "From the analyst's noting of the sequence of [the patient's] associations, the rising and ebbing of his feelings, the shifts of [his] way of experiencing the analyst, the patient becomes aware of the unique dynamics of the sequence of his thoughts and feelings as they unfold in each hour. He can appreciate that the analyst's attentive interest is focused on how his 'mind works,' that is, how he experiences conflicts, how he reveals them, and how he defends against the painful affects associated with them" (Lichtenberg and Slap, 1977, p. 302). Third, "To interpret means to make an unconscious phenomenon conscious. More precisely, it means to make conscious the unconscious meaning, source, history, mode or cause of a given psychic event" (Greenson, 1967, p. 39). Understanding inner conflicts, focusing on how the mind works, and revealing unconscious meaning and cause tilt toward the cognitive both in the analyst's assessment and interpretative aim. Perceiving and interpreting the analysand's transference reactions that are experienced by him in a self-selfobject regulatory interaction can be regarded as no less cognitive when it is distinguished from non-analytic efforts to provide remedial caretaking (Wolf, 1976).

The clarity of the full cognitive value of Kohut's psychology of the self is obscured, I believe, by the proposal that for one sector of the personality a theory of structural intrapsychic conflict is applicable, while for another, a regulatory theory of arrested development and reliance on a selfobject is applicable. I believe that both the traditional conflict and innovative regulatory theories of self psychology have explanatory value; each can be used as a conceptual strategy for organizing the data obtained in psychoanalysis. If a false dichotomy—a rational insight theory for intrapsychic conflict vs. emotionally tilted theory of selfobject regulation—is the result of a faulty theoretical compartmentalization, then the problem cited by Valenstein (1978) would be resolved if the theoretical strategy of self psychology were expanded to a full account of the whole person—a trend that I believe may already be under way.

Let me illustrate by referring to clinical theory. An obsessional man may react automatically with controlling manifestations in response to real or fantasied rebuffs to his tenuous efforts to express affection. Traditionally we view him as involved in an intrapsychic conflict between his oedipal libidinal desire and his fear of castration. He resorts to a compromise formation—he regresses to a fixation point at which he can gratify his libidinal desire by controlling possessive reactions to his mother, and avoids the feared danger from his oedipal genital strivings. This, however, is not the entire story of his oedipal period failure.

Besides the specific conflict represented in his obsessional symptomatology, there will be repercussions from failure he has had in his broader relations to his parents—he will sense one or both as having been inept or faulty in their support given to master this developmental task. In other words, a conflict is not confined to its drive-defense compromise representatives; it also involves some disturbance in the normal regard for the self and idealization of the selfobject. Put in a way I find useful, *the psychoanalytic concept of an intrapsychic conflict represents the particularizing of specific elements out of a developmental regulatory failure, and the sense of low self-esteem and of an unempathic parent represents the generalizing of the problem to the self-selfobject interactional unit.* Thus I believe a conflict is not fully interpreted when its unconscious components are made conscious. There remains to be recognized and interpreted its more general aspects—the failures attributed (accurately or not) to the parents, or reacted to as coming from the general supportive environment.

Likewise, I believe that if we find that a man presenting obsessional symptomatology reveals in the transference major areas of regulatory difficulty broadly attributable to empathic failures throughout his entire training period, we need to listen and interpret at this level. Likewise, conflicts determining the obsessional symptomatology would require interpretation in due time. In my experience, detailed analytic work with regulatory difficulties commonly exposes analyzable drive-defense-superego conflicts organized in specific symptoms. I believe it is logical to assume an increased proneness to conflict when a general disturbance in regulation occurs; the conflicts may center particularly on issues of disturbed self-confidence in sexual and assertive function. As we recognize the indications of conflictual tendencies moving to the foreground of the analysand's associations, we would then aid him with insightful interpretations directed to the specific intrapsychic conflict, whatever its form.

To conclude, the psychology of the self provides convincing evidence that a regulatory theory is a useful, broad conceptualization for explaining psychoanalytic data; the theory of intrapsychic conflict also retains the explanatory value traditionally attributed to it. I do not believe each is best used by regarding it as the explanation for a separate sector of the personality (Kohut, 1971). Rather, I believe both can serve as *alternative shifting perspectives* for organizing and conceptualizing different experiential data as it is revealed by the analysand in the course of analysis, and perceived by the analyst through the empathic vantage point.

The Empathic and Other Vantage Points

The original ideal of "unbiased" analytic listening was meant to most closely approximate the vantage point believed to be optimal for the nineteenth-century natural scientist.[2] Neutral, impartial, evenly suspended attention to everything there is to observe places the analyst *outside* the immediacy of interaction (regulatory or otherwise). He resides above the scene as benevolent fair-minded appraiser, or as patients often depreciatingly describe it, like an experimenter watching a rat in a maze. The dehumanizing sound of these precepts was never meant as a denial of the analyst's disciplined concern—only as a guidance for it. Likewise, the precepts were never meant to disassociate analytic technique from the orienting features of analytic theory. Thus, in following the dictum to stand at a point equidistant from id, ego and superego, the analyst knew that it meant he was to particularly observe the defensive activity of the ego. He was to identify and interpret this activity first, penetrating layer by layer from the surface down—the "onion-peeling" technique. At the bottom lay conflicts related to specific developmental challenges—the mastery of oral dependence, anal ambivalence, castration anxiety, penis envy, primal-scene exposure, etc. The degree of dystonicity was the sign of readiness for the recognition of defense. Thus the patient who reported how well he was doing in some area of his life might have been responded to with silence by the analyst-observer; while absorbing the report as information, he might have too readily inferred the patient's defensive use of avoidance, and therefore waited until the analysand returned to his problems.

The empathic vantage point, by emphasizing "experiencing with the patient's experience," prompts the analytic listener to ask: "*What is the patient expressing?*" This, I believe, is a more basically unbiased question than what the patient is defending against and how he is doing it. The answer to the question, "What does empathic entry into

---

[2]In the post-Einstein era, scientists have had a far greater appreciation that data perceived is relative to the position of the observer *within* the total experimental unit. This alters the belief that in order to be neutral and objective the natural scientist must be *outside* the interactional field, a view assumed to be self-evident at the time of Freud's training as a scientist.

the patient's experiencing tell me he is expressing?" may well be, in some instances, the same as that inferred by the analyst-observer pictured above, namely, that the patient needs to protect himself against a deeper problem when he says that he is doing well. Often, however, a perception closer to the analysand's intention-in-depth may be that he is saying this not to defend himself, but to invite my sharing a moment of pride and pleasure at his or our joint accomplishment. The analyst-observer might infer this too, but I believe the analyst employing the empathic vantage point is better positioned to do so. Likewise, I believe the empathic vantage point allows the analyst to note that the patient who expresses disappointment with him or a parent most often is not invested in asking the analyst to define objective reality as in a natural science reality test. He is expressing the subjective "realness" of his experience as a necessary cooperative compliance with the basic principle of free association, and it is his expression of his subjective reality that alone constitutes the information required for effective analysis at that moment.

The empathic vantage point as advocated by the psychology of the self gives considerable importance to listening for and interpreting the transference. In its emphasis on transference it agrees with traditional analytic practice. It differs by expanding the definition of transference to include the broader regulatory aspects, that is, the generalized references to "selfobject" functioning by the analyst as experienced by the patient. I include in this expanded definition the earlier manifestations of normal and pathological forms of expressive or communicative relationship to significant past figures, including the infantile and later versions of the interactive dialogue with the primary caretaker and the triangular oedipal intercommunication.

The empathic vantage point employs the process of empathy as its principal means and the manifestations of transference as its principal data. There are points of agreement but also differences between this position and that of other analysts who advocate a central focus on transference as the preeminent analytic approach. According to Gill (1978), the analytic method follows three principles: First, the analyst encourages the transference to expand as much as possible. Second, he does so by interpreting resistance to transference awareness through interpretations of allusions, especially those associations not manifestly about the transference. Third, he demonstrates that the analysand's way of experiencing events in the actual analytic situation reveals the patient's preexisting bias. The core analytic work takes place in the here-and-now by combining cognitive recognition of the analysand's distortions with the benefit of a new experience at variance with the analysand's biased expectation. Gill reasons that since the analyst is at the center of the transference, he is in the unique position of observing it at its initiation and throughout its development. Thus, he is able to draw on information intimately accessible to him; accordingly, he is apt to be more accurate in his interpretations than if he were to interpret outside the transference sphere. The empathic vantage point seems to me to share with Gill a sensitivity to the nuances of the use of the transference to produce analytic change. It does not carry with it the "transference-only" restrictiveness that, I believe, would under some circumstances be at variance with the empathic feel for the patient's dominant state of mind. The primary distinction, however, is the expanded definition of transference to the regulative effect on self-state that is not specified by other authors (Gray, 1973; Gill, 1978).

Another vantage point for analytic listening is the analyst's introspection. In this listening mode, the analyst will passively or actively shift attentive focus to his own stream of consciousness. Lichtenberg and Slap suggest that through this introspective focus, the analyst attempts:

> to assess changes in the functional state of mind which for him represents an optimal degree of analytic perceptiveness. Often he must be patient with himself during moments when for some reason his attentiveness fails. A longer shift of focus from (empathic) listening may mean he is having associations through which, by reflecting on them, he can gain valuable information about the analysand. He must be able to use his introspection to distinguish these productive associational shifts from lapses in his optimal attentiveness that indicate repetitive or persisting countertransference interferences with his perceptiveness. In the latter case, at an appropriate time (often outside the hour), he must use his introspection toward the self-analysis of an unresolved conflict [1977, p. 300].

This view of the analyst's attention to his own state of mind retains for introspection a part in both cognitive and emotional aspects of analytic work. It avoids the pitfall of an illusion, that the analyst can use his inner reactions as an accurate register of the analysand's inner state, as if in merger or by some mechanism such as projective identification the analysand operates as a "homunculus" inside the analyst.

The analyst may take three different stances with respect to the patient: an "outside" observer, an interested companion, or a listener *within*. In the first, his predominant position is outside the patient's state of mind. He is an accurate and objective observer of the patient's intrapsychic conflict and disturbed relationships to past and present objects. From time to time he will make a transient identification with the patient (i.e., employ the empathic process) to better sense the analysand's inner state of mind, particularly his emotions. From this external vantage point, augmented by intermittent use of the empathic process, the analyst can determine the nature of the patient's defenses, the drive being defended against, and the context of object relationships in which the conflicts arise. He can recognize how the patient distorts the analyst's statements and intentions; how he experiences occurrences in the analysis through the filter of his past and present sexual and aggressive wishes; how he attempts to induce affirmations of love, favor, or esteem, or provokes negative responses and exaggerates their humiliating effect or attributes to them a malevolent motivation. This stance allows the analyst to interpret to the patient what the analyst perceives him to be doing intrapsychically and interpersonally. Roughly speaking, Kernberg's (1975, 1976) descriptions of his clinical interventions suggest that he advocates "outside" positioning in order to offer effective interpretations of the patient's defenses, drives, and their imbeddedness in pathologic object relations. Especially with the borderline patient, this stance is construed to allow the therapist to confront the patient's defensively disguised primitive aggression with the therapist's own undisguised, controlled, and integrated assertiveness, particularly at moments of high tension.

When the analyst uses such an interpretive approach outside the patient's own way of experiencing, a difficulty sometimes arises. When the analyst correctly interprets a patient's struggle with his aggressiveness, anger, greed, or erotic cravings, the patient often feels attacked and harassed. This defensive mobilization of "counteraggression," provocations, depreciation, envy, negativity, and narcissistic rage may feel to him to be manifestations not of problems he is investigating with the analyst, but secondary to the treatment's exact repetition of the negative attitudes of earlier objects. Experientially, to the patient it can be as if he were being excited or expansive or negativistic or independent as a child, and his mother coldly or hotly fixed him in both their minds as out-of-step, establishing and reinforcing a negative identity image that could have become the basis for a self-fulfilling prophecy. Of course, this difficulty of the patient's misidentification of the analyst's designation of his drive urge as a criticism linked to the past generally is overcome by the analyst's skill, perseverance, and real concern for the patient's welfare. However, its strong potential as a danger cannot be ignored, especially when interpretations are conceived and phrased from the standpoint of an "outside" observer.

A more serious liability of the analyst taking this stance is that it is more difficult for him to sense, identify, and give coherence to altered, frequently disconnected mood and bodily states that patients often experience, especially those with severe strain or stress traumas. From any stance, it is difficult for the analyst to understand the timing, meaning, and motivation involved in the patient's changing self-states—from expansive and elated to deflated and depressed, from idealizing to depreciatory, from separate and capable of some degree of ambivalence to split off as a good self with a good object or as an angry self with an angry object. When the analyst is positioned as an "outside" observer, it is especially hard for him to remain in touch with the patient during these transitions and to sense the source or stimulus for them.

A second stance the analyst may take is that of an interested, sympathetic companion listener. This is the stance the analyst takes when he greets his patient and when he says goodbye. It is most useful for the times during the treatment sessions when the intrapsychic and interpersonal tension is moderate. From this position the analyst may add greatly to the patient's self-awareness by frequently asking him orienting and clarifying questions. Examples are: Can you tell me more about the image of yourself in your dream: Can you give an example of a time you felt that way? How old were you? How did you understand what I meant? The analyst may paraphrase or summarize the patient's statements to ensure and promote congruence of meaning. He may name and identify a feeling-state or attitude to increase recognition and distancing that designating promotes.

I believe that interventions the analyst makes from this stance are especially useful in maintaining and encouraging both intrapsychic and interpersonal connectedness with narcissistic and borderline patients. The disadvantage is that if the therapist attempts to remain in the mode of relatedness of the interested companion inappropriately, that is, at times of high intrapsychic and interactional tension, he may inadvertently induce or seduce the patient into a defensive, repetitious, empty ritual of avoidance of his regulatory problems and conflictual areas.

The third stance is the one I have attempted to delineate—the mode of perception in which the analyst, as *systematically* as possible, positions his listening to be from *within* the patient's state of mind. This vantage point of empathic contact with the patient's own experiential perspective offers the analyst the advantage, when successful, of perceiving the whole context of how the analysand is sensing himself and others, how he senses the source of his affective-cognitive state, and what he feels are his possible responses to his state (i.e., whether he experiences himself as having active choices or feels entrapped and overwhelmed into passive surrender). The analyst can perceive at any given moment whether the analysand is regarding him as the desired source of regulatory help or as the target of a conflictual sexual or aggressive urge.

A particular advantage is that the analyst is optimally placed to perceive the patient's pain and confusion when he experiences altered self-states, as well as to help identify the blotted-out stimuli for the transitions and fluctuations of such states. Sensing in this way, of course, is extremely difficult. The analyst who attempts it faces many problems of technique that require considerable training and many assaults on his personal stability that put him in jeopardy of unconscious countertransference reactions. (This is a broad subject beyond the scope of this paper that touches on issues of training and sensitivities that are hopefully liberated, accentuated, and encouraged in the analyst's personal analysis.)

Two specific problems should be mentioned that may occur when the analyst listens from an empathic vantage point. First, when sensing a patient's pain or confusion about an altered self-state, the analyst may be led into incorrect maneuvers. He may attempt to soothe, or admire, or praise, or placate, rather than to actively interpret the patient's wish for those responses, how that wish fits into his disturbed capacity to regulate himself, and how the regulatory disturbance may be related to conflicts that need to be understood. Second, especially with a patient who has an unstable sense of self and is prone to mobilize rage as an integrating feeling (Lichtenstein, 1971), the analyst might become hesitant to upset or intrude into a split all-good transference state, thus leaving underinterpreted the patient's aggressive reactiveness and its meaning to his self-regulatory disturbance.

Despite its difficulties, I believe that the empathic vantage point is the optimal basic perspective for analytic work, and that needed facets of the others can be integrated into it. Listening from within the frame of reference of the patient's feelings and thoughts enables the analyst to observe and interpret in a manner that permits him to construct an "observation platform" on which both can stand.

However, the patient may not feel comfortable on this imaginary shared platform. The closeness may seem overstimulating. The fears of losing the sense of mutual support may seem too great to acknowledge its existence. The analysand may fear the sharing as a risk of his independence, or he may want to turn it into a situation for demanding some form of gratification. Each of these responses would call for further empathic observation and interpretation.

Sometimes the patient will respond to having his experience articulated and feeling understood by being willing to remain on the "platform" with the analyst and being responsive to further interpretation based on empathic observation. The analysand would then continue to provide associations, his point of view being one of working within the dialogue of an effective self-selfobject interaction. *It is at these moments that I believe the analyst is able to make very rapid shifts in his vantage point to avail himself of the benefits each stance offers as a source of information-gathering.* He may fleetingly establish a kind of mental set in which, like an "outside" natural scientist observer, he visualizes an affectively-charged interaction between the patient and others, then shifts his empathy to each.

The analyst may let his attention fall on how the analysand is experiencing him, even though the patient's focus seems not to be on the transference. The analyst's quickly oscillating attentiveness may also shift to his own responses to the shared closeness: Is he feeling smug because of his success, apprehensive that it will end? He may move away from the emotional side of his empathy or introspection and suddenly see from the shared platform a whole vista of the experience of the hour, the prior hours, and the already-made reconstructions of the past; from these he may recognize a new set of integrations. When he resumes interpretive contact with the analysand, he will first return to the empathic vantage point. He will thus response to the patient, not with what he has learned from any of the other vantage points, and not by superimposing his theoretical frame of reference, but by placing himself solidly back into experiencing within the patient's experience.

Case Illustration

I shall illustrate my use of these concepts through a clinical vignette. Dr. A. is an unmarried physician in her thirties. She entered analysis at the suggestion of her most recent boyfriend. She said that for years she had contemplated analysis because she felt a great deal of hostility toward her parents, but could not understand why. She also indicated that she would become attracted to and involved with a man and then feel it necessary to get away. In her history she described several prolonged attachments to men who, while bright and successful, appeared to be unusually emotionally dependent and clinging.

The material I shall report occurred during one week at the beginning of her second year of analysis. In her Monday hour, Dr. A. complained of a tense weekend. That morning a friend had noted that she looked out-of-sorts and asked her what the matter was. She agreed she felt irritable and down but didn't know the source. She wanted to break up with her boyfriend, but he always pleaded with her not to. He made her feel guilty, but could be great company when not depressed. On Tuesday she cancelled her hour, citing an emergency she had to respond to. On Wednesday (an early morning hour that she frequently missed), Dr. A. began in a desultory tone, saying she was surprised she had come, she hadn't wanted to. She described a disturbing dream, as follows: She was going to watch a scene, like a movie being made. A women with beautiful long black hair, resembling her mother's, was tied in a chair. There was a series of frames put up around the woman, similar to a square with an open end, each frame widening out. A bear with light brown fur was introduced at the far end; the way it was set up the bear was drawn to the woman as if in a funnel. As Dr. A. watched, she felt very tense and agitated. The bear came right up to the woman and bit her. The whole thing was disgusting.

During a brief pause my thought was that the dream depicted a primal scene—Dr. A. was the child observing her bear of a Polish father sexually attacking her South American mother, the sexual content being misperceived as an oral-sadistic attack. Her spontaneous reflection that in contrast to the bear (whose fur was like her and her father's blondish hair), the woman had long black hair (just like her mother's) seemed to add confirmation. I recognized that my association was based on a match between the manifest content of her dream and an important theoretical developmental issue. The match did seem impressive, and I was not ready to discard it. However, as I returned to an empathic sensing from within the patient's experience, I could feel no convincing evidence for it. I resumed an attempt to listen from within.

Dr. A. added no further direct associations and began complaining about the analysis. How long would it take? A year had passed. She knew she was better in some ways, but there was no end in sight. Her tone became more irritable. I believed I could make a connection between the experience I empathically sensed and a portion of the dream. I suggested she might feel like the bear who was introduced into a situation where, because of the way it was constructed, she was drawn nearer and nearer to a person fixedly waiting in a chair. "Oh you," she said, "I hadn't thought of that. Yes, Yes."

With the belief that I had established a platform for joint observing, I added that we had talked many times about her feelings of being trapped and that we knew they were a source of resentment and anger. She agreed and described how such discoveries in analysis always amazed her, but despite satisfaction often made her more tense. I felt she was responding to the empathic sharing, and I suggested that finding out things with my help may have drawn her to me, then made her feel more trapped into a commitment to stay. She responded, "Yes, then I want to say something snotty to you." I paraphrased, "Bite me with sarcasm," and she chuckled good-naturedly at the hour's end. My comment was, I believe, a minor technical error. Rather than interpreting why she wanted to express sarcasm, I gratified a wish for a shared "provocative" interaction.

On Thursday she described a vivid incident from the night before when a man sitting in a booth next to her in a restaurant had blown clouds of cigar smoke over the partition. She had politely asked him to divert the smoke. The man responded provocatively. An ugly alteraction almost resulted. She associated this to incidents of anger and feelings of having to prove herself against those who might take advantage of her. I considered the transference implications of her anger. An analogy to my minor error of the day before occurred to me, but my feeling from within the patient's experience was different. The smoke incident seemed too specific a source for her emotions, and the feel her general responsiveness to me too positive to sense a subjectively interpretable connection. I felt it best to wait and see if this occasion was similar to other times when we jointly could recognize that I was the person she felt was provoking or taking advantage of her. At those times, I had sensed she directed more of her feeling toward me. By waiting, I could also sense whether another issue was emerging.

As she talked I felt her becoming progressively more distant, not hostile, but more discouraged. When the subject matter seemed to her like "old stuff" we'd been over many times, I wondered if, as in her dream, she was feeling more like an observer watching a scene or a movie being made than a participant. She said, "Yes, and I feel just as tense and agitated as I did in the dream." She added with a change of mood, "You know, I had really wanted to get back to that dream but this thing happened in the restaurant and I got so angry that I got thrown off." I suggested sbe might want to get back to working on the dream the next day.

On Friday Dr. A. said she hadn't been sure she'd be able to come because an emergency had arisen, but she had worked it out quickly. I took this to indicate that she felt a positive intention toward the analytic work. When she stated that on the way to the session she had been thinking about her dream, I noted the desire she had expressed at the end of the hour, the frustration the day before in not getting back to it, and her resolving the emergency. She reviewed material about her attraction to men and then feeling trapped, noting similar feelings with her present boyfriend.

I asked for her associations to the "bite." In an interested fashion she stated, "That was strange. The bear bit the woman on the side [pointing to her left lower rib cage]. I expected blood to come out but instead it was a clear liquid. That was the strange part. My mother was always so puzzling. She did the right things—she stayed home to look after me. She saw to it that I was sent to private school, college and medical school. She told me she wanted me to meet a nice boy and marry him, yet I blame her. I resent her and I don't know why." I brought her back to the dream image of expecting blood from a person and getting a clear liquid instead, adding there was a common expression for that. "Oh, my God," she answered excitedly, "ice water in her veins. That was it! I would bring a boy home for her to meet him and she'd be so nice while he was there and then in her cold haughty tone, she'd say, 'Did you see that boy's manners? He didn't know how to greet people and his shirt was soiled.' There's no warmth in that!"

I noted the intensity of her feeling, her excitement. Following up previous analytic work on her headlong plunges into feelings of outrage, she used my recognition of her mounting excitement as an indication of that potential, and calmed down a bit. (I believe the calming effect to be the result of her expanded capacity for regulation of her affect storms as a result of the prior analytic work—not the result of implicit suggestion, explicit parenting or counseling.) She stated, "I know if I let myself go all the way I'll be disgusted with myself for losing control." I sensed that she had sufficient hold of her excitement to continue to share in the interpretation of the dream. I then noted her disgust as onlooker of the bear's biting. "Yes." Then, more calmly, she added, "You know where the bear bit her—it was where her heart is. I don't know; it's so puzzling." I felt that in her several references to "puzzling" she was expressing to me her inability to describe the elements of a contradiction (a conflict). She was curious about it, but her vista from the shared platform did not allow her to go any further in understanding her mixed feelings.

In the immediate analytic work she had moved from the general sense of anger at her parents, to the specific feeling of her mother's coldness toward her independent strivings. Therefore I felt it was compatible with her needs and receptivity to me to attempt to interpret her conflict as she experienced it intrapsychically at that moment, as specifically as her associations allowed. I noted the many times she had described feeling drawn to her mother by her physical attractiveness, as embodied in her beautiful long black hair, and by her many indications of interest and attention exemplified by sponsoring Dr. A.'s schooling. But I also pointed out her feeling that her mother failed to sustain with warmth Dr. A.'s efforts to emerge more independently, live away from home or move to another city, and that Dr. A. regarded her as especially cold in response to having a boyfriend. In the imagery of her dream, it was as though her mother opposed her having the frame of her life truly open. She ended, stating with a sigh: "That's the way I've felt with everyone I've ever tried to be close to."

In putting the interpretation in the manner I had—that she was both drawn to and angry with her mother—I was staying as close as I could to the patient's way of experiencing her conflict at this time. I was aware that at another time Dr. A. would need to understand that she saw aspects of her mother in her lovers, and that behind the heterosexual shading of her love relationships lay a homosexual trend. I also knew that she would subsequently be able to experience herself "drawn to her mother"—not in the passive mode of that expression and the imagery of the dream, but actively, intentionally seeking her for a variety of aims including sensual ones. Interpreting a conflict by using empathy facilitates working through that aspect of the conflict; as a result, unresolved aspects of that conflict are more apt to later come into the foreground of the patient's experience.

Summary

(1) The empathic vantage point does not overemphasize responsiveness to emotionality and underemphasize cognitive elements, either in the analyst's listening or interpreting. A misunderstanding of this nature could be eliminated by the recognition that the processes utilized by the analyst who takes an empathic vantage point are those usually described as empathy, intuition, and secondary process thought. Alternatively, this misunderstanding could be eliminated by a develop-

mental view of empathy as both affective and cognitive from its inception in the mother-infant dialogue.

(2) By providing new insights into psychopathology, Kohut's psychology of the self includes the basis for an extension of interpretation, in the secondary process sense, into the vicissitudes of regulation within the self-selfobject interaction.

I believe that regarding a regulatory theory as explanatory for one sector of the personality, and a theory of intrapsychic conflict as explanatory for another, invites a belief that one sector is responded to by a technique tilted toward the experiential and the emotional, while the other is balanced between the emotional and the cognitive. I prefer to regard the concept of intrapsychic conflict as particularizing specific elements out of a developmental regulatory failure, and the sense of altered self-states and of an unempathic parent as generalizing the problem to the self-selfobject interactional unit. Looked at in this way, the theory of regulatory needs and the theory of intrapsychic conflict can be regarded as alternative shifting perspectives for organizing and conceptualizing different experiential data as they originate from the patient in the course of analysis.

3. The empathic vantage point, one in which the analyst orients his listening stance from *within* the perspective and state of mind of the analysand, is compared with the traditional natural science vantage point of the observer positioned outside, the vantage point that emphasizes transference based on intrapsychic conflict, and the vantage point of the analyst's personal introspection. Three different stances for the analyst—outside the analysand's state of mind; as an interested, sympathetic companion listener; and inside the analysand's mental state—are compared for their advantages and disadvantages as modes of perception of the patient's communications and as launching points for formulating and communicating interpretations. Through a general discussion and clinical example, reasons are given for considering the empathic vantage point as the optimal perspective for psychoanalytic work.

REFERENCES

Arlow, J. & Brenner, C. (1964), *Psychoanalytic Concepts and the Structural Theory*. New York: International Universities Press.

Basch, M. (1977), Developmental psychology and explanatory theory in psychoanalysis. In: *The Annual of Psychoanalysis*, 5:229–266. New York: International Universities Press.

Beres, D. & Arlow, J. (1974), Fantasy and identification in empathy. *Psychoanal. Quart.*, 43:26–50.

Condon, W. (1977), A primary phase in the organization of infant responding. In: *Studies in Mother-Infant Interaction*, ed. H. Schaffer. London: Academic Press, pp. 153–176.

Fenichel, O. (1941), *Problems of Psychoanalytic Technique*. New York: Psychoanalytic Quarterly.

Freud, A. (1936), *The Ego and the Mechanism of Defense: The Writings of Anna Freud*, 2. New York: International Universities Press, 1966.

Freud S. (1909), Analysis of a phobia in a five-year-old boy. *Standard Edition*, 10:3–152. London: Hogarth Press, 1955.

——— (1912), Recommendations to physicians practicing psychoanalysis. *Standard Edition*, 12:109–120. London: Hogarth Press, 1958.

——— (1926), Inhibitions, symptoms and anxiety. *Standard Edition*, 26:77–174. London: Hogarth Press, 1959.

Gill, M. (1978), The transference in Fenichel's *Problems of Psychoanalytic Technique*. Presented at the American Psychoanalytic Association Meeting, December 15.

Goldberg, A., Ed. (1978), *The Psychology of Self: A Casebook*. New York: International Universities Press.

Gray, P. (1973), Psychoanalytic technique and the ego's capacity for viewing intrapsychic activity. *J. Amer. Psychoanal. Assn.*, 21:474–494.

Greenson, R. (1967), *The Technique and Practice of Psychoanalysis*. New York: International Universities Press.

Kernberg, O. (1975), *Borderline Conditions and Pathological Narcissism*. New York: Aronson.

——— (1976), *Object Relations Theory and Clinical Psychoanalysis*. New York: Aronson.

Kohut, H. (1959), Introspection, empathy, and psychoanalysis. *J. Amer. Psychoanal. Assn.*, 7:459–483.

——— (1971), *The Analysis of Self*. New York: International Universities Press.

——— (1977), *The Restoration of the Self*. New York: International Universities Press.

Lichtenberg, J. & Slap, J. (1977), Comments on the general functioning of the analyst in the psychoanalytic situation. In: *The Annual of psychoanalysis*, 5:295–312. New York: International Universities Press.

Lichtenstein, H. (1971), The malignant no: Instinctual drives and the sense of self. In: *The Dilemma of Human Identity*. New York: Aronson, pp. 293–322.
Moore, B. & Fine, B. (1967), *A Glossary of Psychoanalytic Terms and Concepts*. New York: American Psychoanalytic Association.
Schwaber, E. (1980), Self psychology and the concept of psychopathology: A case presentation. In: *Advances in Self Psychology*, ed. A. Goldberg. New York: International Universities Press, pp. 215–242.
Valenstein, A. (1978), Position paper on Fenichel's *Problems of Psychoanalytic Technique*. Presented at American Psychoanalytic Association Meeting, December 15.
Wolf, E. (1976), Ambience and abstinence. In: *The Annual of Psychoanalysis*, 4:101–116. New York: International Universities Press.

Discussion

JOHN E. GEDO, M.D.

I EXPERIENCE THE WORLD OF Jean Genêt's *The Blacks* as I prepare to respond to Joseph Lichtenberg's essay: most people are preoccupied with the struggle to overthrow the old imperium, but, for me, the real action takes place in the jockeying for power among the inheritors. The era of positivism is over; its psychoanalytic manifestations can hardly find defenders among the active contributors on the current scene. Contemporary epistemology is preoccupied with the role of the observer in determining the nature of his (or her) observations; Lichtenberg admirably defines the shifting perspectives among which psychoanalysts must forever choose one or another in order to formulate their interventions. If Lichtenberg still advocates giving the vantage point he calls "empathic" pride of place among the ones available, we may well look upon his choice as a late salvo in the victorious campaign to free psychoanalysis from the vestiges of the laboratory tradition in which it was born—a farewell to Brücke and Charcot.

For me, the particular value of Lichtenberg's contribution lies in his *refusal* to abandon the alternatives to the empathic vantage point in the psychoanalytic situation. In decided contrast to those who would restrict analytic work to its hermeneutic aspects, Lichtenberg stresses the necessity to integrate a number of additional observational activities with our efforts to comprehend the analysand's subjectivity. At crucial junctures, the proper perspective may, after all, be that of the natural scientist (however shorn of nineteenth-century certainties!) At others, the analyst's optimal stance is that of "an interested, sympathetic companion listener." In his illuminating clinical illustration, Lichtenberg demonstrates the shift into a natural science mode of observation: "I sensed that she had sufficient hold on her excitement to continue to share in the interpretation of the dream." As he points out, he did not arrive at this conclusion simply on the basis of empathizing with the patient's current condition; he used comparative observations, taken over long spans of time, to infer that she had gained an "expanded capacity for regulation of her affect storms."

For didactic purposes, Lichtenberg discusses the alternative vantage points of the psychoanalyst sequentially. *In vivo*, of course, they are all simultaneously in continuous operation. In other words, we may reach the conclusion that an analysand has difficulties in tension regulation by correlating the occurrences of his vascular headaches (or mucous colitis, or asthmatic attacks) with episodes of passively endured stimulus overload; in this way, our work parallels that of an ethologist. We may then decide to intervene to bring this correlation to the patient's attention—I trust there can be no question about the advisability of doing this empathically. To succeed, this move must be based on accurate assessment of the patient's emotional position at that given moment (in particular, on the status of the manifold transferences that characterize the analytic relationship)—an achievement contingent on continuous monitoring of these shifting developments from the empathic vantage point.

Lichtenberg gives proper weight to potential abuse of the "ethological mode" (if I may so label it). Yet he pays less attention to analogous dangers in the overuse of the empathic one. He *does* allude to common countertransference errors in response to perceiving the extent of the analysand's distress, especially the propensity to enter into enactments of a loving parent's expectable behavior when confronted by a distressed child. The other potential complication in the use of the empathic mode of observation Lichtenberg singles out is neglect in elucidating the patient's reactive aggression. Obviously, Lichtenberg does not pretend to discuss these issues comprehensively; in my judgment, however, he focuses too narrowly on errors of the more elementary kind—not to be expected from experienced analysts, one would hope. I should like to supplement his suggestions by offering an example of a more insidious mistake, based on an analyst's failure to step out of the empathic vantage point.

Some time ago I undertook to reanalyze a man with severe marital problems who had terminated a lengthy analysis several years before. His difficulties with his wife had been in evidence during the first treatment, but it was hoped that her own therapy would eliminate them. When we started to work together, the patient was infuriated with her infantile behavior but helpless to deal with it effectively because he was afraid that she would be shattered if he set limits on it. From the empathic viewpoint, the main issue was clearly the patient's fantasy about his own potential destructiveness—a fantasy he had learned a good deal about in his first analysis. What he had *never* heard was any challenge to his conviction that his wife's seeming vulnerability was a façade, although his accounts of their troublesome transactions conveyed a very different impression from the one he consciously espoused. By listening to the material in the mode Lichtenberg calls that of the interested companion, I was able to pinpoint how my patient was allowing himself, masochistically, to be tortured and exploited by a clever delinquent. Needless to say, the analysis took on a very different complexion from one that had focused on his apparent sadism! My point is that the analyst should bring to bear observations from as many differing perspectives as possible in order to elucidate the clinical material in fullest light.

Lichtenberg takes pains to free the concept of empathy from the disrepute that may have gathered around it as a result of one-sided claims made for its value as a process promoting affective communication, without regard for the necessity of articulating what is happening in secondary-process terms. In this regard, Lichtenberg differentiates his own use of the concept from that of Kohut (not to mention some of Kohut's students, who fail to use the terminology of "self psychology" with any consistency or precision). The entire analytic community might, I daresay, find Lichtenberg's usage acceptable; if it were adopted, however, the specifically Kohutian flavor of discussions of this subject would evaporate.

I agree with Lichtenberg's judgment that the empathic vantage point is particularly valuable when the analyst is confronted with primitive mental states (see Gedo, 1981a, Chapter 6). But this observation does not mean that Kohut's specific hypotheses about these realms of mental life are preferable to any others. (In recent psychoanalytic discourse, disagreement with Kohut's viewpoint has sometimes been equated with being unempathic!) And when Kohut himself tried to illustrate his use of "empathy" in the clinical setting in his later writings, the process he described referred not so much to the observer's vantage point as to continuous alertness about patients' needs for a "selfobject." It was by no means clear that these preconscious operations involved the affective-perceptual-cognitive networks through which one communicates with infants, rather than the application of psychoanalytic schemata in a deductive manner.

I do not wish to imply that I disagree with Lichtenberg's statement that for certain patients "the sense of an empathic synchrony with the analyst constitutes a major resource for self-regulation," and I concur in his judgment that this empirical discovery was the most important of Kohut's clinical contributions. Elsewhere (Gedo, 1981a, Section II), I have discussed at some length my disagreements with the psychological system Kohut erected on this foundation. Here, I must confine myself to a brief caveat about exclusive reliance on the empathic vantage point even in these circumstances. That strategy led Kohut to the construction of his schema of archaic mental life as a set of subjective wishes (summarized by Lichtenberg). In a posthumously published paper, Kohut (1982) epitomized this option as the conception of human existence in terms of *homo psychologicus*.

I believe this choice unduly narrows the observational field and eliminates from consideration precisely those data concerning the most archaic modes of behavioral regulation, which do not possess (symbolic) mental representation. These biopsychological operations form the bedrock of human behavior; the archaic subjective states emphasized by Kohut are, by contrast, epiphenomena. To put the matter more concretely, we cannot discover the analysand's failure to renounce mutually exclusive goals through exercising our empathic processes; we must infer the presence of deficits in self-regulation, which underlie the symbiotic strivings that fill the psychological field in such cases, through the detached observational methods of a natural scientist.

Lichtenberg also takes Kohut to task for erecting a false dichotomy between a putative psychology of intrapsychic conflict and one focused on issues of self-regulation. I agree that a more all-encompassing view is necessary, as suggested in the hierarchical model of mental life developed in my collaborative work with Goldberg (Gedo and Goldberg, 1973; see also Gedo, 1979, 1981a, 1981b). This is what my advocacy of centering psychoanalytic psychology on the concept of "self-organization" amounts to: we must find a unitary theory in which "conflicts" can simultaneously be seen as partial failures in regulation at some lower (more fundamental) level of the hierarchy of functions. I thus find Lichtenberg's proposals for the technical handling of the shifting requirements of analytic patients fully in accord with the hierarchy of technical modalities I have outlined in my previous writings.

REFERENCES

Gedo, J. (1979), *Beyond Interpretation*. New York: International Universities Press.

_____ (1981a), *Advances in Clinical Psychoanalysis*. New York: International Universities Press.

——— (1981b), Measure for measure: A response. *Psychoanal. Inquiry*, 1:289–316.

———& Goldberg, A. (1973), *Models of the Mind*. Chicago: University of Chicago Press.

Kohut, H. (1982), Introspection, empathy, and the semicircle of mental health. *Int. J. Psycho-Anal.*, 63:395–408. Reprinted here as Chapter 4.

20 Empathy: A Mode of Analytic Listening

EVELYNE SCHWABER, M.D.

If the historian will submit himself to *his material instead of trying to impose himself* on *his material, then the material will ultimately speak to him and supply the answers.*
—Barbara Tuchman, *In Search of History*

AS DIFFERENT THEORETICAL MODELS arrive on the psychoanalytic scene, it becomes more critical, I believe, for the clinician to maintain at the forefront of his or her efforts the elucidation of how he or she gathers the data of depth psychology. The recent exploration of the concept of empathy insofar as it addresses this effort, is a welcome pursuit. However, considerable ambiguity, multidirectional and ofttimes value-laden meaning has arisen regarding this concept, perhaps catalyzed by work with patients representing widening realms of psychopathology. Outside the clinical situation (and within as well), empathy has been described as a mode of human relatedness; as a way of understanding, knowing and responding; and as an early and ubiquitous developmental nutrient. Alternatively, within the clinical situation, it has been thought of as a method of observation, a technical modality, or an adjective describing one—sometimes part of the ana-

---

Reprinted from *Psychoanalytic Inquiry*, 1:357–392 (1981).
I would like to covey my appreciation for the many helpful suggestions in clarifying and conveying my ideas, offered by Drs. Merton Gill, Joseph Lichtenberg, Judy Kantrowitz, Samuel Kaplan, and Paul Schwaber.

lytic ambience, and sometimes the matrix of the analytic method. Moreover, these differences in meanings often seem to reflect differing perspectives in the theories underriding them.

If we were to reserve the term empathy, within the clinical situation, as a method of *observation*—of gathering depth-psychological information—perhaps we could reduce what may be unnecessary controversy over the relationship between its use and its theoretical basis. Understood as a specific, scientifically-trained mode of perceiving the data, and distinguished from the communications which may follow from it, its intrinsic nature would warrant clarification independent of the particular theory upon which the clinician draws. Although theories may offer us models by which to organize our data and hopefully widen our perceptual scope, and although each theoretical system may suggest a definition of the listening stance within its own framework, I believe that the theory does not determine the nature of its application.

I will consider the concept of empathy here in its clinical usage as synonymous with a mode of analytic listening, and share with you some reflections.

I

At a recent panel discussion[1] I presented some clinical material to illustrate a particular focus of attunement to perceptual cues. Portions of this are excerpted[2] as follows:

> Mr. R., a young man in his early 20's, was referred to me as an 'exceptionally gifted photographer,' unable to proceed with his work because of the appearance of somatic symptoms—stomach distress, headaches and dizziness—for which no organic etiology was found. He also complained of a feeling of 'detachment,' an uncomfortable, sometimes frightening sense of being very far removed from things. Mr. R. was a pleasant-looking, thoughtful and intelligent young man, who seemed to have a ready gift toward self-reflection, although he hadn't previously attempted any introspection. He felt great trepidation about returning in analysis to the first 13 years of his life, from which he felt quite removed.

---

[1]*Construction and Reconstruction: Clinical Aspects*, panel of the American Psychoanalytic Association, San Francisco, May 4, 1980. See also Schwaber, 1983a.

[2]Some of this material, both of the author and of the discussant, is paraphrased.

Indeed, whenever he attempted to look at pictures or listen to tapes of himself as a child before the age of 13 he experienced unbearable dizziness and other of the described symptoms; similarly, once on the couch, these symptoms often recurred.

Mr. R. often told of the importance to him of photography, a subject about which he spoke with great affective involvement. In one hour he said: "I can remember even way back having the experience of elation. I can remember it being triggered by how it might look photographically, as in a beautiful scene or in music. When I see something that looks good, there is a very strong desire to take a picture and kind of freeze it there, as with a beautiful sunset. It's an experience all of a sudden of my sensibilities becoming really heightened, like I'll notice the pores of someone's skin and it looks great, and I want to take a picture and catch it . . . I know a psychiatrist who became interested in photography and took it up more and more . . . on his vacations . . . finally giving up psychiatry. . ."

I said (since my own vacation was imminent and there had been no reference to it): "I wonder if my vacation may have been stirring such thoughts, of my waning interest in my profession." Mr. R. replied: "I'm not sure how to understand what you mean. I'm thinking of the joke of the two psychiatrists meeting in an elevator. I wonder if you know the joke, and if you do, will you answer . . . [he spoke more slowly] . . . I think you responded defensively to the idea of a psychiatrist switching to photography . . . I didn't mean to be critical. . . ."

It seemed his train of associations here was derailed; somehow we had gotten off the track. Our time was up, and as he walked out, I noticed that he completely avoided looking at me and his body seemed rather strikingly shrunken in its stance.

One may consider here that I touched on an area of anxiety about separation that he profoundly resisted, which is why he responded as he did. But even if this were so, together we came to understand that the specific trigger of his response included a perception of me, how it felt to him that I said what I did when I did . . . perhaps a historically meaningful recreation.

What was it, then, that he had *felt* about *my comment?* He saw me as defensive . . . meaning, that from *his* vantage point, I seemed to be responding out of needs or concerns of my own, rather than of his. He spoke then of the joke of the two psychiatrists meeting in an elevator. I assumed he was referring to the one about the psychiatrist who, being told by a colleague, "Good morning,"thought "I wonder what he means by that." (I am aware that there are several jokes with different content, although with similar underlying messages.) I did not see at the time what I was later to understand—that the idea is that the first psychiatrist is so caught up in his own work and ideology as to be unable to comprehend the point of view and interest of the person relating to him. This underlying message emerged gradually as he spoke in subsequent hours of his girlfriend's (and later his mother's) lack of interest in his work—a kind of self-preoccupation he experienced about them. Then I could see more clearly that when I responded from within the issue of my profession and my vacation, it was this old injury which I had recreated.

The shrunken stance, the avoidance of eye contact, the halting speech were all aspects of detachment—defenses against and expressions of certain feelings stirred within him. These were also specific responses to perceptions which had their own particular history for him, thereby helping to illuminate for us his image of the early, forgotten, dizzying world of his childhood and the experience of himself within it.

In one hour, the patient came in complaining that he felt that his girlfriend had been withdrawing, that she wasn't touching him very much, and so he did not feel like talking. Words came slowly and dissipated. He paused; I said nothing, and then told of hearing music and silently listening to it. I asked him to say more about this and he reflected, "It seems my hearing music came when I was waiting for you to comment and you didn't." What was he waiting for in such a comment from me, and what did it mean to him that I was silent, I wondered. He said, as he then thought about it, that he felt 'untouched' by me, too, and feeling that he needed soothing, chose an old familiar pathway, listening to music—an auditory mode, as my words would have been, though this time on an imaginary level.

Again, he needed to defend via a familiar retreat from threatening feelings towards me, about which we had yet much more to learn. But in my effort to help him elucidate his perception of me—of my silence as untouching—and his feeling-state that evoked a heightened need for my responsiveness, Mr. R. was able to clarify what had been initially only a vaguely observed perception and inner state, and later to place these in their historical perspective. We were thereby offered a closer view of the contextual sense of the childhood experience and the pathway which he had found-out. We learned of his turn to music in childhood to ease feelings of isolation and insignificance—at first only vaguely articulated states. Music, like the Brahms to which he was 'listening' on the couch, was something his father loved. Listening to music in the hour, then, offered a symbolic representation of a comforting connection to his father, perhaps especially sought in the wake of such painful feelings.

In the ensuing discussion and critique of my remarks,[3] the following comments were made regarding the above-mentioned section:

The [first] hour [above] begins with evidence of the patient's vivid imagery and his intense feelings for his pictures. In the midst of his enthusi-

[3]The discussant was Samuel Abrams, M.D., to whom I wish to express my appreciation for his permission to publish this material.

asm, he mentions having heard of a psychiatrist who became so involved with photography during his summer vacations that he eventually abandoned his profession. The analyst recalls that her vacation is imminent and that there has been no reference to it even obliquely—at least, until now. She intervenes: "I wonder if my vacation may have been stirring such thoughts, of my waning interest in my profession." The patient replies, "I'm not sure how to understand what you mean." He thinks of a joke about two psychiatrists, wonders if his analyst has become 'defensive,' speaks more slowly, apologizes, and leaves, 'shrunken in stance.' The analyst recognizes that the train of associations has become derailed; she *correctly*[4] assumes that the patient's reactions, whatever their other determinants, will first have to be recognized as an outgrowth of his perception of her comment.

It's hard to be sure where exactly the patient was a moment before the intervention . . . I think the analyst was probably *correct* in inferring that her vacation was very much on her patient's mind. Frankly, I do not hear him saying that he feels he has already lost his analyst to her vacation, but she reacts to his associations as if he were making such an accusation.

In my judgment, her intervention is not quite there. I *empathize* with Mr. R.'s being unable to understand it, with his becoming fretful and distressed. However, her comment is not quite so bad, either. She rightfully asserts that the patient's reactions must first be understood as the expression of his perception of her statement, and particularly since it is probably an *incorrect* one. An analyst imposing his mistake upon his patient is almost as bad as his arbitrarily imposing his theories. [Author's comment: a point which I had addressed earlier.] Proper technique directs that he acknowledge the *error* frankly or implicitly and go ahead with the work of the analysis. In this instance, that work should include an attempt at ascertaining the idiosyncratic basis for the patient's response. After all, his is not the only possible reaction to the inexact comment.

Dr. S. gets down to analytic business and addresses herself to *this* [italics in original] patient's specific response to her lapse. She listens to the story of the aloof girlfriend, to the recollections of the distant mother, to the report of the patient's childhood strategy of being comforted by music in the face of painful silences. Dr. S. realizes that her patient must *distort* her routine silent analytic listening when the time has come for him to do so. She asks him directly what that silence means to *him* [italics in original]. He describes his highly personal, unique *distortion* of her silence, experiencing it as being 'untouched,' and retreats to compensating and consoling musical sounds. [The analyst] holds her genetic and dynamic stance. She recognizes that her patient is retreating from

[4]Italics are mine throughout the paper, except where otherwise indicated.

> her along an old and familiar path. The patient is imposing distortions on the relationship, distortions derived from within the intrapsychic constellations that determine who he is, and she pursues those distortions, viewing them as products of his mental activities.

Thus, it is argued that I demonstrate a "typically classical analytic stance." How is it, then, that I am suggesting a shift in listening perspective? To pursue this dialogue, let us look again at the comments offered and, in doing so, consider yet another question: What may be the vantage point here which the discussant is implicitly utilizing in his understanding of the material?

In the first vignette the point is made that the analyst's intervention was an error; judging it to be so, the patient's response is deemed more readily understandable. There is an implication that the analyst's capacity to "empathize" with the patient's response may serve as a measure of its validity, in reality.

In the second example, the analyst's response, that of "silent listening," is judged as "routine," to which the patient's reaction of injury is thereby understood as realistically unwarranted—a "distortion."

Thus, via the introduction of the view of the 'outside' listener, i.e., attempting to objectify what is correct or real, a distinction is made between these two examples. In the first vignette, the analyst's response was in error, and in the second, it was not; in the first then, the patient's response could be empathically understood via the analyst's identification; in the second, this implicitly not being the case, it was deemed a distortion.

Once such an 'outside' view is introduced in the effort to understand the material, might not another 'outside' observer judge these two events differently? He might, for example, believe that a tactfully worded question about my impending vacation was very much in order at this late date; in contrast, he may feel that a response of silence to a patient like Mr. R., who has been telling of the pain of feeling untouched, was not warranted. And so, each listener, employing his own view of reality as a standard, may in turn judge that of the patient.[5]

From Mr. R.'s point of view, each of my responses—whether as defensive or as untouching—were *similarly* felt as errors, injuries whose specific meaning lay in the subjective sense of their historical recreation.

---

[5]Recognizing that either gender is intended, impersonal pronouns will be limited to masculine singular throughout this paper, in order to facilitate reading.

I offer this dialectic in consideration of the extent to which implicitly or explicitly analytic listening has employed the use of two realities—that of the observer from the 'outside,' and that from within (albeit the expressed province of our analytic concern lies with the latter—the patient's subjective reality).

II

It is a truism that Freud's monumental shift from the seduction to the fantasy theory of neurosogenesis marked a critical turning point in the history of psychoanalysis. Internal, that is, subjective, reality became the decisive clinical domain. Freud (1917) wrote, "The fantasies possess *psychical* as contrasted with *material* reality and we gradually learn to understand that *in the world of the neuroses it is psychical reality* which is the decisive kind" (p. 368, italics in original).

Although this shift in the clinical purview of the analyst has had significant implications for theory and technique, analytic listening as illustrated in the preceding discussion has nonetheless continued to maintain a view of 'material' reality alongside that of the patient's subjective view. Stein (1966), for example, has written:

> Our approach differs from other psychotherapies in that we explicitly avoid reality testing—at least in the usual sense. We need not tell our patients that they have misjudged a life situation, nor do we as a rule give in to the temptation to *correct* a *misapprehension* of some analytic event. Instead, we attempt to *correct*, by analysis, those *distortions* of self observation which become evident in the analytic situation. By attaining a clearer vision of his own mental processes, by unsparing honesty with himself, we hope that our patients' distortions of perception of the outer world will be reduced to a minimum [p. 276].

We may see in these comments an implicit distinction made between our technical and our observing positions. Technically we avoid reality testing, while, however, we listen with a keen sense of what is objectively real. Such words as: 'misjudged,' 'misapprehension,' 'distortions . . . to correct,' address this idea—the analyst using his own view of reality to assess that of the patient. The vantage point of the objective 'outside' listener gathering the data is thereby maintained. Other concepts such as therapeutic alliance (which addresses that aspect of the patient's view which allies with 'outside' reality), reality testing, magical thinking, reality principle, the 'real' relationship, each is a further indicator of this 'two-reality' outlook in our analytic listening and theorizing.[6] The concept of transference, understood as 'distortion,' sharply illustrates this perspective; the analyst, given of course that he has paid careful heed to his countertransference responses, simultaneously maintains a view of himself as 'objectively' different from the qualities which are 'projected' onto him by his patient. Thus, there are two realitites—one internal, the other external; one that the patient experiences or perceives, the other that the analyst 'knows.' However we may choose to deal with this technically, analytic listening, embedded in this dual vantage point, must then ultimately imply that the aim is to help the patient gradually shift or 'correct' his view as he attains more mature functioning.

Writing on the development and distortions of empathy, Shapiro (1974) offers a clinical vignette:

> After three years of analysis, the patient decided to marry and repeatedly mentioned his intention to telephone a former woman friend to tell her of his plans since he knew, he said, how she would feel if she heard the news from someone else. What might be designated as his empathic knowledge was held with great certainty, *but I wondered if his supposition about her reaction was accurate.* Was the planned call really charitable? Since he had had an intimate relationship with her for four years, it was possible that his call informing her of his forthcoming marriage to someone else might be taken as an act of hostility. She might interpret it as 'rubbing-it-in,' as a narcissistic wish to know that she was still 'pining' for him, or as some other interactional maneuver.
>
> Only after his delay in communicating with her and his reflection that he hoped she, too, might be planning to marry, did I confront him with his use of projection in the guise of empathic understanding. . . . Following this interpretation that he was assuming he knew what this woman would feel because under similar circumstances he would be hurt, the patient was able to consider a broader range of possible responses that he had formerly omitted. He was no longer certain of his empathic understanding [pp. 5–6].

Shapiro later states:

> The day following the confrontation and interpretation of his 'empathic understanding,' he began the hour by describing the humiliation and

---

[6]It is not the domain of this paper to challenge the utility of these concepts or the view of a 'reality' observed from without, in the theoretical *application* of our clinically derived insights. Rather, I wish to focus attention on their *implicit* impact on the process of the derivation of these insights.

In a recent publication (1983) Spruiell has similarly noted that many of these 'reality' references are "no longer conceptually tenable."

> sense of weakness he had experienced when his fiancée berated him for a failing [p. 13].

Here, Stein's caution not to tell a patient that he has misjudged a life situation appears not to be heeded. The patient's subjective experience was that he knew how this friend would feel; the analyst, concerned with the "accuracy" of this feeling, considered and eventually shared his view of reality—different from that immediately expressed by the patient. The "temptation," as Stein aptly labels it, for the analyst to take this course, is likely to occur precisely if, in our listening stance, such an 'outside' view is maintained.[7]

The meaning, within the transference, of the patient's repeated telling of his intention to telephone his former friend, with the idea of making the news easier for her to take, was not elaborated for the reader. One can but speculate here as to whether the patient's comment the following day may have reflected a sense that his analyst, like his fiancée, had "berated him for a failing."

If this is indeed so, that Freud's shift to intrapsychic reality as the domain of study did not take the decisive form initially proposed, then the question may be raised as to why this has been the case. I shall offer some reflections on the matter.

Freud's scientific outlook paralleled that of the scientific observer of his day, studying and measuring the data from the 'outside'—data for which there is some ultimate measurable reality, independent of the observer.[8] Consistent with this outlook, the psychoanalytic view did not regard the impact of the analyst-observer—his responses, silent or stated, as perceived by the patient—as *intrinsic* to the field of obser-

---

[7]Gray (1973) has written cogently on the analyst's "perspective of attention," persuasively arguing for adjusting the perceptual focus "so as to observe data limited essentially to *inside* the analytic situation . . . " (p. 477), that is, to the immediate psychical implications of what the patient is communicating, rather than to aspects of the patient's external or 'outside' situation.

[8]"Classical physics," Heisenberg (1934) has written, "was built on some fundamental suppositions which appeared to be obvious starting points of all exact science. . . . One was led to the tacit assumption that there existed an objective course of events in space and time, independent of observation; further, that space and time were categories of classification of all events, completely independent of each other, and thus represented an objective reality, which was the same to all men . . . " He later notes, "The fundamental assumption of classical physics, whose natural consequence was the scientific concept of the universe of the nineteenth century, was first attacked in Einstein's special theory of relativity."

vation. Thus, it lacked a systematic place within the unfolding data, and specifically, in the understanding of transference.

Similarly, in the evolving elaboration of the nature of early psychological development, assuming the presence of the 'average expectable milieu,' the influence of that milieu—as *perceived* by the child—on its emerging intrapsychic organization, did not become an intrinsic part of the establishment of psychoanalytic developmental theory. When, for example, Freud's patients told of their childhood seductions, no place remained for the systematic inclusion of perceptual cues in the elucidation of their intrapsychic experience, once the seductions were relegated to fantasy.[9] The external event was to be assessed in terms of an 'objective' measure, whether that of the analyst or of the adult patient reporter. If it did not match the fantastic descriptions, then the patient's wishes, impulses and defenses, and the child's immature psychic organization, were seen as accountable for the discrepancy. As the early conflictual experiences reemerged within the transference, they were similarly understood as discrepant with current 'objective' reality. For as we have seen, the transference, from the perspective of the analyst-observer standing outside the field of observation, did not include the analyst's contribution to the patient's perception as fundamental to its very nature.

Thus, as depth-psychological meaning was understood to concern the world of 'inner' reality, the *inner experience of the surround* did not retain a systematic inclusion in clinical data-gathering—neither in the understanding of transference nor in the reconstruction of developmental history. Perception became relegated to a secondary phenomenon, *distorted* by virtue of the *already* present internal happenings—to be freed from this distortion as acceptance of a more 'realistic' outlook ensues. As long as this notion of 'distortion' continued, analytic listening retained "material" reality within its domain.[10]

---

[9]Cf. Schimek (1975), who has written, ". . . the original reality of a childhood seduction can be an actual interaction with a parental figure, which the child, and sometimes the adult, perceived, experienced, and reacted to as a seduction—even if it did not meet some objective adult criteria of a deliberate sexual act. This is what is usually meant by psychic reality . . . but . . . such a meaning cannot readily be fitted into Freud's conceptual structure, even if it expresses much of the spirit of his clinical approach" (pp. 860–863).

[10]It is interesting that Freud, in his later years (1940), did write that within our own science "reality will always remain unknowable" (p. 196). He was here speaking of the difficulty we as analysts have in freeing ourselves from the "language of our perceptions" (p. 196), which he saw as an inherent "limitation of our science" (p. 196). He did not yet speak to the patient's perceptions of the input of the analyst as intrinsic to the field of observation.

The clinical literature has been replete with interest in the role of the milieu in the formation of psychic structure. Writing on reconstruction in psychoanalysis, Kris (1956) was a strong voice for the inclusion of the milieu in the understanding of inner experience:

> I shall turn to findings to which child analysis has made the decisive contribution: to the importance of the early relationship of parent and child and more *specifically the reaction of the child to peculiarities of the parent's personality*. In our analytic work with adult patients we are only rarely able to include this factor. In my experience we succeed only in the course of long and on the whole successful analytic treatments, since interpretations which take the nature of the parents' personality into account obviously require particular caution and a wealth of affirmative impressions, such as—only the prolonged analysis of reactions in the transference situation can provide [p. 68].

Here, although Kris strongly recommended its inclusion in clinical work, he did not, however, specifically articulate that by the "parent's personality," he meant only the patient's subjective view of it. As long as this distinction was not clearly made, interest in the role of the milieu has carried with it the implication that decisive concern has been with "material" reality.

Loewald (1970) has suggested that we utilize a view of a "psychic field," a "mother-infant psychic matrix," in understanding development. He has written:

> Despite the revolutionary insights implied in Freud's formulations of narcissism, identification, ego and superego formation; despite the early recognition of the fundamental role of transference and resistance in both analysand and analyst; despite increased understanding of the analytic process and of early developmental stages—despite all these, psychoanalytic theory still clings to the model of a given psychic apparatus and starts out with the assumption of the existence of a primitive *individual* psyche. The fact that on the physical and biological level we observe a separate organism at birth does not imply that we also deal with a separate psychic organization, however primitive, at birth, and with imminent psychic energies and forces which, as instinctual drives, become secondarily related to objects. I suggest that we seriously consider the proposition that instinctual drives, as psychic forces, are processes taking place *within a field*—the mother-infant psychic matrix; and that their character as instincts as well as the character of the emerging individual psyche is determined by the changing characteristics of that field and of its evolution into differentiated but separate psychic fields [p. 59].

We may consider here the rather profound implications for our clinical listening. The translation however, of this idea of psychic "processes taking place within a field," from that of the "mother-infant matrix" to the analytic situation in which analyst and patient may be viewed as equivalently part of a "psychic field," not only for regressive states, was not specifically addressed.[11]

Loewald has been on the forefront in articulating the view of transference as including the object world in "interaction with the psychic apparatus" (1960). In maintaining a model of an outer world which may be "distorted" by unconscious processes within the patient, however, he implicitly suggests the vantage point of the external observer.

Thus, the fundamental impact of the 'outer'—as viewed from the perspective of the observer 'within' in elucidating the nature of the internal world—although articulately recognized, was still not systematically included in the conceptualization of transference.

In the last two decades there have been some striking new directions traversed in the field of infancy research, which are having a significant impact on our psychoanalytic thinking. In a recent review of a panel on infancy research (Sander, 1980), Galenson's remarks are reported as follows:

> She pointed out that the symposium papers represent studies which are remarkably different from the bulk of infancy research of 15 or 20 years ago. Although they all employ many of the same scientific criteria of replicability, hypothesis testing and quantifications, the issues they address are different from earlier studies and the issues are addressed differently. First, in each one, the infant is considered as part of an *interactional system*, and, secondly, this system is viewed in its development over time, as an unfolding process. The words rhythmic, regulation, recurrence, etc. occur in each study description. Established psychoanalytic theories regarding psychosexual development do not provide for many of the new research data [p. 191].

Indeed, Sander (1975) had earlier decried the tendency inherent in the psychoanalytic view to see "the organization of behavior as the property of the individual rather than of the more inclusive system of which the individual is a part" (p. 147).[12] Summarizing some of his own work (in the review article cited above, 1980), he wrote of the child's very early construction of a perceptual world, out of

[11]Cf. a view of analyst and patient as a 'contextual unit' (Schwaber, 1979, 1980a).

[12]See also Schwaber, 1980a and b.

> the unique strategies of regulation of the infant-caretaker system. . . . The importance of psychoanalysis—of an understanding of early development, its variations and the uniqueness of each adaptive mother-infant system—lies in the clues it gives us as to how to begin *to recognize in the transference the archaic nature of the regulatory process that was unique for that system as it was consolidating [p. 198].*

Thus, Sander, in consonance with Loewald's remarks about psychic processes within a field, utilizes the concept of the 'mother-infant system,' and further suggests the recognition of such a system, including its 'regulatory process' within the transference. This view of transference now draws upon the experience of the outer as it impinges on the inner, revealing a dimension of developmental history of far-reaching import.

In his early paper on empathy, Kohut (1959) noted the presence of the empathic observer as defining *in principle* the psychological field observed. Kohut's later writings on narcissism (1966, 1968, 1971, 1972, 1977) spoke cogently of the unwitting repetition in the analytic situation of the noxiously experienced early milieu, noting that the meaning of this repetition within the patient's psychic organization can be systematically analyzed.[13] This point of view resulted in a sharpened focus on the *specificity* of the analyst's contribution in the understanding of transference. As heightened attention was thereby paid to the impact of perceptual cues on the organization of the patient's immediate experience, this process was seen as recreating a history of such perceptions and the concomitant responses evoked by them (Schwaber, 1979, 1980a, 1983a, 1983b).[14]

I believe it was Kohut's rigorous use of empathy–introspection as the primary mode of data-gathering, suspending the inferential imposition of a reality from without, which led him to the discovery of the varieties of transferences that he subsequently elaborated. It was not

---

[13]See, for example, the case of Miss F. (Kohut, 1971, pp. 283–293); (see also Ornstein and Ornstein, 1975, 1980).

[14]More recently, Gill (1979) writing from a different vantage point—that of the centrality of the analysis of the transference within analytic technique—has similarly underscored the need for sustained and systematic alertness to cues of the "current stimulus" evoking a transference manifestation. Noting that "any transference must have a link to the actuality of the analytic situation" (p. 278), Gill also sees the analyst and patient as engaged in an effort to arrive at a "consensus about reality," rather than there being "some fictitious absolute reality" (p. 282). Gill and Hoffman's two volumes, "Analysis of Transference" (Int. Univ. Press, 1982), in which these ideas are further elaborated, were not yet available at the time of this writing.

that empathy, as Kohut defined it, was a specific discovery of self psychology; it was rather that its fundamental use as a *perceptual* mode—not as a technical stance nor as something directly synonymous with a developmental need—permitted the systematic unfolding and elaboration of another realm of subjective experience.[15]

Elsewhere (1979), in an effort to further elucidate our understanding of empathy, I have drawn upon the terminology of the self-psychological viewpoint, specifically the "selfobject" concept, in suggesting a definition. However, I have employed this concept in a rather sharply defined, perhaps somewhat idiosyncratic, way, "as a mode of ordering clinical data," i.e., bringing together . . . the self and the object, there is suggested a system . . . something I have called a 'contextual unit'—between patient and analyst. Thereby, it is not to be viewed as a construct having to do exclusively with failures of differentiation between self and object nor to failed recognition of the autonomy of each—but more fundamentally as one which recognizes the immediacy of the surround as being intrinsic to the organization and perception of intrapsychic experience" (Schwaber, 1980a, p. 215).

Although I have found it particularly useful to conceptualize empathy within such a framework, this need not imply either a fundamental change in its meaning or that the theory employed will by itself determine the listening stance. Indeed, as with examples using other theoretical views, some of the clinical case reports utilizing the self-psychological framework have similarly implied a superimposition of the analyst's perspective from without, rather than maintaining the consistent focus on the subjective reality of the patient.

As I have commented earlier, empathy is not the domain of any one theoretical view; any theory, once elaborated, can again be used to impose its own view of reality from without. Arguments between proponents of different theoretical systems do not, by themselves, address the fundamental issue of how the clinical data are being observed.

III

In further pursuit, then, of this question—How is the clinical data being gathered?—let us return to another dialectic:

---

[15]This view has received further confirmation in some of the newer findings of infancy research (see Stechler and Kaplan, 1980). See also Lichtenberg's cogent comments in this issue, Ornstein (1979), and Schwaber (1980b).

Myers (1977) has described a patient with a particular symptom, micropsia, appearing within the analytic situation. Although his stated emphasis was not specifically on the listening perspective, the author's close attention to clinical detail—the analyst's and the patient's responses in describing singular moments—helped to illuminate the contextual nature of the material, and thereby to offer an added opportunity for the reader to make his own inferences.

The particular somatic-sensorial symptom, micropsia, was descriptively defined as a state in which things appear smaller than usual and more distant. Myers noted its appearance after his interpretation of the patient's defense against his aggressive oedipal wishes. The following is an example of one episode:

> In the last session of the week before the weekend break, [the patient] was late for an appointment after I had been forced to change the time of the hour.
>
> He expressed intense anger at the time change and spoke of feeling abandoned by me. Obsessions emerged about the presumed differences between the analysis of children and of adults. He speculated about what kind of father I must be and saw me as warm and loving, which seemed unmasculine to him and different from his own father. He then expressed doubts about whether or not to give his current woman friend a gift, something he had never before done with a woman. It seemed obvious that he wished to give her the gift, but he was frightened because it seemed adult and masculine. The fear of being a man like me led to his adopting a childlike tone, and he meekly voiced the wish that I might turn off the air conditioner because it was chilly. He said that he could not expect me to do this because he paid me such a low fee. When I pointed out that he was portraying himself as a child, as a defensive response to the fears aroused by exhibiting himself as a man to me, he spoke of experiencing micropsia again.
>
> At this time he perceived the books on my shelves as appearing smaller, and once again he was reminded of the latency episodes . . . which usually occurred . . . when he would contemplate being separated from his mother. He spoke of his present wishes to be little with me, to be my child, and of how 'belittled' he had felt by my interpretation, which he took as an injunction to become an adult. . . . He [talked of the injury to his eye] before the onset of the latency micropsia, by a 'bocce ball' thrown by his father [pp. 583–584].

Myers then tells about the link with the patient's testicular movements and concludes that the episode was precipitated by "anger at the analyst-father arising from an oedipal-level conflict . . . the rage arousing intense castration (and separation) anxiety" (p. 585).

What are the implications for the listening perspective expressed here? The patient's symptom was understood as a manifestation of a defensive compromise against the experience of conflictual affect, which was addressed by the interpretation. That is, the fact that he could no longer maintain his feelings in repression was seen as precipitant to the episode. The transference, permitted its free unfolding, is thus viewed as predetermined by already present instinctual and defensive derivatives and the perceptual distortions which they introduce. Since the experiential specificity of the analyst's contribution is not elaborated as intrinsic to the episode, then implicitly the analyst stands 'outside' observing and interpreting the patient's inner reality.

As an alternative, let us look again at the moment—*in context with* the analyst—in which the symptom appeared. It was when his first comments to the patient were that he was "defensively portraying himself" as a child. The patient then replied that he felt "belittled" by *this comment*.

Reviewing his initial remarks, after talking of feeling abandoned the patient seemed to have been wondering whether the analyst would be more warmly available to a child, either as doctor or as father, than he was to him. We might consider whether the symptom, which communicated the experience of painful affect, would have appeared had the analyst responded to his quest, i.e., rather than seeing the patient's childlike behavior as defensive, had he articulated the seeming wish to be responded to with the kind of warmth that the analyst might give to a child. Indeed, when the analyst had at first said nothing, the patient spoke of feeling 'chilly.' One may conjecture that perhaps that very feeling state, as well as the micropsia, arose in the context of a painful perception of the analyst as having 'failed' to understand the patient's quest. Thus, to Myers' statement that the episode was precipitated by "anger at the analyst-father arising from an oedipal-level conflict," might be added—when the analyst *responded* in a way that recreated the inner representation of the father's earlier response to such a conflict. (The father is described in this vignette as neither warm nor loving, and, at least inadvertently, injuring his son.)

It should be noted that there is no intended implication here that the analyst can, by closer empathic approximation, necessarily forestall the appearance of the symptom. Unless it has already been recognized, the analyst cannot know ahead of time what may be uniquely felt by his patient as injurious. A failure in empathy is not synonymous with an error in techique; empathic failure speaks to the subjective experience of the patient and cannot be assessed in any other way.

The perspective of the analyst 'within'—as part of the 'system'

(Sander, 1975)—would attempt to elucidate the subjective sense of how the interpretation felt and how the analyst was perceived, as an inherent aspect of the moment of appearance of the symptom. The patient's view of the analyst as 'belittling,' recognized as an expression of the patient's perceptual reality, would become the explicit focus of further exploration. This perspective is also exemplified in the case of a patient of mine.[16]

> Mrs. G. first experienced episodes of micropsia in her analytic hours, when in the course of our work together, she had begun to feel more socially outgoing. One day she told me of how successful she felt at her new job, and then began to compare her work to mine. I wondered, within the context of the emerging material, if she was perhaps thinking about surpassing me and whether that might not stir up a familiar conflict. The symptom appeared. The walls of my office seemed further away, objects in the room smaller. There was a sense of spatial disorientation.
>
> As with Myers' patient, so, too, this episode could be formulated as arising in the context of emerging aggressive (oedipal) wishes with concomitant intense anxiety within the transference. In accord with the view that the transference included the experience of the meaning of my remarks as an integral part of the recreated past, I then wondered: How did my comments, interwoven with her experience, bear on this episode? Mrs. G. reflected, "Whenever I shared anything with my mother that I felt good about, she'd say something to take it away, some comment directing me elsewhere—whenever I showed something off to her. What just happened with you happened with mother all the time. I was sharing with you my most adult self and you talked about a conflict, like suddenly in barges my mother and takes it away."
>
> The patient began to recall this symptom as one familiar to her from her childhood and on occasion since then. She could remember it at age five or six, with the image of her mother standing in the doorway to her room at night in the darkness—sometimes holding an enema bag, sometimes when she was masturbating—a sense of mother's 'hovering, evil presence,' so small and so distant.
>
> "I always felt myself to be an oddball," she said, "different from peers and from parents . . . Mother used to think I was an odd egg . . . I always felt the need to find someone who had experienced things like me . . . I used to have the sense—like I wasn't completely female . . . when I got my period, it was like despite the fact that I'm not really a woman . . . like they were all sitting around waiting for my breasts to develop . . . if mother discovered an injury, she'd be wildly

[16]This material is from the panel referred to in footnote 1. It also appears in Schwaber, 1983a and b.

upset. . . Masturbating gave me a clearer sense of myself . . . it was a way to really feel my own body, but it also made me feel shame and terror. . . ."

Dreams of spatial disorientation or disconnection came to increased prominence, and we learned that Mrs. G. was told that her mother had not 'touched' her very much as a baby, propping her bottle for greater sterility. Thus, we could begin to reconstruct a view of how the symptom became a defensive choice, weaving the little girl's affect-laden competitive and growth-oriented strivings with her perceptions of the responses to them. Recreating the disorienting imagery of the darkened room where it first appeared, the bodily confusion evoked by the enemas she had received and expressed also within her masturbation experience, and the feeling of spatial disconnectedness from the 'intrusive' or else 'non-touching' mother who was felt somehow as negating the child's blossoming feminine strivings, the symptom represented a particular phenomenon to be observed and given *meaning* in the presence of the analyst. More specifically, it was the analyst—who was felt to be non-accepting of Mrs. G.'s wish to share herself and had put to question the patient's sense of her very femaleness.

IV

Empathy, then, in line with the ideas proposed, is that mode of attunement which attempts to maximize a singular focus on the patient's subjective reality, seeking all possible cues to ascertain it. Vigilantly guarding against the imposition of the analyst's point of view, the role of the analyst and of the surround, as perceived and experienced by the patient, is recognized as intrinsic to that reality; the observer is a part of the field observed. As a scientific modality, empathy employs our cognitive, perceptual, as well as affective capacities.

Arising out of the earliest sensory and tactile communications between mother and child, empathy has a rich and complex developmental history (Shapiro, 1974). As an essential psychological nutriment, it remains throughout life a fundamental mode of relatedness (Kohut, 1975). Thus, unless pathologically stunted, it is a ubiquitous human capacity, which must be trained for rigorous, scientific use.

The analyst's empathy draws upon modalities which are significant components of the essentials of parental empathy—attunement to and recognition of the perceptions and experiential states of another. However, it would be misleading to employ these terms (i.e., the analyst's and the parent's empathy) synonymously, or to suggest that the one "corrects for" the failure of the other, for they speak to two very different contexts.

We may further consider that although empathic capacity arises out of a dyadic matrix, it does not mean that issues concerning dyadic aspects of relationships are necessarily more relevant than triadic ones to our empathic understanding. Similar modalities of attunement are utilized and the contextual considerations equally salient, no matter which developmental or conflictual themes are being addressed. In the case of Mrs. G., for example, observing the perception of the mother's response to her budding oedipal strivings as it was recreated in the transference, lent added dimension to the understanding of how she experienced this developmental phase. The symptom of micropsia gained specificity when viewed within this context.

On the other hand, patients whose primary pathology rests with earlier developmental concerns have helped us to deepen our understanding of this listening mode by their particular sensitivity to our efforts at empathic attunement. For many whose difficulty lies in the sense of uncertainty or lack of reality about their inner experience, a detailed attempt at recognition and articulation of what may be only vaguely felt affects, states or perceptions is especially meaningful.[17] For patients with a variety of character dynamics, sharpening the focus on the meaning of their communications may help to highlight phenomena which have more general relevance than may otherwise be appreciated.

Examples are as follows:

> Mr. A., a young professional man, seemed from the outset to have great difficulty in free-associating for any length of time without the sense of an ongoing dialogue. With varying degrees of pressure, he would interrupt his associations to ask innumerable questions of me, such as, opinions about how he may get a certain girl to go out with him, what he should say to his boss, and other of my thoughts about what he should do. Because I didn't answer him directly, he often became quite angry with me, berating me for not making him feel better. What would my answers offer him? I wondered. Mr. A. wished of me "that you make things more clear . . . a part of me wanting you to plan and structure so

---

[17]Commenting on my use of the phrase "For many," Gill expressed concern that it seemed to him I was backing away from my thesis: "The emphasis on elucidating the patient's subjective experience is important in all patients, and I'm not sure that I would agree that it is any more important in those who have some uncertainty about their inner experience" (personal communication, 1981). I am in full agreement with these comments, and mean primarily to convey that there are some patients who may highlight for us issues of ubiquitous importance.

> I can just follow behind . . . It's really that there's a kind of emptiness, I think . . . like an anxiety, and if you answer a question, it relieves it somewhat. . ." I asked: "You mean that when the underlying anxiety mounts, you ask a question, to seek relief. . . ?" "Yeah," he answered. "It happens without even thinking about it . . . I don't know quite how to define the feeling . . . wanting you to define it for me . . . I don't feel the emptiness . . . I think mostly I don't let myself feel it . . . Yeah, that's when I ask a question. . ."
>
> Early in her analysis, Mrs. G. also frequently seemed to be under great pressure to have me answer questions. Her questions were about myself, for example, whether I saw a particular movie or read a certain book. "I'm thinking of this lovely poem in *MS.* magazine. Did you read it? Do you know the poem I mean?" she asked in one hour with apparent urgency. "Such a strong wish," I said to her, "to have me answer directly. Can we look at what that means?" "There is something to that," she replied. She paused, then noted, "I—feel—now a strangeness about myself—alone—different; that's why I don't write; it's not mutual—not mutual makes me feel strange. It's like coming home from school and telling my mother what happened; she'd just sit there and listen, like from another world. Something about asking you if you had read that poem is like that. It would have been so nice growing up if mother had said, 'Yes, I had the same experience; I know about that.' My mother never told me things like that; like she grew up in a big fishtank different from mine. If you had said something about the poem, I'd have felt better; otherwise, I get this goldfish-in-the-tank feeling. One looks at it, admires it, feeds it. What I'm saying is, I want to get out of the bowl."
>
> Later she was to say, "When I asked you what you've read, what you've seen, it is really, 'Do you experience the same bodily feelings I do?' "

We may recognize here that the issue of whether or not to answer the question directly was not the relevant analytic concern. Empathy is not defined by the offer of an objectively-based direct response. It entails the search for the subjective meaning of the question—in this case, perhaps the acknowledged *recognition* of her wish that I share with her something about my interests and my femaleness.

Empathy requires some resonance of essential human alikeness with the experiential and perceptual world of our patients. Reflecting on our clinical experience, we may recognize that the capacity for empathy (given that there aren't defensive processes mitigating against it) varies to a large extent in proportion to the similarity between the psychological-physiological experiential world of the observer and that of the observed, and that the extent of this similarity defines the limits beyond which empathic observation cannot reach

(Kohut, 1959). Observing the infant's state, or listening to the colloquialisms of someone whose native language differs from our own, are examples of such occurrences in which certain leaps of inference have to be made beyond the limits of empathy as we are standing outside the frame of reference of the other. I have found this to be similarly true in trying to understand some of the physiologically-based bodily experiences of the opposite sex, whereas with one's own sex, one can more readily respond from within the patient's experience.[18]

Sometimes, if we find ourselves struggling to seek a resonance of alikeness, this very difficulty may be a clue that the concern which is salient touches on a very early developmental issue. The empathic gap widens for us as we listen to phenomena "telescoping" issues bearing on presymbolic expression.

The work with Mrs. G. offered further illustration of some of these ideas:

> In the early hours, her mother emerged repeatedly as a frightening, alien figure. She said, "Mother envies me, would take from me or spoil what I have—like a dark fungus. . . ; I always felt she would hex me; she was riddled with anxiety and could never touch with any comfort. . ." Despite this unfolding imagery, it was often difficult, however, to understand the quality Mrs. G. was trying to convey, of mother's present-day injuries. When she described mother's words, they didn't seem to communicate to me the terrible feelings they evoked. For example, when the patient learned to drive, mother remarked, "Isn't it wonderful, you learned to drive a car!" Mrs. G. felt wounded, 'shattered' by this. She said it felt as though mother was again responding to only a part of her rather than to the *whole* of her, which would have included other feeling states, like the fear and anxiety that go with learning to drive.
>
> Thus, there was a discrepancy between the image she portrayed and the one she experienced—at least, some difficulty in my capacity to understand her experience. I thought about the possibility that the patient may have had defensive reasons for insisting on a negative image, and we did know that she sought an ally against her mother. But this was an inferential explanation which did not arise from data offered by the patient, and which I realized I may have been especially tempted to seek, precisely because there was a gap—which I would hope to bridge—in my capacity to gain attunement.

---

[18]Elsewhere (Schwaber, 1978, 1981) I have described the difficulty in gaining empathic attunement with the experience of survivors of the Holocaust because of the "unimaginable" assault on mind and body.

(Indeed, when there is such difficulty in gaining empathic recognition, the tendency may be to try harder to bridge this gap between our understanding and the patient's experience, seeking an explanation from without. But awareness of this very process within us can be illuminating.)

Perhaps, then, the very fact of the difficulty could be seen as meaningful in its own right. If so—that is, accepting the perceptual validity of this imagery, from the patient's point of view—it may lead us to consider that the degree of mother's felt 'injuries' lay in her quality of being, rather than in the words she chose, and that what is being 'telescoped' in these latter-day incidents goes back to very early, perhaps preverbal communications. Further, the sense of discrepancy which I experienced in listening to the patient's associations may offer a clue as to the difficulty others, too, may have in following her. It thus may help us to understand the isolation and aloneness she described herself feeling in social interaction, particularly with women. It may speak to why her search for experiential similarity between us felt so crucial, and may bear on the 'untouched' quality that Mrs. G. had experienced and expressed.

There is another dimension in considering my difficulty in trying to make sense of the imagery Mrs. G. conveyed. It spoke to the feeling I had that I so often seemed to lose her, to how I had to grope and struggle to find my place in *her* experiential world, while yet trying to maintain my own self-reflective vigil, for there was a quality of affectlessness about Mrs. G., a kind of lifelessness, with no manifest warmth. Unfortunately, often only retrospectively did I become aware that I had been impatient, fatigued or bored; perhaps in some way, these were self-protective withdrawls *out* of the intense immersion in her experience. Often the clues to such responses on *my* part were signaled by subtle shifts in the patient's communications—as a change in tone, or sounding more mechanized, or some shift in the style of her stream of associations. In my attempt to maintain sight of the context between us, these clues helped me to more honest self-reflection, to discover that I had stepped out of her frame of reference. What she was thus conveying was an intense, though not articulated sensitivity to my responsiveness, which she communicated in the particular manner described. This seemed to indicate that for her, maintaining 'connectedness' was a central issue—lending added dimension to our understanding of her oft-stated wish for direct dialogue with me. For the analytic work to take place in an affectively meaningful way, the vicissitudes of this issue—whatever *else* was being addressed, had to become a central focus.

Thus, the very effort to elucidate the nature of the difficulty in my search for empathic recognition of Mrs. G.'s subjective experience proved to be an essential aspect of our work together.

That we must rely on some echo of experiential alikeness does not mean, however, that we are to share the patient's experience as our own. To place ourselves in the other's shoes, into what he or she is feeling, is not the same process as considering what *we* would feel if *we*—who *we* are—were in those shoes. It requires a considerable degree of self-awareness to make this crucial distinction, to know what belongs to our own conceptual or perceptual frame of reference so as to reduce the risk of superimposing it. Empathy, then, is not equivalent to identification, although this occurs in its pathway.[19]

Thus, a critical aspect of this mode of listening is the necessity for the analyst to pay very close heed to his own affective responses, so as to be alert to whether he has shifted his view to an outside perspective on reality—either his own or that of others in the patient's external world. Often, the turn to a theory-bound inference can be an important clue to such a shift, whether triggered by some affective communication of the patient or by something arising within ourselves. In either event, it warrants further search.

An example is the case of Mr. R., whom I had discussed at the outset. When I later reflected on my question to him about my vacation, I recognized that I had experienced his communication to me about the psychiatrist-turning-to-photographer as implying that I might lose interest in him while I was away. Not immediately cognizant that I felt challenged, I rallied to my defense. To paraphrase myself, "What! Do you believe I will not think about you while I am away?" (I justified my response with the objectively valid theoretical idea that it is important to help a patient deal with his feelings about a separation.) Thus, I introduced *my* perspective here to deal with something stirring within *me*. Had I stayed with *his* point of view, I might have heard him express a wish that I, too, could appreciate and share his strong interest in photography—perhaps especially since I was going away. Or, I might have wondered what *he* was experiencing at this time that led him to seem provocative (Schwaber, 1980b).

This perspective is quite different from one in which the analyst would view his affective response to the patient as a clue to an uncon-

[19]Cf. Freud (1921): "A path leads from identification by way of imitation to empathy, that is, to the comprehension of the mechanism by means of which we are enabled to take up any attitude at all towards another mental life" (footnote, p. 110). Among others who have written on this issue, see also Arlow (1979), ". . . identification with the patient must give way to thinking *about* the patient" (p. 65).

scious motivation on the patient's part,[20] or in which an identification with the objects in the patient's life is an intrinsic feature of empathy.[21] To be sure, that I responded in a manner similar to the other women in his life may have been evoked by Mr. R.'s recurrent pattern of relating under specific affectively-charged circumstances. Had I been alert to the feeling of provocation, however, I may have recognized that this very feeling meant that I had taken on the vantage point of the 'object' acted upon, rather than that of the patient—with whom I was thus *out* of empathic contact. Further, becoming aware of such a response to the patient, and observing its resemblance to that of others in his life, may deepen the analyst's understanding of the patient's dilemma as he experiences his relationships.

As I have commented earlier, responses of this kind on the analyst's part, which seem out of tune with the patient's vantage point, are inevitable aspects of analytic work. However, it is by our sharpened attunement to the patient's often subtle shifts in state or affect—maintaining the contextual view—that the very sense of injury as well as the particular way of reacting to it (i.e., the nature of his *defensive* modes) are brought to heightened illumination. The change in the tone and spontaneity of Mr. R.'s associations when I asked about my vacation, and the silent, then acknowledged listening to music when he spoke of feeling untouched, were clues to inner experience intimately interwoven with his perception of the surround, which then became gradually articulated.[22]

---

[20]Cf. Schafer (1959), who has described a component of empathy which asks the question: "How does this patient want me to feel?" (p. 347); also Sandler (1976), writing of the "*complementary* role in which [the patient] casts the analyst," notes: "the patient's transference would thus represent an attempt by him to impose an interaction, an interrelationship . . . between himself and the analyst" (p. 44).

[21]Cf. Beres and Arlow (1974), who note, in keeping with the views of H. Deutsch, that "in empathy the analyst may identify not only with the patient, but with his objects as well" (p. 42).

[22]In terms of the analyst's own self-reflection, certainly it behooves him to search within *himself* for evidence of the patient's perception of him. Indeed, such close attunement to the patient's perceptual cues can offer a significant opportunity to deepen one's own self-awareness. However, whether or not the analyst feels he can find within him or herself some affective validation of the patient's perception—as Mr. R.'s comment to me that I seemed defensive—is a concern distinct from the analytic one, dealing solely with the patient's reality.

Thus we see that the intensified focus on certain aspects of nonverbal phenomenology, such as shifts in affect or state, may offer a potential vital clue to what may have been a silent or not yet defined perception of us. The emergence of some presenting fantasy or other imagery, or the appearance of a symptom—as with the episodes of micropsia—may similarly serve to signal a particular perceptual experience. Sometimes a seemingly passing word or phrase may bear such a clue—even to a perception only anticipated. The following dialogue is an example.

Mr. A., in an hour in which he seemed to be particularly pressured in his search for dialogue with me, reflected on this, saying: I felt more isolated this weekend, so I have to recontact with you . . . I'm sure it doesn't relate to your leaving this Thursday and Friday. . . Don't get your hopes up.

I asked: What do you mean—'hopes'?

Mr. A.: So you'd be able to give me an explanation to be satisfied . . . so you'd have an explanation. . .

I (trying to ascertain what implication he was conveying, about his view of me): You seem to be suggesting that my motives for being helpful might in some way be to meet *my own* needs; to be helpful—to do for *you*, so as to satisfy *me*.

Mr. A. (speaking in a more comfortable, less demanding tone now): It's interesting. . . My association to that is, I don't want to get better, because it makes you better . . . I used to say that to my other therapist . . . that if he were to cure me, it would widen the gap between us rather than narrow it . . . I think of my mother . . . her wanting to look good as a mother, so if I was a good son, it would reflect on her—which is similar to how it is with me and my students; if they don't pass, I feel it reflects on me as a teacher . . . like with my mother, having to wear a tie if we go to a party or something—mother insisting that I do; so it was clear it was for her. . . Or she'd come in my room and demand that I clean it up, but it was *my* room. . . Still, parents do that. . .

I: You mean there was an aspect of her doing that, or having those expectations that seemed to be out of *her* needs, rather than yours?

Mr. A.: Right! You know, that's been a longstanding argument between us . . . her needs versus mine . . . so, many of the motives for me to not wear a tie might be in order to not give in to her. . . There's always that question mark. . . Am I doing it for her, or purposely against her?

I: As you said before (about how it would feel here if you were getting better), there would be some question of, is it for me?, or, if not better, is that perhaps against me?

Mr. A.: Right! So how will I ever know?

I: You mean you feel some sense of inner uncertainty as to what your own motives and feelings are. . . Somehow, mother, or someone is al-

ways in the picture.
Mr. A.: Yeah.

When the patient sharpens his own attunement to his inner states and perceptions, even as they are reflections of the analytic moment, he begins to recognize them as familiar and as having historical relevance. He is then more likely to initiate the rediscovery of his own history, enriched by the contextual specificity of his perceptual world and the attendant meanings assigned to it, with a relativity which shifts with the vicissitudes of the transference, yet has inherent continuity.[23] There will be a decreasing need for inferential leaps on the analyst's part, while the patient feels a deeper conviction of his own sense of reality.[24]

Consistent with the notion that our listening stance attempts to minimize the introduction of an 'outside' view, there is a shift in the understanding of transference. Rather than being defined as a distortion to be modified, transference is here understood as a perception—interwoven with the emerging intrapsychic concerns—to be recognized and articulated. Such a perspective—of the observer from within—would hold as spurious the division of an 'inner' from a 'real' reality, and the notion that we must ultimately help the patient to disengage our real selves from his psychic view of us. In the course of the analytic process, the patient may himself discover further options in his own shifting views.

Empathic listening then implies the analyst's capacity to view himself as being used and responded to in the context of the patient's immediate intrapsychic experience. This perspective sharpens the focus on the analyst's contribution, silent or stated, as it influences and orders the nature of the patient's responses—transference, memory, essentially what may be regarded as "ongoing regulation within a system" (Schwaber, 1980b). Loewald's "psychic field," like Sander's "mother-infant system," would now be seen as intrinsic to the understanding and elucidation of transference.

---

[23]Cf. Gray (1982), who writes of the role of memory as "an internal event of immediate intrapsychic importance" (p. 647). See also Schafer's (1979) views on the "construction of multiple histories [of the past] . . . just as one establishes different versions of the present" (p. 15).

[24]Loewald (1981) stated: "As is true in infancy and childhood, mirroring recognition is essential in making experience viable. . . . Validation . . . affirms and confirms the dignity, the reality and truth of an experience and of its particular mode. It is, one might say, the reality-test of inner experience, of psychic reality" (p. 29).

Galenson's concern (Sander, 1980) about the disparity between established psychoanalytic theories and the newer infancy research data would thereby be addressed, as the frame of reference of the infant researcher, utilizing the concept of a system "developing over time, as an unfolding process," and employing such words as "rhythmic, regulation, recurrence," becomes part of the clinical conceptual framework. The very nature of this mode of attunement brings into more systematic focus the vicissitudes of such phenomena as a sense of realness, certainty, connectedness, autonomy, and others bearing upon ubiquitous, individually organized, early issues and patterns which indelibly color ongoing development. Thus, at whatever developmental level a conflictual or adaptive concern is being addressed in our analytic listening, its depth and specificity can be more fully grasped within the perspective of a contextual continuum.

REFERENCES

Abrams, S. (1980), Discussion: *Construction and reconstruction: Clinical aspects*, panel of the American Psychoanalytic Association, San Francisco, May 4, 1980. (Unpublished manuscript.)

Arlow, J. (1979), The role of empathy in the psychoanalytic process. *Bull. Assn. Psychoanal. Med.*, 18:64–69.

Beres, D. & Arlow, J. (1974), Fantasy and identification in empathy. *Psychoanal. Quart.*, 43:26–50.

Freud, S. (1917), Introductory lectures on psycho-analysis. Part III: General theory of the neurosis. *Standard Edition*, 16:243–248. London: Hogarth Press, 1964.

——— (1921), Group psychology and the analysis of the ego. *Standard Edition*, 18:67–143. London: Hogarth Press, 1955.

——— (1940), An outline of psycho-analysis. Part III: The theoretical yield. *Standard Edition*, 23:144–207. London: Hogarth Press, 1964.

Gill, M. (1979), The analysis of the transference. *J. Amer. Psychoanal. Assn.*, 27[Suppl.]:263–288.

Gray, P. (1973), Psychoanalytic technique and the ego's capacity for viewing intrapsychic activity. *J. Amer. Psychoanal. Assn.*, 21:474–494.

——— (1982), "Developmental lag" in the evolution of psychoanalytic technique for psychoanalysis of neurotic conflict. *J. Amer. Psychoanal. Assn.*, 30:621–655.

Heisenberg, W. (1934), *Philosophic Problems of Nuclear Science*. New York: Pantheon, 1952.

Kohut, H. (1959), Introspection, empathy, and psychoanalysis. *J. Amer. Psychoanal. Assn.*, 7:459–483.

_____ (1966), Forms and transformations of narcissism. *J. Amer. Psychoanal. Assn.*, 14:243–272.
_____ (1968), The psychoanalytic treatment of narcissistic personality disorders: Outlines of a systematic approach. *The Psychoanalytic Study of the Child*, 23:86–113. New York: International Universities Press.
_____ (1971), *The Analysis of the Self*. New York: International Universities Press.
_____ (1972), Thoughts on narcissism and narcissistic rage. *The Psychoanalytic Study of the Child*, 27:360–402. New York: Quadrangle.
_____ (1975), The psychoanalyst in the community of scholars. In: *The Annual of Psychoanalysis*, 3:341–370. New York: International Universities Press.
_____ (1977), *The Restoration of the Self*. New York: International Universities Press.
Kris, E. (1956), The recovery of childhood memories in psychoanalysis. *The Psychoanalytic Study of the Child*, 11:54–88. New York: International Universities Press.
Lichtenberg, J. (1981), The empathic mode of perception and alternative vantage points for psychoanalytic work. *Psychoanal. Inq.* 1:329–355.
Loewald, H. (1960), On the therapeutic action of psychoanalysis. *Internat. J. Psycho-Anal.*, 41:16–33.
_____ (1970), Psychoanalytic theory and the psychoanalytic process. *The Psychoanalytic Study of the Child*, 25:45–68. New York: International Universities Press.
_____ (1981), Regression: Some general considerations. *Psychoanal. Quart.* 50:22–43.
Myers, W. (1977), Micropsia and testicular retraction. *Psychoanal. Quart.* 46:580–604.
Ornstein, A. & Ornstein, P. (1975), On the interpretive process in psychoanalysis. *Internat. J. Psychoanal. Psychother.*, 4:219–271.
_____ _____ (1980), Formulating interpretations in clinical psychoanalysis. *Internat. J. Psycho-Anal.*, 61:203–211.
Ornstein, P. (1979), Remarks on the central position of empathy in psychoanalysis. *Bull. Assn. Psychoanal. Med.*, 18:95–108.
Sander, L. (1975), Infant and caretaking environment: Investigation and conceptualization of adaptive behavior in a system of increasing complexity. In: *Explorations in Child Psychiatry*, ed. E. J. Anthony. New York: Plenum Press.

_____ (1980), Reporter: New knowledge about the infant from current research: Implications for psychoanalysis. *J. Amer. Psychoanal. Assn.*, 28:181–198.

Sandler, J. (1976), Countertransference and role-responsiveness. *Internat. Rev. Psycho-Anal.*, 3:43–47.

Schafer, R. (1959), Generative empathy in the treatment situation. *Psychoanal. Quart.*, 28:342–373.

_____ (1979), The appreciative analytic attitude and the construction of multiple histories. *Psychoanal. and Contemp. Thought*, 2:3–24.

Schimek, J. G. (1975), The interpretations of the past: Childhood trauma, psychical reality, and historical truth. *J. Amer. Psychoanal. Assn.*, 23:845–865.

Schwaber, E. (1978), Reflections in response to "A psychoanalytic overview on children of survivors," by J. Kestenberg. Presented at Symposium on *The Holocaust: Psychological Effects on Survivors and Their Children*, Brandeis University, Waltham, Mass., May 1978.

_____ (1979), On the 'self' within the matrix of analytic theory—some clinical reflections and reconsiderations. *Internat. J. Psycho-Anal.*, 60:467–479.

_____ (1980a), Self psychology and the concept of psychopathology: A case presentation. In: *Advances in Self Psychology*, ed. A. Goldberg. New York: International Universities Press, pp. 209–242.

_____ (1980b), Response to discussion of Paul Tolpin. In: *Advances in Self Psychology*, ed. A. Goldberg. New York: International Universities Press, pp. 253–262.

_____ (1981), Narcissism, self psychology and the listening perspective. In: *The Annual of Psychoanalysis*, 9:115–132, New York: International Universities Press.

_____ (1983a), Construction, reconstruction, and the mode of clinical attunement. In: *The Future of Psychoanalysis*, ed. Goldberg, A. International Universities Press, pp. 273–291.

_____ (1983b), A particular perspective on analytic listening. *The Psychoanalytic Study of the Child*, 38:519–546. New Haven: Yale University Press.

Shapiro, T. (1974), The development and distortions of empathy. *Psychoanal. Quart.*, 43:4–25.

Spruiell, V. (1983), The rules and frames of the psychoanalytic situation. *Psychoanal. Quart.*, 52:1–33.

Stechler, G. & Kaplan, S. (1980), The development of the self: A psychoanalytic perspective. *The Psychoanalytic Study of the Child*, 35:85–106. New Haven: Yale University Press.

Stein, M. H. (1966), Self observation, reality, and the superego. In: *Psychoanalysis—A General Psychology*, ed. R. M. Loewenstein, L. Newman, M. Schur, & A. Solnit. New York: International Universities Press, pp. 275–297.
Tuchman, B. (1979), In search of history. *Radcliffe Quart.*, March, pp. 33–37.

Discussion

MERTON M. GILL, M.D.

ALTHOUGH I AM IN ESSENTIAL AGREEMENT with the thrust of Evelyne Schwaber's remarks, I would like to separate several issues that are somewhat condensed in her presentation, question certain implications, and highlight some points that may be lost in the glare of her major argument. In the beginning, for instance, Schwaber articulates two clusters of definitions of empathy. One grouping is "as a mode of human relatedness; as a way of understanding, knowing and responding; and as an early and ubiquitous developmental nutrient." The other is "as a method of observation, a technical modality, or an adjective describing one—sometimes part of the analytic ambience, and sometimes the matrix of the analytic method." The distinction between these two clusters I find somewhat obscure.

Schwaber states that she intends to focus on empathy as a method of observation, and her essay as a whole suggests that her distinction between the two clusters is that the first relates to empathy as a general concept describing how human beings relate to one another, whereas the second defines empathy in the analytic situation, as listening with the primary interest of understanding the patient's psychic reality. What I find not entirely in keeping with this conclusion is her explanation that Kohut was able to discover the varieties of transferences he subsequently elaborated because he used empathy "as a *perceptual* mode—not as a technical stance." Earlier Schwaber equated a method of observation with a technical modality, so I must assume that "technical modality" and "technical stance" are not synonymous. Perhaps by "technical modality" she means a way of listening, whereas by "technical stance" she means listening with a particular theory about psychic functioning in mind.

By calling empathy a mode of analytic listening, Schwaber could be misunderstood as proposing a comprehensive description of empathy and how it is achieved. She is not. What she is arguing seems most succinctly stated in her formulation: "Empathy . . . is that mode of attunement which attempts to maximize a singular focus on the patient's subjective reality. . . . Vigilantly guarding against the imposition of the analyst's point of view, the role of the analyst and of the surround, as perceived and experienced by the patient, is recognized as intrinsic to that reality." There are three central points in this formulation:

1. The purpose of listening—what one is listening for—is to try to understand the patient's psychic reality. It would be hard to disagree with this conclusion, at least as a first step in the therapeutic process. But what one then does with this understanding one believes one has gained of the patient's psychic reality is another matter, to which I shall return.

2. The analyst must recognize " 'the immediacy of the surround as being intrinsic to the organization and perception of intrapsychic experience,' " i.e., the patient's psychic reality. Since the surround in the analytic situation is the analyst, as well as the setting, the same point is expressed in terms of the transference when Schwaber states: "Rather than being defined as a distortion to be modified, transference is here understood as a perception—interwoven with the emerging intrapsychic concerns—to be recognized and articulated." As she notes, this is the same view I have expressed in a paper on transference (Gill, 1979). The analytic situation is a contextual unit. It constitutes a field in which the input from the analyst significantly contributes to the patient's psychic reality. Schwaber means this in more than the trivial sense that the patient's psychic reality is precipitated by something the analyst has said or done, or even by something the patient believes about the analyst.

3. A common error made by analysts is to conclude that a patient's psychic reality is correct or distorted. To do so, Schwaber contends, amounts to declaring that the analyst knows what the correct external reality is. In that belief the analyst is in effect not realizing that his (or her) understanding is *his* own psychic reality rather than an objectively correct assessment of external reality. Schwaber also argues, though without quite making the sequence of steps in her argument

explicit, that saying that an analyst can only know his own psychic reality is another way of saying that the analyst is a participant in a context, i.e., in the analytic situation.

Again, these points may convey the misleading impression that Schwaber is offering a general discussion of empathy. But what would be required for a fuller discussion of empathy would be what I might call the other side of a dialectic. It is also discussed in Schwaber's paper, though less systematically than the points just summarized. For to understand what a patient is experiencing the analyst must consult his own experience too. As Schwaber puts it: "Empathy requires some resonance of essential human alikeness with the experiential and perceptual world of our patients."

Schwaber discusses this side of the dialectic mainly in terms of the difficulties encountered in being empathic when one's background or sex is different from the patient's. She is thus describing a different, though related, aspect of how empathy is impeded when the analyst adopts the attitude of an objective external observer—different from the one she described in saying that the analyst should not assume he has the correct understanding of reality. Indeed, when the analyst and patient are highly discrepant as people, the analyst may well be more likely to take into account the "relativity" of reality.

A consideration of these two different obstacles to accurate empathy enables us to distinguish a misreading of what the patient is experiencing from a misreading of what accounts for the patient's experience. An occidental analyst may be mistaken in what an oriental patient feels because of the cultural difference, but this is to be distinguished from the analyst's concluding that a patient who feels belittled by an interpretation is distorting reality because, in the analyst's view, he had no intention of belittling the patient.

This latter distinction relates to another which must be made concerning whether the analyst sees himself as a participant in an interaction. He can do so and still make the error of assuming that he knows an objective external reality. In the vignette taken from Myers' (1977) case of micropsia, the analyst knew that it was what he had said that made the patient feel belittled. But he concluded that the patient had distorted reality, that the patient was wrong in believing that the analyst had intended to belittle him.

In the case of a cultural discrepancy, the analyst may have no idea that something he has said has offended the patient because he is unaware that his remark is regarded as offensive in the patient's culture. Yet the analyst who genuinely accepts the idea that he is a participant in an interaction will assume that he has played a role in the patient's psychic reality—even if he has no idea what it was.

Stated in terms of empathy, it is generally agreed that the analyst attempts to empathically grasp the patient's subjective experience, but not that the analyst must take his own participation in the analytic situation into account in order to grasp the patient's experience. Nor is it generally accepted that the analyst's view of the situation is his own psychic reality. Although it is acknowledged that the analyst's view may be right or wrong, it is assumed that a competent analyst is usually right. When he is wrong he is said to be displaying countertransference. But the crucial point is that it is generally agreed that there is an objectively correct reality about which one may be right or wrong, not *two* psychic realities—the patient's and the analyst's—each with its own plausibility.

In this light, one might add to Schwaber's comparison between Myers' case vignette and her own—perhaps chosen because they both deal with micropsia (although they need not have to demonstrate her point). Myers recognized that the patient's psychic reality was that he felt belittled by the analyst's remark. Not so incidentally, he knew this because the patient volunteered the information. Had the patient been reluctant to voice this—if, for instance, he had feared that the analyst would be offended at being accused of belittling the patient—we might be even more in the dark than we are. And had the analyst not pursued how he was "being used and responded to in the context of the patient's immediate intrapsychic experience," the interpretation of the appearance of the micropsia might have been even more arbitrary than it was.

What would Schwaber's recommendations have called for? The analyst should have pursued the patient's experience of having been belittled. He probably would have learned more about the patient's experience of the interaction, i.e., about the patient's psychic reality. And his explanation of why the patient experienced his remark as belittling might have been more related to what the patient was saying before the analyst's interpretation (e.g., that the patient could not even expect the analyst to turn off the air conditioner because he paid such a low fee). In fact the conclusion Myers offers to the reader to account for the patient's response to the interpretation is the very same as the interpretation that the patient experienced as belittling. The interpretation was that the patient portrayed himself as a child to defend against the fears aroused by exhibiting himself as a man to the analyst; Myers' conclusion is that the patient was angry at the analyst-father because of his oedipal conflict and that the anger aroused intense castration (and separation) anxiety.

Without embarking on an attempt to unravel this complex web, it is possible to make some relatively simple and direct statements couched in terms of Schwaber's points: (1) The analyst did not pursue the patient's psychic reality. (2) The analyst did not see himself as a participant in the patient's experience, except in the very peripheral sense that he considered the patient's feeling of being belittled to have been precipitated by the interpretation. Instead, he essentially attributed the patient's response to a preexisting oedipal conflict. (3) In effect the analyst considered the patient's experience of having been belittled a distortion of the meaning of the intervention. That is, he took it for granted that he was not belittling the patient. How could a self-respecting analyst belittle a patient? The analyst regarded his view of reality as correct and the patient's view as a distortion. The analyst therefore concluded that he was entitled to make an interpretation of an intrapsychic conflict. Am I implying that the patient was right—that he *was* belittled? No, I am implying only that the patient's psychic reality (that he was belittled) is *plausible* and that the analyst's psychic reality (that he was not intending to belittle the patient) is also plausible. What is to be done?

To begin with, the very process of attempting to reach and sometimes successfully reaching an understanding of the patient's psychic reality has its own intrinsic value. As Schwaber wrote in another paper (1981), which deals with the same theme as this one: "There is no more growth-promoting occurrence than that of feeling that one's inner core of wishes, fears, hopes, defenses—that one's perspective of reality—is recognized and acknowledged" (p. 18). I have no intention of belittling the value of such an experience. But to leave it at that would seem to make of psychoanalysis no more than the experience of being understood. Indeed, it may be that such a conclusion plays a role in many analysts' rejection of the kinds of ideas Schwaber presents, for they are seen as relegating psychoanalysis to a cure by empathy.

The usual view regards the first phase of the analysis of transference as pointing out the patient's distortions of "reality." It is Schwaber's contention that Freud, and the analytic profession as a whole, failed to take psychic reality seriously enough and "continued to maintain a view of 'material' reality alongside that of the patient's subjective view." She singles out the following quotation from Freud: "The fantasies possess *psychical* as contrasted with *material* reality and we gradually learn to understand that *in the world of neuroses it is psy-*

chical reality which is the decisive kind" (1917, p. 368). Obviously, Freud did not deny material reality. He said that psychic reality is the decisive kind in the world of the *neuroses*. Presumably, then, a guiding assumption of analysts is that, with the exception of lapses called countertransferences, they are not in the world of the neuroses—that is, they are capable of knowing the material reality and are therefore justified in deciding when the patient's psychic reality is a distortion of the material reality.

Yet Schwaber seems to have some unresolved misgivings about deemphasizing the role of material reality in psychoanalysis. For she notes: "It is not the domain of this paper to challenge the utility of these concepts [therapeutic alliance, reality testing, magical thinking, reality principle, the real realtionship] or the view of a 'reality' observed from without, in the theoretical *application* of our clinically derived insights. Rather, I wish to focus attention on their *implicit* impact on the process of the derivation of these insights." The remark is somewhat obscure. Is she distinguishing between analytic theory and analytic practice? Does she mean that although in any specific exchange in the analytic situation one cannot distinguish between what is psychic reality and what is material reality, one can use the concept of a material reality to make psychoanalytic generalizations? Or does she simply mean that in any particular analytic exchange the analyst must be very careful before he concludes that he now knows the material—or, as it is more usually called, the objective—reality?

In any case, Schwaber emphasizes that in the analytic situation the analyst cannot presume to know material reality. Does this mean that insofar as the assessment of reality is concerned, patient and analyst are equals? How, then, do they resolve disagreements about what something means? Is the experience of being understood the only help the analyst can give the patient? How does that lead to change?

I will mention a possible answer, only to discard it. The analyst knows more than the patient does about human motivation; the analyst has a general conviction of the ease with which one may be mistaken about one's motivations; and the analyst, having been analyzed, has greater knowledge of his own motivations. All this may be true; yet that would not justify our concluding in any particular instance that the analyst is assessing reality correctly while the patient is distorting it. Moreover, the differences cited may not be true for a particular patient-analyst pair. Does an analyst analyzing an analyst have to be a superior analyst to the one being analyzed?

The difference between the analyst and the patient lies, rather, in their differing psychological positions in the analytic situation. The patient has come for help. He exposes himself as thoroughly as he is able. The analyst has the position of advantage, both literally and metaphorically. He need not expose himself deliberately, though of course he does so inadvertently in many ways. He is under less pressure and is therefore able to maintain greater distance and objectivity than the patient. In general the patient accepts this difference of position and is therefore willing to give a degree of credence to the analyst's assessment of reality when it differs from his own even though in other circumstances he would not. Still, in any particular exchange the analyst must seriously reckon with the possibility that, without knowing it, he is imposing his own view of reality. Indeed, if the analyst takes this attitude, the patient is more likely in general to be ready to consider the analyst's differing view seriously.

But none of this means that the analytic situation is appropriately conceived as one in which the analyst corrects the patient's distortions of reality. It is, rather, that if a useful working relationship exists, a disagreement between patient and analyst will be dealt with by examining it.

I would characterize that examination as negotiation about the discrepancy in the psychic realities of the patient and the analyst. If, in Myers' case, the analyst proceeded to look for how the patient's feeling of being belittled was plausible in the light of the interaction between analyst and patient, the patient might be inclined to consider that his conclusion (that the analyst was belittling him) was not unequivocal. Other views were possible. The patient might then be inclined to ask himself why he had experienced the analyst's remark as a belittling one. He would thus be led to investigate his preexisting and chronic expectations—that is, to begin the process of resolving the transference. An important feature of such resolution, and it gets a good deal of attention in Schwaber's illustrations, is the appearance of genetic material. Such material helps persuade the patient that in many instances where he and the analyst differ the patient is being influenced by his preexisting psychic structure. But, as I shall point out in several examples, the clarification of the patient's psychic reality should not be abandoned too soon in favor of examining genetic material, lest the analyst again fall into the error of imposing his own psychic reality on the patient.

To return to the illustration from Myers: a continuing examination of the patient's psychic reality in the present might have led to ideas quite different from those which the analyst imposed on the patient. As Schwaber points out, these ideas might have concerned, in first approximation, a wish to be responded to with warmth rather than an oedipal conflict. To say this is by no means to deny that this first approximation might be on the road toward revealing an oedipal conflict. But uncovering the conflict in this way may make recognition more meaningful to the patient than if it is prematurely imposed upon him.

Let us turn to how Schwaber handled her case. She, too, made an interpretation to which the patient (Mrs. G.) responded with micropsia. Mrs. G. did not tell Schwaber how she experienced this interpretation, contrary to Myers' patient, who said he felt belittled. But Schwaber, following the principle that empathic listening "implies the analyst's capacity to view himself as being used and responded to in the context of the patient's immediate intrapsychic experience," asked how the patient experienced her remark. She learned that Mrs. G. experienced the analyst as barging in and taking away her pleasure in showing off an accomplishment. The patient's experience was the very opposite of the analyst's prior interpretation. Schwaber had interpreted that Mrs. G. was concerned about surpassing the analyst. Mrs. G.'s experience can be understood, without too much inference, as feeling that the analyst had belittled her; perhaps she experienced the analyst as the one who was afraid of being surpassed. Had this interpretation been made, it would have been a reversal of the interpretation preceding the micropsia. That would have provided a striking contrast to Myers' vignette, in which his understanding remained unchanged.

But, in Schwaber's account, Mrs. G.'s experience that the analyst, like her mother, barged in and took away her attempt to share an accomplishment is not followed up in the present. Instead, there is some interesting genetic material about Mrs. G.'s experiences with her mother. In sum, Schwaber sees this as enabling a reconstruction of the micropsia as a "defensive choice, weaving the little girl's affect-laden competitive and growth-oriented strivings with her perceptions of the responses to them . . . the 'intrusive' or else 'non-touching' mother who was felt somehow as negating the child's blossoming feminine strivings." Maybe so. But what Mrs. G. had been talking about before the analyst's intervention was how successful she felt at her new job and how her work compared with the analyst's. I suggest that Schwaber failed to stay long enough with her own principle—that she failed to pursue the patient's psychic reality in the context of the patient's immediate experience. For that experience was that the analyst had barged in to take away from Mrs. G.'s showing her achievements. I suggest that Mrs. G. may have fled from the immediacy of her complaint about the analyst to complain about her mother. And I suggest that the analyst may have followed her because as a person she preferred not to see herself as possibly in competition with her patient. Perhaps Schwaber has yet to thoroughly accept the principles she espouses and to more fully apply them in her work. Certainly genetic material is important in the resolution of the transference. But one must also be aware of how readily it can be used to defend against the present of the analytic situation. To give another example: in discussing Mr. R.'s experience of her interventions as errors, Schwaber indicates that their "specific meaning lay in the subjective sense of their historical recreation." That is not necessarily correct. Their specific meaning might reside in the immediate interaction between the patient and the analyst, whatever contribution to that meaning was made by the patient's past.

Turning to another topic, I question the relationship Schwaber sees between her ideas and Kohut's. She claims that Kohut speaks of "the unwitting repetition in the analytic situation of the noxiously experienced early milieu." What does this mean he recognizes in terms of the principles she advocates? Kohut sees the analyst as a participant, but so do many others. He sees the patient's experience as justified, but so do others when the analyst's behavior is characterized as countertransference. (And Kohut does see the analyst's behavior on which he focuses as countertransference. A good part of *The Analysis of the Self* [1971] is devoted to the countertransferences to mirroring and idealization.) Kohut did not discover selfobject transferences. The difference between his view of selfobject transferences and the prevailing view is that he believes selfobject transferences are the result of improper early parental handling. The prevailing view emphasizes that these transferences stem primarily from an intrapsychic conflict. Kohut advocates restraint and delay in interpreting selfobject transferences not only to permit them to develop clearly, but also to convince the patient that the analyst can be trusted to feel and respond differently from the early figures.

How is Kohut's idea that the empathic observer defines the psychological field related to Schwaber's ideas? Only indirectly—in two ways. First, it can be related to Schwaber's conviction that the primary task of the analyst is, if only initially, to understand the patient's psychic reality, for such understanding, according to Kohut, must always include empathy, or "vicarious introspection," as a major ingredient. The second point of relationship lies in Schwaber's emphasis on Kohut's description of "the unwitting repetition in the analytic situation of the noxiously experienced early milieu." She suggests: "This point of view resulted in a sharpened focus on the *specificity* of the analyst's contribution in the understanding of transference.

At the same time Schwaber recognizes that she is using the concept of selfobject in what she calls a "perhaps somewhat idiosyncratic way." That is because she is *not* using it as a "'construct having to do exclusively with failures of differentiation between self and object nor to failed recognition of the autonomy of each—but more fundamentally as one which recognizes the immediacy of the surround as being intrinsic to the organization and perception of intrapsychic experience.'" Schwaber does well to emphasize this difference between herself and Kohut, for Kohut quite explicitly restricts the contribution of the analyst to the patient's experience in both transference neuroses and narcissistic and more serious disorders to a precipitant. He does not, like Schwaber, call it "intrinsic" to the patient's experience. He writes:

> Persistent introspection leads in the transference neuroses to the recognition of an inner struggle between infantile strivings and inner counterforces against these strivings: the structural conflict. The analyst, to the extent that he is a transference figure, is not experienced in the framework of an interpersonal relationship but as the carrier of the analysand's unconscious endopsychic structures. . . . Persistent introspection in the narcissistic disorders and in the borderline states thus leads to the recognition of an unstructured psyche struggling to maintain contact with an archaic object or to keep up the tenuous separation from it. Here, the analyst is not the screen for the projection of internal structure (transference), but the direct continuation of an early reality. . . . He *is* the old object [1959, pp. 217–219].

To say that the analyst is the old object is no more intrinsic to what he actually is than to say he is a screen. Kohut indicates that all transferences are repetitions, but not all repetitions are transferences. He means that although the patient's experience of the analyst in the narcissistic disorders is a repetition, this repetition does not conform to the definition of a transference figure as a carrier of the analysand's unconscious intrapsychic structure. It is true that Kohut emphasizes the analyst as making an intrinsic contribution in his concept of transmuting internalizations. Indeed, it is this emphasis which has resulted in the accusation that Kohut's analyses are psychotherapies, operating through interpersonal interaction. This criticism is an example of how many analysts more readily recognize noxious interpersonal interaction than benign interpersonal interaction, which—though universally and necessarily present in any analysis—is as though it were nonexistent, equivalent to the blank screen or neutrality.

Yet Schwaber is somewhat inconsistent in her recognition of the difference between her view and Kohut's, for she argues that Kohut's rigorous use of empathic introspection led to the discovery of the varieties of transference he elaborated. She does not distinguish sharply enough between a central focus on subjective experience and the analyst's realization that he can know only his subjective reality. As Schwaber correctly points out, case reports by self psychologists may betray the imposition of the analyst's perspective, just as case reports from other perspectives may. That is, a self psychology framework does not necessarily guard against the analyst's imposing his perspective. It is of course true that every analyst works within some perspective. The decisive point is how aware he is of his perspective and how he tries to take it into account.

Several other miscellaneous points caught my attention in reading Schwaber's paper. It is, for instance, interesting that perceptive discussions of the mother-infant relationship as a contextual unit can readily be found in the literature. Yet, as Schwaber intimates in referring to Loewald (1970), this thinking does not necessarily carry over into a consideration of the patient-analyst relationship as a contextual unit—except in the trivial sense that the analyst's interventions precipitate responses in the patient. The analyst may reason, as I quoted Kohut as doing, that the patient's structure is fixed and his psychic experience, insofar as it is transference, is not regarded as significantly related to the current interaction, however important a role a past interaction may have played in the genesis of that structure.

One must recognize that the analyst's participation in the field, or what Schwaber calls the contextual unit, may be primarily by way of the setting of the analytic situation rather than any action or intervention within that setting. The analyst's silence and the pressure that engendered for a response from Mr. A. and Mrs. G. illustrate the contextual unit determined by the setting. If one fails to perceive this point, one may see these illustrations as referring only to the patient's psychic reality, not to any contribution the analyst makes to that reality.

Another point is that the patient's response to an intervention need not be directly expressed (as with Myers' patient); it may be expressed indirectly by allusion. A nice example is offered in Schwaber's discussion of Shapiro's (1974) case vignette. According to Shapiro, "The day following the confrontation and interpretation of his 'empathic understanding,' [the patient] began the hour by describing the humiliation and sense of weakness he had experienced when his fiancée berated him for a failing" (p. 13). Schwaber suggests that the patient's comment "may have reflected a sense that his analyst, like his fiancée, had 'berated him for a failing' " in his interpretation in the preceding session.

Schwaber also makes the important point that it is dangerous to assume that if one feels a particular way that shows that the patient is attempting to make one feel that way. It is true that one may be "role-responsive" (Sandler, 1976) to the patient's attempt to create a pattern of interpersonal relationship. But it is also true that just as the transference is not solely a response to the analyst, so is the countertransference not solely a response to the patient. That Schwaber experienced her photographer patient as suggesting that she would forget about him on her vacation does not necessarily mean that he was hinting that she would. Nevertheless, it is true that the analyst's feelings may give important clues to the patient's subjective experience. Indeed, as I suggested earlier, this is essential for an understanding of the patient's experience.

I close with a comment on Schwaber's reference to "Freud's monumental shift from the seduction to the fantasy theory of neurosogenesis [which] marked a critical turning point in the history of psychoanalysis." Had Freud been convinced of the ubiquity of what Schwaber calls a contextual unit, he would have looked for what had happened between the parent and the child which the child might have experienced as a seduction. In examining psychic reality, then, one must assume that a patient's account may relate to something that is equivalent in psychic reality to what the patient claims, even if not literally so. Schwaber cites Schimek (1975) as articulating this point clearly. It has also been aphoristically stated by Levenson (1972), who said: "If the patient claims that the analyst is poisoning his soup, this may mean that he feels he is being fed a poisoned relationship" (p. 80).

Lest my remarks obscure what I consider to be Schwaber's important contribution, I end by again quoting the essence of that contribution: "Empathy . . . is that mode of attunement which attempts to maximize a singular focus on the patient's subjective reality. . . . Vigilantly guarding against the imposition of the analyst's point of view, the role of the analyst and of the surround, as perceived and experienced by the patient, is recognized as intrinsic to that reality."

REFERENCES

Freud, S. (1917), Introductory lectures on psycho-analysis. Part III: General theory of neurosis. *Standard Edition*, 16:243–248. London: Hogarth Press, 1964.

Gill, M. M. (1979), The analysis of the transference. *J. Amer. Psychoanal. Assn.*, 27(Suppl.):263–288.

Kohut, H. (1959), Introspection, empathy, and psychoanalysis. In: *The Search for the Self: Selected Writings*, Vol. 1, ed. P. H. Ornstein. New York: International Universities Press, 1978, pp. 205–232.

——— (1971), *The Analysis of Self*. New York: International Universities Press.

Levenson, E. (1972), *The Fallacy of Understanding*. New York: Basic Books.

Loewald, H. (1970), Psychoanalytic theory and the psychoanalytic process. *The Psychoanalytic Study of the Child*, 25:46–68. New York: International Universities Press.

Myers, W. (1977), Micropsia and testicular retraction. *Psychoanal. Quart.*, 46:580–604.

Sandler, J. (1976), Countertransference and role-responsiveness. *Int. Rev. Psycho-Anal.*, 3:43–47.

Schimek, J. G. (1975), The interpretations of the past: Childhood trauma, psychical reality, and historical truth. *J. Amer. Psychoanal. Assn.*, 23:845–865.

Schwaber, E. (1981), Variations in psychoanalytic thought. Presented to 19th Annual Conference of Council of Psychoanalytic Psychotherapists, New York, Oct. 18.

Shapiro, T. (1974), The development and distortion of empathy. *Psychoanal. Quart.*, 43:4–25.

21 The Process of Empathic Response

HERBERT J. SCHLESINGER, Ph.D.

I

In common usage, empathic has several implications. We use the term frequently to characterize an individual of whom we approve. We describe him as an "empathic person." By this appelation, we usually mean this person has a sensitive regard for his fellow man, likes people, is aware of and accommodates to their needs, is sympathetic with their causes and alert to how they are feeling. The person so described is, in short, a good human being.

In another common usage, we advise our students to "respond empathically to their patients." By this we mean, first of all, that they should attune themselves to the affective component of the patient's communications and comment upon it in their interventions, in addition to or sometimes rather than the content. We advise the young analyst to focus on *how* the patient *feels* about what he is saying, not merely on what he is talking about. When the student has grasped this point of view, we call his affect-focused comments "empathic."

This last usage is subject to easy corruption. A common vulgarization is to speak of "giving the patient empathy"—to speak

Reprinted from *Psychoanalytic Inquiry*, 1:393–416 (1981).

of empathy as if it were an oozy substance that could be applied like butter to an otherwise unappetizing piece of dry toast. In this usage, affect, empathy and rapport start to sound interchangeable, and the term loses any specificity of meaning. I shall not dwell upon these aberrations further.

I have no particular quarrel with the general honorific usage that permits us to describe people or their comments as empathic. My concern is rather that neither of these usages captures the essential technical significance of the term for psychoanalysis or psychotherapy. From the technical point of view I shall take, empathic both refers to tuning in and *remaining attuned* to the changing meanings of a patient's experiencing. To place the sense of responding empathically as a process, I shall first discuss the process of psychotherapy.

We are accustomed to thinking of psychotherapy as a process and as having several aspects that we can consider independently. Thus we speak of the *content* of a patient's communications and the *affective tone*. We consider separately the patient's communicative *intent,* i.e., what he wants to tell us about, and his tendentious *purpose,* i.e., what he wants to do to us, how he plans to act upon us, change us, or get us to do something to, for or against him. We also consider separately the *form* and the *medium* in which communication is cast.

This much is true for all interpersonal communication. When we speak specifically about therapeutic communication, we must introduce another point of view—that of transference, repetition and neurosis. We have learned that it is essential to "look through the transference" at what the patient is saying, the affect with which he says it, and his wish to act upon us or to have us act upon him. We see further that the patient is not free to communicate in any way he chooses but must relate to us within a script written a long time ago, which the patient is condemned to repeat endlessly, casting himself and every new person into the preordained roles they must occupy with respect to each other. The patient thus does not necessarily influence us in ways he consciously wants to, but in ways that he must. He is as much a victim or character in the script as are we. While he is unwittingly the author and director of the therapeutic drama he must play out, he is at the same time a character playing a role.

This metaphoric formulation sounds like a description of the Pirandello play *Six Characters in Search of an Author,* and indeed all the characters in the patient's script are looking for their author. But that is not all they are looking for, and at times it seems that even when they meet their author they are unwilling to recognize him. All of the characters in the patient's script are, of course, aspects of the patient himself. Transference is a way of externalizing one's infantile conflicts in an attempt to solve them by repeating established non-solutions. The resulting drama is played out in life rather than through memory on one's internal stage.

If we recognize that the patient is forced by his neurosis to endlessly replay a script with characters who are fixed in conflicting roles (another way of saying that the patient avoids experiencing *intra*psychic conflict), then we are in a better position to understand the complexity of the patient's communications. They reflect the mixed messages and multiple conflicting contents and affects that correspond to the multiple conflicting roles and characters in the script of the neurosis.

What significance has this précis of the theory of neurosis? At the very least it should be clear that if we regard psychoanalysis as a process, it is not sufficient to advise a student to "go with the affect." *Which* affect should he go with and, if he is accurate in his empathy and the patient responds differently but also affectively, with *which* affect should he go next? In the therapeutic interaction the analyst is assigned roles required by the patient's unconscious script. If he is to allow, and even facilitate, the patient to communicate with him through transference, he cannot reject the multiple and successive roles assigned him, though some may seem alien or distasteful, but must allow himself to be molded into different respondents. It is essential for the analyst to be able to sense what the patient is doing to the transference object, as well as what the transference object is doing to the patient. He must be able to experience in signal amounts the affects of the transference figures and the patient in these interactions.

We recognize that all of these transference figures are aspects of the patient himself externalized as a function of the patient's neurosis. What could it mean then to suggest that the analyst should empathize with *the patient?* The patient is not a unitary figure. Indeed, the analytic situation is designed to facilitate the observation of his divided selves. Would it not be necessary at least to specify *which aspect* of the patient or *which transference figure* the analyst should empathize with? Clearly, the analyst must choose whose affective experience to resonate with. Responding empathically in such a multi-person field can be a complicated affair. To anticipate a later development in this argument, it follows that if the analyst is accurately and appropriately[1] empathic with one of the parties in the drama, the action may shift, the script may change, or a seemingly new script may be substituted. The analyst may find himself cast in a different role or may discover an unsuspected attribute of the role he has already been playing. Being empathic in a therapeutic situation must be viewed as part of the interpretive process.

The task of the analyst is even more complicated than the previous description and metaphors might convey. The persons in the transference are not the only persons involved. In addition to the characters of the patient's infantile romance, there are also likely to be the patient's boss, spouse, children and other actual persons in his life. Last, but by no means least, there is the analyst himself, who in addition to being a rack upon which transference imagos can be hung, is also a real person. What has empathy to do with these additional characters?

II

Could we think of the analyst being empathic with other persons who are in current relationships with the patient? Since

[1]Appropriately implies that the empathic intervention is also well timed and properly dosed.

we are speaking about communication in the therapeutic relationship and have already allowed that the analyst can empathize with split-off parts of the patient projected as transference imagos, it is only a slight extension to allow the usage that speaks of empathizing with current real persons in the patient's life. After all, "real" other persons "exist" in the therapeutic interaction only to the extent that they are remembered, whether or not they are mentioned specifically. Their presence then is on much the same basis as transference imagos.

Relationships are internal as well as external affairs. In the therapeutic interaction, the current representation of the other "real" person is more important than his "actuality," about which the analyst may know very little. The analyst after all is aware mainly of his own feelings, and through resonance and accurate empathy, to some extent of the patient's feelings. His understanding of current persons in the patient's life can only be through empathy with their representations as the patient brings them explicitly or implicitly into the therapeutic situation. A common example is the feeling the analyst occasionally gets that he now knows what the patient's wife has to put up with.

I think it is fair usage, and therapeutically useful, to consider how the analyst might apply his capacity to empathize with the patient's wife, children, present-day father and mother, siblings, boss, and other current persons in the patient's life outside of the treatment situation. This conception might be easier to accept if I would not insist upon the idea of empathizing with other "real" persons. Since I have already conceded that it is the *representations* of these others with whom we empathize, the distinction between them and transference imagos may seem slim. I would therefore be willing to consider empathizing with other "real" persons as a variation of the process of empathizing with aspects of the patient that for the moment are projected as transferences. Let us consider a case example:

> The patient, a young male afflicted with severe stomach cramps and headaches as well as outbursts of temper, is

complaining about the treatment he gets at the hands of his boss, whom he feels is on the verge of firing him. The patient has complained in this way often enough and done enough work about it to be able to entertain the possibility that he is provocative and "asking for it." At the same time, the patient is deeply invested in defending a shaky sense of self which requires that he distinguish himself clearly from important others who might otherwise "absorb" him. It is clear that the current problem with the boss is a present version of a struggle with the patient's father of childhood, and that the patient is trying to keep this conflict out of the relationship with the analyst. At this point, explicit references to the conflict in the transference are quite heavily defended against. The patient grudgingly accepts the analyst's help and has become more dependent on him than he likes. He tries to keep this relationship "real," and would become frightened if the analyst were to tactlessly assert that the feelings about the boss are "really" about the analyst. For this reason, much of the treatment at this point is being conducted within the metaphor about the boss which both expresses and defends against the transference.

The analyst hears his patient struggling with transference feelings and resolving the struggle temporarily by displacing the feelings onto his boss. He would like to facilitate the patient's tolerance for transference, but for the moment can only work toward this goal by facilitating the expression and exploration of his conflict in a safer context—as displaced to the boss. Thus, at a point when the patient seems to be winding down in his tirade against the boss, the analyst switches from his previous style of intervening (in which he had empathized with the patient's feeling of being tormented by the boss) to say, "you must be quite a handful for your boss to deal with."

The patient looks surprised for a moment, then grins and shows obvious pleasure as he lets himself relish what a problem he has been for the boss.

Let us interrupt this clinical account to ask how we can understand the analyst's intervention, why he took that approach, and why it had the effect it did. The analyst seemed to "switch sides" in this intervention. The position from which he speaks seems not so much from over the patient's shoulder looking at the boss, as over the boss' shoulder looking at the patient. But the patient, paradoxically, does not now experience the analyst as tormenting him, as he so recently accused the boss of doing; rather, he seems to enjoy the idea that the boss is discomfited. If we put the analyst's intervention in a more general form, it might sound like this: "You have really been giving the transference figure a hard time and making him suffer." Notice that both the original form of the analyst's intervention and this transformation contain the same content—but subject and object have been reversed. Would either form of the intervention be likely to have the same effect at that point? I doubt it; the remarks differ in more than reversal of subject and object. The one comment speaks of how the boss *feels* in the interaction with the patient, the other about what the patient is *doing* to the boss.

I am sure that the intervention as originally given aroused far less resistance than would the transformed remark; the latter could be heard as criticism of the patient, the analyst joining with the boss in attacking him. Given the patient's acceptance, even relish of the first intervention, we could guess that it would not be long before he could respond favorably to the transformed version as well.

The analyst was attempting to broaden the therapeutic process, to see if more aspects of the patient's conflict could be dealt with in the boss metaphor than the patient seemed capable of doing unaided. The analyst understood that the patient's tirade against the (displaced) transference figure was meant not only to punish him for his previous "tormenting" of the patient; it served also to maintain contact with him (and with the infantile father), a beloved and needed figure albeit for the moment a dangerous one. The patient's fury with the transference figure is based in part on his conviction that he does not matter to his father figure, cannot influence him or change him. He is in that sense helpless and impotent in the relationship with the transference figure. Since he cannot be loved, he will be a nuisance.

While these inferences are very likely correct, they could hardly be heard or accepted by the patient at this point. But the analyst's intervention does take a small step toward opening up that aspect of the transference to exploration. While empathizing with the boss' feelings about the patient, the analyst's remark expresses clearly that the patient *has* had an impact on the boss and has gotten through to him. This intervention was made when the patient had just about exhausted his invective, was no longer as frightened that the boss would retaliate (in the transference), and was starting to look a bit sad. The analyst intuitively understood the shift in the patient's affective state as the beginnings of his feeling that it doesn't do any good to blast in this way—it would have no effect on his father. Thus the analyst spoke to that point and put his understanding empathically. This intervention, which explicitly empathizes with the probable affective state of the boss vis-à-vis the patient, also empathizes with the wish of the patient to have an impact, to produce an affective state in the boss. The feeling the analyst attributes to the boss is the one that would be easiest for the patient to accept at that moment.

> As the hour progressed, and the patient was able to sustain his ability to move around in his relationship with the boss and from time to time recognize that he had had similar feelings and wishes toward his father, the analyst was able to test out a bit more of the patient's tolerance for aspects of the transference, while still remaining in the boss metaphor. Thus, the analyst was able to say: "You really do know how to get his goat."
>
> The patient could now make use of this comment that spoke of *his activity* in the relationship with the boss, and tended to open up the issue of the patient taking responsibility for the kind of impact he had had. At a later point, the

analyst found it useful to shift again to an explicit empathic position with the boss, saying, "I bet he has no idea of how complex his relationship with you is."

This last intervention, like the first we looked at, also serves several functions. It underscores the work just done between the analyst and patient, for it is the patient who now has a newly enriched understanding of the complexities of his relationships with bosses and fathers. It is also the patient who has just learned that it is safe to look at these complexities and to see himself as acting upon these transference figures, and not solely as the victim of their unheeding power. There is a bit of narcissistic balm in the analyst's alluding to the boss as feeling a degree of helplessness and bafflement in his relationship with the patient, and it is also true, although probably truer of the patient's father than the boss, or for that matter, the analyst. It also implies another aspect of the transference; the analyst's intervention implicitly attributes to the boss (more accurately to the father) a *wish* to understand the patient. The boss and father in this intervention are construed as more than, and other than, malevolent powers. The analyst's intervention alludes to a frustrated but well-intentioned parent at his wits' end to understand his child. What is more, put in this way, the patient is able to agree; by granting the transference figure this enhanced stature, he gains stature himself.

Another way to look at this analysis of the situation is to note that the patient gains some strength and courage to deal with the relationship to the transference figure through his work with the analyst. He also is obtaining some gratification by doing so. The gratification is not only from the sense of mastery that accompanies insight. Some also derives from the way the analyst phrases his interventions. His description of the interactions with the transference figure is stated honorifically. As the patient hears the interaction described, he is helped to feel that he came off pretty well. The bit of narcissistic pleasure adds to the therapeutic effectiveness of this exchange.

One of the lessons of this case example is that it is not sufficient to describe one's activity with the patient as "empathizing with *him*." The patient is not unitary. To the extent that he is involved in conflict, he is not a whole. It is necessary to specify which aspect of the patient, which side of the conflict one is empathizing with, and one's purpose for doing so.

To put it differently, responding empathically often amounts to taking sides in a conflict. I think this point is self-evident. Yet viewed in this way, it must surely seem to conflict with the usual admonition given the analyst or psychoanalytically-oriented therapist that he should be "neutral," that he should stand equidistant between id, ego, and superego. How can we resolve this paradox?

I believe the paradox is generated by unwittingly slipping from one model of the therapeutic interaction to another. If one takes a view of the analytic interaction as a whole, the analyst's position can certainly be described as neutral. From this vantage point he does not take sides in conflict, but "presides" (Menninger and Holzman, 1973) in the manner of a judge at a trial, in charge, as it were, of keeping the analytic process "fair." From the standpoint of the analytic process itself, however, the analyst is constantly shifting his position in an effort to facilitate movement and prevent stagnation. One might say that it is the "function" of neurosis, or more precisely resistance, to slow things down, to make sure that the interaction cycles repetitively through the well-worn transference channels. One way to think about the analyst's task is that he attempts to encourage new occurrences, to open choices for the patient where only compulsion has reigned previously. Toward that end, he will strive within the bounds of tact, dosage, and timing to "unbalance" things, to promote a degree of tension in the therapeutic interaction that will activate movement.

This tension can be thought of in different ways—between patient and analyst, between transference and reality, or put equivalently, between the various aspects of the patient that are in conflict. The purpose of working with transference, after all, is to promote the open, verbal expression of conflict in the therapeutic situation. By expressing conflict verbally the patient is enabled to experience it, observe it, and to the degree possible, master it. By master, of course, we mean not to exterminate the conflict but to recognize the validity of competing interests within one's personality, their historical sources and present relevance, to come to terms with them in ways that are more syntonic with reality, and to make considered conscious decisions about them rather than automatically repeat unconscious ones.

It is a corollary of these considerations that a "balanced" intervention cannot be empathic. This stand may seem unjustifiably dogmatic, but consider the following: The usual effort of the well-meaning beginning psychotherapist or psychoanalyst is to try to be "fair" in his interventions. Taking the concept of neutrality as a technical maxim, the beginner will offer interventions in the form of "you feel 'x,' but you also feel 'y'" (e.g., you love your father, but you also hate him). The effect of an intervention cast in this form depends on "where the patient is" with respect to that conflict. Often the patient will respond indignantly to the suggestion that he feels "x," but is quite aware that he feels "y." After the patient has been in treatment for a while and has come to recognize at least in theory that he feels both "x" and "y," he may nod agreement, but generally nothing follows from it.

The balanced intervention summarizes matters and for the moment puts an end to the process of exploration. The interpretation that tries to incorporate both sides of the conflict in the same intervention does not facilitate the patient's own activity in examining his feelings. The rueful recognition that conflict is an inevitable part of the human condition, which such an intervention expresses, is an existential statement, not an analytic interpretation. It is a general fact in clinical work that patients do not experience both sides of a conflict at the same time; they feel one side or the other. In those few instances when both sides simultaneously emerge strongly in consciousness, the experience is unmistakable, painful to the point of being unbearable, and at least momentarily paralyzing. It is not the ordinary experience of patients in treatment. Since both sides of a conflict are not generally in consciousness together, a balanced intervention, to the extent that it alludes to an unlikely feeling state, will by definition not be empathic.

On the other hand, the analyst who empathizes with only one side of the conflict, who says to the patient "you feel 'x,'" because that is the feeling dominant at the moment, will hear his patient respond in one of several ways: (1) It may facilitate the patient feeling "x" more deeply, while elaborating the experience verbally. Recall that in the example above, the patient's first response to the analyst's empathizing with his anger and disdain for his boss was of this kind. Note also that the unbalanced intervention may facilitate a broadening of the expression of feeling in the transference, or the past, or in present reality as a metaphor. (2) If the patient has nearly exhausted feeling "x", or put more accurately, if his continuing about "x" has created so much internal tension such that "y" is now demanding to be expressed, if he has gotten too far off center in terms of his own ambivalence, then one will hear the patient back off about feeling "x." The patient may seem tired of it, worried, wistful, uneasy, or irritated without knowing why. The patient may suddenly change the subject as if no longer interested in "x" or potentially in "y." These indications will also tell the analyst that the patient may be ready to consider that he also feels "y" because "y" is now closer to awareness, or that he is resisting experiencing "y." The analyst might first want to empathize with the peculiar state (e.g., uneasiness) that the patient feels with respect to "x" (and potentially "y"); he might note empathically that the patient's feelings seem to be changing. Or he might comment that the whole situation seems to be more complicated than previously considered. Or he might say, "The last thing you said suggested to me that you feel the boss may have some reasons of his own for acting as he does."

In short, the pendulum of ambivalence will tend to swing back and forth unless interfered with. If the analyst gives it a light push in the direction in which it is already going, he can be sure that before long it will swing back of its own accord, and/or the patient will show signs that he resists expressing the other side of the conflict. If the analyst tries to push the pendulum both ways at the same time, stasis results.

When I suggested that the analyst might well choose to empathize with the uneasiness of the patient, I was alluding to a general principle. The general advice given analysts and therapists is that they should "empathize with the patient's ego," and such an intervention could be regarded as an example of doing so. This general advice, which would seem to rule out empathizing with id or superego, and thus provides an unvarying vector for our empathic interventions, also involves confusion about conceptual models. It is one thing to propose that the analyst should always be on the side of the ego, and by extension, never side with id or superego; it is quite another to recognize that both id and superego are *only* accessible through ego—the doorway or gateway to the personality as-a-whole. We have no independent access in the therapeutic situation to id or superego.

The intervention around which I focused this discussion empathized with the way the patient was feeling as his conflict was becoming more fully expressed. He for the moment had stretched himself as far in the "x" direction as was comfortable for him, and was starting to feel uneasy at having expressed so much hate for his boss (as a surrogate for his father). He was in danger (in fantasy) of either destroying the father, alienating him, or losing his love. He thus began to feel a need to make restitution, or express the other side of the ambivalence—in short, to restore a more comfortable state of neurotic balance. At that point the analyst commented on the discomfort the patient was starting to feel, clearly empathizing with the patient's experience of the moment, but not taking sides in the conflict. One might describe him as empathizing with the ego.

In summary, since the structural model assigns conscious experiencing to the ego, all of the analyst's interventions must be directed toward or through the ego, whatever their ultimate intent and destination might be. For example, it is conceivable if the patient's response had been of a positive kind, the analyst's next intervention might have been, "You seem to be recalling a time when your boss was quite different, when he excused you from a distasteful chore out of consideration for your wishes." To the extent that the analyst's intention is to facilitate expression of the other side of the ambivalence—in this instance to express some derivative of love rather than hate—we might regard this direction as "toward the id." On the other hand, also depending on the patient's response, the analyst might observe, "I think you have gotten worried about how angry you have been about your boss," or "It makes you feel terrible to have spoken so hatefully to me about your boss." I think both of these comments can be described as tending toward empathy with the superego, through the ego.

Thus, while responding empathically to the patient requires that one be able to identify what the patient is trying to do, what he hopes for, and what he fears might happen, it is essential to recognize that all of these issues are involved in conflict; they will be in an affective dialectic as the patient successively occupies positions that are ambivalently defined. If the analyst permits himself to "go with" the patient, or rather, with the dominant affect of the patient at each moment, he will find that after a while the other side of the ambivalence will manifest itself, and can be empathized with in turn. This approach also permits the analyst to assess the extent to which the patient is resisting expressing "y." Any of the suggested empathic interventions could thereby serve to open an exploration of resistance (Schlesinger, 1982).

III

In the previous sections, a conceptual position has been implied that I will now make explicit. It should be clear that empathy is not a *content* of communication. When we speak of the analyst responding empathically to the patient, he does not communicate *about* empathy. Neither is empathy a *form* of communication. While we speak vulgarly about "empathizing" with the patient, and thus imply that empathy might be a formal aspect of analyst-patient communication, the proper usage is adverbial; the term modifies the way in which we interact with the patient.

Empathy describes the *position* from which the analyst interacts with the patient. This positional sense of empathy refers to the interpersonal space in the analytic situation. If we agree that therapeutic communication involves conflict and transferences and that the patient is engaged in reliving aspects of his life and reenacting his unconscious fantasies through the dramatic personae projected onto the analyst and onto himself, then we can consider that the geography of the analytic situation can better be described as a field rather than a line connecting analyst and patient. It will often feel to the analyst and to the patient that there are several persons in the room. As the analyst related himself to the patient empathically, he has to choose which imago, or transference object, to stand behind and empathize with. This then is the sense of empathy defining a position. Where on the analytic field does the analyst choose to stand, as it were, when he responds to the patient?

To clarify this conception, I must digress for a moment to discuss an auxilliary but essential concept—the therapeutic split. The concept of splitting, first described by Freud (1927, 1940) in connection with fetishism, was given its therapeutic sense by Sterba (1934), and was later developed by Zetzel (1958). The term describes the essential capacity of the analyst (and the patient) to experience and observe simultaneously. In the present context, it refers to the capacity of the analyst to accept the patient's transference, to allow himself to feel what it is like to be the opposite party in the patient's reenacted fantasy, and at the same time to experience himself as the analyst (or "therapeutically," a usage preferred by some). Thus, part of the analyst is (or ought to be) free to move about the therapeutic space, and to speak for—or in the position of—or within the affective experience of—any of the participants in the transference drama.

It should be clear from the above that responding empathically can and perhaps ought to be conscious, deliberate activity. The analyst may choose to what extent and with whom he will empathize at any time. In this last regard we must not forget that the analyst himself is a figure with whom he (the "therapeutic ally") can empathize. The analyst, of course, may choose well or poorly; it is possible to misidentify a dominant affect and the person or imago who is feeling it. For the present, let me just say that in his selection the analyst may be right or wrong to varying degrees. Although errors may be of an infinite variety, I would like to stress one dimension of the therapeutic interaction along which adequacy of empathy could be scaled or measured. This dimension is defined by *identification* with the patient at one pole and *alienation* from the patient at the other. The middle ground, which we might also think of as the analyst's relatively conflict-free area of empathy, describes the space within which the analyst can move freely and voluntarily with respect to the characters in the transference drama. The pole that I have called "identification with the patient" may be reflected in interventions that are sympathetic rather than empathic. When identified with the patient, the analyst is no longer free to choose his position—he has effectively merged for the moment with the patient. I believe that identification as well as alienation are the result of the analyst's transferences or countertransferences, or the defenses against them.

Alienation describes the other pole of the "adequacy of empathy" dimension. If we can assume that the clinician does not lack capacity for empathy, then alienation usually reflects a momentary or more chronic defense against empathy, or perhaps against identification (again a matter of the analyst's transferences). As he moves about in the therepeutic interaction empathizing now with one party and then with another, the analyst will also find himself moving relatively closer to identification or alienation from the patient or one of his projections. He should be able to assess his own being drawn closer or repelled further from the patient both as reflecting the wishes and fears of the patient expressed in the transference and in terms of his own transferences and countertransferences. In short, the pushes and pulls that the analyst experiences can be used by him diagnostically to learn about the "state" of the analytic process.

Referring to the analyst's empathic activity as conscious and voluntary may make it seem that it is planned perhaps more regularly than many analysts experience it. The amount of cognitive awareness that analysts have about the choices available to them in empathic responsiveness will vary from time to time. As I will discuss below under interferences with empathizing, the sense of choice is experienced most clearly when the analyst is reasonably "detached" from the patient. When he is himself strongly moved by affect, whether positive or negative, it is difficult for him to maintain the therapeutic split. We might speak of the split becoming "rewelded" by strong affects. The analyst is not free to respond empathically when his own need to defend himself is too great.

I have been describing the conditions that must obtain in order that the analyst be able to respond empathically in the analytic situation. He must maintain the therapeutic split, which implies accepting the patient's tranferences, experiencing (in signal quantity) the affective responses of the transference imagos, as well as those of the therapeutic ally and the portion of the patient that is the counterpart of the transference imagos. Empathy then describes the position from which the analyst participates in the therapeutic interaction.

Perhaps this is a place to mention that the capacity to split in the interests of the analysis is not only essential for the analyst, but also for the patient. The ability to experience and observe is essential for the development of insight and to objectify one's experience. To be able to put oneself in the position of one's fellow man is an important capacity of mature persons. It is a capacity which often is inhibited, defended against or poorly developed in those persons who become our patients. The encouragement of empathy in patients is therefore a common goal for all psychoanalysis and psychotherapy. In the sections below I will also discuss the interferences with, and resistances against, empathizing.

IV

The following vignette was offered to a seminar to illustrate empathic therapeutic communication:

> The patient was seen in the clinic for several sessions. He was a man in early middle-age who had been charged with sexual abuse of a prepubescent daughter. She accused both him and her adolescent brother, but only the patient was prosecuted. The patient denied all allegations, was furious with the daughter and said, partly by way of defense, that he didn't even like her.
>
> There was ample indication of disturbance in the family, other than the charged offense. The patient was on some combination of welfare payments that netted him enough so that there was little incentive to work. His typical pattern had been to pull up stakes and move whenever things got tough. He was in the process of facing a court appearance since he was pleading guilty on advice of counsel and expected two years deferred prosecution. The patient was hospitalized on several occasions for suicide threats and other crises. He did not seek treatment under the duress of the court, but apparently as part of an effort to mitigate the court's attitude towards him. The focus of the treatment thus far, however, had not been on the issue of the offense.
>
> The therapist summarized the beginning of the hour she was presenting by saying that the patient came in "bitching" about the mail service. They had not delivered his checks; therefore the family could not eat, nor could he send the younger child to school. The therapist added that she responded in general to his complaining by "empathizing"

with his plight, commiserating with how badly things were going for him. She did not hear the metaphoric complaint about how badly *all* authorities were treating this fellow. In responding softly and attempting "to get with him," she dissociated herself from the potential transference accusation implied in the patient's denouncing the post office for malfeasance. Should this style of intervening be described as empathic?

The therapist's soft answers, intended to "turn away wrath," were not empathic in the sense I have been upholding. The patient could be heard as complaining in advance about anticipated bad treatment with the intention to intimidate the therapist. As the hour progressed, we could hear that he did succeed in producing in the therapist the kind of all-giving person that he liked to deal with, by manipulating her into a position of identifying with him. The therapist offered sympathy, not empathy. Her interventions avoided the transference and expressed a countertransference need to defend herself against the patient's implicit accusations and the guilt they aroused. She said in effect, "I am not one of your persecutors; I am on your side." By taking this position of identification with the patient, the therapist decreased the distance between them, dissipated the slight tension that ought to exist between patient and therapist, and mollified the patient by accommodating to his wishes and fears. She was coerced by him without being aware of it. She said she felt comfortable during this hour, unlike the previous hours, probably because of her accommodations.

As the hour progressed, there were additional displaced accusations having the same flavor as those about the post office; it became clear that while the patient wanted to manipulate the therapist into becoming a warm and comforting presence for him, he was also in conflict about this wish. The patient noted at one point that he could not accept anything from someone who expected something from him in return. He only wanted things from people who liked him, which is to say, who did not insist on reciprocity, and who had low expectations of him. The therapist fulfilled these conditions fully during this hour.

The patient's mixed feelings about this wish emerged through complaints about his wife, about whom he first said, "Every time I try to do something, she shoots me down." Subsequently, however, he said that his wife always agrees with him, no matter what he says. Clearly, the wife too had been manipulated into a position of identifying with him, and he expressed contempt for her for being an easy mark. Similarly, while he presented himself at one point as one who needed relief and alms in order to get by, at a later point he said that he was angry at people who underestimated him and told him he couldn't do things. He liked to prove them wrong and was writing a book to "show them."

Earlier he indicated that he would move when things got "too hot" for him and that he would move immediately if he had the money. As he fantasied submitting his book for publication, he added that if it weren't accepted, he could carry on. He took a succession of incompatible positions that had a kaleidoscopic quality.

Finally, the therapist reported herself confused when one of the patient's switches apparently was too much for her to absorb. For the rest, she was too close to him to notice that he repetitively had shifted his ground. Because the therapist could not maintain the therapeutic split, she was unaware of the degree to which the patient was acting upon her and dictating her responses. She was thus unable to utilize the patient's behavior with her therapeutically.

There were any number of points when the therapist could have taken a position somewhat distant from the patient, and could have commented on his actions and expectations in relation to the transference figure. While doing so, she could have tested whether the patient was capable of taking a more objective position himself and testing the reality of his suggestions. Responding empathically to a patient is only possible when the therapist can split himself into transference figure and therapeutic ally. Empathizing in this sense is not a capacity of transference figures who, after all, are figments of the patient's imagination and whose moods are defined by the transference scenario. The transference figure does not have independent freedom of movement. The therapeutic ally, however, can move independently. If the therapist (therapeutic ally) can separate himself from the transference figure, he can comment on the interaction between the transference object and the patient. This ability of the therapeutic ally to comment from several positions amounts to the ability to respond empathically.

This clinical vignette illustrates that a major source of interference with empathic communication is the loss of the therapeutic split. If we can assume that the therapist in this example had a basic talent for doing pyschotherapy, including the talents that underlie empathic communication, e.g., sensitivity and ability to identify the feelings of others and view the world through their eyes, we must then be able to account for the temporary (at least) loss of this capacity.

The therapeutic split can become "rewelded" when the analyst's defensiveness, or need for defense, increases past a certain amount. This increase in defense demand generally follows a heightening of the analyst's affect level (whether anxiety, guilt, anger, erotic, or nurturant interest, etc.), when the analyst becomes caught up in transference or countertransference with the patient. When the analyst or therapist is for the moment (or chronically) preoccupied with the need to defend himself, he obviously is less available to his patient. Regardless of the nature of his defenses, or his defensive style, the result is a loss of working distance and freedom of movement for the therapeutic ally, and an overidentification either with the patient or a transference imago. The analyst then feels forced into acting with or against the patient, or more typically, finds himself inhibited from acting.

In the example above, the therapist became identified with

the patient, or more accurately, with a transference imago that stood for a wish in the patient to be indulged and coddled. We cannot know from the material provided whether the therapist took this stance solely because of the coerciveness of the patient's transferences, because of defenses against anger toward the patient as a consequence of his behavior with her, because of the charges against him, because of guilt about these matters, or for other reasons. At any rate, in that position she was too close to see or comment on the interaction taking place between the patient and the transference figure. There are hints in the material that the patient found the therapist's unvarying solicitude burdensome. He spoke with contempt about his wife who agreed with him on everything and he spoke darkly about people who underestimated him and what he can do. But remaining so defensively close to the patient, the therapist could not sense that the patient was by no means monolithic in his needy demanding, but had shifted widely and frequently in the successive stances he took. We might even speculate that some of them were intended to shake himself loose from the therapist.

Perhaps I can illustrate with some potential responses how this point of view toward empathy could have been implemented. An empathic response in the situation described would embody the patient's fear and expectation of being misunderstood, deprived, or otherwise mistreated by an authority who has the power to give or withhold from him (as does the post office). The response could be direct and interpret the displacement from the transference (e.g., "You're afraid the clinic [and/or I] might turn out to be like the post office"); or it might attempt to facilitate the fuller development of the patient's fantasy by empathizing narrowly with his feelings within the metaphor about the post office; or it might be made slightly more general, within the notion of an "umbrella" intervention that covers the situation described by the patient and a little bit more, (e.g., "How do they expect you to get your family fed and clothed and sent to school if they don't delivery your check on time?"). In the latter examples the ally looks over the shoulder of the patient at the transference object and empathizes with his feeling of distrust and anger at that person. These responses also would facilitate further denunciation of disappointing authority figures, with the expectation that the patient's distrust and anger would soon generalize to include other persons who are actually or potentially withholding and disappointing, perhaps even the therapist.

In principle, the latter alternatives would fit better at a stage earlier in the interpretive process, since the intervention that interprets the post office metaphor toward the transferenc e would likely abort the further development of the patient's fears and foster testing of reality. The initial empathic response thus begins a process of exposing and unraveling the tranference by dealing first with the resistance against transference expressed in the patient's metaphorically-expressed anger.

To continue to explore possibilities, the analyst could also have spoken from the position of the displaced transference figure. Again leaving the displacement uninterpreted for the moment, the analyst could have said, "They don't give a damn if you are inconvenienced." I offer this last for completeness' sake to illustrate that the therapist could speak for the transference figure and that such a response could also be described fairly as empathic.

Each accurate and appropriately empathic intervention by the analyst should be followed by a shift in the patient's position. The analyst's subsequent comments must take account of these shifts. This is merely another way of saying that there is no such thing as a uniformly empathic position; empathizing must be viewed as a process. The process of empathizing implies "going with" rather than "opposing" the prevailing affect (Schlesinger, 1982).

Summary

The capacity to communicate empathically with patients is the basis of psychoanalysis and psychodynamic psychotherapies. Empathy is not part of the content of therapeutic communication;

we rarely talk to patients about empathy. Rather, it is an aspect of the process of communication itself. Viewing empathic communication as a process implies that the analyst's position with regard to the patient changes as the patient's position changes. This empathy is thus not a uniform trait of analysts, or a class of therapeutic communications. The interventions we call "empathic" are those which are accurately attuned to what the patient is feeling and expressing at each moment.

The term "empathic," as it describes the analyst's responses to the patient, specifically refers to the *position* from which the analyst responds. Usually this will be one of looking over the patient's shoulder at the transference figure, while sharing the surface emotion expressed. "Empathic'" can also describe the position of looking over the shoulder of the transference figure toward that aspect of the patient making the projection.

Essential to empathic communication is the ability of the analyst to maintain the therapeutic split. Interferences with empathizing generally involve a loss of therapeutic split, usually when the analyst's own defensive needs become excessive.

REFERENCES

Freud, S. (1927), Fetishism. *Standard Edition,* 21:152–158. London: Hogarth Press, 1961.

——— (1940), Splitting of the ego in the process of defence. *Standard Edition,* 23:273–278. London: Hogarth Press, 1964.

Menninger, K. & Holzman, P. (1973), *Theory of Psychoanalytic Technique,* Second Edition. New York: Basic Books.

Schlesinger, H. (1982), Resistance as process. In: *Resistance: Problematic Patient Behavior in Psychodynamic and Behavior Therapies,* ed. P. Wachtel. New York: Plenum.

Sterba, R. (1934), The fate of the ego in analytic therapy. *Internat. J. Psycho-Anal.* 15:117–126.

Zetzel, E. (1958), The therapeutic alliance in the analysis of hysteria. In: *The Capacity for Emotional Growth.* New York: International Universities Press, 1970.

Discussion

ALAN Z. SKOLNIKOFF, M.D., and MARDI J. HOROWITZ, M.D.

WE DEFINE EMPATHY AS a state of mind. As such, it has multiple components, including perceptual, emotional, conceptual, and behavioral ones. The perceptual component entails a direction of attention toward specific representations of the patient or his (or her) objects. The emotional one includes attractions or repulsions toward the patient or his objects at any given time. The conceptual component involves an integration of emotional and cognitive aspects, and the behavioral one contains either imitative or interactive trials of action.

Herbert Schlesinger sees empathy as a process within the mind of the analyst. It is one of tuning in and staying tuned to the meanings of the patient's experiences and behaviors. What does this add to our psychoanalytic understanding of empathic activity? The key point on which we agree with Schlesinger is a recognition of *empathy* as a shifting focus within a repertoire of self- and object schematizations. If we were to regard analytic patients as each having only a single self-concept, then whenever we were empathic, we would feel as they felt in a situation. But we recognize that our patients have multiple self-concepts and multiple patterns of relationship. Their conflicts are often struggles between different, simultaneous emotional potentials in the same situation. To respond empathically, one must choose between various ways of reacting within a given interpersonal situation being described by the patient. One must choose between a variety of role relationship models simultaneously being applied to a situation by the patient—including those relationship models or self-concepts that the patient dreads, wards off, or uses for defensive purposes, as well as those on which the patient is basing his most realistic adaptive reactions. Schlesinger appropriately emphasizes this aspect of choice in the empathic state of mind.

The set of the various self-images, object concepts, role relationship models, including aims, is what Schlesinger refers to as the unconscious script. In this script, enacted in the evolution of a transference neurosis, the analyst is often assigned not one but several roles. These may occur or unfold in a storylike sequence. Again, part of the analyst's empathic response entails a choice as well as a reaction to provoking stimuli. We allow ourselves to experience not only the successive roles assigned by the patient, but the experience of the patient at the other end of the real or imagined transaction. Within the process of empathy, Schlesinger includes a "feeling into" the roles of original transference figures (such as a parent) and current transference figures (such as a boss), as well as the countertransferences provoked by the patient.

As illustrated in Schlesinger's first clinical vignette, the process of empathic responding is one in which the patient is also asked to learn. As Schlesinger puts it, "The analyst seemed to 'switch sides' in this intervention" when he said, "'you must be quite a handful for your boss to deal with.'" The analyst is taking the position of looking over the boss' shoulder toward the patient, and asking the patient to take that view as well. For this patient, as for many in analysis, this may be a relatively new experience.

In the course of most analyses, patients are encouraged to experience empathy for themselves, viewed as children. As part of their newly continuous (rather than repressed or dissociated) life stories, they also have empathic responses for their parents responding to them as children. With an adult mind, they now have capability for such recognition. In the transference neurosis, this aspect of learning is one in which the patient recognizes the pressure of his transference provocations on the analyst, and how that may feel to the analyst.

Schlesinger clarifies one of the mechanisms by which the analyst's mental processes give rise to mini-emotional experiences (one might call them "trials of emotion"). These mini-emotional experiences form the basis for what is said to patients, and experienced by them as empathic. The analyst constructs a conceptual space, occupied by various self- and object concepts. In this space the self of the patient is identified with or occupied by the self of the analyst. This is why the empathic state of mind is called "being in the shoes of another." But the analyst does not just stand in those shoes. The analyst moves about this conceptual space, perhaps using imagery. He imitatively and imaginatively experiences a given situation in many ways, as various transactions between several figures.

We believe that the analyst chooses, consciously or unconsciously, provoked or unprovoked by the patient, to change the vantage point. The analyst reexperiences, repeats the transactional situation from the points of view of various self- and object concepts. The emotional experiences from each point of view are then related to other models in the mind of the analyst, ones that concern the trains of thought inferred to be stymied by conflict in the mind of the patient.

This conceptualization allows inference about the often unconscious decision-making process within the analyst that may precede his first conscious thought about what may later become an interpretation given to the patient. The analyst is unconsciously examining and reexamining the patient's core conflicts in terms of various self- and object concepts within the modeled mind of the patient. This is done in the empathic state of mind—which is, we think, what is meant by free-floating attention. When this examination coalesces into a model of the relationship between the varied self- and object concepts that has high explanatory power, or that points toward resolution, then the analyst can consciously represent this information. He reappraises the pattern consciously for his own "that's it" or "that's not it" responses, again modeled on the patient's behalf.

Once again the analyst may shift roles and speak as the analyst giving an interpretation to the patient. Sometimes, however, interpretations are worded as if the patient were thinking what the analyst says. Instead of saying, "You are afraid to be angry with me," when that is empathically recognized, the analyst may simply conjecture, "Afraid to be angry," ommitting the pronouns that signal the position of the analyst as subject (me) to the patient as object (you). This may be a conscious decision not to assign subject or object, or it may be that the analyst does not yet know what the direction in the mind of the patient is.

We believe that Schlesinger's description of the process of empathy is helpful in pointing toward such varied functions, and helps us avoid reification of the term itself. His focus, however, is limited to the conscious aspects of the empathic process, and this may give the misleading impression that the psychoanalytic process proceeds in an orderly way. We believe that an unconscious part of the empathic process precedes the clearer understanding of the patient's situation that Schlesinger illustrates in the clinical vignette of the patient and his boss.

Schlesinger, for instance, indicates that the analyst can and should maintain the therapeutic split, meaning the ability to experience and observe simultaneously. If the analyst is moved by strong affects, whether positive or negative, he cannot maintain this split. In Schlesinger's view, the analyst should maintain the position of accepting the transferences (observing them more than experiencing them) rather than participating. As we see it, although the analyst attempt to maintain this therapeutic split, in reality, during the course of the work, before achieving an understanding of the patient's transferences, the analyst is unconsciously participating in his mind with the patient in a re-enactment of the transferences. Here we agree with Sandler (1981) and McLaughlin (1981) that the analyst is not able to maintain a perfect intrapsychic neutrality but has his own inner "transference" (countertransference) to the patient. As the work with the patient continues, however, the analyst retrospectively recognizes his participation and thereby regains the therapeutic split.

Schlesinger emphasizes maintaining "the middle ground between alienation and identification with the patient." We contend that in reality the analyst is not always able to maintain the "middle ground," but is moved by emotion and may even transiently experience confusion because he does not understand what the nature of the interaction is between him and the patient. Through continuing self-analysis, an understanding of the role relationships gradually emerges, the therapeutic split is regained, and the middle ground is reestablished.

The analyst's departure from "the middle ground" is often attributed to a lack of experience or an incomplete analysis. Yet most of our detailed information on the psychoanalytic process comes from studies of supervision or from observations that omit the analyst's ongoing subjective reactions to the patient. Case studies in the literature or at conferences rarely include an ongoing account of the analyst's subjective emotional reactions. When a subjective reaction is pointed out, it usually is to indicate an "error" or "countertransference." Windholz (1980; Windholz and Oremland, 1971) has described a method by which the analyst's subjective reactions may be studied prospectively. It is called consensual analysis. The treating analyst reports weekly to a nonparticipating observing analyst and describes the process, especially his own subjective reactions to the patient. This information is compared with that written after each session. The analyst's capacity to then retrospectively and prospectively analyze these subjective reactions, which constitute a departure from the middle ground, would seem to yield a more accurate representation of the psychoanalytic process.

Our definition of the empathic process thus includes the analyst's capacity to permit subjective reactions to emerge in the service of understanding the role relationships the patient is eliciting in him. These roles may shift rapidly and may not be immediately understood by the analyst. The capacity to observe these experiences (regaining the therapeutic split) finally leads to understanding and eventually interpretation.

Let us return to Schlesinger's clinical vignette and look again at the patient and the analyst. We agree that the analyst is confronted with the question: "Which aspect of the patient or which transference figure should I empathize with?" In the example given, the analyst "switches sides" and empathizes with the patient's representation of the boss by saying, " 'you must be quite a handful for your boss to deal with.' " This comment appears to facilitate the treatment in that it offers the patient the perspective of having the power to torment his boss as well as to feel tormented by him. We agree that this intervention appears empathic in the complete sense that Schlesinger describes it.

We would argue, however, that frequently the means by which the analyst arrives at such an understanding may not be under conscious control. Let us imagine some steps that might lead to such an understanding: the analyst might, over a period of time, personally find this patient difficult to deal with, consciously assess this, but still find remarks coming to mind that reveal his own irritation. Retrospectively and prospectively, through the empathic process, he might realize that the patient is evoking in him the role of tormentor, which fits that of the childhood father and the current boss. The analyst might try to point this out in the transference, but to no avail—the patient refuses to acknowledge any negative feelings toward him. The analyst might then feel frustrated, recognizing the patient's inability to deal with the negative feelings within the transference. In attempting to deal with this frustration, he might consider how to communicate in a safe way to the patient what feelings the patient is evoking in him. The thought that the patient might tolerate negative feelings toward the boss, as well as the boss' negative feelings toward him, might be a relief to the analyst. Even though this would be a displacement of the transference, it would permit the analyst to stay emotionally engaged. He might hope that the patient's response to his remark will presage a capacity for him to eventually experience and observe the negative transference feelings directly.

We agree with Schlesinger's emphasis on the analyst's capacity to identify and understand the multiplicity of self- and object concepts that are portrayed. We would, however, expand his concept of how the analyst achieves this empathy by underlining the important role of the affective component, which is often unconscious. This component may be experienced even before it is integrated into a cognitive and conceptual understanding of the interaction with the patient.

REFERENCES

McLaughlin, J. (1981), Transference, psychic reality, and countertransference. *Psychoanal. Quart.*, 50:639–664.

Sandler, J. (1981), Character traits and object relationships. *Psychoanal. Quart.*, 50:694–708.

Windholz, E. (1980), The consensual analysis. Presented at 69th Annual Meeting of American Psychoanalytic Association, San Francisco, May.

——— & Oremland, J. (1971), Some specific transference, countertransference, and supervisory problems in the analysis of a narcissistic personality. *Int. J. Psycho-Anal.*, 52:267–275.

22 Empathic Understanding

N. GREGORY HAMILTON, M.D.

Which of us has looked into his father's heart?
Which of us has known his brother?
—Thomas Wolfe, *Look Homeward, Angel*

EMPATHY IS OUR VEHICLE for understanding one another in a meaningful way. To examine this phenomenon more closely, I will present two examples of empathic understanding. These will be used to demonstrate how empathic understanding, in these instances, can be reduced to four elements: (1) observation of a patient, (2) observation of a child, (3) observation of the observer's experience, and (4) relatedness, a term which has to do with parallels among the above three observations.

Since experiences are only meaningful within their contexts, before proceeding I should mention that I work intensively with a few, severely ill, yet verbal schizophrenic patients in an attempt to understand them. Additionally, I enjoy playing nightly on the living room rug with my barely verbal son. And finally, I am undergoing psychoanalysis myself. All three of these factors may contribute to my view of the following experiences.

Example 1

Ms. A., a schizophrenic patient who still retained a keen desire to be understood, explained her terror of being devoured by a Cyclops. She vaguely felt that this Cyclops might actually be her therapist or herself, and she was afraid.

Reprinted from *Psychoanalytic Inquiry*, 1:417–422.

At the end of the day I remained disturbed by my patient's distress and by the threat to the therapeutic process which her uneasiness posed. Nevertheless, she seemed safe enough for the night. Setting my concerns aside I returned home for an evening meal with my family. After the meal my sixteen-month-old son and I played at stacking blocks. We cooperated and our movements complemented one another in the delicate task. Then, stopping, my son (who resembles me in complexion, hair color, and body habitus) looked up with a wondering eye. He pointed to one of my eyes and I spontaneously closed it. My visual experience, of course, remained the same with one eye closed as it had been with both eyes opened. As I looked out at the world, including my son who then put his hand over one of his own eyes, I felt washed over by a familiar and yet unfamiliar sense of enchantment, as if I were looking at my childhood self in a mirror. I realized, then, the very simple fact that I took in the world as a single visual experience. The visual field is single. How commonplace!

To a child, I concluded, his first experience of himself must be that of a single-visioned being. Eventually, he learns he has two eyes, but vision is single. It must take a fair degree of experience to associate that single visual experience with two eyes. Visually, as orally, then, the child must first experience his seeing apparatus as single, schematically represented in Figure 1.

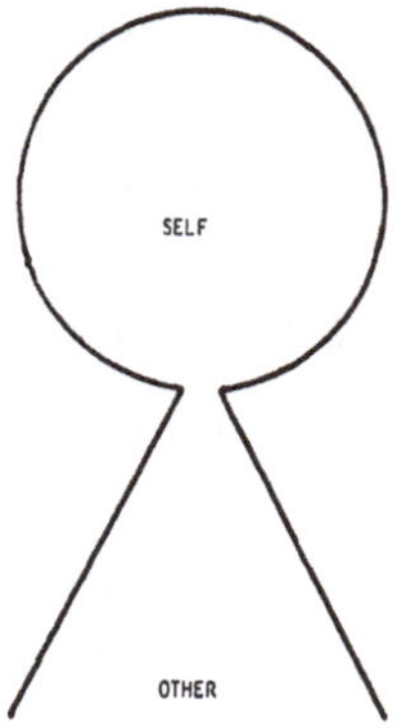

FIGURE 1

Such an experience must antedate the child's later ability to see himself with two eyes, following which he learns to represent himself in some such fashion, as represented in Figure 2.

FIGURE 2

It seems only natural, then, that my unhappy patient would associate primitive longings with a primitive self-image such as the Cyclops, represented in Figure 3.

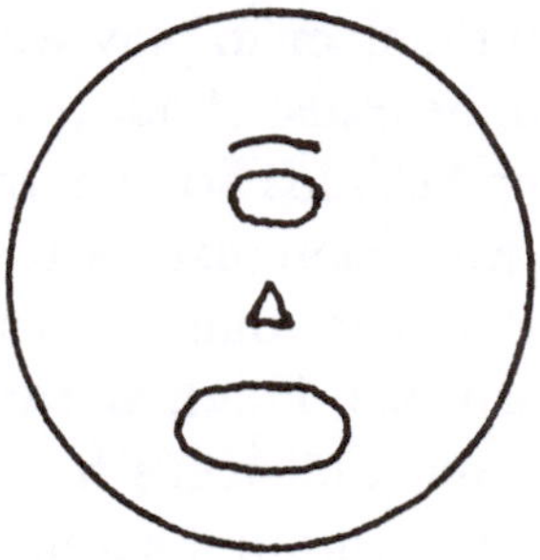

FIGURE 3

Not surprisingly, when I later presented this idea to my patient, mentioning it as an interesting fantasy of some possible pertinence to her experience, it helped her return to a more abstract and integrated mode of thinking.

Example 2

Several months later, after another regressive episode, the same schizophrenic patient complained that she had lost her feeling of reality and of relatedness to me, her therapist. This loss followed a recent attempt to reunite with an old lover. The attempt had resulted in a rejection, which in turn led to a renewed delusional preoccupation.

Over the period of a week's work, the patient again began to experience me as a caring therapist. She then stated that she wished I would hold her, but she realized she was too big for me to hold like a baby and that I would never be her mother or father.

In the next hour her feeling of therapeutic communion (Goldstein, 1954) renewed, although she kept her eyes downcast throughout the hour, as she had for most of the week. Eventually, however, she looked longingly at me, stating, "I am feeling cared about very much and it terrifies me. The closeness frightens me." She went on to say that she felt exquisitely vulnerable. In particular, she felt in danger of losing me.

After finishing the rest of my day's work with charts, medications, and administrative tasks, I returned to my family and dinner. Again, I sat on the floor to play with my son and some small toys. This time in the midst of our play, my toddler looked longingly at me, putting both his arms in my arms. Playfully, I pulled him closer until my vision just started to blur. At the moment when the limit of my eye's ability to focus finer was reached, my son looked faintly anxious. He then leaned rapidly forward, kissed me on the lips, and pulled his head back again with a pleased gaze. As he entered within the limit of my visual accommodation, his visage had disappeared, and my visage must have disappeared for him as his did for me. His response was to open his mouth, make tactile contact, and retreat to reestablish visual contact.

The experience, I thought, was one of increasing visual closeness interrupted by a rather startling visual object loss and followed by oral contact. When, out of interest, I repeated the movement, once more my toddler's expression changed to one of slight anxiety before he darted forward to kiss me, then retreated laughing, all right on cue. The movement was reminiscent of how he had earlier approached his mother's breast: seeing it, opening his mouth, and then lunging toward the breast, sucking greedily as if he had been suddenly drawn in by a vacuum.

Again, a feeling of reminiscence and quiescence swept over me. I felt that I had remembered something visually and tactilely. I felt I had remembered a fusion experience including slight anxiety at the turning point between visual object loss and physical contact. Again, this experience helped me understand the anxiety and longing of my patient.

Discussion

Now, we can examine these illustrations of empathic understanding to determine the contributing sources of information:

Working from the surface, we find the first source of information to be observation of a single patient. That is, as the patient described her experiences to me, I in turn observed her. This source of information is the same as that used in any medical history-taking. For example, we ask patients if they experience discomfort or if they experience paroxysms of nocturnal dyspnea, and so on. This source of information, then, seems entirely commonplace and acceptable.

Similarly, the second source of information seems commonplace. It was none other than observation of a child's behavior. Ethologists have quite fruitfully used such techniques of naturalistic observation. As for the study of humans, Freud (1900), of course, referred to his observations of infants, but in a less systematic fashion. Recently, Mahler, Pine and Bergman (1975) have been among the psychoanalysts to employ the observation of infants combined with what Mahler terms "coenesthetic empathy."

Third, I observed my own subjective states, including sensations which had the quality of memories. It is this element, then, which distinguishes empathic understanding from other forms of scientific observation and gives it its subtlety and power. Freud (1905) also utilized this element of empathic understanding in his investigation of verbal phenomena, although he did not fully exploit his technique for investigation of preverbal phenomena.

The fourth element is relatedness. Sullivan (1953) termed this element "the interpersonal field." Because Sullivan's term has electromagnetic and ethereal connotations, I prefer the word "relatedness." In the examples I have provided, relatedness refers to parallels between the reported experience of my patient, the observed behavior of my son, and my own subjective experiences. More broadly, relatedness also refers to my communication with colleagues, past and present, including this written communication.

Summary

Two examples of empathic understanding were examined and found to be derivable from four elements: (1) observation of a patient; (2) observation of a child; (3) observation of the observer's experience; and (4) relatedness, a term which refers to parallels among the above three observations. This view demonstrates empathic understanding to be basically similar to other modes of understanding.

REFERENCES

Freud, S. (1900), The interpretation of dreams. *Standard Edition*, 4 & 5. London: Hogarth Press, 1953.

_____ (1905), Jokes and their relation to the unconscious. *Standard Edition*, 8:9–236, 1960.

Goldstein, K. (1954), The concept of transference in the treatment of organic and functional nervous disease. *ACTA Psychotherapeutica*, 2:334–353.

Mahler, M. S., Pine, F., & Bergman, A. (1975), *The Psychological Birth of the Human Infant: Symbiosis and Individuation*. New York: Basic Books.

Sullivan, H. S. (1953), *The Interpersonal Theory of Psychiatry*. New York: Norton.

Discussion

JOHN J. HARTMAN, Ph.D.

N Gregory Hamilton has given us two charming and sensitive examples to illustrate his concept of empathic understanding. His thesis rests importantly on the use of his own emotional experiences in coming to his conclusions. He remarks, for example, "I felt washed over by a familiar and yet unfamiliar sense of enchantment, as if I were looking at my childhood self in a mirror." And: "Again, a feeling of reminiscence and quiescence swept over me. I felt that I had remembered something visually and tactilely." Hamilton believes that these kinds of experiences distinguish empathy from other kinds of knowledge, and that relatedness is necessary to reach and disseminate this kind of knowledge.

In my opinion, it is no coincidence that Hamilton chooses examples of the interplay between his experience with his very young child and with a schizophrenic patient to discuss empathy. Greenson (1960), among others, has noted that empathy involes a temporary fusion of self- and object representations, permitting an affective experience of another person in order to gain understanding of that person. This fusion is analogous to the early mother-child relatedness. Dealing with children, whose self- and object representations have not fully consolidated, and schizophrenics, whose capacities in this area fluctuate so rapidly, enhances just this kind of experience. Hamilton's ability to tune in to the emotional experiences of his day, to allow himself to experience others affectively, and to bring out of this a coherent and helpful understanding is a credit to his ability as an observer and as a clinician.

Although Hamilton does not attempt a comprehensive definition of empathy, his comments raise several questions in my mind about the use of the term "empathy." As a term, "empathy" has evolved in such a way that it means many different things to many different people. Hamilton states: "Empathy is our vehicle for understanding one another in a meaningful way." There is an implication here that empathy is the only vehicle clinicians have for understanding others in a meaningful way, and this highlights a problem in our clinical literature. There has been a tendency to idealize empathy both as an observational tool and as a therapeutic mechanism. When empathy is idealized, even unwittingly, a polarization of empathy and insight often results. To my mind, these are inextricably connected. Hamilton might well have added a fifth element to his discussion of empathy: the use of the affective experience of relatedness with cognitive functions to bring greater cognitive understanding of the other person. What makes empathy a therapeutic concept is the *use* to which it is put in the clinical situation to enhance understanding.

I do not believe that Hamilton would disagree with this. But he fails to spell out clearly that empathic understanding is not the only kind of understanding relevant to clinical work. Guiora (1967), for example, has distinguished empathy from inference and intuition in the clinical process. Knowledge useful to the patient can also be gained from the theory of psychopathology, the patient's history, the course of treatment, the therapist's experience with similar patients, cognitive awareness of the current and past transference, free associations, and other factors which are subject more to a cognitive inferential process than empathy. In Hamilton's case, this kind of knowledge would also include infant play, Greek mythology, anatomy, and physics. Empathy may be of special value in dealing with preverbal phenomena, with more disturbed patients in general, and with all patients at particular times in their treatment. But empathic understanding is not our only vehicle for understanding patients. And empathy and understanding are not synonymous.

Indeed, the idealization of empathy, to the exclusion of other factors in the understanding of patients, poses some major methodological and clinical problems. In emphasizing his own affective experiences, Hamilton seems to use them as evidence of the correctness of his insights. His "sense of enchantment" serves not as data, but as almost conclusive evidence of the validity of his assertions. Further evidence to support his claims comes from the integration and enhanced functioning of his patient. It is not clear to me how Hamilton thinks this came about. Was it the conveying of his insight gained through empathy that helped his patient, or was it the empathic experience itself? Or could it have been some other factor, not elucidated by the data presented? My question concerns the nature of evidence in our clinical work. Particularly in working with preverbal phenomena, it is very easy to construct a version of psychic reality which may or may not correspond to that of the patient. How are we to assess the correctness of our conclusions for the particular patient or for their generalizability to other people? I claim no answer to this question, but I do urge a certain caution in using empathy exclusively to apprehend psychic reality. The persuasiveness and sensitivity of Hamilton's paper ought not to narrow our vision of this thorny problem.

In the actual clinical situation, this issue poses some further problems. The difficulty lies in distinguishing an empathic response from countertransference and identification (Beres and Arlow, 1974). Empathy is not only a mode of understanding but also a form of object relationship, as Hamilton describes in such an intriguing way. But as an object relationship, the empathic experience can color certain other clinical manifestations, or prevent them from emerging. In my experience, it is not uncommon for empathy to defend against or mask hostility and other derivatives of the agressive drive in either the patient or the therapist. There is considerable controversy about the technical handling of aggressive impulses in more disturbed patients. It is especially difficult to be empathic with patients in whom aggression seems so intense. By the same token, it may be a relief for therapist and patient alike to experience affect states of great closeness, warmth, and mutual understanding. Empathic understanding, in my view, is not an end-point but a mutual experience, which itself may become the subject of further inquiry into and understanding of the possible unconscious fantasies and impulses it may screen.

REFERENCES

Beres, D. & Arlow, J. A. (1974), Fantasy and identification in empathy. *Psychoanal. Quart.*, 43:26–50.

Greenson, R. R. (1960), Empathy and its vicissitudes. *Int. J. Psycho-Anal.*, 41:418–424.

Guiora, A. Z. (1967), Toward a systematic study of empathy. *Compr. Psychiat.*, 8:375–385.

23 Empathy, Antipathy, and Telepathy in the Analytic Process

RENÉ MAJOR, M.D., and PATRICK MILLER, M.D.

Editor's Introductory Note

JAMES THURBER described a man who had all his books translated into French because he thought they lost a great deal in the original. Aware that much is lost in translation into English, we have tried nonetheless to maintain in this paper by Drs. Major and Miller the flavor of thought in current French analytic circles.

Drs. Major and Miller review the common phenomenon of uncanny intersubjectivity, as Freud did when he considered telepathy. Thus, their ideas can be placed along the axis away from simple emotionality towards unemotional examination of thought transference. Their conceptualizations are rooted in Freud's early theories, particularly the shift from autoerotic and thing representations to object-related and word representations, with the capacity for both regression and progression along that line. A concept basic to their premise is that the unconscious of the other plays a formative role in the developing unconscious of the subject. This formative impact is evidenced

Reprinted from *Psychoanalytic Inquiry*, 1:449–470 (1981).

both developmentally and clinically. From this base, well-accepted in their psychoanalytic group, they present a study whose subject, *but not whose technique of study,* may seem magical to some readers.

In a recent paper, Major (1980) gave an account of logical processes in interpretive work of analysis and the type of communication it implied between analyst and analysand. As Freud (1923) emphasized, the analyst's work of interpreting (*Deutungsarbeit*) the analysand's unconscious paradoxically implies that the analyst surrender himself to his own unconscious mental activity; he must follow the drift of the analysand's unconscious through his own unconscious. This mode of communicating presupposes that the analyst will indulge episodically in a process of regressive reflection. This regression will not be a temporal one, but a formal and/or topographical one.

We must consider that the analyst's state of episodic, formal and/or topographic regression—a tendency towards empathic communication by the analyst with the analysand—may be increased to the point of producing telepathic phenomena, or phenomena comparable to those observed in telepathic communication. When this occurs, the analyst is usually stunned by confrontation with the "uncanny," as if something from a symbolic order suddenly entered into the real world.

When the empathic communication is combined with the antipathic communication, the latter introduces a chain of representations or signifying network. By countering the *Einfühlung* ("being with" through feeling), it makes the empathic communication more apparent. The combination of empathic and antipathic communication produces an encounter or nonencounter of two chains of signifiers: that is, an "inter-pret"[1] of representations. Alternatively, suggestive interpretation may occur by imposing a signifier belonging solely to the analyst's history or mythology.

[1] French pun on interpret and loan (*prêt* in French).

At first in the interpretive work, a thought transference (*Gedankenubertragung*) occurs that causes an unconscious wish to undergo a topographical change. The *"lieu of the Interpretand"* is an intermediary space belonging neither to the analyst's sphere of mental activity alone, nor to that of the analysand, but to a medium where the drift of the one's unconscious is caught up with the other's. This process can be compared to what we observe in the telepathic experience.

In the second phase of the interpreting process, the representations produced by thought transference undergo, as in dreams, the attraction of the scopophilic instinct. The analyst sees himself as the subject and as the object of an action suggested in the fantasy—a fantasy related to the analysand's fantasy. The analyst's state of dreamlike narcissism, if not shaken by guilt (i.e., the voice of moral conscience), is disturbed at least by the voice of the analysand. One or the other, or one *and* the other draw him away from his "dream," like the dream Freud cites of a father's guilt and the candle which falls onto his child who asks, "Father, don't you see I'm burning?" (Freud, 1900, p. 509).

Thus a third stage of the interpreting process brings the representations from the scopophilic sphere to the "acousophilic" sphere. Empathic and antipathic communication are thus relayed by the acoustic image (signifier) that can produce an "inter-pret" (a loan between). This is an interpretation of the telepathic experience that has just taken place, in which the analyst, as upon awakening from a reverie, has surrendered himself to his own unconscious mental activity.

The Telepathic Kernel of the Dream

Let us consider what could be called the *telepathic kernel* of the dream.

> A father had been watching beside his child's sickbed for days and nights on end. After the child had died, he went into the next room to lie down, but left the door open so that

> he could see from his bedroom into the room in which his child's body was laid out, with tall candles standing round him. An old man had been engaged to keep watch over it, and sat beside the body murmuring prayers. After a few hours sleep, the father had a dream that *his child was standing beside his bed, caught him by the arm and whispered to him reproachfully: 'Father, don't you see I'm burning?'* He woke up, noticed a bright glare of light from the next room, hurried into it and found that the old watchman had dropped off to sleep and that the wrappings and one of the arms of his beloved child's dead body had been burned by a lighted candle that had fallen on them [Freud, 1900, p. 509].

We tend to take for granted the fact that visual perception of the fire or olfactory perception of the smoke could have awakened the father. But in that case, we may ask ourselves why the same sensory perceptions did not awaken the old man who was supposed to be watching over the child. The watchman was indeed sitting beside the child's body. Why, at the risk of being burnt himself, does he continue to dream, blind to outside reality? Of course we must suppose, as Freud did, that the sleeping man knows that he is both sleeping and dreaming. If the bright light really is in any way responsible for bringing him out of the dream, why does it awaken one of the sleeping men rather than the other—the one who is sitting farther from the flames? What makes the difference between the two dreamers is each one's psychical reality in regard to the dead child. The words of the dream, "Father, don't you see. . . ?" seem more likely to strike the dreamer's senses through the reproachful voice of conscience, than the vision which is to dazzle him. How could the father prolong the life of his child in his dream if the *corpus delicti* itself had disappeared when he woke up?

We may wonder, without being able to decide, if someone that we see alive in his body and his words is living his own life. Or is he living like an automaton? Or has an insistent gaze managed to breathe life into a body that did not seem to contain any life or that seemed deprived of it? This is so strange that even death itself seems unable to decide.

As Freud said:

> This is a dream which has special claims upon our attention. . . . The explanation is simple enough . . . but as soon as we endeavor to penetrate more deeply into the mental process involved in dreaming, every path will end in darkness. There is no possibility of *explaining* dreams as a psychical process since to explain a thing means to trace it back to something already known . . . we shall be obliged to set a number of fresh hypotheses which touch tentatively upon the structure of the apparatus of the mind and upon the play of forces operating in it [1900, p. 511].

Can't we suppose that the child's body constitutes a psychical space covered by the father's dream process? "By inserting the unconscious between what is physical and what was previously called 'psychical,' psychoanalysis has paved the way for the assumption of such processes as telepathy" (Freud, 1933, p. 55).

A colleague told us how she had been awakened at an hour of the night when she never wakes up, by a dream that her son, asleep in another room of the apartment, was suffocating. She got up and rushed towards her child's bedroom just in time to save his life. The child had not been able to cry out. No visual, acoustic, or other signal could have awakened the mother.

As for the dream of the burning child, it must be noted that it was related to Freud by a woman who dreamt it after having heard it told by a lecturer who probably got it from the father who had originally dreamt it. "Its content made an impression on the lady and she proceeded to *re-dream* it" (1900, p. 509). Did Freud re-dream it himself and then give it to us to re-dream? We may wonder if there is dream transmission in psychoanalysis on the model of thought transmission.

What is a telepathic process, according to Freud?

> It consists in a mental act in one person instigating the same mental act in another person. What lies between these

> two mental acts may easily be a physical process into which the mental one is transformed at one end and which is transformed back once more into the same mental one at the other end. If there is such a theory of telepathy as a real process, we may suspect that, in spite of its being so hard to demonstrate, it is quite a common phenomenon [Freud, 1933, p. 55].

We think, as Freud did, that the phenomenon of thought transference is so close to telepathy that without much violence it can indeed be regarded as the same thing. It claims that mental processes in one person—ideas, emotional states, conative impulses—can be transferred to another person through empty space. This is the *intermediary space* which we spoke of: belonging neither to the analyst's sphere of mental activity alone, nor to that of the analysand, but a space where, in a three-phase process of interpretation, the drift of one's unconscious is caught up with the other's.

If the telepathic phenomenon can occur with persons in totally different spaces, even separated by a long distance (which is usually the case when a communication of a dramatic event is reported), it is not surprising that it should occur in the analytic situation with persons who are involved in a significant relationship in which they have surrendered to their unconscious mental activity.

A Foreign Body in the Mind

The following are examples from our clinical practice:

I am speaking with Gabriel, a hospitalized schizophrenic patient with a long psychiatric history. Since we have only recently met, I suggest that he tell me the chronology of his hospitalizations. He replies: "It began because I knocked over a pile of records. . . ." Exactly as he is saying this sentence, an image like a photograph or a still frame in a film fixes itself in my mind—the Boulevard St. Michel, the corner of the rue Racine, the Gibert bookshop. When I say "fixes itself," I mean that it enters like a foreign body; I don't know what to do with it; it does not seem to be connected to any associative chain. The interview goes on. After about ten minutes Gabriel comes back to the incident, "I was on the Boulevard St. Michel. I was walking by Gibert's. I stopped to look at some records. I knocked over a pile, but not on purpose, as I was turning around. . . ."

This can be contrasted with an example taken from an analytic session with a neurotic patient. That day the patient was barely lying down on the couch when I found myself thinking of nosebleeds—what would happen if my nose started bleeding and I didn't even have a handkerchief. Very quickly associations flew past: menstrual period, bisexuality, Freud and Fliess, and in my astonishment I thought, "This is really strange; nosebleeds aren't part of my personal psychosomatic baggage." Then the patient started to talk, and as he spoke, little by little, his nose became stuffed up and he spoke more and more through his nose. And when he got up from the couch, he extracted a gigantic handkerchief from his pocket and said to me, "Couldn't you give me one of those things you shove up your nose. . . ?" The session had centered on his refusal to accept the passivity implied by his position on the couch. In short, here we were involved in a signifying logic of fantasies, an 'inter-pret' (inter-loan) of signifiers, *without* experiencing a sense of the uncanny or even the sense of something strangely familiar to us. Let us say that as analysts we have learned how this kind of inter-pret of signifiers comes about. Thus, we see that this experience in a mind receptive and prepared functions in a completely different manner from the Gibert bookshop experience.

The case of the Gibert bookshop involved something like a photograph or a single frame from a film that fixed itself in the mind like a foreign body. Indeed, the telepathic experience always involves a foreign body in the mind, something that seems at the same time both intimate and strange. And we are amazed at knowing about something that usually remains unknown to us. The same amazement arises from knowledge that can be transmitted in dreams about the state of body organs that are silent in the waking state. Thus, we have come to wonder whether the archaic mode of communication which makes use of telepathy is not the product of an excess of contradictory knowledge that derives from the acquisition of language, and has this "jamming" of the archaic mode of communication made it possible to develop a relative independence of one individual from knowledge of happenings in another's body? We know that children assume at first that their parents know what they are thinking.

That is why a telepathic experience that occurs during the analytic process allows us to hypothesize that the other's body exists as a topographical locality of thought. The telepathic experience that occurs outside the analytic process carries with it a feeling of having a foreign body in the mind. Alternatively, it may convey a feeling of *an empty space*[2] (temporarily empty of representations). The empty space favors communication at a distance of knowledge that is usually kept at a distance.

The Empty Space and Its Border

We shall try to touch upon the special quality of certain countertransferential bodily experiences aroused during psychoanalytic work. These experiences of the analyst can be compared to empathy or telepathy, but they constitute a negative version of these phenomena. They concern the communication (in the literal sense of the term, i.e., the reproduction "in vivo") not of images, nor of words or groups of words, but of the phenomenon of *non*(re)presentation. During the session, the analyst experiences moments when his thoughts are shattered, his associative capacities become destroyed, and he is unable to fantasize. These moments cannot be circumvented: there is nothing; and nothing else can be done, thought, or dreamt of. These "borderline" states tend to vanish as soon as the sessions are over, and the analyst is usually left physically exhausted.

Maurice, the patient who inspired these remarks on "border-

[2]The empty space involves negative hallucination as a primary experience, a subject which cannot be developed in the limits of this paper.

line states of countertransference" was a professionally successful engineer, but his life had become more and more barren. His existence was so overrun with obsessional defense mechanisms (obsessive thoughts, magic formulas, rituals) that he felt more and more impoverished and sought help in "staying alive." Because of his monotonous voice and his unappealing story, only one detail of these interviews stands out, one of particular emotional and instinctive vividness. M. sometimes would get a sudden delightful feeling throughout his whole body when certain men (always older than he and of a higher social status) spoke to him. They had to use a certain tone of voice, and the setting had to be within a work context and without any intention of sexual seduction. For months on end, the patient came regularly to his sessions, and paid punctually. He hardly lay on the couch before he began to speak continuously until the end of the session without silence or the slightest pause. It was not possible to find the right moment to slip in a word of interruption, the only possibility was for the analyst to speak in the middle of the analysand's sentence. The unremitting discourse was also totally abstract and conceptual. No reference was made to anecdotes of daily life; there were no dreams, no fantasies.

What can be said afterwards about this mass of words? Almost nothing. Everything slips away; everything dissolves. Prey to the "borderline states" I mentioned above, for the analyst all diversionary tactics are futile. It is impossible to fantasize, dream, or think of something else because the essential (psychical?) reality experienced is that it is impossible to think (dream, fantasize, etc. . .). This has nothing to do with boredom—it is something much harder to name. If one tries to take notes during these sessions in an attempt to register or capture that which seems to slip away from any grasp, it is even worse. Rereading the notes leaves only empty words, dead words which transmit nothing of the massive experience. It is thus a matter of "coping" with this reality, which one hesitates to qualify as psychical, considering how physical it feels. Simultaneously, during most of the sessions, M. gave off an extremely strong body odor. This odorous effusion seemed to be like a somatic illustration of projective identification. It served as a primitive mode of communication, more closely related to antipathy than to empathy or telepathy.

It would take too long to give a step-by-step account of this analysis; furthermore, this is not our purpose here. Let us just say that gradually we managed to understand that what was being transmitted to the analyst was the equivalent, one could say the enactment, of an emotional experience derived from the subjective position the patient had lived through during his early childhood. A second boy, born after the early death of a sister who was the second child, M. had been entrusted at a very young age to the care of his father's sister and mother. Every Sunday brought a visit from his mother, accompanied by his father and brother. At the end of the afternoon, they departed leaving him suffering unbearably from the separation. To put an end to this pain (and being unable to kill his mother—"the cause" of it), his only alternative was to kill all psychical activity—not to think, dream, or fantasize anymore. Thus failing for words, he had had to transmit to me through the impossibility of any verbal representation, something equivalent to these psychotic moments. In struggling with these feelings (i.e., against the death threat directed at psychical life), I was to develop them ideationally and set them back into a story. All of this had to be experienced in order to be able to say something effective. To be authentic, my words had to be formed from within our shared experience, not imposed from the outside. Only then could the interpretation make reality acceptable to the patient.

It could be argued that everything I describe as a "countertransferential" bodily experience is only a manifestation of my resistance as an analyst to "hearing." That of course poses basic questions about clinical practice, what it brings into play for the analyst and what he allows himself to use in his psychical reality, including bodily responses, even primal ones. Our hypothesis in the above case is that the resistance (to the analysis and the transference), i.e., the experience of the annihilation of mental activity, would have been considered as the analyst's defense (as is generally done, for example, in saying that the analyst wants to fall asleep to escape from the analysand's unconscious aggressiveness, etc.). However, if the analyst hadn't agreed to take on this covert reality *without understanding anything about it,* including into his body itself, he would not have been able to locate it as a part of the other's reality. It would certainly have prevented this patient from being able to say one day (two-and-a-half years after the analysis began), "You know, in my childhood I was so stifled by reality that I couldn't dream. I feel that when I come here I can start to dream. And when you interrupt the session you're the one who keeps me from dreaming."

Freud always insisted that in psychoanalytic work the analyst uses his unconscious to decipher the patient's unconscious, in other words, the ideational representatives of secondary repression, possibly even the inaccessible primary repression. But it is imaginable that in the analytic situation (by analogy to the dreamer's situation) regression could go beyond this topography, that is to say, into a mythical origin predating the primary repression beyond its "border." Another way of posing this question would be: Can the instinctual that comes before any phantasmic elaboration be conceived? These questions don't seem purely speculative to us. They refer to problems of psychoanalytic practice that remain obscure, such as the involvement of the analyst's "body," especially in the course of treatment of psychotics and borderline states.

In following the concept of regression developed by Freud in *The Interpretation of Dreams*, the most fruitful path seems to be to go deeper into the notion of formal regression. In speaking of formal regression, Freud pondered the backward movement "from a complex ideational act back to the raw material of the memory traces underlying it" (1900, p. 543). This clearly concerns passage from the "psychical" to the "bodily," "which makes possible the cathexis of the system *Pcpt.* in the reverse direction starting from thoughts to the pitch of complete sensory vividness" (p. 543). Freud indicates that this process which takes place in dreams, only occurs partially during wakefulness and "never extends beyond the mnemic images" (p. 543). Nevertheless, in the analytic setting, there may be moments of formal regression that extend to the "raw material," i.e., the sensory image. But in the analytic situation this happens with two subjects who deliberately leave the borderline between themselves evenly-suspended. (This is the point of the experience.) Then wouldn't part of the analytic work (unconscious) be to reelaborate representations? This reelaboration of representations would start from the revitalization of "sensory images" that have been rediscovered through formal regression. In this case wouldn't the phenomena of empathy or telepathy be first steps on the path of reelaboration? Freud said that a dream might be described as a substitute for an infantile scene modified by being transferred onto a recent experience. The infantile scene is unable to bring about its own revival and has to be content with returning as a dream. Then wouldn't certain "sensory images" have to be content with returning, in the course of analytic work, as empathy or telepathy in the analyst! From this it can be seen how primary identification, as Freud (1923) expressed it much later in the terms of another topography, can be reactivated in the course of the psychoanalytic process: "At the very beginning, in the individual's primitive oral phase, object cathexis and identification are no doubt indistinguishable from each other"(p. 29).

It is certainly no coincidence that the text of Freud's that has appealed to us most is the one in which *the very notion of topography* is developed, "The scene of action of dreams is different from that of waking ideational life. . . what is presented to us in these words is the idea of psychical locality. I shall entirely disregard the fact that the mental apparatus with which we are here concerned is also known to us in the form of an anatomical preparation. And I shall carefully avoid the temptation to determine psychical locality in any anatomical fashion" (1900 p. 536). Anatomy is disregarded, but the body remains in its sensory vividness. Freud often indicates to us that the densest, most opaque part of the dream, that which most resists meaning, is exactly the part which carries the most truth for the dreaming subject. The now famous metaphor that came to him to explain it—the dream's navel—is both bodily and "fleshly" suggestive of the relationship between one flesh and another. The relationship between one flesh and another is precisely that which is unknown to us, but which perhaps is reactivated during the psychoanalytic experience.

Telepathy as a Common Phenomenon

Freud said:

> If there is such a theory as telepathy as a real process, we may suspect that, in spite of its being so hard to demonstrate, it is quite a common phenomenon. A short time ago Dorothy Burlingham, a trustworthy witness, in a paper on child analysis and the mother (1932) published some observations which, if they can be confirmed, would be bound to put an end to the remaining doubts on the reality of thought-transference. She made use of the situation, no longer a rare one, in which a mother and child are simultaneously in analysis, and reported some remarkable events such as the following. One day the mother spoke during her analytic session of a gold coin that had played a particular part in one of the scenes of her childhood. Immediately afterwards, after she had returned home, her little boy, about ten years old, came to her room and brought her a gold coin which he asked her to keep for him. She asked him in astonishment where he had got it from. He had been given it on his birthday; but his birthday had been several months earlier and there was no reason why the child should have remembered the gold coin precisely then. The mother reported the occurrence to the child's analyst and asked her to find out from the child the reason for his action. But the child's analysis threw no light on the matter; the action had forced its way that day into the child's life like a foreign body. A few weeks

> later the mother was sitting at her writing-desk to write down, as she had been told to do, an account of the experience, when in came the boy and asked for the gold coin back, as he wanted to take it with him to show in his analytic session. Once again the child's analysis could discover no explanation of his wish [1933, p. 56].

The reader will have noticed that Freud, in relating the experience told by Dorothy Burlingham, uses the words "foreign body"—"The child's analysis threw no light on the matter; the action had forced its way that day into the child's life like a foreign body." To continue the parallel between our ideas and those of Freud we might ask about the lack of explanation to this day of aspects of Freudian psychoanalysis and of the enigmatic sentence used by Freud to end his lecture, "And this brings us back to psychoanalysis, which was what we started out from" (1933, p. 56).

The analytic situation seems particularly suited for receiving telepathic messages, "that kind of psychical counterpart to wireless telegraphy" (Freud, 1933, p. 36). We can contrast that instinctual immediacy of empathic communication to the immediacy, at a distance, of telepathic communication. Paradoxically, empathic communication occurs mostly in analysis when the other is at a distance from his own unconscious (as a means of rediscovering identification through a network of signifiers), while telepathic communication occurs mostly in psychotic states where the analysand seems to have more direct access to the analyst's unconscious.[3]

Most of the dreams of a woman one of us had in analysis contained elements representing events that happened at the same time in her analyst's life. He had every reason to believe that his analysand had no way of knowing of the existence of these real life events. No information gained, either during the analysis or after, was able to refute the conclusion that the pa-

[3]There are many incidences of thought transference in Beatrice's revival of a lost part of her history in *Rêver l'autre* by René Major, (1977).

tient had astonishing knowledge in her dreams, and *only* in her dreams. It is worth noting that the patient did not want to dream because what she had seen in her dreams at night would be confirmed by events in her own daily life. Although the patient presented a significant psychotic nucleus, she was a fairly well adapted, highly trained professional person. Although her dreams would be pertinent to the subject of this paper they contain confidential material concerning the analysand's life as well as the analyst's, and therefore cannot be used at this time.

Thought Transference and Father Transference

In the case of Herr P.,[4] alias von Vorsicht (Mr. Foresight), related to us by Freud (1933), we can clearly see all the indiscretions in the analyst's maintaining his and the patient's personal privacy. Recognition of these kinds of indiscretions allows us to comprehend how events in the analyst's life may appear in the patient's dreams. In Freud's case, the indiscretions of information revealed to Herr P. go from David Forsyth (who arrives from London and is supposed to replace Herr P. in analysis with Freud), to Ernest Jones (who met Herr P., knows Forsyth, and rejects telepathy as a foreign body in psychoanalysis), to Anton von Freund (the eminent Hungarian psychoanalyst who lives in the same hotel as Herr P. and whom Freud visits and tells his patient about). This patient, as a foreign body in Freud's mind, sees what is going on inside, and has a foresight like the virgin who nicknames him "von Vorsicht." There is virgin territory, empty space, in this analysis. "I had long before proposed our stopping the treatment, but he has wished to continue it, evidently because he felt comfortable in a well-tempered father-transference to me" (p. 48). What is a well-

[4]In order to follow the argument presented here, it would be useful for the reader to refamiliarize himself with Lecture 30 of the *New Introductory Lectures,* entitled "Dreams and Occultism" (Freud, 1933), as well as Freud's other writings on telepathy (1921, 1922).

tempered father transference? "His case did not promise any therapeutic success" (Freud, 1933, p. 48). Is there anything that links thought divination or thought betrayal (*Gedanken erraten, Gedanken verraten*) in this case to unanalyzability? Freud further said, "I shall have to suppress much that would have greatly increased the convincing force of the observation. It is an example in which the fact came clearly to light and did not need to be developed by analysis" (p. 47).

Does this mean that telepathy or teleanalysis could replace psychoanalysis? And what is the relationship between thought transference and father transference? Or mother transference? Is it a relationship that nourishes father transference and mother transference or a relationship which invalidates them—a relationship of non-relationship? In this case, thought transference, both in the direction analyst → analysand as well as in the other direction, analysand → analyst, could well be the keystone of the analysis of *power* in psychoanalysis. In an editor's note, Strachey writes, "This case is the one which should have been the 'third case' to be included in 'psychoanalysis and telepathy.' The circumstances of its omission were explained by Freud in the paper... as was indicated there, the original draft has survived.... It should be added, however, that since that volume of the Standard Edition was published the manuscript has once again unaccountably disappeared" (1933, pp. 47–48).

We have grounds for believing that because of telepathy, a letter or a text doesn't reach its destination. Jones (1957) suggests that telepathy must be rejected as a foreign body in psychoanalysis so that sender and receiver may stay in the same circuit of father transference; thus thought transference may always be linked to the father's thought as father of thought. But what is the "foreign body" in the head of psychoanalysis (Jones was then president of the International Psychoanalytic Association), if not political considerations? It is said and believed that the political is foreign to psychoanalysis.

It is undoubtedly not a coincidence either that the correspondence between Freud and Ferenczi which most closely deals with the question of telepathy has not yet reached its destination—the reader. After so many years, it still remains a hidden correspondence.[5] Perhaps it would tell us something about the contents of the experiments Freud alludes to in a letter to Jones on March 15, 1925: "Ferenczi was here recently on a Sunday. The three of us [Anna Freud was the third] carried out experiments with thought transference." (Who had those two been analyzed by?) "They were remarkably good, particularly those in which I played the medium and then analyzed my associations. The matter is becoming urgent for us" (1957, p. 393).

"On the day that letter was written," writes Jones as if he had had telepathic knowledge of it (the kind which is not unusual when you've been on the same couch), "I [Jones] had sent a circular, one in which the following passage occurred":

> I cannot share Ferenczi's optimism about telepathy being used as objective proof of the contentions of psycho-analysis. On the contrary, in England at least, a great part of the opposition to psycho-analysis is based on the imaginary idea that psycho-analysis operates with agents ("the psyche") which are supposed to be independent of the body. The prejudice against telepathy is also so strong that any mixture of the two subjects could have only one effect, that of delaying the assimilation of psycho-analysis. As the latter aim is the one nearest to Professor's heart, I find it comprehensible that he should personally defer any interest he may have in telepathy and I can only welcome his decision. At the same time, this is a sacrifice we cannot expect from all other psychoanalysts, but we can reasonably hope that anyone wishing to write on telepathy will make it clear that he does so independently of psycho-analysis and does not wish to infer that the truth of one stands or falls by the truth of the other.

[5]Six letters from the correspondence between Sigmund Freud and Sandor Ferenczi have recently been published in *Zur Psychoanalyse der Objekt-Beziehungen* (Jappe and Nedelmann 1980). In a footnote it says that, "the legatees do not intend to publish other abstracts of that correspondence in a foreseen future" (p. 140).

> This would be a simple act of justice to those psycho-analysts who, like myself, are far from convinced of the truth of telepathy, and who cannot therefore welcome the possibility of their convictions about psycho-analysis becoming involved with something else with which they do not agree. I should take up the same standpoint against any entanglement with any variety of philosophy, politics, etc. [p. 393].

Jones' letter apparently had some effect, for when Ferenczi in that same week told Freud he would like to give an account of his telepathic experiments to the next Congress, the Hamburg Conference of 1925[6], Freud wrote back:

> I advise against it. Don't do it. Your experiments are certainly not any more striking or free from doubt than those that have been incorporated in the literature, which so far have not received credence. The only new thing in your lecture would be the personal element and the personal influence that must radiate from it. By it you would be throwing a bomb into the psychoanalytical house which would be certain to explode. Surely we agree in not wanting to hasten this perhaps unavoidable disturbance in our development [pp. 393–394].

In a circular letter Freud wrote:

> Our friend Jones seems to me to be too unhappy about the sensation that my conversion to telepathy has made in English periodicals. He will recollect how near to such a conversion I came in the communication I had the occasion to make during our Harz travels. Considerations of external policy since that time held me back long enough, but finally one must show one's colors and need bother about the scandal this time as little as on earlier, perhaps still more important occasions [p. 394].

[6]The Congress which promoted the rules for training analysis and psychoanalytic transmission. Cf. Eitingon's report to the Business Meeting (authors' note).

Hereupon Jones wrote to Freud, saying among other things:

> You also forget sometimes in what a special position you are personally. When many things pass under the name of psycho-analysis our answer to inquirers is 'psycho-analysis is Freud,' so now the statement that psycho-analysis leads logically to telepathy, etc., is more difficult to meet. In your private political opinions you might be a Bolshevist, but you would not help the spread of psycho-analysis by announcing it. So when 'considerations of external policy' kept you silent before I do not know how the situation should have changed in this respect [p. 395].

In answer to Jones, Freud wrote:

> I am extremely sorry that my utterance about telepathy should have plunged you into fresh difficulties. But it is really hard not to offend English susceptibilities. . . . I have no prospect of pacifying public opinion in England, but I should like at least to explain to you my apparent inconsistency in the matter of telepathy. You remember how I had already at the time of our Harz travels expressed a favorable prejudice towards telepathy. But there seemed no need to do so publicly, my own conviction was not very strong, and the diplomatic consideration of guarding psychoanalysis from any approach to occultism easily gained the upper hand. Now the revising of the *Interpretation of Dreams* for the *Collected Edition* was a spur to reconsider the problem of telepathy. Moreover my own experiences through tests I made with Ferenczi and my daughter won such a convincing force for me that the diplomatic considerations on the other side had to give way. I was once more faced with a case where on a reduced scale I had to repeat the great experiment of my life: namely, to proclaim a conviction without taking into account any echo from the outer world. So then it was unavoidable. When anyone adduces my fall into sin, just answer him calmly that con-

version to telepathy is my private affair like my Jewishness, my passion for smoking and many other things, and that the theme of telepathy is in essence alien to psychoanalysis [pp. 395–396].

The Kernel of Truth and the Other as a Foreign Body for Narcissism

Freud maintained that telepathy might be the kernel of truth in the obscure field of occultism. We have quoted these excerpts from the Freud correspondence with Jones to show that "power" in the psychoanalytic movement itself was challenged by the question of telepathy. We believe that the telepathic kernel of dreams challenges the analyst's power, the "subject supposed to know," because it assumes the analysis of the modes of communication of knowledge. The kernel of truth in thought transference challenges the very notion of transference. The kernel of suggestion in transference is based upon a *lack* of knowledge of unconscious thought transmission.

During the same year (1921) in which Freud wrote "Psychoanalysis and Telepathy" (the text that was only published after his death), he was also interested in group psychology and in the question of empathy: "another suspicion may tell us that we are far from having exhausted the problem of identification, and that we are faced by the process which psychology calls 'empathy' (*Einfühlung*) and which plays the largest part in our understanding of what is inherently foreign to our Ego in other people" (p. 108).

The other, when experienced as a foreign body for the ego, thus could be grasped only by a process of *empathy* in which an *immediate passage is made into the other*, crossing a space empty of representations related to the paternal or maternal complex. This empathic relationship is located short of, or beyond, transference. It implies passage through the reflexive mode of the verb and the instinct: to see oneself and hear oneself in the other, to transfer oneself into the other (*Sich einfühlen in*). This is how we understand the question that presented itself to Freud in *Group Psychology and the Analysis of the Ego* (1921). How, indeed, did the original Narcissus come to *alter himself,* to invent himself as an object? Is it not by empathy, and also by antipathy —removing himself from the place of his entrancement, by an entrancement within himself of his love and hate?

Freud said that personal (or egotistical) instincts are transformed into social instincts when they are combined with erotic components. This transformation to social instincts is the same as Narcissus' move to the object by combining egotistical instincts with erotic components. But how in this move does the other become constituted as one's father or mother? We believe that it is the naming process that constitutes the other as father or mother, where the father or mother is constituted "in the possessive." By maintaining in this naming process a de-naming process, the possibility is offered for a link beyond the mother[7] and beyond the father in the possessive (as psychic entities) to the outside others. Thought transference short-circuits communication by reference to the father's thought system. And if the unconscious exists because of the requirements of the social collective—which affirms something entirely different from a collective unconscious—dreams are the mind's most asocial product inside the "socius." Accordingly, it is hardly astonishing that dreams, especially the navel of dreams, disregard identifications that usually jam all telepathic communication.

It is also in this sense that we understand that Freud, starting from the observation of breaks and gaps in the "natural" continuity of human groups, formed the hypothesis of a social instinct (*soziale trieb*). Freud wondered if the social instinct is primary, or if it originates in a restricted group such as the family. This question challenges nothing less than the essential relationship of the child to its parents. Is it constituted by the law of the father? Or can we suppose that the father or the mother—as objects—are created when love or hate recede into the subject?

The analytic social tie is only formed against a background

[7]The French for beyond the mother is *outre-mère* and in French it associates to *outremer*, meaning overseas.

of *non*relationship—of nonoccurrence of any tie in an asocial context. Woven of all social ties, composed of sexual instincts that are or aren't inhibited in terms of aim, the analytic tie—the tie which unties, anarchic in its essence—will untie all these ties by untying itself. In order to do so, analytic transference must be based on a relationship of nonrelationship. This is what the analytic situation activates. But it is the dream's umbilical cord that is tied to the unknown, up to the point where the unknown becomes an event for the unconscious. What binds the dimension of the other lies in the dream's navel. It is this umbilical knot that reopens for the subject a tie, a communication, through the chain of unconscious representations. By inserting the unconscious between the physical and the psychical, we learn to know that we already knew what we thought we did not know.

REFERENCES

Freud, S. (1900), The interpretation of dreams. Standard Edition, 4 & 5. London: Hogarth Press, 1953.

_____ (1921a), Group psychology and the analysis of the ego. *Standard Edition,* 18:65–143. London: Hogarth Press, 1955.

_____ (1921b), Psycho-analysis and telepathy. *Standard Edition,* 18:175–194. London: Hogarth Press, 1941.

_____ (1922), Dreams and telepathy. *Standard Edition,* 18:195–220. London: Hogarth Press, 1955.

_____ (1923), The ego and the id. *Standard Edition,* 19:12–63. London: Hogarth Press, 1961.

_____ (1933), New introductory lectures on psycho-analysis: Dreams and occultism. *Standard Edition,* 22:31–56. London: Hogarth Press, 1964.

Jappe, G. & Nedelmann, C. (1980), *Zur Psychoanalyse der Objekt-Beziehungen.* Vienna: Frommann Hollzboog.

Jones, E. (1957), *The Life and Work of Sigmund Freud,* Vol. 3. New York: Basic Books.

Major, R. (1977), *Rêver l'autre.* Paris: Aubier Montaigne.

_____ (1980), The logical process of interpretation. *Internat. Rev. Psycho-Anal.,* 7:397–403.

Roustang, F. (1983), *Psychoanalysis Never Lets Go.* Baltimore, MD: Johns Hopkins University Press.

Discussion

STANLEY A. LEAVY, M.D.

In considering René Major and Patrick Miller's remarks, one must remember that they write against a background of Lacanian discourse that pervades all aspects of contemporary Parisian psychoanalytic thought—either by sympathy or antipathy, one might say. Summarizing in a language more familiar to English-speaking analysts may be of help.

Major and Miller propose that the analyst's regression in following the unconscious stream of the patient's thoughts, while aiming at empathy, may also produce telepathic phenomena. In all interpretive work, they believe, an intermediary space exists, where the drift of one unconscious is caught up with that of another. The analyst then sees himself (or herself) as the subject of the analysand's fantasy. Finally, these representations appear as signifying words—as acoustic images shared by the two.

In citing the dream of the burning child reported by Freud (1900), Major and Miller point to Freud's (1933) comment that the unconscious, as a state between the physical and the psychic, makes telepathy understandable. The body of another person is a psychic sphere open to the empathic process. Mental processes can be transferred through the intermediary space in which the interpretive work takes place. Examples are given of visual images in the analyst's mind that appear in the patient's associations. In other situations, an exchange of fantasies seems to take place. The telepathic experience involves a kind of "foreign body in the mind," deriving from an archaic mode of communication, normally "jammed" by language. Another's body becomes a topographic locality of thought.

According to Major and Miller, in certain countertransference states of antipathy (the opposite or, rather, complement of empathy), the analyst's mind is in a state of nonrepresentation. In the example of the severely obsessional patient, the unremitting monotony of his thoughts produced in the analyst the same absence of psychic activity that the patient had come to use defensively ever since his childhood. This, too, is a state in which a parallel experience occurs in both patient and analyst.

Is it possible, the authors ask, that the regression in the analyst may go back to a mythical origin, predating primary repression, when "the instinctual that comes before any phantasmic elaboration" might be conceived? This would amount to a passage from the psychic to the physical. Both empathy and telepathy are steps toward psychic re-elaboration, proceeding from the deep quasi-umbilical relationship that is reactivated during analysis. "Paradoxically," Major and Miller note, "empathic communication occurs mostly in analysis when the other is at a distance from his own unconscious . . . while telepathic communication occurs mostly in psychotic states where the analysand seems to have more direct access to the analyst's unconscious."

If telepathy occurs, could it replace psychoanalysis, by substituting transfer of thought for the transference? Such a consideration, the authors indicate—along with the dangerous prejudices against analysis already rampant—prompted Jones and Freud to keep the subject quiet. It was, after all, a question of power, for the telepathic kernel of dreams challenges the analyst's power to interpret through knowledge. If there is a passage from one mind to another across "a space empty of representations related to the paternal or maternal complex" (i.e., transference), then "the empathic relationship is located short of, or beyond, transference." Thought transference, Major and Miller explain, communicates by bypassing the signifying process that is instituted at the time the infant acquires the names of father and mother as signifiers. Transference and dreams thus foster a return to the intermediate space between the physical and the psychic.

I don't suppose that anyone will read Major and Miller's article without recollecting instances of thought transference or even discovering such an instance in an ongoing analysis. That phenomenon itself ought to give us pause, for it suggests one of two possibilities: we may ordinarily overlook instances of telepathic communication because of resistances to or rationalizations of them, or when they do occur, they assume the guise of wish fulfillments. The whole matter can easily be dismissed if we remain strict empiricists and show that telepathy does not withstand statistical scrutiny. After all, it is hardly remarkable that of all the innumerable isolated thoughts in the minds of the patient and the analyst, an occasional one is matched in the other. The trouble with strict empiricism, however, is that if we apply it to psychoanalysis in general—and not just to this troublesome element—not many of our interpretations will stand up. So, although we have to allow for the possibility that it is all happenstance, we ought to continue proposing other explanations.

Major and Miller postulate a "space" in which the junction of minds takes place. They draw on Freud's statement: "What lies between these two mental acts may easily be a physical process into which the mental one is transformed at one end and which is transformed back once more into the same mental one at the other end" (1933, p. 55). We might represent it thus:

Mental Act 1 → Physical Process → Mental Act 2

The process seems analogous to the change in state when a sound, say, is transformed at the transmitter into an electronic state, and then retransformed into an acoustic state by the receiver. Yet this analogy is misleading because it is wholly physical. The only way to fit it to our use would be to insist that mental processes are also essentially physical, in which case I do not see why we call it *psycho*analysis.

Now, Major and Miller do not always use the word "space" in this obviously empirical fashion. A space in which "the drift of one unconscious is caught up with that of another" is probably a phenomenological space—that is, the largely preconsciously conceived distance between the participants in the dialogue. This is a very important space, and we know from experience how it may change in extent, quality, and content without any alteration in the natural surroundings. But how can anything at all, conscious or unconscious, pass across it? Unless we start out by postulating the telepathic communication we are trying to explain, it must be through some kind of signification, primarily through spoken words. Usually we do not have much trouble admitting this signification when we are on the patient's "wavelength"—when we and the patient come from different starting places of thought to a set of common ideas. The fact that some people are better at this than others is as mysterious as any other talent, but no more so. In such cases of empathy, we can usually fairly well identify the set of signifiers that tipped us off in the right direction. It is when we come to telepathy that we get into trouble, and that, too, suggests something worth thinking about: we may be responding to signifiers that are hidden rather than manifest—like scrambled messages over the telephone wires.

I do not have answers to my own questions, but an instance out of my clinical experience may be enlightening. In the beginning of a session, Mr. A., a young man with no psychotic organization, expressed his sadness and depression—at first around the anniversary of the death of his father many years before (which had become vividly revived in the transference) and then around a rejection he had recently suffered at the hands of some trusted superiors. Something he said made me wonder aloud whether he did not expect the same treatment from me. He saw the point but did not say anything further about it. At this time a stray thought entered my mind, from a concern of mine that had just preceded the hour. It went like this: "I might have to write something in French on the typewriter, which is always a nuisance because of the accents. And what *is* the French word for typewriter? Is it *machine à écrire? La machine?* Of course, the Italian is *la macchina*, the Latin *machina* (fem.) as in *deus ex machina.*"

At this juncture I became conscious of my lapse of attention and returned to Mr. A., who continued to unfold the story of his recent disappointment. Five minutes later he was still on the subject, but he then mentioned that one of the trusted elders might have offered a solution to the problem that had so troubled him. And that, he said, "would be a *deus ex machina.*"

Of course the voicing of the Latin phrase might have been a coincidence, but some other considerations are noteworthy. I do not recall that Mr. A. had ever before used a Latin word, or any foreign word, in my presence, although it is possible that he knew of my interest in languages. Still, nothing whatever that I said aloud to him in the session could have given him a cue for the phrase. I had not betrayed my lapse of attention by anything I said, nor do I think, on recollection, that I was blatantly silent, so to speak, when I ought to have said something. Barring coincidence then, I suggest the following explanation: I empathically heard Mr. A.'s complaint as a transferential allusion—*I*, too, might fail him; indeed, as a much older man, I was almost sure to do so by dying at some time (which we had discussed in earlier sessions). Then, with my lapse of attention, I *did* behave like the superiors who had not kept their promise to him. Here I have to assume that I did give him some cue of my preoccupation, although I cannot remember it. Or perhaps I was not *sym*pathetic enough at this depressed moment. At all events, I was not being father (*deus*), and that was called for. Another transference figure from outside the analysis had suggested a solution.

This explanation is incomplete, however, unless we suppose that the phrase I had formed in my mind and not uttered (but which was after all not entirely out of tune with what my patient wanted of me) was somehow "overheard" by Mr. A. And that in its repeated form, it asked, "Why are you, too, ignoring me just when I need you?"

Still, my explanation remains defective. What I have done is to surmise what might have been *signified* by the signifier *deus ex machina* (the missing father, missing at the anniversary of his death, missing in the neglect from the father-figures, missing in the transference). But I have not accounted for the *choice* of the signifier. Perhaps some scrambling of phonemes occurred, which, urged by the exigencies of the situation, formed in the patient the gestalt that had originated in me. Yet that is pure speculation.

It is no purer, however, than that of Major and Miller, who effectively lean on a physical transmission of ideas at a distance. They have imagined what this *might* be like, and quite persuasively—up to the point of guessing at what the actual physics of the event might be. Here they are wisely silent. May it not be that telepathic communication, if it exists, is one of many subjects that are of interest to psychoanalysis but have to be studied outside of psychoanalysis?

REFERENCES

Freud, S. (1900), The interpretation of dreams. *Standard Edition*, 4 & 5. London: Hogarth Press, 1953.

——— (1933), New introductory lectures on psycho-analysis: Dreams and occultism. *Standard Edition*, 22:31–56. London: Hogarth Press, 1964.

Noise: A Reply

RENÉ MAJOR, M.D., and PATRICK MILLER, M.D.

FIRST OF ALL, a word about the Editor's Introductory Note to our article on "Empathy, Antipathy, and Telepathy in the Analytic Process." It states: "A concept basic to their premise is that the unconscious of the other plays a formative role in the developing unconscious of the subject." This assertion—if we exclude the questionable notion of a "developing unconscious"—ensues directly from the Freudian conception of language learning, in which the child's feeling that others have "made" speech in him (or her) and, with it, thoughts is indeed justified.[1] Need we add that infantile dialect, within which lie the fantasies of the unconscious, seizes onto the parents' unconscious, and that thought at the outset is unconscious? One has only to read Freud's (1920) observations on little Ernst to be convinced. If such a tendency did not already exist, it would be difficult to understand that in the analytic situation "the drift of one unconscious is caught up with that of another" (Freud, 1923).

"This base," explains the Editor's Introductory Note, is "well-accepted in their psychoanalytic group"—suggesting that *in our group* (in the U.S.) this is not "well-accepted." So be it. Undoubtedly, this is repayment in kind for prejudices just as firmly rooted in France concerning the theoretical bases of what the "American way" of psycho-

---

"Noise," a bilingual signifier, serves as question to be added to the debate. (In French, *chercher noise à quelqu'un* means to pick a quarrel with someone.)

[1]See Freud's remarks on the occasion of Tausk's presentation of "The Influencing Machine" (1919).

analysis is. In order to dispel any misunderstanding, we must clarify our view. The American editor (with the best of intentions, we have no doubt) warns the American reader that across the ocean strange things can be heard: noises about the big noise (Lacan). This caveat is reiterated by Stanley Leavy: "In considering René Major and Patrick Miller's remarks, one must remember that they write against a background of Lacanian discourse." Let us spell this out. Neither of us has ever belonged to Lacan's school, although we have read Lacan as we have read Freud (and Ferenczi, Klein, Winnicott, Waelder, Hartmann, Kris, Loewenstein, Kohut, Kernberg, and so on).

The Editor's Introductory Note (we must insist!) concludes: "they present a study whose subject, *but not whose technique of study*, may seem magical to some readers." The word "magical" provides an opportunity for us to quote Lacan: "Magic is the truth as cause in its aspect of efficient cause" (1966, p. 871; our translation). This assertion is demonstrated in the use of the performative (see Austin, 1962). If the chairman of a meeting says, "I declare this meeting open," the meeting is in fact opened by these words. What this implies is that these words are pronounced by someone with the necessary authority. And this brings us back to transference. Going beyond the opposition between true or false statements and those which are acts in themselves, any statement (and analytic practice confirms this) tends to achieve an unconscious effect on the other (person).

We do not wish to pick a quarrel with (*chercher noise à*) the American editor, but if he thinks the American reader believes that we (the French authors) believe in something the American reader doesn't believe in, he may also think the French reader believes that the American author believes in something else that the French reader doesn't believe in. All this is to say that we thought we could get out of the alternative belief or nonbelief in telepathy. Just like the question of belief in the unconscious. We can say that God is unconscious. That doesn't mean we believe in God. But the names "God," "unconscious," and "telepathy" exist, and they must signify something. We contend it is difficult to imagine a theory of the unconscious without a theory of telepathy. In any case, this question is raised directly by Freud.

The question of belief or nonbelief in telepathy is interesting for another reason. It runs through the history of the psychoanalytic movement. Jones believes that he doesn't believe in it, or that one shouldn't. Ferenczi believes that he believes in it, or would like to be believed by Jones, who will pass him off as crazy. It is a crazy story, passed on from generation to generation (by tele- "pathy"?), and it continues to haunt psychoanalytic thought. Will it be said that people do not have the same (theoretical) ghosts in England as in Hungary? As for Freud, we must say that he is willing to analyze phenomena relating to what is called "telepathy" but is worried that this will cast doubt on his theory of dreams. He hesitates. "I am afraid," he writes to Ferenczi, "that you are in the process of discovering something important"—nothing less than a "psychogenesis of physics" (unpublished). If Freud had a second life to live, this is the question he would tackle. In the theoretical field, this debate also covers the question of the preeminence of fantasy or trauma (a long-term fight between Freud and Ferenczi for which no surrender has been recorded).

Coupled concepts, such as fantasy and reality, chance and determinism, belong to an old paradigm—to use Kuhn's (1970) idea—within which certain issues have been able to develop. Today, microphysics and molecular biology force us to question these coupled concepts. A new paradigm emerges, which refuses to declare apparently impertinent[2] questions off-limits. This is why we find it difficult to follow Leavy when he suggests that "telepathic communication, if it exists, is one of many subjects that are of interest to psychoanalysis but have to be studied outside of psychoanalysis." Especially because this new paradigm was generated by psychoanalysis. Indeed, the questions of inside and outside, of reduplication of the outside inside the subject, of precession of judgment of attribution over judgment of existence (as set out by Freud [1925]), introduce a topology in which the object must be inserted into the subject's division and the subject is internally excluded from its object. So that the only subject considered by psychoanalysis is the subject of science.[3]

Discontinuities in the psychic function can assume several forms. But it is Freud's anticipatory vision that maintains: "By inserting the unconscious between what is physical and what was previously called 'psychical', psycho-analysis has paved the way for the assumption of such processes as telepathy" (1933, p. 55). The external variables are precisely the coordinates of *space* and *time*. According to primary processes, communication brings into play a new paradigm of continuities and discontinuities in space and time. This is what is actually meant by so-called telepathic communication. Can't these conjectural variables be calculated exactly? If the production of occurrences can be correlated to the production of speech, it is not unreasonable to hypothesize that self-organizing systems that store up variable data on speech may establish a closer link between these data and certain

---

[2]Both uses of the word are intended here: irreverent *and* irrelevant.

[3]It is true that Lacan emphasized this. Rightly so, we think.

occurrences. The correlation of perceptive values with an architecture of molecules would go through a multiple determination of the signifier. And here we encounter the *deus* or the unconscious *ex machina*. On the "other stage,"[4] the dream stage, the machine directs the director.

It is precisely on this question that we find Leavy conjecturing on what might be signified by the signifier *deus ex machina*, exchanged by his patient and himself. Does the subject choose the signifier, or does the signifier produce the effects of fading or unfading on a subject? In the latter case, if we hypothesize precession of the signifier or the unconscious representative, the effect of signification is not to be found in the signified (which would fall into the pairing of the concepts inside/outside, fantasy/reality, signifier/signified) but in the substitution of one signifier for another. This is also the question *outside* psychoanalysis as well as *in* psychoanalysis.

It is difficult for us to conceive of well-established limits to what is outside and inside psychoanalysis. Especially now that the boundaries formerly set up around the so-called natural sciences and the so-called social sciences are falling away (one has only to raise the question of the social status of physics or biology and, inversely, of the biophysical roots of socio-politico-psychoanalysis). The subject of knowledge is not the reflection of natural or psychic laws. Knowledge carries with it a multitude of paradigms, conceptions, theories. The same theory can be scientific or dogmatic. Freudian theory is a good example of this. Since it hasn't given itself the means to reflect on, to question itself, it is all the more subject to the hazards of "foreign affairs." And in the course of its history it has stumbled against, among other things, a theory of telepathy. It is this problem that interests us, and it was not brought up in either the editor's or Leavy's discussion—undoubtedly because of fascination with or the rejection of the phenomenon, and the dichotomy constantly set up between the analytic institution and the institutionalization of session protocol. For us, the same appeals for subservience, the same power stakes, show up in both.

References to empiricism (which, let us not forget, is a philosophy) or calls, like Simon's (1981), to "let me see the evidence" (have you ever seen the unconscious?) fail to move us. And how, then, could we believe that the occurrence in analysis of such-and-such unexplained phenomenon necessarily confirmed an unresolved conflict in the therapist, Beres and Arlow (1974) suggest. Let's be serious. Might the range of generalization of the Oedipus complex be limited to Freud's

[4]In French, *scène* signifies both "scene" and "stage."

own oedipal conflict? That the occurrence of "telepathic-type phenomena" between patient and analyst is connected to "some important unresolved communicative issue that is not being apprehended by ordinary means," as Simon emphasizes, simply means that when things cannot be said one way they are said another way. By other means. Must we refuse to examine those other means of communication? On whose behalf? On behalf of a theory of transference established as dogma?

Moreover, Simon himself begins to have doubts. Although he states: "There must be a certain tension . . . between the expectation that empathic communication can succeed and the fear that it may not," he continues: "I am uncertain whether such a tension would inevitably represent a repetition of a previously existing pattern in the patient's life, or whether it might arise as a function of the unique and novel nature of the psychoanalytic relationship." It is just this question that preoccupied us when we wondered how the analytic tie is liable to untie all preexisting ties and to untie itself. We had to assume that analytic transference is based, outside of repetition and ordinary means of communication, on *a relationship of nonrelation* (in *time* and *space*, precisely). This entails some consequences: from the standpoint of unconscious logic, children create parents just as parents create children, and the analysand "makes" the analyst as much as the analyst "makes" the analysand. Between them, there is always the Other,[5] to whom the discourse is addressed. How else can we imagine a way out of the didactic repetition of "the well-tempered father-transference?"

This is, indeed, a question of method for us, "a technique of study"—which is not magic at all.

REFERENCES

Austin, J. L. (1962), *How to Do Things with Words*. New York: Oxford University Press.

Beres, D. & Arlow, J. (1974), Fantasy and identification in empathy. *Psychoanal. Quart.*, 43:26–50.

Freud, S. (1896), Letter 52 in: Extracts from the Fliess papers. *Standard Edition*, 1:239. London: Hogarth Press, 1966.

——— (1920), Beyond the pleasure principle. *Standard Edition*, 18:3–64. London: Hogarth Press, 1955.

[5]Cf. Freud's *der Andere*, in a letter to Fliess (1896, p. 239).

——— (1923), Two encyclopaedia articles. *Standard Edition,* 18:235–259. London: Hogarth Press, 1955.

——— (1925), Negation. *Standard Edition,* 19:235–239. London: Hogarth Press, 1961.

——— (1933), New introductory lectures on psycho-analysis. *Standard Edition*, 22:3–182. London: Hogarth Press, 1964.

Kuhn, T. S. (1970), *The Structure of Scientific Revolutions*. Chicago: University of Chicago Press.

Simon, B. (1981), Confluence of visual image between patient and analyst: Communication of failed communication. *Psychoanal. Inquiry*, 1:471–488. Reprinted here as Chapter 24.

24 Confluence of Visual Image Between Patient and Analyst: Communication of Failed Communication

BENNETT SIMON, M.D.

IN THE COURSE of an analytic hour, early in the second year of analysis, a rather odd image came to my mind; a few minutes later, my patient was envisioning a strikingly similar image (though with some striking differences as well). Each image would have been worthy of comment in its own right, but the confluence of the two was indeed startling. In the course of further analysis and self-analysis, it became clear that this incident indicated a state of silent, deep empathic communication between my patient and myself. However, it also became clear that what we were communicating included statements of reproach, isolation and misunderstanding. In short, while being in close touch via this imagistic level of communication, we were also each caught up in autistic reverie—a meditation on loneliness.

First, I shall present an account of the session. Then I shall offer what I came to understand about this incident during the subsequent few weeks. What emerged from both the immediate

Reprinted from *Psychoanalytic Inquiry*, 1:471–488 (1981). An earlier version of this paper was presented at the 1980 Cambridge Hospital Psychotherapy Symposium, "Communication in Psychotherapy." I wish to thank Dr. Joseph Lichtenberg for his attentive comments on that version.

and the more delayed reflections was a crystallization of previously unorganized thoughts and impressions about some core issues in the patient's development and their transference manifestations. I will also include, though not as the central part of my discussion, some further insights about the patient that emerged much later, at the time of reviewing and writing this material.

Finally, I will locate the issues raised by this clinical vignette in the broader context of the nature of empathic communication and miscommunication between patient and analyst.

The Clinical Vignette

The patient, a gifted young scientist, married and father of two small children, had originally sought treatment because of mild recurrent depression, and an increasing awareness of his self-demeaning stance and attendant self-destructive behavior. He wanted, among other things, to be more articulate and communicative in his dealings with his loved ones, colleagues, and himself. He experienced an undercurrent of isolation and loneliness, and at times felt as if there were a kind of plastic shield between himself and those around him. He felt different from others and didn't know how to express a sense of commonality on occasions when he did feel close to them.

The background of the session was as follows: The patient had missed the first two sessions of the week (four sessions per week) because of a parapraxis on his part. He had informed me some time before that he would not attend these two sessions in order to go to a convention, and I proceeded to fill the hours. A few days before the sessions in question, the patient remarked that he was glad he had cancelled his plans. I told him I had not known of the cancellation, and after a few minutes, informed him that, in accordance with his instructions, I had filled the hours. With this realization, he became somewhat annoyed with himself, but at that juncture we were not able to learn more about his parapraxis.

In the session itself, the patient described his trip to a scientific convention where he had read a paper. (He had gone there for a weekend rather than for four days.) The paper had gone well, although he feared it was above the heads of many in the audience. He related several pleasurable meetings with old friends, slightly marred by his competitive feelings. On the plane back, he said he had "pulled out all my old neurotic tricks. The stewardess was very attractive; I ended up first grabbing the drink she was handing to my neighbor, and then in realizing my error, spilled my drink all over my lap."

I now interrupt his narrative to report something of my own stream of thought: "Lusting after the stewardess—spilling the drink. Hmm, fouling his own nest—There's a French word for that—*chenouille*, or something—DeGaulle used to use it about the French and their politics—meetings with colleagues, rivalry—convention—I should write a paper I've been meaning to get together—expand my thoughts on the *Odyssey,* hero as an only child—I can do it now—Why don't I fill in much more detail?—Odysseus' rivalries as sibling rivalries—his lies, one of his lying names, Aithon—'firebrand'—J. told me it is also the name of a bird, which in folklore, somehow everts its stomach and then eats it—good point for my thesis on oral aggression and sibling rivalry in the poem—arresting image—How does that work?—image keeps coming—funny, irrelevant—(I envision a cormorant-like bird everting its stomach, as if through its belly button)—Better pay attention to the patient (I'm losing his drift)."

I then proposed to the patient what I had earlier started to say to myself—that his attraction to the stewardess seemed to unhinge him. He replied, "Yeah; I hate to admit this, but I think I was really most upset about missing those two sessions." After a silence he continued, "I have an image now of something I heard in a lecture on the black widow spider—the supreme sacrifice of the mother. She turns her stomach out and her own digestive juices start to eat away at her body so that the little spiders can eat her up."

The extraordinary similarity (and the interesting difference) between my image of the bird eating his stomach, and his of the spider digesting herself, hit me like a thunderbolt. This was an event to be shouted about, discussed—with whom? The patient? No, let's listen more before we answer the question. The patient at first had no idea of the connection between his image and all his preceding associations, but was quite taken by it. He went on in a very affective (and moving) way to expand upon his discovery, namely, that he was very upset that he had given away his two sessions (and I added, thereby "stewing in his own juice"). I thought to myself—it really matters to him; he missed being here and was much more profoundly disappointed than he could have believed. He sees how he has not been valuing the analysis enough, and has hidden from himself just how important analysis is. His wish is that he could better translate the understanding he acquired into personal change. I said, "Perhaps you have been devaluing the analysis and thereby interfering with that translation." He replied, "That's a good point. I guess it's also true that this may be an example of my finally changing—that I'm changing in my feeling."

After a bit more discussion, I asked him again about his image—what about the children eating the mother? He said he thought he had been in analysis too much for the sake of his children; he didn't want them to have to suffer from their father the way he suffered from his. Maybe he's resentful; there's not enough for him; there is too much sacrificing his substance for the sake of others.

Thus, from the patient's perspective, the significance of his parapraxis and of this particular session was that he became much more aware of how much analysis meant to him, and how much he had been keeping his feelings about me and my importance to him at a distance. In addition he was beginning to have an awareness of at least one motive for minimizing the analysis, i.e., resentment that he was doing this for someone else. The image struck him as odd, but did not become the center of his interest in that session; nor did it surface and demand further exploration in subsequent sessions. I did not tell him then or later about my image and astonishment at our almost simultaneous mental events. For me there were two important points in this session. For the moment they can be epitomized as *his discovery* —how much analysis meant to him—and *my discovery*—a fascinating phenomenon to understand, integrate into treatment, and consider reporting to colleagues.

Explanations of the Event

I will now consider my attempts at explanation of this event, which began to arise in my mind in small part during the session itself, but occurred largely during the next few days and over several subsequent weeks.

(1) My own stream of association was thematically closely parallel to his, though on a separate track. It included rivalry, success, and showing-off a product, but also the possibility of destroying one's self in the process—first, fouling one's own nest, and then the specifically oral image of devouring one's self.

(2) In his transference, there was undoubtedly a competitive element with me. On my part was some awareness of feeling competitive with him as well as feeling admiration for his work.

(3) The congruence of such idiosyncratic images (even though he had brought up related images before) suggests an intensity of affect and a joint preparedness to experience something not previously acknowledged. In particular, the patient came to realize his profound disappointment and (less explicit in this session) his deep craving and need for sessions. I myself had not adequately realized the depth of his neediness and the effectiveness of his defenses against disappointment. One proof of my countertransference was that with various rationalizations I kept postponing to tell him about several sessions that I would probably cancel the following month. I believe I was reluctant to encounter and uncover his great neediness.

What about the difference between his image and mine? For want of more specific evidence, I shall pass over the significance of the contrast between a bird and a spider, and examine two aspects of the differences: (1) His image involved children devouring a parent (mother), while mine involved seemingly no interpersonal transaction, only auto-cannibalism, and (2) his image came from science and mine from mythology. As for the detail of the children, he had already elaborated on his sense of himself as a parent perhaps sacrificing too much of himself, and added some material about his mother sacrificing herself (to the father's predatory behavior) for the sake of her children.

There were several specific implications of this fantasy for the relationship between us. For one thing, he must have felt that I had given away his sessions to other patients, i.e., his substance was being devoured by his siblings. Second, he implied in talking of my patients that he and I shared a parental concern about them. In this version, one transference issue was that I as father allowed him as mother to be devoured by the children. (My image is a *male* creature, his a female.) My image did not include, in the manifest content, any theme of children (although my own prior associations involved themes of sibling rivalry and oral greed). In fact, I had not focused on the fate of the two sessions, or how I had used the time, but more on his self-destructive behavior. (Had I squandered some of my substance, allowed myself to be eaten up—by virtue of not filling the hours with paying patients, but with a meeting and with a supervisory hour?)

In any case, an examination of the difference between his image and mine suggested to me that I had been neglecting some aspect of sibling rivalry, or neglecting a particular fantasy of the two of us as parents of "the other children." Conversely, it may well be that I also was registering (via my image) a complementary aspect of his fantasy—an archaic self-devouring, relatively undifferentiated or pre-object fantasy. The simultaneous presence of our separate versions indicated that his (repetitive) self-destructive behaviors were fed by two fantasies, a fantasy of himself as *alone* in the universe (and in the analysis), having to gain sustenance only from himself, and a fantasy involving the dangers of sustaining himself with supplies stolen from siblings.

The available data did not allow for any finer resolution, nor for a clear sense of how these two fantasies might have been interrelated. Much later, I came to realize from other material that the self-devouring fantasy was also an oral version of an oedipal, incestuous theme—self-devouring was equivalent to incest, i.e., consuming your own substance instead of getting fresh sustenance from the outside.

As for the contrast between the manifest sources of our respective images, science and mythology, I placed this in my mind within the context of what had been only a partially crystallized understanding of the nature of our interactions. One of the patient's initial complaints was that he was a bit too prosaic in his life, including his inner life. He wanted more music, more poetry, more color. (Music had been an important part of his earlier life, and he had neglected this interest for many years.) Poetry was incomprehensible to him, and he could not paint or draw. All he could do was think about science. Two clinical observations are relevant here. One is that this patient had an extremely vivid and rich dream life (though he reported somewhat fewer dreams than my other patients). His dreams included arresting images, startling affects, colors, lights, action, and what I imagined must have been transformations of past and current life traumas. However, the yield of interpretation of these dreams was rather meager. There seemed to be formidable resistances to dream interpretation and to integrating the understanding of dreams into the ongoing stream of his inner life. We had discussed this issue several times as a source of frustration both to him and to me, and clearly an important aspect of his makeup to be understood.

Second, within any given session, he might easily interrupt an ongoing stream of associations (or a dialogue between us) to bring up some scientific observation, either an insight into a problem in his own field or some other area of science. Or, he might comment on the physics of a noisy radiator, or a weird sound from a vehicle passing in the street. At one level, these were intrusions; to me they were annoying disturbances in getting down to the real business of analysis—passions, images, conflicts, symptoms. At another level, this behavior was a terribly important part of the patient's life and clearly had defensive, adaptive, communicative, as well as transferential and historical meanings. At times, he genuinely engaged my curiosity in thinking about these scientific, technical phenomena.

Both in regard to the place of his dreams in his life and the place of these scientific and technological interpolations in the sessions, he and I had oscillated between two stances. The first was one of assuming a contest or competition between his interests (scientific) and mine (imaginative, psychoanalytic). He would apologize for the difference, characteristically act deferentially, and try and comply with what he took to be my needs and wishes. An attitude of father-son rivalry was clearly being enacted in this manner (his father having been a popular teacher of literature). The other stance was of a more comfortable dialogue between "colleagues" who, though in different fields, were genuinely curious to learn about one another's area and to enlarge the boundaries of mutual understanding. This too mirrored a piece of the past—times of genuine respectful dialogue between him and his father, and times of great comfort and closeness to his mother, when he could explain scientific matters to her; although uncomprehending she would convey her admiration and sincere wish to be able to understand and communicate with him.

Thus, in brief, his personal history was being played out in the analytic sessions. The core problem in his growing up was the issue of whether his own style, different from his father's and mother's, would be the focus of competition and misunderstanding or of complementarity and increased understanding.

For my part, the evolution of my own understanding of these issues in the analysis grew with time, and was accompanied by some fragments of self-analysis. For example, I came to reconsider my own childhood interests in science, and understand how these interests could at times separate me from parents and peers, and at other times help bring me closer with the people I clearly cared about. These self-analytic considerations, in turn, also related to the earlier discussion of the difference between his image and mine—his involving multiple personages, and mine involving only one.

The difference in styles (science vs. mythology) indeed carried an implication similar to the difference in the number of agents in our two respective images—*both differences encoded the issue of loneliness versus intimacy.* My image had in part been shaped by a reactivation of my childhood scenes of painful loneliness, brooding, and "eating my heart out" (and compensatory overeating) in relation to peer difficulties. Also involved was the attendant worry about how much I had contributed to such painful situations. Had I in the present (once again) played a role in the "loneliness" from his missing the sessions—for it emerged that *I* had also missed him more than I had been aware of? Had I done something to engender a situation of my being separated from a close friend or a parent, or from my "favorite child"? Thus, the confluence of our images also conveyed a sense of two lonely children, sitting and playing near each other, each conflicted about drawing closer, about clearly indicating a desire to be and play together. Pride, fear of rejection, and competitive feelings both separated and united us.

The Question of Telling the Patient

Then, what about telling the patient that I had anticipated his image (or an important aspect of it)? Might that have helped bridge the gap and brought us closer, or at least brought out into the open our feelings and conflicts? Both by training and temperament I was reluctant to share such information without considerable deliberation. My thoughts at the moment ran something like this: Stop and think about what this means before you blurt it out! A premonition like this might not be all that wonderful nor simply convey what a gifted intuitive therapist you are, but in fact might reveal a serious communication problem between you and the patient. Perhaps you are valuing your "intuition" much more than what the patient is struggling with. Further, for this patient your telling him of your image, after he told you of his, might be taken as another example of his competitive inferiority and prove very difficult to analyze. Also telling him of your image would have certainly derailed him from talking about what was pressing on his mind—the realization of his disappointment and how much he had missed coming. In short, at a time when the patient is getting much more in touch with his feelings of wanting and needing you and beginning to communicate them more openly with less shame, fear and humiliation, you underline your cleverness rather than feeling for his plight.

Conversely, to tell him might have focused dramatically on the issue of communication between us. After the initial startle, perhaps I could really have begun to show him something of my thinking and foster the process of his learning to analyze himself (after all, one very important goal of treatment). Telling might also have been a "corrective emotional experience" —presenting him with a kind of sharing to which he was wholly unaccustomed. Overall my decision was not to tell, in large measure because most of what I have written thus far in this paper about transference and countertransference I did not know at that moment. It is worth noting that this particular session and my understanding of it constituted an important, but not necessarily dramatic turning point in the analysis. Rather, it was part of a phase of consolidation and deepening of our analytic experience.

The Psychoanalytic Literature on ESP

I shall turn now from this vignette to the material taken from another vantage point, namely, the psychoanalytic literature on extrasensory perception (ESP) and telepathic phenomena in the clinical setting. Clearly, whatever the outcome and understanding of such an event, it is necessary to raise the question of how in the world it occurred in the first place.

By now there is an extensive and stimulating literature on the subject of how the analyst comes to understand the patient—the matrix of communication, feeling and empathy out of which interpretations and other interventions are formed in the mind of the analyst. Particularly useful both for its review and conceptualizations is the study of Balter, Lothane, and Spencer (1980) summarizing and extending Isakower's notion of "the analyzing instrument." Important ideas and clinical vignettes can also be found in the work of Ross and Kapp (1962), Miller (1972), Jacobs (1973), Beres and Arlow, (1974), Shapiro (1974), Greeenacre (1975), Spiegel (1975), Kern (1978), Arlow (1979), Kernberg (1979), Lester (1980) and Post (1980). Kohut and his associates have contributed importantly to this subject by their emphasis on the central role of empathy both in the development of psychopathology and in the analytic process (Kohut, 1977; Goldberg, 1978, 1980).

Rather than review this rich literature in detail, I will address a particular aspect of the question of how communication takes place between patient and analyst, namely, the relationship of extrasensory perception and telepathic communication to psychoanalysis.

During the early years of psychoanalysis there arose a keen interest in psychoanalysis and the occult, which especially concerned incidents similar to and more dramatic than the one I described, and their possible relationship to telepathy and extrasensory perception. There were lively debates in the literature about whether psychoanalysis helped demonstrate the existence of ESP, or whether seemingly telepathic phenomena could be "explained" by the powerful forces existing between patient and analyst, i.e., transference and countertransference. Devereux (1953a) offered a marvelous collection and commentary on these issues.

A particularly vivid example was reported by Helene Deutsch (1926). While listening to her last patient of the day, she found herself distracted by thoughts of her eighth wedding anniversary celebration that evening. She reproached herself for inattention to her patient (as I had done with my patient). The next day the patient reported a dream at the beginning of the session: A family is celebrating its eighth wedding anniversary. The couple is sitting at a round table. She is very sad, and the husband is angry and irritated. In her dream, the patient knows that the sadness of the woman is due to her childlessness. (Dr. Deutsch had been struggling with issues of her own childless state.)

After ruling out the possibility that the patient knew these facts about her life, Deutsch proceeded to an interesting discussion of the transference and countertransference issues in the case, especially as heralded by the patient's dream. Exactly how the patient "knew" these particular concerns of hers, or why at that juncture in the analysis such a phenomenon should have occurred, was not specifically explained. The controversy about whether or not such phenomena require an explanation in terms of ESP (or can be most parsimoniously explained by it) has not been satisfactorily resolved. While the debate has not continued in print for the last decade or so, a few therapists have kept the issue alive in presentations and clinical discussions. Some particularly interesting work has been done in trying to understand the conditions under which ESP-like phenomena seem to occur most readily.

I myself do not believe in ESP and telepathy; in fact, I am more of an "atheist" than an "agnostic" on the subject. Intellectually I am open to saying, "let me see the evidence," but I really cannot claim at an emotional level to have an open mind on the subject. I should therefore note a clinical observation: A few of my patients over the years have either surmised my attitude on this subject and/or learned of it from direct comments; they have then proceeded to produce all sorts of telepathic-like dreams, memories, or free associations in the course of therapy, which made me quite nervous about my adamant "atheism" in this area. I have also noted that some self-reproach for not paying attention to the patient seems to be a common experience of the therapist as a *prelude* to the occurrence of ESP-like phenomena. A colleague, Dr. James Skinner, who does believe in parapsychological communication and has collected what he believes to be extensive documentation, has concluded that ESP-like perceptions on the part of patients about events in the life (or in the mind of the therapist) tend to occur at junctures where the therapist is in fact *less available* to the patient; the patient, it seems, must exert a special effort to remain in contact with the therapist.

It may seem a bit ironic to argue that occasions of deep and extraordinary communication between patient and therapist are to be explained in the context of *failures* of communication. I believe, however, that the latter may be an important element. Nevertheless, one must at least start out by looking for explanations of how the phenomena happen, not just for factors relating to communicative disturbance.

A careful study by Seitz (1975) is most instructive in this regard. He describes instances after termination with a patient when upon thinking of that patient, he would be contacted the next day. There were enough of such occurrences as well as those when he thought about a terminated patient who did not contact him, that he was able to conduct a "controlled" retrospective study. He came to several interesting conclusions:

(1) The phenomenon occurred almost exclusively with patients who had been in psychoanalysis, not psychotherapy (although there were many instances of patients in psychoanalysis where the coincidence did not occur). That is, a certain intensity and depth of contact had to have taken place for the phenomenon to occur. (I and other therapists have observed such phenomena with patients in psychotherapy as well as in analysis.)

(2) There were *anniversary reactions* that both the therapist and the patient were experiencing. He was generally able to discover this by reviewing treatment notes, either on his own or with the patient who had just recontacted him. Patient and analyst were attuned unconsciously to a timetable of important events that could be reconstructed from past material but which was obscure for either therapist or patient, or often both.

(3) These incidents usually represented a confluence of unresolved conflict in the patient and a related unresolved conflict in the therapist; or more accurately, a conflict partially resolved but liable to be reawakened or intensified by particular circumstances. Other authors, especially Beres and Arlow (1974), viewed such coincidences as signifying unresolved therapist conflict. The activation of a conflict in the therapist similar to that in the patient undoubtedly served as a pathway of empathy via the therapist's unconscious identification with the patient.

The "countertransference" may thus be a therapeutically useful tool, if properly understood, analyzed, and utilized by the therapist.

(4) In the years since he first noticed and began to study this post-termination phenomenon, its incidence had gradually decreased; it now occurs only rarely! He has several possible explanations, though he is not sure about their validity. One is that the author has learned from this study how to pick up unresolved issues at the time of termination that earlier in his career he might not have noticed. A second possible explanation is that over the years he as an analyst may have become less involved with his patients!

To me, the manner in which such telepathic-like events occur is impressive and awe inspiring—not altogether explicable, but not altogether mysterious either. Both verbal and nonverbal cues are involved, and certainly a *progressive* attunement to each other's emotional functioning is important. In examining my notes and recollections about this particular incident with the image of an animal eating itself, it became clearer that not only were there important cues in the session, but that material existed throughout the course of treatment which provided the ingredients, as it were, for the patient and me to produce such images conjointly. In fact, it is noteworthy (and Seitz emphasizes this), the degree to which the therapist's *astonishment* is based upon repression of knowledge about the patient he had had at hand. Undoubtedly major shifts of defenses must take place both in therapist and patient as a precondition to the formation of such conjoint images or pieces of knowledge.

In retrospect, this particular incident may well have been phase-related in a peculiar kind of way. One colleague, Payne, upon hearing this clinical material, correctly dated the incident to late in the first year or early in the second year of analysis. (See also Lester [1980] for interesting comments on patient's use of visual images and their relation to the depth of the analysis.) Indeed, following this incident, over weeks and months the analytic process noticeably deepened. Concomitantly, the patient's more exotic dreams and imagery began to appear less frequently and the manifest content of the dreams became more ordinary, as it were, and conveyed more intense and integrated affect. The patient began to regard his dreams less as objects for my curiosity to be given over to me for my study, and transmitted a greater sense that the dreams were his, that he owned them, and that the feelings, memories and interpretations of these dreams were indeed part of him. It is possible this particular incident might be a species of the genus of mental events marked by a greater preparedness to participate on the part of the patient, and a greater receptiveness on the part of the analyst in response to it.

Thus, we find ourselves again at the question posed earlier in the discussion—Is there some *difficulty in communication* that may be signaled by this kind of nonverbal, imagistic experience? I have indicated that there indeed were significant problems of understanding and being understood which were replayed in the analytic situation of my patient. Among the issues that gradually became clearer to us was the extent that he not only felt "off somewhere else," but experienced others as similarly situated; or he perceived them as trying to be with him but chronically frustrated and having to resort to brute confrontation, almost violence, to get through to him. The history of understanding and misunderstanding in his life, of failed and successful empathy, and of benignly and sadistically motivated empathy, had to be progressively elucidated.

In the course of analyzing my reactions during and after this session, I came to realize more about my own history of failed and successful understanding and the vicissitudes of empathy in my relationships, especially the importance of unsuccessful empathy in learning and growing. One outcome of this self-analysis was, in fact, a fuller appreciation of the similarities and differences between the patient and myself and how this could provide a basis for mutual understanding.

Reflections during the analysis as well as retrospectively also sensitized me to the complexity and specificity of different modes of understanding in the course of the patient's development. Although he had styles of knowing and communicating that were preferred, he did not have only one "channel" available. Rather, he had a great capacity for poetry and empathy in his scientific work, and was certainly not devoid of these capacities in his close personal relationships. His different styles also reflected a history of different identifications that shifted in importance with phases of development.

Analysts too have histories of using different modes of understanding and empathizing, including various personal identifications ranging from early infancy to current analysts, teachers, and colleagues. Kernberg (1979) in particular has emphasized that different therapists have different genetic and situationally related strengths in empathy. (See Greenacre, 1975; Shane, 1980; Balter et al., 1980.)

The above considerations about personal histories and styles of patient and analyst may be tantamount to restating the obvious, particularly when the work of Kohut and his students has done so much to increase consciousness about the central role of empathy in psychoanalysis. Issues of failed and successful empathy are prominent in virtually all discussions of analytic technique. The need to understand the vicissitudes of empathy in the patient's life is indeed implicit throughout contemporary case reports (Goldberg, 1978).

Conclusion: A Hypothesis

What, then, is the relationship between certain telepathic and empathic phenomena in analysis? The line of thinking I have developed in this paper can be summed up as a hypothesis. An important variable in the timing of telepathic-type phenomena occurring between patient and analyst is the existence of some important unresolved communicative issue that is not being apprehended by ordinary means. There must be a certain tension (preconscious? unconscious?) between the expectation that empathic communication can succeed and the fear that it may not. In stating this hypothesis, I am uncertain whether such a tension would inevitably represent a repetition of a previously existing pattern in the patient's life, or whether it might arise as a function of the unique and novel nature of the psychoanalytic relationship. If my hypothesis is correct, then the argument *for* telling the patient about the analyst's side of the experience is made stronger, so that this struggle between hope and despair about being understood can be analyzed. Such a hypothesis, of course, does not aim at providing a complete explanation for telepathic-type phenomena in analysis.

To conclude, I wish to emphasize the degree to which the term "empathy" is a rather sweeping and nonspecific kind of explanation. If, as Hume suggests, "explanation is where the mind rests," then using empathy as an explanation would indeed allow our minds to rest far short of the kind of detail we should expect in the analytic situation. It is useful to treat "empathy" as having a conceptual status similar to that of the term "internalization." (See Schafer, 1976, 158–178, 351–354.) "Empathy" is an attempt at explaining the process whereby one person comes to understand and know something about the other without everything being made explicit, but it is also a term that signals the operation of a *fantasy* about such communication. As a fantasy, one must analyze its history and meaning for each patient, just as Devereux (1953b) has argued, one must analyze the meaning of a patient's conviction that some telepathic process has occurred. As a theoretical explanatory term, one must assume that it is unlikely that empathy is a unitary phenomenon; rather, there must be an "anatomy of empathy." Both developmental and detailed clinical studies of the patterns and rhythms of failed and successful communication alert us to the multiplicity of mode, channel and style by which we come to know one another.

REFERENCES

Arlow, J. (1979), The genesis of interpretation. *J. Amer. Psychoanal. Assn.*, 27:193–206.

Balter, L., Lothane, Z. & Spencer, J. H., Jr. (1980), On the analyzing instrument. *Psychoanal. Quart.*, 49:474–504.

Beres, D. & Arlow, J. (1974), Fantasy and identification in empathy. *Psychoanal. Quart.*, 43:26–50.

Deutsch, H. (1926), Occult processes occurring during psychoanalysis. In: *Psychoanalysis and the Occult,* ed. G. Devereux. New York: International Universities Press, 1953, pp. 133–146.

Devereux, G., ed. (1953a), *Psychoanalysis and the occult.* New York: International Universities Press.

________ (1953b), The technique of analyzing "occult" occurrences in analysis. In: *Psychoanalysis and the Occult.* New York: International Universities Press, pp. 391–417.

Goldberg, A., ed. (1978), *The Psychology of the Self: A Casebook.* New York: International Universities Press.

________ (1980), *Advances in Self-Psychology.* New York: International Universities Press.

Greenacre, P. (1975), On reconstruction. *J. Amer. Psychoanal. Assn.*, 23:693–712.

Jacobs, T. (1973), Posture, gesture, and movement in the analyst: Cues to interpretation and countertransference. *J. Amer. Psychoanal. Assn.*, 21:77–92.

Kern, J. W. (1978), Countertransference and spontaneous screens: An analyst studies his own visual images. *J. Amer. Psychoanal. Assn.*, 26:21–47.

Kernberg, O. (1979), Some implications of object relations theory for psychoanalytic techniques. *J. Amer. Psychoanal. Assn.*, 27:207–240.

Kohut, H. (1977), *The Restoration of the Self.* New York: International Universities Press.

Lester, E. P. (1980), Imagery and transference in the analytic process. *Internat. J. Psycho-Anal.*, 61:411–420.

Miller, I. (1972), Inhibition of empathy caused by unconscious fantasy. *Internat. J. Psychoanal. Psychother.*, 1:107–116.

Post, S. L. (1980), Origins, elements and functions of therapeutic empathy. *Internat. J. Psycho-Anal.*, 61:277–288.

Ross, W. D. and Kapp, F. T. (1962), A technique for self-analysis of countertransference. *J. Amer. Psychoanal. Assn.*, 10:643–657.

Schafer, R. (1976), *A New Language for Psychoanalysis.* New Haven: Yale University Press.

Seitz, P. F. D. (1975), ESP-like experiences of a psychoanalyst: A possible psychological mechanism. *Psychoanal. & Contemp. Sci.*, 4:189–209.

Shane, M. (1980), Countertransference and the developmental orientation and approach. *Psychoanal. & Contemp. Thought,* 3:195–212.

Shapiro, T. (1974), The development and distortions of empathy. *Psychoanal. Quart.*, 43:4–25.

Spiegel, L. A. (1975), The functions of free association in psychoanalysis: Their relation to technique and theory. *Internat. Rev. Psycho-Anal.*, 2:379–388.

Discussion

JAMES C. SKINNER, M.D.

Bennett Simon's essay, particularly the incident of parallel imagery he reports, sounded an echo in my own experience. Under what conditions, I wonder, do such startling phenomena occur? Suggested answers to this question, such as coincidence or increasingly parallel streams of thought induced by subliminal cues, lack explanatory power. Instead, the phenomena Simons describes seem impossible to explain in terms of any sensory processes we are familiar with.

Some years ago I, like Simon, was startled to hear a patient describe a dream that corresponded—not just in overall substance or in a single detail, but in many details—to an event in my own life on the preceding day, of which the patient could not possibly have had knowledge. A week or two later, the patient repeated this curious correspondence and soon after I became aware that another analytic patient was also reporting dreams that were startling replications of events in my life. I began to tape-record both patients' analytic sessions. Eventually, as I became aware that certain recurrent aspects of the events in my life seemed to be portrayed in my patients' dreams, I introduced a prediction on the tape before recording the session. Altogether there are some 30 examples of such corresponding dreams in my files, from which I have selected one example.

> The patient reported a dream in which he seemed to be in an art store. He came across a portrait of himself and was amazed to find it there. Since he didn't remember ever sitting for a portrait, he realized that it must have been done from a photograph. In any case, he admired the

technique and thought it was a handsome painting. The artist appeared and told him that it was worth about $1,000. The patient now commented to me that although he would have liked to own it, that was too high a price for him to pay. He described himself in the dream as sitting on a stool, looking at this portrait of himself; it seemed a very strange experience. The artist then went away, presumably to work on something for him (the patient), perhaps some molding or something like that. In any case, the artist was using a saw and, in the process of making this molding or whatever, cut himself. He came to the patient and asked him, "Can you see where I've been cut?" On inquiry, the patient said that he understood this to be a kind of test, that the artist knew where he had been cut but wondered if the patient could notice it and find the cut. At first when the patient looked, he couldn't see anything because the man had a white shirt on; he didn't see any signs of blood. Then the the man pulled up the sleeve of his left arm and showed him that he had a deep cut or laceration in the arm. He must have gotten it by reaching forward across the saw. The artist then began peeling away the layers of skin from around the cut and chopping at the edges with a knife, as one might do a piece of meat. The patient tried to dissuade him from this and eventually succeeded, instructing him to go to a hospital. The artist then went off on a trolley car to the hospital.

On the morning before this patient's dream I was visiting my mother and we were invited to see a neighbor's antiques. The evening before, this woman had told us about an accident that her husband had had while working on a paint box for her in his workshop. Somehow, he got his left hand into the circular saw and cut off three fingers. She described the difficulties in getting him to the hospital and mentioned how self-controlled and casual he was while she was so upset she could hardly find the car keys. When we went over to her house the next morning, she first showed us some paintings she had done from photographs my mother had lent her (photographs taken by my brother years ago). She was especially proud of a painting done from a photograph of an old man carrying a basket. Her husband was very interested in photography, and he and I spent a lot of time discussing a unique process he used to create different effects in his photographs. I felt as though I were being particularly charming and as though he were admiring me. A number of his pictures were displayed in the dining room, and we spent some time looking at them. Later on, as we left the house, my mother asked me if I had noticed his left hand and the scars remaining from the accident. I said that I had not, and she said, "It's just as well."

It is through examining such experiences that I have developed some convictions about the conditions under which they occur. Many writers, including Balint (1955) and Servadio (1955), have remarked on how inexplicable correspondences between the analyst's life and the patient's dreams or associations seem to occur at times when the patient feels cut off from communication with a meaningful "other"—the therapist. With Simon's patient, this condition appears to be true. Yet in my material, although often true, it is not invariably so, as far as I can tell in retrospect. Such correspondences also seem to occur when I have given a "special gift" to someone other than the patient.

In one of the first corresponding dreams in my experience, an analytic patient "responded" to my having shared some details of my personal life with another patient (with whom I was terminating) by having a dream in which I shared the same details with her. The patient with whom I was terminating was planning a trip to England. In my last session with her, I impulsively told her, as though to advise her, something of the trip to England my wife and I had made some years ago. I felt a guilty pleasure in doing so and was filled with a sense of how pleased with me the patient must be. My other analytic, "deprived" patient thereupon brought in a dream in which my wife and I were strolling with her and told her all about a trip we were going to take to England. Surrounding this dream, in time, were intense fantasies of intruding magically into the sexual life of my wife and me and disrupting our pleasure.

It is interesting to note that the results of recent experiments with card guessing or other tests for extrasensory perception seem to be intensified—showing greater statistical significance—when the "receiver" is in a state of sensory deprivation. This condition—the "Ganzfeld state"—may be achieved by placing ping-pong balls cut in half over the eyes and then illuminating them with a rather strong source of light and equipping the "receiver" with earphones through which "white noise" is heard (Kreitler and Kreitler, 1974; Stanford *et al.*, 1976; Terry and Honorton, 1976). It is also of interest that most of the coincidences in my own practice have occurred in the classical analytic situation, which does include some sensory (as well as emotional) isolation for the patient. In the experiments mentioned, however, it is unclear whether it is the lack of confusing or a masking background "noise" that contributes to the increased accuracy of the "receiver's" guesses or whether a feeling of being cut off in an emotional sense might result in a greater need to establish contact.

The two patients who produced the majority of the correspondences I have studied were both patients for whom contact and fusion were particularly important. One patient disclosed, midway through the analysis, that he had entered treatment with the fantasy that by in some way getting close to the therapist, he could share in what he assumed to be the therapist's prospects for immortality. Specifically, he felt that the analyst must have overcome all risk of psychosomatic illness and that he (the patient) could also reach that goal. His dreams often carried this theme, even portraying the therapist and himself as immortal. The other patient, who had strong homosexual desires, also spoke clearly of a wish for fusion. In both patients, their dreams, associations, and life histories reflected particularly difficult and painful experiences with the task of individuation.

As I mentioned earlier, I have also noticed that the reported correspondence may awaken or startle me out of a preoccupation with matters other than the patient. A recent example of this gave me a kind of double-take. The patient had reported associations to a dream, which corresponded to an event in my life the day before. Then, on a different track, he described how he had often tried to get his father's attention, to distract his father from reading the newspaper when he (the patient) had something of importance to communicate. At that very moment I was preoccupied with looking at a picture postcard on the table behind the couch, which held a striking correspondence to the patient's dream. One might argue that the patient, sensing in some way the therapist's lack of attention (or, in other cases, the therapist's having given something "special" to someone else), reached across the ordinary sensory boundaries to share in the therapist's life and at the same time to acquire his sole attention once more.

All of this implies that the patient, the "receiver," establishes an empathic relationship out of his (or her) own need and in some way reaches out and "steals" a portion of the therapist's day residue for his own dream construction. It is important, however, to consider the other partner in this unusual relationship—the therapist, or the "sender." What can one say about his needs and the conditions surrounding the incidents "purloined" by the patient?

Almost invariably, the incidents in my own life that found a correspondence in my patients' dreams had been experienced by me with a special kind of pleasure. Initially, I tended to call this a "regressive feeling"—almost an infantile feeling. There was a sense that other people were very pleased with me without asking anything of me—that I was enjoyed and loved without qualifications or demands. A certain excitement surrounded these incidents; I felt a certain power but, even more, a sense of self-satisfaction fused with nostalgia for something I could not name. As I came to describe this affect more clearly, I attempted to predict which events would appear in my patients' dreams, and I achieved some success with this criterion. In my notes I labeled it a "mirroring effect" (this was years before I heard of Kohut's mirror transference). And, as notes reflect, the most striking correspondences occurred when my sense of being mirrored with approval was the strongest. (It is of interest that in one of my examples and in one shared with me by a colleague, an actual mirror appeared both in the incident in the therapist's life and in the patient's dream.)

Recently, in reading Kohut (1971), I came across the passage in which he speaks of a child seeing the "gleam in the mother's eye" and feeling unqualifiedly loved and accepted. This, it seems to me, is the feeling I have described in these incidents. Why should this particular condition be important for this peculiar kind of empathic response? According to Kohut, mirroring is important in a child's use of the external object. It does increase the analyst's self-absorption and thus may make him even more "unavailable" in the patient's dream life. Or is he more available? Does the patient become the mirror in which the analyst's act is reflected? There have been a few instances in my own work when this seems to have been true, when I have been thinking of the patient at the time I had the experience that later appeared to be reflected in the patient's dream. My thought on those occasions was essentially: "If only he could see me now." It was as though I were seeking some satisfaction from the patient which I could not realize in the ordinary course of a therapeutic relationship.

Much of my discussion has centered on an assumption that the patient—the presumed "receiver"—is gaining access to information I have "transmitted." Another model has recently been proposed by Stanford (1974a, 1974b). He focuses much more on the needs of the person who has the parapsychological experience and whose needs are satisfied by the information received. One may argue that the patient as a receiver has needs to be in touch with the therapist and that these needs are satisfied, even though he has no conscious recognition of borrowing material from the therapist's life to use in his own dream. But what about the needs of the therapist? I have spoken of a peculiar sense of "regression," of nostalgia and of being "mirrored," as very much part of the experiences reflected in a patient's dream. There is also, to be sure, an element of "magic." My use of the word "nostalgia" suggests that, for me, those experiences did not just provide satisfaction but echoed with a longing for some lost state or relationship, impossible to define. This feeling seems similar to deep longings I remember from childhood and adolescence, longings that followed dreams of my own in which I performed "magic."

A few more examples may clarify my meaning. In working with one borderline patient, I found it useful to have her depict her feelings about herself and others on a large blackboard; I would then actively participate in correcting some of these portrayed views. When I asked her to *draw* one of her dreams, I discovered that many more visual details, rich with associations, emerged; they had been lost in the verbal translation. Since that experience, I have quite frequently asked patients to draw their dreams on the blackboard—including the two analytic patients who produced the majority of the "corresponding" dreams. In drawing a dream, one of these patients portrayed his feeling of losing the closeness of various parts of himself by depicting them as increasingly distant from each other; he spoke of a longing for an earlier, more tightly related arrangement. Some time later I read a book in which the author spoke in almost Jungian (collective unconscious) terms of the relationship of all individuals and organisms to each other. To illustrate this, he had described a group of fish which remained separated—moving in different directions—when feeding, but when startled, immediately formed themselves into a school—all oriented in the same direction and related one to the other. The next morning this patient reported that he had dreamed I had an aquarium in my office, which became the center of attention for both of us in the way the blackboard often had been. He dreamt I spoke in a "cosmic" way of somewhat mystical matters and of the relationship of each fish to the others. This example not only illustrates the link of the common "ground," which I described in my own nostalgic childhood fantasies, but also the possible importance of the shared focus of attention between analyst and patient. One might compare this to the shared concerns of which Simon speaks in attempting to explain shared visual fantasies.

Let us return now to my question: What might the needs of the therapist, or "sender" be? Stanford (1974a) suggests that the universe may somehow function at times in a beneficent fashion so that events occur in a way that meets felt needs. A number of experiments seem to demonstrate that "extrasensory" acquisition of information is more likely to occur when there is a strong need on the part of the individual to acquire that information (Braud, 1976). If one extends this idea of need to include the need for a specific experience, it is easier to understand why, as in my material, seemingly trivial information may be acquired.

What I am emphasizing is the strength of the desire to have such an experience, not just the details of the experience itself. The wish may be not only for something magical but also for a closeness that is not allowed in one's adult life but can be realized in this particular fashion. I myself, for example, dreamt one night of having a prophetic dream of disaster, which (in the dream) was then fulfilled upon reading the morning newspaper. In the dream I was excited and delighted by this experience. The next morning one of my patients reported a dream that seemed to be curiously fulfilled by an actual experience after awakening. In a sense, the wish fulfillment expressed in my dream was fulfilled by the patient in his experience. Further, I suggest that these experiences represented a "completion" of myself in some way, without a full relationship to an outside object; in some sense there is a closed circle of self-fulfillment which, as I described earlier for one of my patients, may represent a longing for immortality.

One of the puzzling aspects of such correspondences is the specificity with which *one* person satisfies the need of the therapist. On only one occasion do I recall that more than one patient seemed to produce corresponding details to an event in my life. Nevertheless, another example suggests that if one adopts Stanford's idea that the order of events benignly meets the individual's needs, one may see a multiplicity of response. On this occasion I had been asked to give a lecture on parapsychological phenomena and their relationship to therapy at a hospital some distance from Boston. The topic was of interest to me and I looked forward to the talk, although with some concern that once more I was involved in an area of discourse that was suspect to many people. The night before the lecture, a colleague, who had not spoken to me of parapsychological phenomena for at least two years, called me to report such an experience with a patient and to ask my advice on whether to share the information with his patient. He knew nothing of my lecture. The next morning, an hour or two before I was to leave, a resident, knowing of my interest in parapsychology, stopped me in the hall to tell me that a patient of his had just reported a precognitive dream. After the lecture, a member of the audience, who had not known beforehand the subject of my talk, reported that the day before one of her patients had reported two parapsychological experiences. Finally, on the day before the lecture, I myself had experienced a striking correspondence between a "gift" to one patient, with whom I was terminating, and a comment of another patient, who was eager to share in my life.

Now, I come back to the point at which I began—namely, Simon's paper and his experience. The isolation and loneliness the patient felt was described "as if there were a kind of plastic shield between himself and those around him." Simon's own associations just before the startling correspondence involved thoughts about a paper that he wanted to write:

> I should write a paper I've been meaning to get together—expand my thoughts on the *Odyssey*, hero as an only child—I can do it now—Why

> don't I fill in much more detail?—Odysseus' rivalries as sibling rivalries—his lies, one of his lying names, Aithon—'firebrand'—J. told me it is also the name of a bird, which in folklore, somehow everts its stomach and then eats it—good point for my thesis on oral aggression and sibling rivalry in the poem—arresting image—How does that work?—image keeps coming—funny, irrelevant—(I envision a cormorant-like bird everting its stomach, as if through its belly button)—Better pay attention to the patient (I'm losing his drift).

The patient responds: "I have an image now of something I heard in a lecture on the black widow spider—the supreme sacrifice of the mother. She turns her stomach out and her own digestive juices start to eat away at her body so that the little spiders can eat her up." It is clear that Simon had allowed his attention to focus on his own interests, in particular, on the *Odyssey* and the hero—and even more specifically, on the "hero as an only child." As Simon himself mentions there are links to his own feelings of isolation and loneliness as a child. Although I can only speculate, he, too, seems to wish for a special kind of distinction, perhaps to be loved and admired for himself, not necessarily only as an analyst. Later on Simon comments: "Thus, the confluence of our images also conveyed a sense of two lonely children, sitting and playing near each other, each conflicted about drawing close, about clearly indicating a desire to be and play together. Pride, fear of rejection, and competitive feelings both separated and united us."

Simon's remarks seem to parallel my own description of the conditions surrounding correspondences that appear to be inexplicable in terms of ordinary sensory processes. His paper is a brilliant discussion of the issues of communication, of failed communication and the nature of empathy. That his inclination is to reject an extrasensory explanation of these incidents in no way interferes with my appreciation of the elegance of his paper. He states: "'Empathy' is an attempt at explaining the process whereby one person comes to understand and know something about the other without everything being made explicit, but it is also a term that signals the operation of a *fantasy* about such communication. As a fantasy, one must analyze its history and meaning for each patient . . . one must analyze the meaning of a patient's conviction that some telepathic process has occurred." I agree. But I also emphasize that the ability to analyze these processes as fantasies does not foreclose the possibility that they exist as actual events. Some of the most virulent criticism of parapsychology has come from professional magicians. As Reichbart (1978) points out, the practice of "magic" and the accompanying need to expose, as fraudulent, any claim for the validity of parapsychological experiences may represent a fear that some kinds of "magic" might truly exist. It is also of interest that in a number of experiments in Canada and England, phenomena that appeared to be parapsychological and inexplicable, according to what we know of natural physical laws, were promoted and often initiated by deliberately fraudulent, "staged magical" effects (Stanford, 1974b).

The exact nature of these occurrences should remain of great interest to all of us. Freud is said to have remarked that if he had another professional life to live, he would devote it to psychic research.

REFERENCES

Balint, M. (1955), Notes on parapsychology and parapsychological healing. *Int. J. Psycho-Anal.*, 36:31–35.

Braud, W. G. (1976), Conscious vs. unconscious clairvoyance in the context of an academic examination. *J. Parapsychol.*, 39:277–288.

Kohut, H. (1971), *The Analysis of the Self.* New York: International Universities Press.

Kreitler, H. & Kreitler, S. (1974), Optimization of experimental ESP. *J. Parapsychol.*, 38:383–392.

Reichbart, R. (1978), Magic and PSI: Some speculations on their relationship. *J. Amer. Soc. Psychical Res.*, 72:153–175.

Roll, W. (1966), ESP and memory. *Int. J. Neuropsychiat.*, 2:505–519.

Servadio, E. (1955), A presumptively telepathic-precognitive dream during analysis. *Int. J. Psycho-Anal.*, 36:27–30.

Stanford, R. (1974a), An experimentally testable model for spontaneous PSI events, I: Extrasensory events. *J. Amer. Soc. Psychical Res.*, 68:34–57.

——— (1974b), An experimentally testable model for spontaneous PSI events, II: Psychokinetic events. *J. Amer. Soc. Psychical Res.*, 68:321–355.

——— et al. (1976), A study of motivational arousal and self-concept in psy-mediated instrumental response. *J. Amer. Soc. Psychical Res.*, 70:167–178.

Terry, J. C. & Honorton, C. (1976), PSI information retrieval in the Ganzfeld: The confirmation studies. *J. Amer. Soc. Psychical Res.*, 70:207–217.

25 Empathy and the Analyzing Instrument

JAMES H. SPENCER, JR., M.D. and LEON BALTER, M.D.

THE LAST DECADE has brought increasing reference in the psychoanalytic literature to the concept of empathy and the part it plays in the psychoanalytic process. To some this growing interest seems to embody a growing consensus about the central place of empathy in psychoanalysis (Ornstein, 1979). Others see empathy as an important aspect of the psychoanalytic process, but believe the current attention to it is potentially dangerous (Arlow, 1979). Still others see a clear and present danger, which warrants a vigorous attack on the current use of the concept (Shapiro, 1981).

The interrelationship of empathy and psychoanalysis has been particularly stressed by Heinz Kohut. He has argued that empathy is the essential, defining characteristic of the psychoanalytic method (1959, 1977), and that the persistent use of empathy, defined as "vicarious introspection," sets psychoanalysis apart as a method for gathering data. This view of empathy and psychoanalysis has been elaborated at length (Kohut, 1971, 1977, 1978), mostly with regard to the related clinical and theoretical ideas about the "self" and the therapeutic effect of the analyst's empathy. The question of the place of empathy and the empathic experience in psychoanalytic data gathering has been discussed by Lichtenberg (1981), Schwaber (1981), and others.

In his writings Kohut has repeatedly stressed the contribution that empathy makes to the psychoanalytic process, but he has devoted less time to the contribution the psychoanalytic situation makes to the empathic process. We intend to emphasize the latter and to describe the way in which certain aspects of the psychoanalytic situation may affect the analyst's empathic experience. In doing so we contend that empathy as it occurs and is used in psychoanalysis differs in certain important respects from empathy in other situations. The differences are specific and qualitative, and it is these differences which give empathy its special place in the psychoanalytic method.

Toward an Operational Definition of the Empathic Experience

The term "empathy" has been used in a variety of ways in the psychoanalytic literature, some of which seem to be mutually contradictory (see Reed, 1984). It has, for example, been called an innate *capacity* (Olden, 1953) and a *means of communication* (Karush, 1979). Although Reed argues that the word contains an essential ambiguity that should be accepted and even valued, it may be worth trying to arrive at a definition that is as operational as possible.

Some of the difficulty in discussing the concept can be resolved if we distinguish among: (1) the *capacity* for empathy (which may have a variety of developmental and other antecedents), (2) the *empathic experience* itself (which is essentially intrapsychic, within one person who is empathizing with another), and (3) the *communication* between one person and another (which enables the second to empathize with the first).

With regard to the first aspect, we note only that some have suggested that the capacity for empathy is directly derived from the earliest preverbal experiences of communication, based on mother-infant merging (Olden, 1953; Kohut, 1966). When seen in this way, empathy tends to become lost to further understanding; moreover, it comes to refer to something that is at the same time an intrapsychic process *and* a mode of communication. Recent papers by Buie (1981) and Edelheit (1978) have effectively taken issue with this point of view.

The importance of the *empathic experience* has been recognized by psychoanalysts for many years. The term has usually been used with reference to a particular kind of intrapsychic experience of the analyst, one in which he (or she) seems to experience the same feelings as the analysand. Definitions of the empathic experience have usually used such concepts as "trial identification" (Fliess, 1942). As Buie (1981) points out, the term "identification" has mostly been used in a descriptive sense, without specific reference to intrapsychic mechanisms.

This view of empathy is well articulated by Beres and Arlow in their paper on "Fantasy and Identification in Empathy" (1974). They consider empathy to involve transient identification with the patient. But they stress that "the empathizer preserves his separateness from the object," and thus differ with those who consider it to be based on merging with the object. In their opinion, the affect involved in an empathic experience is "in the nature of a signal affect, a momentary identification with the patient which leads to the awareness, 'this is what my patient may be feeling' " (p. 35). They then go on to develop an original point, which may further explain at least some empathic experiences. Suggesting that the "signal [affect] portends the emergence of an unconscious fantasy" (p. 35), they use a clinical example to show how the emergence of an unconscious fantasy in a patient may evoke a similar unconscious fantasy in the analyst. Here they refer to Arlow's previous work (1969a, 1969b) or how "the data of perception have the power to reactivate or facilitate the emergence of unconscious fantasy activity" (1974, p. 36). Extending this earlier emphasis on the patient and the way in which real life perceptions (experiences) may reactivate the patient's particular unconscious fantasies, they conclude:

> Clinical material obtained in the treatment situation may be examined from the vantage point of these principles. The sensory input, the analyst's perceptions, consists of the patient's productions. A measure of the analyst's empathic capacity lies in his ability to be stimulated by the patient's unconscious fantasy when the analyst himself is not yet aware of the existence or the nature of the patient's unconscious fantasy [p. 45].

The emphasis on empathy as a transient identification, an "adjunct to our technical procedure," represents the traditional psychoanalytic view. The concept of "signal affect" and the clinical examples imply that empathy should not be considered a technique that is deliberately used but rather a phenomenon that occurs in psychoanalytic sessions as a result of certain technical procedures. Furthermore, the idea that a signal affect is followed by the emergence in the analyst of an unconscious fantasy similar to the one active in the patient accounts for the emotional aspect of the analyst's empathic experience and the way in which it may be specific to the patient. Finally, this idea contributes toward a definition of empathy in terms of psychoanalytic concepts rather than using the term "empathy" to define psychoanalysis.

Although Beres and Arlow have made an important contribution to a psychoanalytic understanding of empathy and its place in the psychoanalytic process they do not specifically address a narrower question: Is there anything unique about the way in which empathy occurs in the psychoanalytic situation, or is it essentially similar to what may occur elsewhere? In their summary they note: "The empathic process which is central to the psychotherapeutic relationship between patient and therapist is also a basic element in all human interaction and finds its highest social expression in the shared aesthetic experience of the artist and his audience, as well as in religion and other group phenomena" (p. 47). Earlier they drew parallels between these shared human experiences and empathy as it occurs in psychoanalysis, but they do not discuss what the differences may be. We believe some aspects of empathy may be unique to the psychoanalytic situation. An examination of these touches on a second question, also raised by Beres and Arlow's paper: To what extent do the unconscious fantasies shared by the patient and the analyst represent: (1) universal fantasies, (2) more specific fantasies that fortuitously happen to be present in both parties, or (3) more specific fantasies that arise uniquely as the product of the psychoanalytic process?

In his recent paper on the nature of empathy, Buie (1981) has also made a major contribution to an operational definition of the empathic experience. He rejects the idea that empathy is "a unique mode for directly gaining information about the patient by means that are independent of visual and auditory perceptions of his behavior" (p. 283), and with it the commonly found blurring of the distinction between the intrapsychic process and the *prior* communication that makes it possible. Buie clearly states that empathy cannot occur without antecedent perception and communication; it is not itself a mode of communication, and it does not occur as a result of extrasensory perception: "The empathic process requires interpersonal communication in order to begin; the patient provides cues about his state of thought and feeling which are perceived by the analyst" (p. 298). Usually, and ideally, in the analytic situation, such cues are provided predominantly through verbal communication.

Buie quotes Freud and others in support of the idea that the empathic experience is based on a process of inference which *follows* such communication: "we can have no *direct* knowledge about the mental experience of another person. We have only inferences which are based upon an assumption that we locate within our own mind something that is analogous or homologous with that mental state of the other person which gives rise to the perceived sensory cues" (p. 292). In this context he discusses four types of internal referent which may contribute to the empathizer's response: (1) conceptual referents, (2) self-experience referents, (3) imaginative imitation referents, and (4) resonance referents.

Buie, however, does not go on to discuss the various kinds of communication that may result in empathy. Nor does he make any particular distinction between empathy in the psychoanalytic situation and in other settings. In addressing the issue of interpersonal communication, then, we shall attempt to show how the nature of empathy in psychoanalysis is partially determined by the nature of psychoanalytic communication.

Communication in Psychoanalysis

It is difficult to conceive of empathy occurring without some kind of communication to the empathizer from the object of his empathy. But the communication need not include free association or any other specifically psychoanalytic activity. Empathy may occur as a result of ordinary conversation or nonverbal communication. In order to elaborate on the place of empathy in the *psychoanalytic process*, we shall first review the nature of psychoanalytic communication, using concepts developed in a previous paper (Balter, Lothane, and Spencer, 1980).

Psychoanalysis is a process that aims at the analyst and analysand gaining as complete an understanding as possible of the analysand's conscious and unconscious fantasies, conflicts, and intrapsychic processes. An analysis begins with the initial understanding of a person and progresses through stages in which this understanding is refined, becoming broader, deeper, and more precise. In this it is not unique. In addition to the refinement of the scope and detail of understanding, however, there is an aspect of the process that *is* unique—namely, the continuing, systematic introduction into this understanding of material that was previously unconscious.

At any stage of an analysis and in any given session, the process of refining our understanding of *conscious* experience and fantasy, and of *unconscious* experience and fantasy, may occur in sequence or simultaneously. It occurs through a process of communication, and this communication is primarily verbal. The analysand talks to the analyst and the latter listens, responding more or less infrequently with interpretations or other interventions.

The analysand's material can be heard in two ways. There is a manifest content, which makes reference to conscious experience and thought. It is usually dominated by secondary-process thinking, although it need not be entirely logical or coherent. It can be listened to and understood by an analyst or anyone else as an ordinary conversation would be. We may refer to this as *conventional* communication between analysand and analyst.

There is, however, a second type of communication, which is not conventional and is in many respects unique to psychoanalysis. Loewenstein (1956) has referred to a kind of coded message or subtext, which is latent in the manifest content of the patient's material and to which the analyst must attend. It will often make reference to unconscious fantasies, memories, and conflicts, and it is dominated to a large extent by primary-procss thinking.

Both these types of communication occur throughout an analysis and throughout any analytic session. They are always concurrent, in that there is always a manifest content and always a latent content, but one or the other may appear predominant at any given point. Conventional communication, for instance, may appear predominant in a narrative account of a previous day's experience or in a patient's attempt to describe an emotion or sequence of thought through introspection, but there may be evidence for the subtext in a tone of voice, a slip of the tongue, or an unusual emphasis. On the other hand, the purest free association, which may very evidently embody the primary process and reference to unconscious fantasy, will also include considerable secondary-process thinking and reference to conscious thought and feeling.

This distinction between *conventional communication*, to which an analyst or any listener should be attentive, and *the subtext*, to which an analyst should be equally attentive, is necessary if we are to clarify some differences between empathy in psychoanalysis and in ordinary conversation. Before approaching these differences, however, we need to further define the kind of communication that is unique to psychoanalysis.

The Analyzing Instrument

The term "analyzing instrument" was introduced by Otto Isakower to describe certain fundamental aspects of the activity of analyzing (New York Psychoanalytic Institute, 1963a, 1963b). It is a construct that effectively describes the way in which certain aspects of the analysand's intrapsychic processes and complementary aspects of the analyst's intrapsychic processes form a communication circuit, which is aimed at making conscious and elucidating the analysand's unconscious fantasy-memory constellations (Balter et al., 1980).

In discussing the "psychological preparation of the patient," Freud describes two changes that must be brought about to establish a particular state of mind in the analysand: "an increase in the attention he pays to his own psychological perceptions and the elimination of the criticism by which he normally sifts the thoughts that occur to him" (1900, pp. 101–102). In elaborating on the second change, Freud concludes that the analysand will find that "innumerable ideas come into his consciousness of which he could otherwise never have got hold." These and all other ideas that come to mind are put into words and communicated to the analyst. This verbal reporting, when added to Freud's two instructions, completes the preconditions leading to what is usually called free association. According to Freud, the state of mind engendered in the analysand "bears some analogy to the state before falling asleep" (1900, p. 102). This state of mind, however, can more generally and operationally be described as a regression of ego functions than as an approximation of sleep. The reason for the appearance of such a regressed state of mind in the analytic situation has been discussed at greater length in our previous paper (Balter et al., 1980). That such a regressed state of mind does appear is daily evident in the content of analytic sessions, content that frequently exhibits a shift toward primary-process thinking, visual and other images, the diminished importance of reality testing and the sense of reality, lessened inhibition of impulse and affect, and so on.

In order to understand Isakower's concept of the analyzing instrument as "a composite consisting of two complementary halves" (New York Psychoanalytic Institute, 1963b), it is only necessary to recognize that in listening to the patient's free associations, the analyst may often be in a regressed state of mind himself, and for much the same reason. Freud (1912) also makes certain recommendations to the analyst about the state of mind in which to listen to the patient's communications:

> The technique . . . consists simply in not directing one's notice to anything in particular and in maintaining the same 'evenly suspended attention' (as I have called it) in the face of all that one hears. . . . It will be seen that the rule of giving equal notice to everything is the necessary counterpart to the demand made on the patient that he should communicate everything that occurs to him without criticism or selection. . . . The rule for the doctor may be expressed: 'He should withhold all conscious influences from his capacity to attend, and give himself over completely to his "unconscious memory"' [pp. 111–112].

The analyst is instructed to direct uncritical attention toward the analysand's communications. In a later paper on technique (1922), Freud also recommends that the analyst give uncritical attention to his own internal perceptions, and in so doing "to surrender himself to his own unconscious mental activity, in a state of evenly hovering attention, . . . and by these means to catch the drift of the patient's unconscious with his own unconscious" (p. 239).

In the above passages and elsewhere, Freud lays down three preconditions for the *analyst* in establishing the required state of mind for the functioning of the analyzing instrument: (1) the concentration of attention on the analysand's communications, (2) the concentration of attention on the analyst's own internal perceptions, and (3) the suspension of critical activity regarding these two objects of the analyst's attention. These preconditions for the analyst, which are similar to those for the analysand, tend to have an effect on the analyst's state of mind, which is also similar: they induce a regression in ego functioning. Isakower has stated that "there prevails a near-identity of the quality of wakefulness in both the analyst and the analysand" (New York Psychoanalytic Institute, 1963b). We would restate this: *The analyst's regression is essentially of the same nature as that which obtains in the analysand.*

The analysand free associating in the state of mind described above and the analyst listening in a comparably regressed state of mind are the two complementary halves of what Isakower calls the analyzing instrument. The activity of analyzing involves many different processes, both intrapsychic and interpersonal. The construct of the analyzing instrument subsumes a set of these processes that cannot exist entirely apart from other processes and may be utilized only intermittently. However, as an entity, it embodies a communicative process that is unique to psychoanalysis.

This communication is unique, not only because the analysand's state of mind during free association tends to become regressed, but also because *the analyst is more likely to perceive connections between words, ideas, and images that are products of the patient's primary process and the derivatives of unconscious fantasies*. This occurs because the analyst's mind, through voluntary adherence to the three preconditions, is itself *in part freed from the constraints of secondary-process thinking, reality testing, and so on*. Under these conditions, the patient's words are more likely to evoke visual, auditory, and bodily images in the analyst—involuntary images that may seem idiosyncratic (i.e., the analyst's own associations) but are ultimately stimulated by the patient's productions. This communication circuit within the analyzing instrument has been well described by Arlow: "In a sense, we dream along with our patients, supplying at first data from our own store of images in order to objectify the patient's memory into some sort of picture. We then furnish this picture to the analysand who responds with further memories, associations and fantasies" (1969a, p. 49).

In sum, the aim of the functioning of the analyzing instrument is the elucidation of the fantasy-memory constellations of the analysand; the means is the voluntary, controlled induction of complementary states of mind in analysand and analyst, allowing communication on a regressed level.

Empathy in Psychoanalysis

Communication within the analyzing instrument can be distinguished from the more conventional communication that occurs in the analytic situation as well as elsewhere. Although it might be difficult to separate one from the other in the transcript of an analytic session, it is usually possible to find evidence for the existence of both types.

This distinction between the analyzing instrument and conventional communication can be useful in addressing the questions raised earlier with regard to empathy and psychoanalysis: (1) How do the psychoanalytic situation and psychoanalytic communication affect the analyst's empathic experience? (2) As a consequence of this, does empathy in psychoanalysis differ from empathy in other situations? And (3) must the analyst and the analysand have similar backgrounds, experiences, or fantasies?

With regard to the first question, empathy can certainly occur as a result of conventional communication in analysis. Transient identification with a person describing conscious anger at an unreasonable boss or conscious disappointment at a rejection can be an important part of the response of any analyst. As such, it may not be specifically affected by the psychoanalytic situation and may not differ substantially from the empathy experienced by a friend or relative of the patient, or from the empathy of a supportive psychotherapist.

On the other hand, an empathic response may occur within the communication circuit of the analyzing instrument. Because the latter is unique to psychoanalysis, one might expect it to have a unique and specific effect on the analyst's empathy, and indeed, this is the case. The transient identification with the patient's experience in the psychoanalytic situation is far more likely to include aspects of the experience not included in the patient's manifest description, aspects of which the patient may be only dimly aware, or not consciously aware at all. As we have noted, adherence by the analyst to the preconditions for the functioning of the analyzing instrument, particularly the suspension of critical judgment, results in a partial regression of mental functioning, and this increases the likelihood that the analyst will "hear" or apprehend the presence of derivatives of unconscious mentation in the patient's material. Beres and Arlow (1974) give a good example of this when they describe an analyst responding to a patient's dream with his own brief visual fantasy of reunion with a loved one. This in spite of the fact that the dream's manifest content did not contain such a reunion. The response proved to be empathic in that it foreshadowed the emergence of a similar fantasy of the patient's which had previously been only latent in the material.

This effect of the analyzing instrument on the analyst's empathy provides an answer to the second question, regarding the difference between empathy in psychoanalysis and in other situations. As just noted, the empathic responses stimulated by use of the analyzing instrument are more likely to include unconscious elements of the patient's experience, and in this important respect they differ from empathic responses to more conventional communication during analytic sessions. The latter have much in common with empathic responses in supportive psychotherapy and in ordinary conversation; the former are unique to psychoanalysis. To phrase this somewhat differently, we may say that the transient identification of the analyst within the functioning communication circuit of the analyzing instrument is more likely to include elements of latent content. On the other hand, empathy in conventional communication, empathy with what the patient *says* he feels and thinks, is more likely to be restricted to manifest content. A discussion of the place of empathy in psychoanalytic method should keep this difference clearly in focus. It points up the importance of the difference between manifest and latent, conscious and unconscious, in any such discussion.

A third question raised by the psychoanalytic literature on empathy has to do with the degree to which the analyst and the patient must have similar backgrounds or similar experiences if the former is to empathize with the latter. Kohut has suggested that similar backgrounds are helpful, if not essential (1959, p. 463). Beres and Arlow (1974) think that empathy occurs when the analyst and the patient share an unconscious fantasy, and their most striking example implies that a corresponding fantasy is already latent in the analyst, ready to be evoked by the patient's material.

Yet just how important is it that the analyst and the patient have had similar experiences or share similar unconscious fantasiesThe answer is both obvious and misleading. Kohut points out that a person cannot empathize with a plant, and we can all agree. Moreover, it would be difficult to empathize with all but the most elementary experiences if the object of empathy were from a completely different culture and spoke an unknown language. On the other hand, there are many analysts whose European backgrounds differ greatly from those of their American patients, and this does not preclude an effective psychoanalysis. It is obvious that there must be some similarity, but equally obvious that it is impossible to make a general statement as to how much.

We suggest that the most useful general statement that can be made is the following: Analyst and analysand must share a common language. A common language implies that they have a common set of words, with denotations and connotations, along with a set of rules for usage. This language acts as an organizer for subjective experience and the world of objects. In short, a common language provides a means by which relatively complex experience can be communicated from one person to another. Without it, such communication must be severely limited, along with the range and depth of possible empathic responses.

Nevertheless, although a common language makes effective communication possible, it does not guarantee that it will take place. It is in this sense that the emphasis on common backgrounds in the analyst and the analysand is misleading. Two people from similar backgrounds, in the absence of effective communication, may jump to the conclusion that they understand each other on a particular point when in fact they do not. The analyst's own personal background and previous experience are obviously antecedents to his empathic response to an analysand. However, *the depth, complexity, and accuracy of the empathic response will depend on how well the object of empathy conveys his experience to the empathizer and how well the latter apprehends what has been conveyed.*

Much can be conveyed by conventional communication in psychoanalysis or elsewhere. A patient who states simply that he has a headache may evoke an empathic response. A mother who is conscious of grief at the death of her child may describe and express her feeling in such a way as to evoke an empathic response in an analyst, even though the latter has not had a similar experience. If this mother's child died during an elective operation, she might be conscious of and convey an experience including grief, anger, and guilt. Again, the analyst might transiently identify with the experience, but his ability to do so would depend even more on the mother's communication and his ability to apprehend what was expressed, complete with nuances.

Beres and Arlow (1974) identify the aspect of an empathic response that is crucial to psychoanalysis—namely, the "sharing" of an *unconscious* fantasy between the analyst and the patient, which we have explained by reference to the analyzing instrument. To reiterate: the partial regression of the listening analyst enables him to apprehend things in the patient's free associations that, taken together, may convey a relatively specific unconscious fantasy or intrapsychic conflict with which he can transiently identify. *If the communication is effective,* the analyst need not have had a preexisting similar unconscious fantasy of his own, except to the extent that all complex, specific unconscious fantasies are derivatives of certain universal fantasies. The nature of empathy in psychoanalysis is primarily determined by the nature of psychoanalytic communication and its accuracy by the effectiveness of such communication, including the effective use of the analyzing instrument. The frequency, accuracy, and usefulness of empathic responses in a particular psychoanalytic treatment will therefore depend more on the effective use of the analyzing instrument than on the fact that the analyst may have unconscious fantasies similar to the patient's.

Our point can be illustrated by an example from Beres and Arlow's paper, in which they provide lengthy quotations from a patient who showed evidence of claustrophobia. In listening to this material, the analyst became increasingly aware of the patient's fear of confinement. But another idea also emerged in the analyst's mind—that the patient was under the influence of a vagina dentata fantasy. As Beres and Arlow point out, the material on confinement "followed immediately upon a train of thoughts dealing with his fearsome mother and her destructive, hawklike beak" (p. 31). It is also interesting to note that words containing the consonants "st" occur repeatedly throughout the material ("stuck," "stop," "start," "restrictions"), along with references to the mother's "sharp tongue" and "cruel mouth." None of this would lead to the idea of a vagina dentata in the logic of the secondary process, but an analyst listening with the regressed ego functions characteristic of the analyzing instrument would be more likely to apprehend the material with the logic of the primary process. In other words, the analyst's thinking within the analyzing instrument may be influenced by acoustic images, displacement, and contiguity, enabling him to respond to aspects of the patient's material that are probably derivatives of the patient's unconscious fantasy—derivatives that are in part the product of the same kind of regressed mental processes on the patient's side. As a result, the analyst is able to empathize more deeply and precisely with the patient than would be possible outside the analytic situation.

The Function of Empathy in Psychoanalytic Method

We have described how empathy may occur in the psychoanalytic situation, certain of its antecedents and characteristics, and in particular how it is related to psychoanalytic communication. That is, we have tried to identify the ways in which psychoanalytic method affects empathy, and how empathy in psychoanalysis may be unique. It remains to ask what contribution empathy makes to psychoanalytic method.

As Reed (1984) has pointed out, there are some psychoanalysts who seem to regard empathy as an important tool in furthering the analytic understanding of the patient, and others who see it as contributing to a kind of nurturant ambiance necessary for analysis to take place. We contend that the analyst's empathic response to the patient can be an important element in the actual process of analyzing. It can play a crucial part in the continuing effort to deepen and broaden the understanding of a patient, specifically of his *unconscious* fantasies and conflicts, although it is by no means the only way to attain this end.

The crucial points in an analytic session or a series of sessions are those where there is a progression from the known to the previously unknown, where analyst and patient together unearth something in the patient's experience, memory, or fantasy that was previously unrecognized or unconscious. This progression may occur spontaneously when the patient's associations lead directly to new material or insight; it may occur in a dream and its associations, through analysis of an aspect of the transference, or as a result of an interpretation or other intervention by the analyst and the patient's subsequent response. In the last instance, the interpretation itself would be seen as a means, not as an end in itself. The common idea that interpretations may be validated by the appearance of new material suggests that their value lies as much in the way they further the analysis as in the way they interpret what has gone before.

One of the controversies around the concept of empathy centers on the danger that the empathic response may be treated as an end rather than a means. The expression "I know just how you feel" can shift from empathy to sympathy just as easily when uttered by an analyst to a patient as when expressed by a mother to a child. And the empathic response to a patient's material, even when nothing is said aloud, may be experienced by the analyst as an end rather than a means toward further analysis. Viewed in this way, empathy becomes an interference to analyzing rather than an element in analytic methodology. It is this danger that Shapiro (1981) and Arlow (1979) warn of, and it is a real danger. But it is also true that an *interpretation,* no matter how accurate and valid, can become a resistance for the analysand or the analyst under certain conditions; yet no one has argued that we should discard this concept or activity.

The value of empathy in psychoanalysis lies primarily in its use as a means of uncovering previously unknown aspects of the patient's experience. In understanding how this may occur, we should recall that an empathic response is usually considered to be an emotional response—one in which the empathizer transiently has the same feeling as the person with whom he is empathizing. In examples of empathic experience, however, there is usually an *idea* explicitly or implicitly associated with the feeling. We do not empathize with grief or anger in the abstract; we transiently identify with the mother who has lost her child or the person whose boss makes unreasonable demands. In such examples, the idea (e.g., the loss of a child) may be a conscious aspect of a patient's experience, but there will usually be unconscious aspects to it, and in some cases the idea is entirely unconscious. As we have seen, Beres and Arlow (1974) cite examples in which the ideational component was embodied in an unconscious fantasy.

In their discussions of affect theory in psychoanalysis, Novey (1959) and Lewin (1961, 1965) conclude that a psychoanalytic understanding of any emotion must include reference to an ideational content, which is invariably present. Brenner (1974) reviews these and other papers and advances a psychoanalytic theory of affect, in which he holds that a particular affect for a particular person can be fully described only if we are able to define a feeling (characterized by a degree of pleasure or unpleasure) that is associated in the person's mind with a particular idea, either or both of which may be conscious or unconscious. Brenner asserts: "All affects have ideational content and a developmental history. To analyze any affect means to discover those ideas and that history" (p. 542). Thus, the analysis of the feeling component of a patient's manifest experience may lead to the uncovering of unconscious ideational material, with which it is associated. We would further assert that the analyst's own empathic feeling responses to the patient's material are often an important means of discovering such unconscious ideational aspects of the patient's mental life.

In the example from Beres and Arlow (1974) discussed earlier, it was suggested that through the functioning of the analyzing instrument, the analyst had a feeling response, which in turn led to the uncovering of a latent unconscious idea. This was an important part of the patient's current emotional experience, a component previously unknown to both patient and therapist. An empathic response may thus act as a "bridge," leading from a known, or more clearly seen, feeling to an unknown, or less clearly seen, unconscious fantasy. Empathy becomes another means—along with interpretation, defense analysis, and other more traditionally recognized analytic procedures—of eliciting and elaborating new material and with it a further understanding of the patient's unconscious fantasy-memory constellations.

Another example, given in our previous paper (Balter et al., 1980), further illustrates how the analyst's empathic response may lead to new material from the patient. A young woman had been describing a dinner party at which several intelligent people had been aggressively discussing different topics. She had felt uncomfortable and very unhappy and found herself wishing that her former lover (a strong, aggressive individual) were there. She was trying, with difficulty, to describe the exact nature of her painful feelings when the therapist suddenly experienced a visual image of the legs of chairs and a table as they would be seen from the height of a small child. He transiently identified with the experience of a small child who felt left out and unable to participate at an adult party. He said so to the patient, who responded with memories of how she had felt as a child in a family that included several bigger brothers. She then went on to recall the wish she had had then to *be* one of her brothers and related this to her present-day wish for her former lover and a feeling at times that he was part of her or she part of him.

In this example, the analyst, while listening to the patient describe her *feelings*, found himself transiently identified with an affective experience containing both a feeling component and an ideational component, both manifested by a visual image. In short, he had an empathic response. The ideational component was new, and it led to new associations from the patient. In this instance, empathy was a *means* to elicit further material from the patient and increase analytic understanding.

Conscious feeling, then, may lead through empathy to unconscious fantasy. In other cases, the ideational component may appear first in the patient's material, and the analyst's empathic response may lead to further understanding of the feeling component. On the night before a session, for example, a patient had been in a high-rise apartment and seen a large, dark cloud which seemed to be approaching the building.

The patient was an unusually independent woman with considerable narcissistic investment in this character trait. The apartment was that of an older friend, and the patient had once taken a serious overdose when left alone there by her friend during a period of depression. The precipitant for this suicide attempt had never been understood. On seeing the cloud, she had a fantasy of King Kong "embracing" the Empire State Building. She described this to the analyst without conscious awareness of any accompanying affect.

Associative material, the analyst's prior understanding of the patient, and his recollection of scenes in the movie where the heroine is held gently by the giant gorilla led to a sudden transient identification with a young woman feeling warm, safe, and protected (as opposed to terrified and hurt). When this was conveyed to the patient, she responded with further associations about a childhood wish for protective "holding" by her father—and then suddenly recalled the terrible disappointment and despair she had felt in the apartment when her older friend had left her alone at a time when she desperately wanted help but could not ask for it because of her need to maintain her feeling that she never needed help from anyone. In this example, then, the analyst's empathic response led from a conscious fantasy to an emotional component, which in turn led to the patient's increased understanding of feelings of which she had only been dimly aware (i.e., the feeling of warmth and safety associated with the childhood wish for her father's protection, and the related angry disappointment when her friend had failed to gratify a similar wish in the more recent past).

In the following example, the ideational component was not a fantasy, but rather a description by the patient of an event from the previous day. The analyst's own unbidden and unexpected emotional response enabled him to recognize a similar emotion in the patient—an emotion that had hitherto been concealed from him and perhaps even from her.

A young married woman had come into treatment for the acute onset of agoraphobia precipitated by the birth of her first child. She was completely dependent on her husband to accompany her everywhere beyond the radius of a city block from her home. For the first few months, he even accompanied her to her sessions. After that, she was able to come by herself. She was always careful to emphasize how devoted her husband was to her and how grateful she was to him. But it was also clear that he bullied her at home, resented her treatment, and generally behaved toward her in an imperious manner. One day, she gravely told of a rather dramatic event on the previous day. Her husband woke up with a severe allergic reaction. His whole face was swollen; his cheeks were puffed out, enormously exaggerated, and the loose tissues around his eyes were so swollen that there were only slits where his eyes had been. As she described at great length her husband's agony, the therapist noticed waves of barely controllable laughter welling up in him. At first he wondered whether he had a sadistic antagonism to the patient's husband because of the latter's attitude toward the treatment. But then he noticed that the patient seemed to be having a slight difficulty in speaking in her usually fluent manner. He realized that she *also* was suppressing laughter, and that he had "acquired" his laughter through "contagion" (Freud, 1921), through identification with the patient's own sadistic enjoyment of her husband's plight, in short through empathy. The therapist could then broach the subject of the patient's anger at her husband and her wish to revenge herself on him. The eventual mobilization of her anger led to the direct amelioration of her phobia.

These examples illustrate the way in which the analyst's empathic response may lead directly to new material and new understanding. Such understanding can, of course, be independently judged concerning its relevance and validity. Clearly, the analyst's empathic experiences can be an effective means to further the analysis, and as such they make a major contribution to our work. We have argued, however, that the nature of these experiences is very much determined by the analytic situation and particularly by the unique nature of the communication between analysand and analyst. This point should be kept clearly in mind when considering the place of empathy in psychoanalytic method.

REFERENCES

Arlow, J. (1969a), Fantasy, memory and reality testing. *Psychoanal. Quart.*, 38:28–51.

_____ (1969b), Unconscious fantasy and disturbances of conscious experience. *Psychoanal. Quart.*, 38:1–27.

_____ (1979), The role of empathy in the psychoanalytic process. *Bull. Assn. Psychoanal. Med.* 18:64–69.

Balter, L., Lothane, Z., & Spencer, J. (1980), On the analyzing instrument. *Psychoanal. Quart.*, 49:474–504.

Beres, D. & Arlow, J. (1974), Fantasy and identification in empathy. *Psychoanal. Quart.*, 43:26–50.

Brenner, C. (1974), On the nature and development of affects: A unified theory. *Psychoanal. Quart.*, 43:532–556.

Buie, D. (1981), Empathy: Its nature and limitations. *J. Amer. Psychoanal. Assn.*, 29:281–307.

Edelheit, H. (1978), On the biology of language: Darwinian/Lamarckian homology in human inheritance (with some thoughts about the Lamarckism of Freud). In: *Psychiatry and the Humanities*, ed. J. Smith. New Haven: Yale University Press, pp. 45–74.

Fliess, R. (1942), The metapsychology of the analyst. *Psychoanal. Quart.*, 11:211–227.

Freud, S. (1900), The interpretation of dreams. *Standard Edition*, 4 & 5. London: Hogarth Press, 1953.

——— (1912), Recommendations to physicians practising psycho-analysis. *Standard Edition*, 12:111–120. London: Hogarth Press, 1958.

——— (1922), Two encyclopaedia articles. *Standard Edition*, 18:235–259. London: Hogarth Press, 1955.

——— (1921), Group psychology and the analysis of the ego. *Standard Edition*, 18:69–143. London: Hogarth Press, 1955.

Karush, A. (1979), Introductory remarks on the role of empathy in the psychoanalytic process. *Bull. Assn. Psychoanal. Med.*, 18:62–63.

Kohut, H. (1959), Introspection, empathy, and psychoanalysis. *J. Amer. Psychoanal. Assn.*, 7:459–483.

——— (1966), Forms and transformations of narcissism. *J. Amer. Psychoanal. Assn.*, 14:242–272.

——— (1971), *The Analysis of the Self.* New York: International Universities Press.

——— (1977), *The Restoration of the Self.* New York: International Universities Press.

——— (1978), *The Search for the Self: Selected Writings*, ed. P. H. Ornstein. New York: International Universities Press.

Lewin, B. (1961), Reflections on depression. *The Psychoanalytic Study of the Child*, 16:321–331. New York: International Universities Press.

——— (1965), Reflections on affect. In: *Drives, Affects, Behavior*, Vol. 2, ed. M. Schur. New York: International Universities Press, pp. 23–37.

Lichtenberg, J. D. (1981), The empathic mode of perception and alternative vantage points for psychoanalytic work. *Psychoanal. Inquiry*, 1:329–355. Reprinted here as Chapter 19.

Loewenstein, R. M. (1956), Some remarks on the role of speech in psychoanalytic technique. *Int. J. Psycho-Anal.*, 37:460–468.

New York Psychoanalytic Institute (1963a), Minutes of the faculty meeting of October 14. (Unpublished.)

——— (1963b), Minutes of the faculty meeting of November 20. (Unpublished.)

Novey, S. (1959), A clinical view of affect theory in psychoanalysis. *Int. J. Psycho-Anal.*, 40:94–104.

Olden, C. (1953), On adult empathy with children. *The Psychoanalytic Study of the Child*, 8:111–126. New York: International Universities Press.

Ornstein, P. H. (1979), Remarks on the central position of empathy in psychoanalysis. *Bull. Assn. Psychoanal. Med.*, 18:95–108.

Reed, G. (1984), The antithetical meaning of the term "empathy" in psychoanalytic discourse. Printed here as Chapter 1.

Schwaber, E. (1981), Empathy: A mode of analytic listening. *Psychoanal. Inquiry*, 1:357–392. Reprinted here as Chapter 20.

Shapiro, T. (1981), Empathy: A critical reevaluation. *Psychoanal. Inquiry*, 1:423–448. Reprinted here as Chapter 5.

26 Therapeutic Empathy and the Treatment of Schizophrenics

PING-NIE PAO, M.D.

> *The Tao that can be told of is Not the Absolute Tao; The Names that Can be Given are not Absolute Names*
>
> *Nameless is the Origin of Heaven and Earth; Naming is the Mother of all Things*
>
> —Lao-tze, *Tao-te-ching*

LAO-TZE POINTS TO a basic human dilemma—in essence, that processes and changes are difficult to describe precisely. In talking about them, names must be assigned but those assigned names often do not fully or absolutely describe what we intend to describe.

In the analytic situation it is imperative that the analyst understand the patient. It is generally accepted that the analyst comes to understand the patient through the use of empathy. What, then, is empathy? Obviously, empathy denotes a process. And, as the name of a process, "empathy" may have the limitations Lao-tze articulated; it may not fully or absolutely describe what we intend to describe. Fliess (1942), one of the first analysts who attempted to define empathy, envisioned it as a process in which the analyst makes a "trial identification" with the patient. But does trial identification really occur? If it does, how does the analyst make this trial identification with the patient? While listening to a patient, does an analyst say to himself: "If my father did this or that to me, as the patient's father has done to him, I would experience such and such. And, therefore, the patient must be experiencing such

Reprinted from *Psychoanalytic Inquiry*, 3:145–167 (1983).

and such." Is this how the analyst reaches an understanding of the patient? Perhaps the analyst's identification with the patient is not a conscious effort, but accomplished in the unconscious or preconscious. Even if we settle the issue of the level of consciousness at which the trial identification takes place, we are still left wondering whether empathy involves the analyst's listening before the trial identification or the subsequent action in making an interpretation.

During the last two decades, my professional time has been equally spent in the office treatment of neurotic patients and the hospital treatment of severely disturbed schizophrenic patients. In working with both types of patients, I have made use of my empathic capacity,[1] although my comments here concern its use with schizophrenic patients. Generally speaking, we may consider three groups of severely disturbed, hospitalized schizophrenic patients: (1) those who are completely out of contact with external reality and are practically mute, (2) those who are now and then out of contact with reality and are visibly in panic, and (3) those who appear in contact with reality but have severe thought disorders.[2] Through examples of my work with these patients, I hope to illustrate the similarities and differences in the use of one's empathic capacity in understanding neurotics and psychotics. In the process I also hope to clarify my own understanding of therapeutic empathy—its scope and its definition.

Illustrative Cases

The three types of patients I have described may sometimes appear as three phases in the treatment course of a single patient. I would have liked to use material from a single patient, but this

[1]For practical purposes, it may be helpful to consider empathy as the application of empathic capacity.

[2]I have intentionally excluded healthier or recovering patients who behave, to some extent, like severe neurotics (obsessional or phobic) or borderlines. They flip in and out of reality only briefly and are quite capable of studying this brief loss of reality.

would have compromised the patient's anonymity. For similar reasons, I prefer not to use material from my own patients; instead, I have drawn on some recent consultations.[3] Despite these restrictions, I hope to make my points clear. My presentation begins with the third group of patients—those most in contact with external reality—because these patients are the most accessible and my interaction with them resembles that with neurotic patients in that it is essentially verbal.

Apparent Contact With Reality
But Severe Thought Disorder

Miss A, a 22-year-old single woman asked to see me for a consultation. She had become insidiously psychotic while in high school but had managed to function at a marginal level until the first semester of college. After several brief hospitalizations, her condition deteriorated and it was recommended that she come to Chestnut Lodge. This was two and a half years before the consultation with me took place. During these two and a half years she had worked with a woman doctor. Recently, she had become an outpatient and had begun to audit a course at a local college.

Although Miss A had asked to see me, once in my office, she did not articulate her reasons for wanting to see me. She appeared well groomed and neatly dressed—on the surface she could pass for a "normal" college student (although very much of the retiring type). After we sat in silence for a couple of minutes, I noted she looked in my direction but not into my eyes. The silence was awkward for me, but she gave no sign of wanting to talk. Figuring I had to initiate the conversation, I ventured: "It has been a long time since we last talked in this office. How have you been? (The last time we had met was when, upon her admission, I had interviewed her in order to select a doctor to work with her.) Miss A smiled—but very faintly. After a short pause, she said: "There is something I want to tell you. Do you know I was raped?" I

[3]One of my duties at Chestnut Lodge has been to serve as an in-hospital consultant.

thought to myself: Did this happen recently? If so, I was surprised I had not been apprised of this event. I searched for some comforting words to say to her but was unable to find any. To my relief, she started again: "There were three boys. Up on the hill. They have ruined my insides completely and I can't have children anymore." Again, I searched for words to say; again, I could not find any. But this time I knew why I was speechless—she was telling me a terrifying, tragic story, but she exhibited no equivalent emotion, nor did she stir up any specific feelings within me.

Miss A paused, as if waiting for me to say something. Sensing that I must say something for our conversation to continue, I speculated: "You are troubled that your insides are ruined?" Without emotion, she answered: "Yes." (I had forced the word "troubled" out of myself and she agreed. Yet I did not detect any trace of her being troubled about this.) There was silence, and I felt very awkward indeed. Not knowing whether I was compelled by a need to clear my confusion or to satisfy my curiosity, I blurted out: "You were raped and your insides were ruined. When did this rape happen?" She cast a quick glance at me, full of annoyance and impatience. I felt really apologetic, again not knowing why. So I added: "I am sorry, for I really don't know" (still thinking it was a recent affair).

After a pause, Miss A answered: "This happened when I was 14." Suddenly, I felt relieved (ridiculous—as if I should feel responsible for her misfortune if it had happened while she was an outpatient at the Lodge!). Yet I was also curious. I could not help asking myself what was going on with this young woman, putting me through all this. Feeling slightly irritated now, I became bolder, remarking: "This happened when you were 14. That was quite a long time ago. Has there been any improvement with your damaged insides—especially with the help of *your doctor*?" My emphasis on "your doctor" was aimed at turning our discourse more toward the here and now. I wanted to direct attention to the psychological level, as well as to find out how useful, in her view, her doctor had been to her.

Still apparently devoid of appropriate emotion, she said: "Do you know my father? He is a doctor. He had tried to help me, I think. He sent me to the beach where there were sharks. The purpose was to have the sharks eat up all of my insides. Then I could have new insides.'' Suddenly, I felt I was with her (although I couldn't specify how it happened). I commented: ''I am glad to know about your father's good intentions to help you.'' She cracked a smile as I went on: ''But I am also interested in—how has your doctor been useful to you?'' She pulled back a bit and straightened herself up—all in a jerky motion. Suddenly, as if she had made up her mind, she stated: ''I came to ask you to give me a new doctor.'' From that moment on she ceased to talk as crazily as she had initially, although her language was still not what one would expect in daily conversation. Most significantly, her voice began to carry emotion.

In response to a question from me, Miss A explained that she wanted a change of doctors because her doctor was a blonde and she herself a brunette. She added that her next doctor should also be a woman but with dark hair like hers. After assuring her that I would be open-minded about her request, I encouraged her to tell me why the hair color should make such a difference. Speaking somewhat in gibberish and in a halting way, she referred to her mother's hair, which was once dyed blonde (unfortunately she could not tell me when) and her father's hair, which was naturally brown. On the surface her talk was nonsensical. As she talked, I could listen to her with only ''half of my mind''; the other half was thinking that her parents had recently separated. This trend of thought led me to inquire about her current life situation—where she was living, etc. By now her speech was practically ''normal'' and she was generous in sharing information with me. I thus learned that her parents had established separate households. Her father now lived with the three older children (Miss A and her two younger brothers of college age), whereas her mother lived with her youngest sister.

As I indicated, Miss A now talked quite ''normally.'' In her description I could sense various emotional tones—sadness, loneliness, longing to be cared for by her mother, jealousy toward her sister, confusion about living with three men, each of whom had his own busy social life. In my mind an idea began to crystallize: Miss A wished to be mothered by her mother but had forbidden herself to entertain such a wish. During her formative years, the wished-for mother had had blonde (dyed) hair. Now, as her conflict was being enacted in the transference, she wanted to get rid of her blonde doctor. With this construction in mind, I directed our conversation to her blonde doctor again. What came out was that her attachment to her doctor was intense and that she really had no strong desire to change doctors. Choosing an opportune moment, I thus said to her that I thought I had some understanding of her problem. Because her living situation left much to be desired, she wished to have her blonde doctor take good care of her so much that she became fearful of her own wish. It was this fear that made her sometimes think of getting away from her blonde doctor.

I watched Miss A closely. She did not disagree with me. Nor did she agree with me. But she looked interested. I went on (now quite forcefully): "In my opinion, there is no call for a change of doctors—at least now. Now, the most important thing to do is for you to tell your blonde doctor all you and I have talked about—more importantly, your wish-fear to receive mothering from your doctor." She nodded. I decided that this would be an appropriate moment for me to conclude our consultation, and I did.

Comments

Using Miss A's communicative style with me, we can divide the consultation into three parts. In the beginning she talked about her "delusions" in an emotionally expressionless way. In retrospect it is quite understandable that having requested to see me, she failed at the outset to tell me the reason for her request. She was in conflict about her blonde doctor but did not really want to leave her. If she came out with the request to change doctors, how could she be sure that I (a stranger to her) would do the right thing? She therefore had to be very cautious and use schizophrenese. But on my part, then and there, responding to her straightforward request to see me, I was not prepared to listen to her disguised communication; nor was I intrigued by her mysteriousness. In retrospect her "delusions" were impregnated with meaning (e.g., the three men at home were causing damaging anxiety inside her). But then and there, I had no idea whatsoever what she was talking about and did not feel entertained. All in all, I had no desire to tune up my empathic capacity for her. To be truthful, I stayed with her merely because it was the professional thing to do. In fact all my activities during this part of the consultation (trying to keep the conversation going, to steer our discussion to her doctor, etc.) were aimed at fulfilling the professional requirement. My predicament was: Here I am—already committed for this hour to her—why not make the best of it? Still, my learned professional (bedside) manner must have been agreeable to her. And because it was, she was willing to shift gears and try to meet me more than halfway. At this point she brought up her father.

Now we come to the second part of the consultation. As I already indicated: Suddenly, I felt I was with her (although I couldn't specify how it happened). On reflection, her comment about her father was really the turning point of the consultation. Her remark—"He had tried to help me, I think"—was followed by a weird story. Had I been duly impressed by her words, which described a horrid scene of destruction, I might have been swept away by thoughts about her father eating up her insides, his aggression, her projection, etc. And the rest of the consultation would certainly have taken quite a different direction. But, in connection with her whole presence at that moment, I was struck by the *way* she enunciated the phrase "to help me, I think"—especially the "I think," Because of this, I commented on her father's "good intentions." When she smiled, I felt I was on the right track. Now I reasoned, though not in my full awareness: She did not have to come to talk to me about her father, for she could and should be talking about him with her doctor. And this line of thought continued (still not in my full awareness): She came to me to talk about her doctor, for that would be a topic she would find it difficult to talk to her doctor about. I thus encouraged her to talk about her doctor.

At this point, after she told me that she wanted to change doctors, her language became obscure again. In retrospect it seems clear that she had touched on a conflict-laden issue and felt too much anxiety to make her story straightforward. But then and there, conditioned by her behavior during the first part of the consultation, I was not intrigued by her "gibberish." In a way, as at the outset, my exploratory questions were still determined by professional habit. The situation began to change, however, as she responded to my questions. I began to realize that although she was still uncertain about her request, she trusted me enough to share it with me. Appreciating this trust, I reciprocated in kind. Then, increasingly, even though my emotions did not vibrate with hers, her answers to my questions began to set off specific trains of thoughts in me. As a result, my questions became more and more focused.

Here we come to the third part of the consultation. Miss A now talked "normally." She was not at all bashful in allowing herself to display a wide range of emotions before me (still a relative stranger). Obviously she no longer found it necessary to deploy defensive measures to inhibit the experiencing of her emotions (see Pao, 1979). In consequence, my emotions began to reverberate with hers and I felt I was interviewing a neurotic rather than a psychotic person.

Possessing empathic capacity and attempting to empathically understand the other person are not matters of the same order. The first is a potential; the second makes use of the potential. *Every* living human possesses empathic capacity—although there are, of course, individual variations. Without this capacity, the person simply could not survive. But as much as this *capacity* is a biological given, its *use* may be facilitated or inhibited during the early years of the mother-child transactions. Thus some of us seem to develop a capacity to be more empathic than others.

Now, to make use of one's empathic capacity to understand another person's needs and wants is not a solo activity. It is a process in which the two participants—the one who desires to understand and the one who desires to be understood—must both participate actively. Together, these two participants will gradually set up a more and more intricate "network" of connected communication. This network includes not only a continuous, to-and-fro exchange (verbal or otherwise) between the two, but also the active mental transactions within each. These mental transactions, unlike those behind an empty social facade or a deep, aversive withdrawal, are aimed—at least at some level—at maintaining the to-and-fro exchange.

With Miss A, establishing this communicative network was a complex procedure, but the potential was there: Miss A wanted to be understood, despite her reservations, and I wanted to understand her, despite my limitations. We began by conversing and exchanging nonverbal clues—facial expressions, bodily movements, gestures. Through these exchanges we both came to feel that we were at least in a friendly environment. And Miss A continued to talk, to elicit and make judgments on my verbal and nonverbal responses. Eventually she let out her thoughts about her father. It may have been her tone of voice or her gestures, whatever—something made her hear her remark about her "father's help" louder than the other material in her horror story. I do not need to go on. Suffice it to say that in a continuous way what I thought, felt, and did was transmitted to her and what she thought, felt, and did (including lessening her defensive effort) was transmitted to me. Whatever was transmitted from me to her started off a new set of thoughts, feelings, and actions in her; and this in turn was transmitted back to me, starting off new thoughts, feelings, and actions in me. And so on. In this way a complicated network of connectedness was established between the two of us. As the consultation went on, it became denser and denser. Eventually we accomplished, for the most part, what we set out to accomplish—namely, for her to be understood by me and for me to understand her.

It may be that it takes somewhat less time for a continuous to-and-fro exchange to develop when the person trying to understand has a better-than-average empathic capacity. But what needs to be stressed is that this communicative network cannot be established at all without the participation of the other person—the one who wants to be understood. And however much one participant may want to keep the to-and-fro exchange going, the other participant may suddenly decide to stop it. If this occurs, the connectedness between the two will be severed. By and large, building each small step toward understanding another person is a tedious job. Yet tearing down the network of connectedness between the two participants can be as easy as flicking a switch. This is true with both neurotic and schizophrenic patients. The major difference is that with schizophrenic patients the building-up process is, as a rule, much more strenuous, and once the breakdown in connectedness occurs, it may well be final. The patient may abruptly conclude: "You have failed me too many times. You'll never understand me. I don't care any more to be understood by you. You and I are finished." Because schizophrenic patients are usually superficially compliant, they may nevertheless continue to attend the therapeutic sessions and go through the required ritual. But they may *never* again make an effort to want to be understood.

Intermittent Loss of Reality Contact and Visible Panic

Miss B, a woman in her early twenties, had been at Chestnut Lodge for about a year. Her first hospitalization had occurred five or six years before her admission to Chestnut Lodge. At that time she was confused, delusional, and hallucinating. Although during the intervening years she required periodic hospitalization, she was able to stay at home most of the time, taking an assortment of psychotropic drugs. Then, when hospitalization once again became necessary, her parents decided on long-term treatment, and she was admitted to Chestnut Lodge. Following her admission, all her medications were discontinued, and she began working with a male analyst, toward whom she readily developed an attachment. In the course of five or six months, as her relationship with her analyst deepened, she began to regress. From time to time, she was confused and "out of it." In response to her hallucinated voices, she inflicted wounds on her body. She attempted AWOL and was assaultive at times. Thus, for security reasons, she was confined to her ward.

Then, unexpectedly, Miss B's analyst decided to leave Chestnut Lodge. Approximately three weeks before his scheduled departure, she called my office and asked to talk to me. Upon receiving her request, I told myself: As she was able to take this initiative, she should have the consultation with me in my office. But when I informed the ward of my intention, I was told it was not possible. Under the present circumstances, she would have to be escorted to my office by two male technicians. My curiosity was aroused: This description did not fit my original appraisal of her. I conferred with the area administrator,[4] and we agreed that with proper handling, Miss B should be able to come to my office without too much difficulty. She was told point-blank: "Since you want to talk to Dr. Pao, you go to his office to talk to him and get your problem straightened out with him." In the end one escort, instead of two, brought her and another patient to the building where my office was located.

That Miss B was very tense could easily be detected from her stiff body, rapid gait, furtive glances, and anxious-looking face. Without invitation, disregarding any social etiquette, she went straight to a chair and simply slumped herself into it. Several minutes elapsed. She shifted her position slightly, so that she was briefly looking in my direction. I caught her eyes for a split-second, before they darted away. Sensing that I must open the session, I began: "Miss B, how do you do, and is there anything I can do for you now?" She replied: "My doctor said he is leaving the hospital." Fully aware of her anxiousness, I was nevertheless misled by her ability to verbalize her "problem" so easily. Thus I said to her: "So you've come to talk to me about leaving."

Suddenly, Miss B straightened up in her chair, as if to jump out

[4]As I have described elsewhere (Pao, 1979), at Chestnut Lodge each patient has two physicians: a therapist and an "administrator" (who is concerned with the patient's daily activities).

of it. She was looking in my direction but not at me. Her face looked pained, like a hurt animal ready to pounce and attack. For a second I was frightened. And I was acutely aware of her size—two to three inches taller than I am, with a large bone frame (this is fact, not my illusion). Anticipating the worst, I regretted my decision to see her in my office—especially as I had asked her escort to wait in the waiting room (some distance from my office), instead of right outside my door. But I knew better than to indulge in fear or regret. I pulled myself together, determined to face whatever was to ensue. Intently, I watched her movements: She lightened her grip on the arms of the chair, then slowly let go of her hold. As she did this, she slumped back into the chair.

For five minutes or so, Miss B appeared "spaced out," staring straight in my direction but without expression. She did not move and seemed miles and miles away. In essence, she assumed a catatonic pose. I figured that I had been careless, that my remark had been too much for her. I decided that the best thing to do now would be to wait and be quiet. So another five minutes passed. Then Miss B stirred. As if awakening from a dream, she gazed at me with a perplexed expression and asked where she was. I explained: "I am Dr. Pao. You wanted to see me and so we are meeting in my office." She looked about, as if to reorient herself. I remained silent, wondering what action I should take now. Several more minutes went by. I noticed that her facial expression now appeared more relaxed.

Finally I decided it was time for me to try again: "You wanted to see me." She nodded. After another spell of silence she began to talk. Miss B told me that she saw a psychiatrist before she came to Chestnut Lodge, that she had taken medicine for a long, long time but was no longer taking any medicine. I expressed appreciation for the information. She went on: "I told them that I could not make the dining room. They said I could. I went. I cut myself—my voice told me to do that." As I searched for words, she continued: "On the ward I curl up like this." She drew her legs up, taking a squatting position in the chair. Then she pushed her head down as low as possible, into the space created by her separated legs. She raised her arms and crossed them over her bent head. It seemed a fetal position.

At this point I uttered some sound to encourage her to go on. To my relief, she did: "I had to—Joan and Mary [both patients] wanted to talk to me. They drove me crazy. Gary [another patient] paced all the time and he drove me crazy. I wanted to go to my room and they [the staff] wouldn't let me." I felt very sympathetic toward her. Suddenly, I remembered another patient, from some years ago: While talking to this patient in my office, I would inadvertently shift my position, or cross and recross my legs. When I did that, she would stop talking and suddenly scream at me, at the top of her lungs: "You have grated my brain." At first I had been completely baffled. This woman could not tell me that the "grating" was related to my movement. (Nor, in my opinion, should my movement have created any noise). I myself immediately tried to link her screams to my verbalized statement—without success. It was only after a long while that I began to see a connection. When I imparted my understanding to her, she told me that what I considered a noiseless movement, she experienced as thunder. Why this noise we would ordinarily ignore should be experienced by her as thunder I never did understand. Why, for instance, didn't she experience my voice (although it was soft) as thunder? At any rate, for some time thereafter I tried to make only minimal movements in order to keep our conversation going.

Because of this memory, I decided that Miss B wanted very much to ward off external stimuli. It occurred to me that at this moment the major external stimulus was her doctor's leaving. Perhaps this was the reason she had requested to see me before her doctor actually departed. So when she paused for breath, I interjected: "You felt that a lot of things going on around you were difficult for you to cope with." She agreed. I hastened to add: "Such as people coming and going." I did not directly state that her doctor would be leaving her; it did not seem necessary to do so, for at a preconscious level she knew what I was talking about. Moreover, if I did spell it out, she would definitely deny me the satisfaction of knowing how she felt.

Miss B's immediate response was: "I have been in this hospital for almost one year." Her voice was full of sadness. "It does take a long time to know someone," I commented. And she replied: "I knew my doctor before I came here for seven years." Noting her evasiveness, I decided to nail it down a little: "Once we know somebody, we feel sad when we have to part—like you previously parted with your doctor in your hometown and now with Dr. X." Although wistful, she shed no tears, saying: "I have been sick for a long time." My response was: "It was unfortunate that you and your doctors had to part, but your partings were not determined by your being sick for a long time. In fact, judging from the way you talk to me, I know you are struggling hard to get well and as long as this struggle goes on you will, I believe, feel a lot better." (Note: to say "feel a lot better" is different from saying "you will get well.") Now, in a childlike way, she asked: "Really?" I answered: "It is my firm belief, and I hope you will continue to do what you have been doing—that is, struggle to get well." She nodded. She was a bit tearful now.

Thinking that this would be the best time to conclude the hour, I said: "You came to ask me to give you a new doctor who could help you in your struggle. I will be very serious in my choice. I hope that you can believe me when I say I will be serious." She looked "soft" and relaxed as she said: "Yes." When we parted, I intentionally offered my hand. With some hesitation, she raised her hand to reach mine. Deliberately holding her hand very tight, I affirmed: "We shall both try." She then returned uneventfully to her ward with the escort.

Comment

In presenting this case, I intended to bring out the patient's tendency to flip in and out of reality as the result of extreme anxiety. Yet during this consultation Miss B broke with reality only once. As a schizophrenic-I patient (Pao, 1979), Miss B might have had sufficient ego strength to hold onto reality despite her extreme anxiety. It is also significant that her break with reality was not a complete one; for instance, she seemed to some extent to control her behavior by "making" herself catatonic and thus averting her automatic response to extreme anxiety—that is, to be destructive toward others or herself. With sicker patients (schizophrenic-II or -III) one would expect frequent breaks with reality during an interview. Moreover, the patient would seem to have less control over this, and it would be more difficult to discern what had precipitated the break (recall the example of the patient who felt her brain was being grated when I uncrossed and recrossed my legs).

In the early part of the consultation I believe I made a serious error in broaching a painful subject with a very anxious patient in a rather callous way. This error, in my opinion, was a technical one, not strictly related to empathy. For at that stage of the consultation, the empathic network had not yet been established. I did not really know Miss B, nor had I received enough of a message from her to establish an empathic understanding of the best way to approach her. In response to my error, Miss B resorted to aggressivity to assuage her pain. I was almost the target of her aggression.[5] Certainly I was glad that she held off her aggression by becoming catatonic for a while. That she could go in and out of this catatonic state with some degree of ego control portended a relatively good prognosis (I sincerely hoped she could benefit from analytic psychotherapy).

When Miss B made a second effort to communicate with me, I was more careful. This care had more to do with my professional experience than with empathy per se, for an empathic network only developed much later in the consultation. The distinction I am making here can be sensed in a shift in attentiveness. In the beginning, when I rely on my professional skills, I am usually aware of extraneous stimuli, such as the hum of a lawn mower or the muffled yet still distinct click of a typewriter in the next room. In con-

[5]Assaults by patients on the unit may often result from a statement or action by a staff member, to which the patient overreacts.

trast, as the empathic network is being established, I become increasingly absorbed in the verbal and nonverbal exchange and in the goings-on in my own mind as a result of this exchange. At these times I am practically oblivious to other stimuli.

To me, the turning point of the consultation occurred shortly after Miss B "reoriented" herself, when I repeated to her: "You wanted to see me." Following my statement, she started to give me some "history." On the surface the "history" was irrelevant, yet I sensed that it was impregnated with important messages. Thus I thanked her for giving me the information. Now she decided to let her hair down, so to speak, and proceeded to tell me, although still in schizophrenese, about being overburdened by too much external stimulation. We were both becoming more and more involved, and a network of connectedness began to be firmly established.

The turning point must be attributed to her effort; it was initiated by her. Fortunately I did not drop the ball this time, as I found meaning in her seemingly irrelevant report of fragmented events in the "history" of her past treatment. Such good luck is not rare. Yet it depends on the intensity of the patient's need to get a conversation going with the other person. More important, it depends on the patient's feeling of hopefulness at that given moment—"Maybe I can yet get my idea across." If this hopefulness had not existed, Miss B would have ceased to make any effort and our consultation would have stopped short, long before we could accomplish our goal.

To suddenly remember an old patient and then make use of this association in the current context is not uncommon in the treatment of neurotic patients. It is only with psychotic patients that we sometimes consider it prudent not to ask exploratory questions. I did not, for instance, ask Miss B what she meant when she said: "I have been sick for a long time." When the patient is psychotic and especially when he or she is very anxious, an exploratory question can often be experienced as a bullet shot; it can have a countertherapeutic effect. My response to Miss B's statement was guided by the emotion stirred up in me—hopelessness. I geared my action toward encouraging her to keep on trying.

Earlier I mentioned that every action should be deemed a part of the empathic process once the communicative network has been established. I would like to stress that omission of an action is also an action. When, for instance, I commented to Miss B in general terms on "people coming and going," I might have instead or in addition, remarked: "Dr. X is leaving." My not stating that "Dr. X is leaving" (which was the purpose of our meeting to begin with) was determined by my understanding of Miss B, gained through the exchanges in the empathic network she and I had established. From this understanding, it was quite clear to me that without making the statement openly, I had already brought to her awareness that Dr. X's leaving was one of her current concerns. And I knew that should I directly state this, I might evoke so many emotions in her that she wouldn't be able to stay calm and carry on our exchange. Such precaution is perhaps less necessary with a neurotic patient.

It is of interest that from the beginning to the end of the consultation my attitude toward Miss B was consistent—consistent in placing the responsibility on her shoulders. At the very beginning, based on the fact that she had made the request to see me, I insisted that she and I should meet in my office—implying that she should take a certain responsibility. At the end I elicited her cooperation in accomplishing a common goal. It's true that at the beginning I simply made an educated guess (and that educated guess could hardly be considered as deriving from empathy). What might evolve from that guess was completely beyond my control. But after having spent nearly an hour with her, my effort to encourage her to take responsibility was empathically determined; then I knew what I could expect from her.

Lack of Reality Orientation and Almost Mute

Mrs. C became acutely psychotic at 19 and was in and out of hospitals for six years, before being admitted to Chestnut Lodge. Upon admission, she was disoriented and very violent, but in a couple of months she calmed down considerably (without drugs).

Still, for most of the day she had to be kept in a quiet room. There she smeared food and feces all over the wall. And she managed to remove most of the wallboard, as well as some of the acoustical tiles from the ceiling. When she met with her analyst, she was in general mute, with occasional outbursts of threatening to attack him.

This was the situation when I paid her a visit. Her room was locked from outside. Inside, there was no furniture, except for a rubber mattress lying in the middle of the room, stripped of sheets. Mrs. C sat on the floor in one corner of the room, where she could not be easily seen through the small window of the door. When I walked in, she had obviously been forewarned by the click of the key and the opening of the door. She appeared alert. Yet, at the sight of me, she immediately lost interest and returned to "reading" the newspaper. (I could not be certain that she was actually reading it.)

I introduced myself—and I sensed that I was very formal, but I did not know how else to act. I explained that I visited various patients from time to time. Mrs. C didn't even look up. When I asked her permission to sit down on the mattress, she ignored me. I did not feel rejected, but I knew I would be ignored—no matter what I said or did. Finding no magic word to break the silence, I decided to remain quiet. Although in the main looking in her direction, I glanced at the damage done to the room—the acoustic tiles missing from the ceiling, the wallboard mostly stripped from the wall, the walls themselves smeared with dirty colors (they had obviously been scrubbed). In silence I entertained some fantasies, reflecting on how, although she was now sitting there quietly, she must have a fierce temper. She looked small, but she obviously had a lot of strength if she had torn off the wallboard. And how did she manage to remove the ceiling tiles? That was a real feat: Why did she do all these things? Perhaps she felt like a caged animal. But she was violent and destructive before it became necessary to confine her to the quiet room. What had propelled her into this display of violence? So my thoughts went.

Suddenly, I noticed that Mrs. C had raised the newspaper in

such a way that her face was hidden from me. I thought a bit, and felt like saying: "Perhaps my surveying this room has made you feel ashamed of what you did and so . . ." But I didn't say anything, for I was completely uncertain that my reproachful thoughts were true. Then I noticed that once in a while she would pull down the newspaper and peek at me. I was glad that she was curious but found no proper words to say. Finally, when she peeked again, I commented: "Yes, I am still here. I hope you don't wish to chase me out." All of a sudden she put down the newspaper and asked: "What do you want?" Before I could answer, she pulled the newspaper up again.

But now, I felt inspired: "You want to hide from me—you want to hide from others by getting yourself locked inside this room. Is there anything you feel that is so terrible? You feel angry, I assume. But I know you had a good reason to be angry. Should a person who is angry be locked up?" From behind the newspaper she roared: "Get out." I didn't experience her roar as malicious or as requiring any action. Thus I found myself telling her quite calmly: "I'd be glad to get out, but I must learn something with respect to your need to hide yourself from me." She roared again behind the paper: "Go ask my father and my husband." I replied: "I don't see how they could know why you want to hide from me." Again she roared, this time more angrily: "They put me here." So I said: "You are very angry because they put you in the hospital. You don't like to see yourself being very angry and you don't like me to detect that you are angry, so you hide your face from me. Isn't that it? Now tell me why you are so ashamed of your anger." She didn't say anything, still hiding behind the newspaper. I pleaded: "Would you let me take a look at your face? Let me see if I'd be frightened by it." She responded in a softer tone, with the newspaper still up: "Get out and leave me alone." Although her voice was not ferocious, there was a finality to it. So I said "okay" and stood up.

As I thought about lingering on for a brief moment, she lowered the newspaper to peek. I seized the opportunity: "I am glad to see your face, which to me is not hideously frightening. In fact, it reflects a kindly soul." To my surprise, she now put down the newspaper, placing it in her lap. Still standing, I said: "I do wish you'd talk to your doctor about why you are so ashamed of your own anger." She said nothing. Unable to curb my curiosity, I asked her if she tore up the room because she was angry. This time I was really surprised; I learned that she was tearing the room apart in order to get out of the hospital. I told her that I understood her wish to get out of the hospital, but she wouldn't succeed in the way she was going about it. If she went through the ceiling, there was another floor; and if she went through the wall, there was another room. Instead, I suggested that I could give her some tips on how to get out of the hospital. She might talk to her analyst about her angry feelings and how ashamed she was about them. Thereupon I bid goodbye to her.

Comment

In establishing an empathic network, nonverbal behavior can play an important role. Although in the treatment of neurotics we tend to use a preeminently verbal exchange, in the treatment of psychotics (especially mute patients) we have to rely greatly on the nonverbal exchange. With Mrs. C, for instance, even when we were sitting silently with each other, a to-and-fro nonverbal exchange was going on. It was through this nonverbal exchange that I got a glimpse of what was going on in the patient's mind. Nevertheless, to really understand the patient, I did have to fall back on our verbal exchange.

The turning point of this consultation was when I caught her peeking out at me from behind the newspaper. Suddenly, it became pristinely clear that my fantasy about her feeling ashamed was "fact." Thus I ventured to say what I said. And later, when she put down the newspaper, I could have proceeded to establish a conversation with her. She might have (who knows?) told me a lot about herself. But something in me told me to say only: "I do wish you'd talk to your doctor. . ." This wasn't so much a concern about siphoning transference material; it was more a concern about the situation she and I were in. I decided that to talk to her indirectly was far better than insisting on a direct conversation. Similarly, when my curiosity about why she had destroyed the room was satisfied, there was a good atmosphere for furthering our conversation. Again I was told by an inner voice not to step beyond a certain threshold, and I obeyed. I felt then that if I went on, I might get some very interesting (perhaps even very important) information about her. But at some point she would feel like withdrawing. At this point our network, tediously built-up, would be shattered to pieces. As a result, she probably would not register anything we talked about, or even remember that for a few moments she had actually talked with someone with relatively little reservation.

Working with schizophrenic patients, the analyst is constantly confronted with the patient's wish-fear dilemma. To strike a balance, one must know (through the empathic network) how long one can get the patient to stay in the network, how much elaboration of certain topics one can expect in one session, and when and where one should terminate the interview. In the consultation with Mrs. C, I had the advantage of leaving when I felt I should leave. In the treatment setting, however, the length of the session is set. If the analyst leaves early, the patient (even without a watch) may interpret it in a specific way, according to his or her need at that moment. Instead, I would suggest turning to a lighter, perhaps irrelevant, topic—one the patient can enjoy and participate in. Then, if possible (and usually it is) near the end of the hour, the analyst can bring the "important" topic back—merely as a refocusing, without any desire to rework it.

It is true that tomorrow, or even a month from tomorrow, the patient may not bring back the "important" topic. That doesn't matter. The analyst's job is to be with the patient in the context of the here and now. It is in this here-and-now context that the analyst and patient should hope to establish the empathic network in each session. And it is because of this empathic network that the patient may drop his or her schizophrenese and talk plainly with us. Of course, only through plain talk can we reach some verbalized, unambiguous, consensual validation. I recall that during my my residency days I was awed to learn that Harry Stack Sullivan or Frieda Fromm-Reichmann could make most schizophrenic patients drop their schizophrenese. Now, although I can't imagine myself ever doing what they did, I do believe that what they achieved was not only possible but will be repeated by many in generations to come. However "original" the quality of empathic capacity is, the use of that potential can be learned (although it cannot be taught).

Concluding Remarks

Katan (1954) unequivocally asserted that in treating a schizophrenic patient, the analyst has to pay attention to the "well" part of the patient. I fully concur with his view. In my contact with any schizophrenic patient, I try my utmost to reach this "well" part, hoping to establish as normal a conversation as I can with any human being. My hope, however, has more often than not been dashed. Elsewhere (Pao, 1979), I have described the striking subjective experience in interviewing schizophrenic patients—that during the interview one may experience a total inability to make emotional contact or an intermittent breaking up of the emotional contact once it is established. I have learned that this breaking up of emotional contact (attaching or linking in Bion's [1959] terms) is the patient's doing. If I am lucky, I can manage to limit this break to a minimum. But the break in emotional contact is very much related to the degree of the patient's illness and the degree of anxiety he or she experiences at that given moment. Thus there are times when whatever I do to establish or to maintain emotional contact appears insignificant.

In the cases described here, I was uniquely successful in averting a break in emotional contact for unduly long periods of time. This contrasts sharply to situations where I interviewed a patient shortly after admission to select a doctor, or where the patient and I had already contracted for long-term psychoanalytic psychotherapy.

On closer examination, what stands out is that, with the exception of Mrs. C, the patients had requested to see me and had already prepared themselves. Again, this suggests that for one person to arrive at an empathic understanding of the other, both participants have to make an effort. To put it in another way: For the analyst's vicarious introspection to be useful, the patient must participate in introspection as well. If the patient exercises too much resistance to introspection, the analyst's vicarious introspection alone can hardly reach any deep understanding of the patient. Still, parallel, simultaneous introspection by the analyst and the patient is an inadequate way to depict the process of empathic understanding. To arrive at such an understanding, what is introspected by one must be transmitted to the other and vice versa. This continuous to-and-fro exchange establishes what I characterize as the empathic network; only when this network becomes increasingly dense can "normal" communication be maintained.

To exchange what is introspected involves actions—both conscious and unconscious. The most conscious action is, of course, the analyst's interpretive utterance. If interpretation refers to making the unconscious conscious, then in treating a schizophrenic patient the analyst must be prepared to make noninterpretive remarks. Without such noninterpretive remarks, the conversation with a schizophrenic patient will soon run dry. When long silence ensues, the network of connectedness rapidly breaks down. And once this breakdown occurs, its repair can be tedious. Success cannot be guaranteed in the same hour—or even in several hours to follow.

REFERENCES

Bion, W. R. (1959). Attacks on linking. *Int. J. Psychoanal.*, 40:308–315.

Fliess, R. (1942). The metapsychology of the analyst. *Psychoanal. Q.*, 11:211–227.

Katan, M. (1954). The importance of the non-psychotic part of the personality in schizophrenia. *Int. J. Psychoanal.*, 35:119–128.

Pao, P.-N. (1979). *Schizophrenic Disorders*. New York: Int. Univ. Press.

27 The Borderline Concept: Pathological Character or Iatrogenic Myth?

BERNARD BRANDCHAFT, M.D., and ROBERT D. STOLOROW, Ph.D.

THE BORDERLINE CONCEPT has, in recent years, achieved enormous popularity within psychoanalytic and psychotherapeutic circles. Despite this rise to stardom, vast differences of opinion and numerous unresolved questions continue to exist concerning just what, if anything, the term "borderline" describes. We shall not attempt to cover the voluminous literature on this subject here (see Sugarman and Lerner, 1980, for an excellent review). Instead, we offer a critique of the currently prevalent view that the term "borderline" refers to a discrete pathological character structure, rooted in specific pathognomonic instinctual conflicts and primitive defenses. In our opinion, an alternative understanding of borderline phenomena emerges when they are viewed from a psychoanalytic developmental and self-psychological perspective.

The term "borderline" is generally used to refer to a distinct character structure that predisposes to faulty object relations, in which the fundamental difficulties are ordinarily attributed to the patient's pathological ego functioning. Typically the borderline personality organization is pictured as a direct structural consequence of the patient's use of certain primitive defenses—splitting, projective identification, idealization, and grandiosity—to ward off intense conflicts over

This paper is dedicated to the memory of Heinz Kohut, who extended our capacity for empathic understanding to previously inaccessible regions of human subjectivity.

dependency and excessive pregenital aggression (which dependency presumably mobilizes). But what is the clinical evidence that supposedly demonstrates the operation of these primitive defenses? And what is the meaning of the excessive aggression to which primary etiological significance is ascribed in the genesis of borderline psychopathology?

The Question of Splitting

The experience of external objects as "all-good" or "all-bad" is generally regarded as a clear manifestation of splitting, resulting in sudden and total reversals of feeling whereby the view of the object is shifted from one extreme to the other. Oscillation between extreme and contradictory self-concepts is similarly seen as evidence of splitting. This fluid and rapid alternation of contradictory perceptions of the self or others is seen as the result of an active defensive process whereby images with opposing affective valences are forcibly kept apart in order to prevent intense ambivalence. But is this assumption warranted clinically? Splitting as a defense actively employed to ward off ambivalence conflicts can come into play only after a minimum of integration of discrepant self- and object experiences has been achieved through development (Stolorow and Lachmann, 1980). A defensive split into parts presupposes a prior integration of a whole. It is our contention that such a presupposition is not warranted when treating patients who are ordinarily diagnosed "borderline." Their fragmentary perceptions do not result primarily from defensive activity, but rather from an arrest in development, which impairs their ability reliably to synthesize affectively discrepant experiences of self and other. Their rapidly fluctuating views of the therapist, for example, do not primarily serve to prevent ambivalence toward him (or her). They are, in part, manifestations of a need for the therapist to serve as an archaic containing or holding object whose consistently empathic *comprehension* and acceptance of these patients' contradictory affective states function as a facilitating medium through which their varying perceptions and feelings can eventually become better integrated (Winnicott, 1965; Modell, 1976; Stolorow and Lachmann, 1980).

It is our view that the lack of synthesis of self- and object experiences characteristic of so-called borderline states is neither defensive in nature nor central in the genesis of these disorders. In our experience, the intense, contradictory affective states that these patients experience within the transference, and in particular their violent negative reactions, are indicative of specific structural weaknesses and vulnerabilities rooted in specific developmental interferences. Archaic mirroring and idealizing needs are revived in analytic transferences, together with hopes for a resumption of development. When these needs are responded to, or understood and interpreted empathically, intense positive reactions occur. Similarly, when these needs are not recognized, responded to, or interpreted empathically, violent negative reactions may ensue. If these angry reactions are presumed to represent a defensive dissociation of good and bad aspects of objects, this in effect constitutes a covert demand that the patient ignore his own subjective experiences and appreciate the "goodness" of the analyst and his interpretations. It precludes analysis of the patient's subjective experience in depth, the elements that go to make it up, and their special hierarchy of meanings for the patient. In contrast when we have held such preconceptions in abeyance, we have found that the intensity of the angry reactions stems from the way they encoded and encapsulated memories of specific traumatic childhood experiences.

The Case of Jeff

A clinical vignette illustrates our idea of a specific vulnerability. When Jeff, a young man of 23, entered treatment, he was in a state of marked overstimulation. He could not sit still for more than a few minutes at a time; his eyes darted from object to object; and he spoke under constant pressure. Although enrolled in college, he had not been able to attend classes or concentrate on his work. Increasingly frightened when alone at night, he had recently begun to take to the streets. There he had been approached for homosexual purposes several times, and this made him more fearful of his own unrecognized wishes and heightened his agitation. In the sessions he gave the impression of wanting desperately to cling to something around which he might begin to reorganize and restructure himself. Consequently, during the first months of treatment it was very difficult to bring any session to a close. His initial resistances centered on fears of being used to fulfill the analyst's needs. When these were interpreted, an early idealizing transference developed. This enabled Jeff to confront the area of primary defect—a failure to have attained a cohesive self and a vulnerability to recurrent states of protracted disorganization. The analysis thus resumed a developmental process that had been stalled.

Jeff's relationship with his father had always presented difficulty for him. The father reacted to any weakness or shortcoming in his son with impatience and contempt. This situation directly entered the analysis because Jeff's father had assumed financial responsibility for the treatment. The arrangement became a source of greater and greater tension between the two, for the father resented the burden of payment, as well as what he saw as evidence of his son's weakness and simultaneously a source of shame for himself. The difficulties in this area increased whenever Jeff made it clear that the analysis was not leading in the direction of making Jeff the son his father had always wished for, but was instead increasing Jeff's determination to develop in his own way.

Although the analyst realized the complications that might ensue, after two and a half years he notified Jeff that he was raising his fees generally. He wanted to discuss the matter with Jeff to see if and how it might be worked out. The request came at a time when Jeff's relations with his father were already strained, though it did not appear likely that this would change within any foreseeable period of time. Jeff's initial response was one of some anger about the unfortunate timing, followed by a remark to the effect that of course he knew how the analyst felt because everything was going up in price. Recognizing Jeff's frequent tendency to substitute an understanding of someone else's position for an expression of his own, the analyst interpreted this, together with Jeff's fear of the analyst's reaction to his expressing his own feeling. (We would emphasize that in our experience such genuine emotional expression is always obstructed, and with it an essential aspect of an authentic relationship, when a patient's affective states are incorrectly interpreted as defensive transference distortions.)

Gradually, over the course of the next few sessions, Jeff was able to come out with his feelings—feelings of hurt, disappointment, and violent anger. The hurt seemed to center on the analyst's failure to *ever* (Jeff's words) consider him first, and the extent to which this experience revived feelings of always having been a burden, a supplicant, someone standing in the way of other people's plans or enjoyment. Jeff was a twin, and he recounted a welter of experiences in which his twin had preempted his parents' attention by being exactly the child they wanted and one who caused them no difficulty.

Jeff's anger at the analyst was related mostly to the poor timing and what that meant to him. He spoke of the bind the analyst's request put him in. Things were already going badly between him and his father. Jeff had just started a new job and had been forced to ask his father for money for new clothes. Each encounter of that kind was humiliating for Jeff. Now he would have to face a review of how long he had been in treatment and how much longer it was to continue. How could the analyst, knowing all this, choose to put Jeff through it!

Frequently, after expressing himself unabashedly, Jeff would huddle up, as if in a corner, his arms protectively wrapped around himself. In response to questions, he confirmed that he was terrified. He was certain that the analyst would be furious with him, call him selfish, and berate him for his lack of appreciation for the analyst.

There now emerged a host of memories in which the timing of Jeff's life (and indeed, his life itself) had to conform to someone else's wishes. He had to go to bed when his father said so to his mother. He had to wait until his father was done with the evening news before speaking to him, and then he could only talk about what his father was interested in. Monday night, football night, was especially sacrosanct—not an occasion when a pleasurable interest might be shared, but one more occasion when Dad was not to be disturbed.

Jeff's mother told him when, what, and how to eat. She chose his clothes for him, where and how he was to sit or stand. He was not to sit on the couch lest the cushions be messed up, nor on his bed for similar reasons. He had to renounce his own inclinations and adopt her wishes regarding what music he was to like. Always before the family left on an auto trip, he was instructed to urinate, and his mother checked to make sure he didn't put anything over on them. Otherwise they might have to stop along the way. And Jeff recalled that whenever he attempted to protest or assert himself, perhaps because something was especially important to him, he was squelched, accused of selfishness and a lack of consideration. He was told his father wouldn't want to come home at all if he kept this up.

For Jeff, the most significant aspect of these repeated experiences was a feeling of absolute powerlessness. Once, when he could not stand it anymore, he went to his room and packed an overnight bag. When he appeared in front of his parents to declare he was running away, no one said a word or made a move to stop him. He then realized that he was stuck—that no one else would want him and that he had to give in.

These experiences formed the background of Jeff's reaction to the analyst's request for an increase. Jeff retained, in its most imperative form, the longing that someone would put his wishes first, and he was highly sensitive to the specific configuration of others' needs being put before his own. He therefore responded acutely and intensely to that configuration when it entered the transference. This response was covered over by a more moderate reaction, in which he apparently attempted defensively to "synthesize" good and bad object concepts. What was crucial, however, was for Jeff to recognize the underlying intensity of his hurt and the experiences behind it, rather than having his reaction regarded as an instance of splitting or a lack of appreciation for the analyst. This recognition opened up an entire area of the transference to analysis and ultimate resolution. Jeff and the analyst came to see clearly the extent to which Jeff had found it necessary to define himself around what was expected, what would please, and what would not offend in order to maintain his object ties. They were able to comprehend the threat constantly posed to any authentic experience of self—the threat of estrangement and isolation Jeff had encountered whenever he asserted himself or attempted to act on his own behalf. The analysis, then, brought out into the open and allowed Jeff to work through the enormous resentment such distortion of self had aroused.

The Question of Projective Identification

Considerations similar to those which we have discussed for splitting apply to the view of projective identification as a primitive defense, characteristic of borderline patients. In projective identification there is a blurring of the distinction between the self and the object in the area of the projected content. Such states of self-object confusion are presumed to be the product of an active defensive effort to externalize all-bad, aggressive self- and object images. Once again, we question whether this assumption is clinically justified.

Projection as a defense actively employed to ward off conflict can come into play only after a minimum of self-object differentiation has been reliably achieved (Stolorow and Lachmann, 1980). Defensive translocation of mental content across self-object boundaries presupposes that those boundaries have been for the most part consolidated. Our experience contradicts such a presupposition for patients diagnosed "borderline." Their states of self-object confusion arise primarily from a developmentally determined inability to maintain the distinction between self and object. In the treatment context it is not useful to view such states as examples of either defensive projection or general ego weakness. Instead, these partially undifferentiated states are best understood as manifestations of revivals with the therapist of a specific need for immersion in a nexus of archaic relatedness, from within which formerly thwarted developmental processes of self-articulation and self-demarcation can be revitalized and once again resumed (Stolorow and Lachmann, 1980).

Frequently we have encountered in the literature a second, and to our minds even more questionable, use of the term "projective identification." There is presumed to be not only a projective distortion of the patient's subjective experience of the object, but also a purposefully induced alteration in the external object's actual attitude and behavior toward the patient. The patient is said to put split-off, disavowed parts of himself inside the external object. This formulation is based on the observation that intense reactions frequently occur in analysts who are treating borderline patients. Because such reactions are experienced similarly by most "reasonably well-adjusted therapists," the reasoning goes, "countertransference reactions in these cases reflect the patient's problems much more than any specific problems of the analyst's past" (Kernberg, 1975, p. 54). It is also suggested that if the analyst is reacting intensely to the patient, such countertransference is a clue to the patient's hidden intention. Kernberg, for example, writes:

> If the patient systematically rejects all the analyst's interpretations over a long period of time, the analyst may recognize his own resultant feelings of impotence and point out to the patient that he is treating the analyst as if he wished to make him feel defeated and impotent. Or when antisocial behavior in the patient makes the analyst, rather than the patient worry about the consequences, the analyst may point out that the patient seems to try to let the analyst feel the concern over his behavior because the patient himself cannot tolerate such a feeling [1975, p. 247)].

These formulations fail to take into account that when the analyst, in his interpretations, insists that the patient's difficulties arise from vicissitudes of aggressive-drive processing, the only alternatives open to the patient are to agree with the premises being put forward or to find himself in the position of *inadvertently* making the analyst feel defeated and impotent. To us, this state of affairs seems to reflect the extent to which the analyst's self-esteem depends on the patient's acceptance of the correctness of his theoretical position, rather than necessarily reflecting any unconscious hostile intention on the part of the patient. Similarly, the analyst's concerns about a patient's antisocial behavior seem to us to reflect the analyst's difficulties in sufficiently demarcating himself from the patient so as to be able to devote himself to the investigation of the meaning of the actions in question.

A description of a typical clinical application of the concept of projective identification is contained in Kernberg's reference to Ingmar Bergman's movie *Persona:*

> A recent motion picture . . . illustrates the breakdown of an immature but basically decent young woman, a nurse, charged with the care of a psychologically severely ill woman presenting what we would describe as a typical narcissistic personality. In the face of the cold, unscrupulous

> exploitation to which the young nurse is subjected she gradually breaks down. She cannot face the fact that the other sick woman returns only hatred for love and is completely unable to acknowledge any loving or human feeling toward her. The sick woman seems able to live only if and when she can destroy what is valuable in other persons, although in the process she ends up by destroying herself as a human being. In a dramatic development the nurse develops an intense hatred for the sick woman and mistreats her cruelly at one point. It is as if all the hatred within the sick woman had been transferred into the helpful one, destroying the helping person from the inside [1975, pp. 245–246].

We hold that conclusions such as this are unjustified and that the underlying assumptions are unwarranted and antitherapeutic. In the first place, there is no evidence that the sick woman is "able to live only if and when she can destroy what is valuable in other persons"; there are only indications that the sick woman does not respond in a way that the nurse-therapist wants or needs. We are familiar in our own practice with many cases in which patients who have recently experienced traumatic loss and disintegration resolutely protect themselves against any involvement until some spontaneous recovery has set in. Second, there is no evidence that "the hatred within the sick woman has been transferred into the helpful one, destroying the helping person from the inside." There is, instead, every indication that the patient's responsiveness was required in order for the nurse to maintain her own self-esteem and to regulate her own psychological functioning. When frustrated, the nurse demonstrated her own narcissistic vulnerability and propensity for rage reactions. We have observed such factors at work in ourselves and regard them to some degree as universal in therapeutic relationships. In our view, their near universality does not warrant their being ignored as originating in the personality structure of the therapist. Nor does it warrant the assumption that these responses are an indication of pathological projective mechanisms on the part of the patient. We have found that the assumption that the patient wishes the therapist to feel impotent or infuriated is much more often than not directly contradicted in our own work. Such wishes, we suggest, occur only when the patient's disagreements, assertions, and primary wishes to have his own subjective experiences empathically understood have been consistently unresponded to. Far more often, the patient's fear of the analyst's narcissistic vulnerability and of being held responsible for the analyst's feeling of frustration constitutes a severe resistance to free association and a prominent motive for defense.

The concept of projective identification is used extensively by analysts to explain any fear that is not readily intelligible as a response to a real danger. It is consistently invoked to explain why patients are so regularly afraid of their analysts. We have found, however, that the analyst's insistence that negative reactions in analysis are to be explained by the patient's innate aggression or envy, or by his projection of aggressively distorted internal objects, can be damaging to the patient, to the unfolding selfobject transference, and to the analysis (Brandchaft, 1983).

The application of the theory of projective identification carries with it the real danger of depriving patients of a means of defending themselves when they feel that the analyst is cruel, distant, controlling, or demeaning. This danger is increased if the analyst, for whatever reason, is unable or unwilling to become aware of his actual effect on the patient, or if he minimizes that effect because of a conviction that he has the ultimate best interests of the patient at heart. Frequently, this conviction in the analyst takes the form of a conception of a "more normal dependent" part of the patient, which is being dominated and excluded by the aggressive part. Such unwarranted, if reassuring, concepts notwithstanding, the tendency to fall back on interpretations of projection to the detriment of the subjective experience of the patient, even where such mechanisms exist, can in practice be shown to foster a dependence on the analyst's perceptions at the expense of the patient's. These interpretations encourage, indeed require, a *pro forma* belief in the analyst's "goodness" and correctness at the expense of the self. They impair the patient's sense of his own self and belief in that self, and they encourage an agreement that necessary and understandable efforts to protect a vulnerable self are indicative of severe pathology and should be given up.

Further Misconceptualizations

Closely allied with the developmental disturbances discussed so far are the idealizations and grandiosity which often pervade the treatment of patients who are called "borderline." Such inflations of the self or others are regularly interpreted as being defensive against dependency and the attendant subject-centered or object-centered aggression. Our experiences indicate that most often the idealizations and grandiosity are manifestations of selfobject transferences (Kohut, 1971, 1977). They are not pathological defenses, but rather revivals with the therapist of the archaic idealizing and mirroring ties which had been traumatically and phase-inappropriately ruptured during the patient's formative years, and upon which he now comes to rely for the restoration and maintenance of his sense of self and for the resumption and completion of his arrested psychological growth.

Having argued that much of the clinical evidence cited for the operation of primitive defenses is actually evidence of needs for specific modes of relatedness to archaic selfobjects, and of the empathic failures of such selfobjects, how shall we understand the "excessive pregenital aggression" that many authors believe is the etiological bedrock of borderline pathology? We contend that pervasive primitive aggression is an inevitable, unwitting, iatrogenic consequence of a therapeutic approach that presupposes that the psychological configurations we have been discussing are in their essence pathological defenses against dependency and primitive aggression. A patient revives an arrested archaic state or need, or attempts a previously aborted developmental step within the therapeutic relationship, and the therapist interpets this developmental necessity as if it were a pathological defense. The patient then experiences this misinterpretation as a gross failure of empathy, a severe breach of trust, a traumatic narcissistic wound (Stolorow and Lachmann, 1980). When vital developmental requirements reexperienced in relation to the therapist once again meet with traumatically unempathic responses, is it surprising that such misunderstandings often bring intense rage and destructiveness in their wake? We are contending, in other words, that the pervasive aggression is not etiological, but rather a secondary reaction to the therapist's inability to comprehend the developmental meaning of the patient's archaic states and of the archaic bond that the patient needs to establish with him (Kohut, 1972, 1977).

An Intersubjective Viewpoint

At this point we are in a position to formulate our central thesis regarding the borderline concept. The psychological essence of what we call "borderline" is *not* that it is a pathological condition located solely in the patient. Rather, *it refers to phenomena arising in an intersubjective field—a field consisting of a precarious, vulnerable self and a failing, archaic selfobject.* In order to elaborate this thesis further, we must clarify the nature of the self disorder that contributes to the emergence of borderline phenomena.

We view the various disorders of the self as arbitrary points along a continuum (see Adler, 1981), rather than as discrete diagnostic entities. The points along this continuum are defined by the degree of impairment and vulnerability of the sense of self, the acuteness of the threat of its disintegration, and the motivational urgency of self-reparative efforts in various pathological states. The degree of severity of self disorder may be evaluated with reference to three essential features of the sense of self—its structural cohesion, temporal stability, and affective coloration (Stolorow and Lachmann, 1980).

In certain patients, the sense of self is negatively colored (feelings of low self-esteem) but is for the most part temporally stable and structurally cohesive. One might refer to such cases as mild self disorders. In other patients, the sense of self is negatively colored *and* its organization is temporally unstable (experiences of identity confusion) but, notwithstanding fleeting fragmentations, it largely retains its structural cohesion. One might refer to such cases as moderately severe self disorders. In a third group of patients, the sense of self is negatively colored, temporally unstable, *and* lacking in cohesion and thus subject to protracted structural fragmentation and disintegration. One might refer to such cases as very severe self disorders. Roughly speaking, patients who are called "borderline" fall within the moderate to severe range of self disorders.

Our concept of self disorder as a continuum or dimension of psychopathology is somewhat at variance with Kohut's (1971) early view that "borderline" refers to a discrete diagnostic entity, which is sharply distinguishable from the narcissistic personality disorders. The borderline personality, according to this view, is chronically threatened with the possibility of an irreversible disintegration of the self—a psychological catastrophe that is more or less successfully averted by the various protective operations characteristic of borderline functioning. This vulnerability to a permanent breakup of the self is the product of a traumatically crushing or depriving developmental history, which has precluded even a minimal consolidation of the archaic grandiose self and the idealized parent imago. Consequently, unlike the narcissistic personality, the borderline patient is unable to form a stable mirroring or idealizing selfobject transference and is therefore unanalyzable by the classical method.

In contrast with this conceptualization, our observations are consistent with those of other analysts who have reported analyses of borderline personalities in which the therapist *was* eventually able to help the patient form a more or less stable and analyzable selfobject transference (Adler, 1980, 1981; Tolpin, 1980). It is true that the selfobject ties formed by those patients who are called "borderline" tend initially to be far more primitive and intense, more labile and vulnerable to disruption, and therefore more taxing of the therapist's empathy and tolerance (Adler, 1980, 1981; Tolpin, 1980) than those described by Kohut as being characteristic of narcissistic personalities. Furthermore, when the selfobject ties of a patient with a moderate to severe self disorder are obstructed or ruptured by empathic failures or separations, the patient's reactions may be much more catastrophic and disturbed, for what is threatened is the patient's central self-regulatory capacity—the basic structural integrity and stability of the sense of self, not merely its affective tone (Adler, 1980, 1981; Stolorow and Lachmann, 1980). Nevertheless, when these patients' archaic states and needs are correctly understood, they can be helped to form more or less stable selfobject transferences, and, when this is achieved, their so-called borderline features recede and even disappear. So long as the selfobject tie to the therapist remains intact, their treatment will bear a close similarity to Kohut's descriptions of analyses of narcissistic personality disorders (Adler, 1980, 1981).[1] When the selfobject tie to the therapist becomes significantly disrupted, on the other hand, the patient may once again present borderline features. What we wish to stress is that whether or not a stable selfobject bond can develop and be maintained (which in turn shapes both the apparent diagnostic picture and the assessment of analyzability) does not depend only on the patient's nuclear self pathology. It will be codetermined by the extent of the therapist's ability to comprehend empathically the nature of the patient's archaic subjective universe (Tolpin, 1980) as it begins to structure the microcosm of the therapeutic transference.

The Case of Caroline

Our conception of borderline as phenomena arising and receding within an intersubjective field is exemplified by the case of Caroline. The "borderline" symptoms that led Caroline to enter analysis were immediately precipitated by severe disturbances in her relationship

[1]In a recent personal communication (1981), Kohut states that he has long held views compatible with those developed here. He writes: "Insofar as the therapist is able to build an empathic bridge to the patient, the patient has in a way ceased to be a borderline case . . . and has become a case of [severe] narcissistic personality disorder."

with her husband. In other words, they arose within a specific intersubjective field—that of a precarious, vulnerable self and a failing, archaic selfobject (her husband). The analyst, however, did not recognize this sufficiently when the treatment began, and his lack of understanding complicated and prolonged the treatment. We have since observed that most often patients enter treatment when there is a breakdown in an archaic selfobject bond, which has hitherto served to maintain, however precariously and at whatever cost, the structural cohesion and stability of the self and the patient's central self-regulatory capability.

Caroline's two previous attempts at treatment had not materially affected the underlying defect in her self-structure. When she entered the analysis described here, she was 42 years old. Her last analysis had ended about three years earlier when her analyst told her he didn't feel he could do any more for her. Since that time she had thrown herself into various pursuits. She had returned to school to finish her education, which had been interrupted many years before when she married. In addition, she had involved herself in some charitable and social activities in an attempt "to feel useful" and to keep herself occupied.

Caroline spoke with a Southern accent, which became more pronounced when she was tense. She was somewhat overweight and attempted to cover this with loose-fitting clothes, which only made it stand out more. For some time she had been in a state of more or less constant anxiety, at times hyperactive and at other times withdrawn, apathetic, and unable to get moving. Early in her treatment, she displayed a frightened little girl look, expressing her evident discomfort and not infrequently her terror. She avoided the analyst's eyes almost completely. In the first weeks, she openly voiced her disbelief that anyone could help her and said she saw no way out of her difficulties.

Gradually it was reconstructed that her present intractable state dated from about 10 years earlier and had followed a deterioration in her relationship with her husband (to whom she had now been married for about a dozen years). Although Caroline had been a reasonably attractive young woman, her shyness and lack of confidence, in concert with a puritanical upbringing, had constricted her social and sexual development. Thus, her husband was the first man with whom she had had a serious relationship. She had been an outstanding student—her remarkable intelligence was to become clearer as the treatment progressed—but she left college when she married in order to support and further the career of her husband, then in law school. Subsequently, when he set up practice, she kept house for him, assisted him in many ways, reared their child, and operated a small business so that they could prosper financially. In spite of this, their relationship became more strained and conflicted, as her husband became ever more displeased with and critical of her—of her accent, her weight, her anxiety and depression. This culminated in a "borderline" state, with progressive lethargy, hypochondriacal symptoms, feelings of deadness that began in her extremities and threatened to engulf her whole body, and frightening delusions about her husband harming, poisoning, or killing her.

Caroline recovered from this early episode in a matter of weeks, but many of the symptoms recurred (though not the delusions) and other symptoms took hold. She began to eat compulsively, and there were periodic withdrawals during which she remained preoccupied with puzzles or needlework for long periods of time. In the early months of treatment, Caroline appeared so distraught and disorganized that the analyst believed that only by seeing her six times a week could he avert a prolonged hospitalization or suicide (to which she made several references).

Whatever the content of the sessions, Caroline reacted to their ending with enormous anxiety and clung to the analyst as the hour drew to a close, speeding up her associations so that he could not interrupt her. When he succeeded in calling the session to a halt, she either continued the conversation until he closed the door behind her or, enraged by his interrupting her, walked out in a sullen pout. Weekends and more prolonged separations produced severe regressive states and numerous dreams filled with disaster—flooding and drowning, houses perched precariously on a cliff edge, supports crumbling, black men pursuing her, and imagery involving a variety of mutilations.

In the first dream that Caroline reported in the analysis, she described her husband and her analyst sitting in the living room. She went to the freezer and took something out. It was the trunk of a frozen corpse with no limbs. She showed this to the men, but they began to have sport with it—tossing it around and laughing.

The early sessions were marked by an almost uninterrupted stream of associations. The analyst found it hard to think, let alone formulate a coherent understanding of any underlying meaning. As this continued for some time, it was difficult for the analyst to escape the conviction that she was projecting her anxiety and helplessness into him in an attempt to rid herself of these feelings.

Gradually, however, it became clearer that she was terrified of the analyst and the treatment—terrified that she would be treated cruelly, driven mad, or abandoned as a hopeless case. These fears were interpreted to her as indications of a lack of trust and reluctance to depend on the analyst. Such interpretations seemed for a time to calm her, and they evoked memories of her early experiences.

Caroline was the first child of her mother and father. They had married when her mother was approaching 40. Her father, four years older, was then a widower with two teen-aged sons, a hard-working accountant who needed someone to take responsibility for their upbringing. As a young woman, Caroline's mother had wanted desperately to escape from the drudgery of her small town life, and her love of music seemed to offer her the opportunity. But she realized rather late that her hopes to become an opera singer or the coach of an operatic prodigy were destined to disappointment. By that time her chances for a good marriage had passed her by, and she settled on Caroline's father, more with resignation than ardor, a bird in no gilded cage.

Caroline was born two years later, in what she was repeatedly told was an extremely difficult labor. Three years after her birth a brother was born. This birth was even more difficult and resulted in severe damage to the mother's pelvic tissues. Afterward the mother took to her bed in a depression that lasted for many months, during which time she was preoccupied with an assortment of hypochondriacal and somatic symptoms. When she recovered, she treated Caroline as if the little girl were an extension of her own defective, diseased self. She reacted to every sneeze as if it were a harbinger of death, took Caroline from doctor to doctor, and kept her out of school for two years. As Caroline and her health became the mother's sole preoccupation, intense conflicts arose. These centered on what foods Caroline was to eat, how much and at what intervals she must sleep, and especially her bowel habits.

As the treatment progressed, the analyst noted that Caroline was somewhat better as each week proceeded, but then regressed toward its end. Weekends, though shortened to a day, remained disasters, with the patient unable to think or function except at a minimal level. The analyst thought that the material indicated Caroline's inability to retain any image of a good object built up during the sessions—she and it underwent a nearly complete deterioration during separations. When she returned to analysis, it was in a state of helplessness. Repeatedly, she then complained that the analysis was not helping her, and frequently, apparently forgetting her condition when she entered treatment, she angrily asserted that the analyst was responsible for her pain and lack of progress.

It was easy for the analyst to conclude that the archaic states of confusion and disintegration into which Caroline lapsed came about because of persistent splitting, that her good internal objects were being kept widely apart from the bad, that synthesis was being actively prevented from occurring, and that she could not simultaneously accept the analyst's goodness and his separateness. She reacted to his unavailability on weekends and to what he believed were thoughtful and helpful interpretations as if they were purposely meant to make her suffer. Attacking him in that way, she anticipated being attacked in return. And she experienced every attempt on his part to explain this situation to her, no matter how cautiously, tactfully, and empathically phrased, as a renewed attack on her.

Another "symptom" appeared in Caroline's treatment. One day, in striking contrast to her usual outfit of jeans and tennis shoes, she appeared in a lovely skirt and jacket, a pretty blouse, and fashionable shoes and purse. Greatly embarrassed, she revealed that she had gone on a spree, bought three outfits, several pairs of shoes, and an assortment of matching accessories. She confided that she did this every once in a while, in spite of herself. She knew that when she went home she would have to hide all the things she had bought and might never be able to wear them, for her husband would be furious with her. He would be frightened and horrified by her excesses. He maintained absolute control over the family finances and regarded her buying binges as symptoms of insanity or as inconsiderate breaches of contract. Moreover, now he would have further grounds for his understandable concern over her treatment.

The analyst felt that if her purpose was to project into him her anxiety over behavior for which she wished to escape responsibility, she could not have devised a more effective means. He was also struck by the excess, the suddenness, and the lack of control, and he tried, without success, to investigate the spree from that perspective. He was to learn later that Caroline did not buy another stitch of clothing for three years.

Caroline's fears of the analyst and the analysis kept recurring. Her dreams were filled with scalding suns, Chinese tortures, and monstrously cruel people. Such images were generally interpreted as transference projections. And gradually some small progress seemed to occur. Her anger subsided somewhat, her anxiety assumed more manageable proportions, and she was able to read and to socialize to a greater extent. Yet whenever her old symptoms returned, she thrashed herself mercilessly. Repeated working through of these themes seemed to the analyst to leave no alternative to the explanation that something in her was opposing success, making it impossible for her to benefit further from treatment, her marriage, and, indeed, her life. She made many starts in many directions, but invariably her enthusiasm disappeared, to be mourned and to become the focus for renewed disappointment and anger with herself. It seemed that continued treatment would only confirm an omnipotent fantasy that somehow some experience would magically solve her difficulties without her having to change.

The analysis, then, appeared to have reached a stalemate. Although basic problems had not been solved, the prospect of termination loomed unmistakably, for it seemed to the analyst that more analysis would only serve to keep Caroline from utilizing the considerable insights she had attained. Rationalizations appeared like weeds after a rain. After all, her background had left her with a considerable toll. The difficulties of her attachment to or detachment from her husband, especially at her age, were all but insurmountable. Her gains, looked at in a certain light, were not negligible, and it seemed certain that she was no longer so vulnerable to the threat of collapse that had brought her into treatment.

In the fourth year of treatment, with many of Caroline's borderline features still intact, the analyst decided to take one last look. It had long been apparent that she was disappointed and felt herself to be a failure, but it was now also becoming clear that she felt that the *analyst* was disappointed in her and that *he* considered her and himself failures. This factor—Caroline's responsiveness to cues of the analyst's feeling about her—had been grossly underestimated. In fact, as was later understood, her imperative need to be liked and approved of and the devastating effect on her of the analyst's disapproval, which she sensed, had been crucial in structuring the first phase of treatment. Her depression, her attacks on herself, and her lack of sustaining motivation all became understandable from this perspective. The analyst could not continue to maintain that her perceptions of him were all projection, for he began to recognize in himself what she had been responding to. This dawning awareness ushered in the second phase of the analysis.

In a subsequent session, in response to Caroline's expression of weariness and thoughts about terminating, the analyst commented that he realized that the process was becoming wearing. But could they take one more good look at what had been occurring before deciding to terminate? Perhaps there was something he had not understood, something that might prove helpful. Perhaps he had conveyed an increasing disappointment in her and in himself, especially around her continuing symptoms, and perhaps that had contributed in an important way to her dejection and disparagement of herself. Caroline responded enthusiastically. Yes, she exclaimed, she had felt awful about the analyst's disappointment, which she had sensed. By this time she should be able to feel better and to control her diet, for she had learned so much. She had attacked herself mercilessly for not having tried hard enough. She was weak and self-indulgent, she said, and must want to spite both her husband and the analyst as she had always defied her mother. When she was on her diets, she could somehow kill her craving for food and not be hungry. But something always happened and she again felt the urge to eat. Then she felt she was a failure and tried harder and harder. When she was finally unable to stick to her diet, she hated herself, for she had let the analyst and her husband down. *Once that point had been reached she was absolutely unable to restrain herself—the more alone she felt, the more she hated herself and the more she felt compelled to eat.*

The analyst was now able to glimpse the transference configuration that had actually determined the course of Caroline's analysis. Together they began to look at what happened to her when she was alone, paying increasing attention now to her subjective experiences and trying to understand them in a different way. There seemed to be a complex and thoroughgoing alteration of her state of mind—a slipping away of self-esteem, feelings of accelerating disorganization and disconnectedness, an inability to concentrate, and increasing feelings of deadness, involving coldness and loss of sensation in her limbs, so that they no longer seemed to belong to her. All these symptoms the analyst came to recognize as signs of a fragmenting process and of an underlying defect in her self-structure. It became apparent how much Caroline had looked to the analyst to maintain her sense of self, needing from him what had not been acquired in her childhood. When the analyst had interpreted her archaic states and transference needs as expressions of pathological splitting and projection, she had become intensely ashamed and self-hating. In their impact on Caroline, the interpretations of pathological defenses had repeated the fragmentation-producing effects of her mother's view of her as defective and diseased.

It was especially important to Caroline that the analyst be pleased with her. She had tried valiantly to get this across to him early in the analysis, but he had regarded this as defensive. He had not recognized as primary her specific need for him to serve as a selfobject who would provide the mirroring, affirming responsiveness that her self-absorbed, depressed, and hypochondriacal mother had been unable to supply during her early formative years. Behind this specific need lay the vulnerability to fragmentation that had pervaded Caroline's analytic experiences. When the selfobject tie to the analyst was disrupted by an empathic failure—that is, a failure of the analyst to understand her subjective experience in its essence—or by a loss of connectedness during weekends or vacations, she could not maintain the cohesion, stability, and affective tone of her precarious self. She fell apart, eating compulsively in an effort to strengthen herself and to fill the defect in her sense of self—trying to recover through oral self-stimulation the feeling that she existed at all.

As the structural weakness was being worked through, Caroline realized at one point that she was becoming addicted to television and radio. When she thought about the vague, apprehensive restlessness she felt in the absence of sensory stimulation, she realized that "empty" did not really describe her feeling. Rather, she recognized "a feeling of deficiency, a lack of some very specific supporting structure which would prevent everything from falling in—some essential piece of myself missing." When the analyst had taken her symptoms as a disparagement of his efforts, as a defensive aggrandizement of herself, or as an indication of greed, she had felt even worse. Feeling blamed, she had relentlessly blamed herself.

As the disturbance in the transference tie was seen and analyzed in this new way, with focus on the fragmented states and the underlying structural deficit, Caroline became more alive, friendlier, much more enthusiastic, and increasingly capable. Her desire to understand her states of mind grew in direct proportion to her sense of the analyst's desire to help her acquire this understanding. She expressed appreciation that the analyst now recognized her vulnerability and the legitimacy of her fears. "The first thing I had to get across to you," she explained when she was certain that he would understand her, "was how important what you thought of me was. Until that happened nothing else could happen. I couldn't disagree with you because I was afraid of worse consequences. So I tried to see and use and apply what you said, even when it made me hate myself. I tried to think you were opening up a new world for me, a new way of seeing things that would work out better in the end. And when it wasn't working out that way, I blamed myself."

With the working through of her fragmented states in relation to their triggering experiences within a disrupted selfobject tie, Caroline's borderline symptomatology and paranoidlike fears dropped away, together with what had previously been regarded as splitting, projection, and a failure to internalize a good object. She and the analyst could now better understand her dream of the frozen torso and her expectations of being laughed at. She had often been terrified as a little girl, but her fears had always been mocked. She could not, for example, let her mother bathe her or wash her hair, and her mother would be furious with her. No one understood why she was afraid of her mother—indeed, afraid of almost everything. She was teased mercilessly by her brothers for being so afraid. "Girls can't do anything," they would say.

As Caroline's vulnerability decreased, there were increasing signs that she was turning once more to the analyst to help her understand her early relationship with her mother, its effect on her, and how crucial elements were being replicated with her husband and the analyst. The analyst could now understand the symbolism of an earlier turning, which he had missed. Her buying binge had contained both her fear and her intense need to be noticed. As a girl, she had turned to her father to be noticed, for it was only through connecting herself to him that she felt she might be able to extricate herself from the traumatogenic enmeshment with her mother. "But he was remote and embarrassed by emotion—even by mother's emotion, and even though he loved mother," she remarked. "When feelings were expressed, he would look away. Then, after a point, he would introduce another subject, as if what had taken place before did not exist." Caroline remembered wanting her father to pick her up, but he never did, except as part of a game. She didn't play right, she felt, so she couldn't be held. And she so wanted him to want to be close to her. She realized now that when the analyst spoke to her gently and smiled when he greeted her, she felt real and warm, not frozen. If she had been feeling bad and hating herself, that made her feel all right.

Caroline had blamed herself when her father hadn't noticed her or loved her. In particular, she had blamed her anger. The anger evoked by her father's unresponsiveness had been enormously threatening to her because of her desperate need for him as a selfobject. Thus, she exonerated him and blamed her reactive anger for his faulty responsiveness. A similar sequence could be observed in reaction to the empathic failures of her husband and the analyst. Her idealizations were not primarily a defense against her anger. Rather, she preserved the vitally needed idealizations *at the expense* of her anger and of her ability to assert herself when her interests were disregarded.

Caroline had turned to her father not primarily as an oedipal love object, but as an idealized selfobject whose responsive interest in her might have opened a compensatory path along which her thwarted development could resume. When this developmental thrust was revived in the transference, her associations led her back to her fourth and fifth years. Her memories clearly showed that what she most needed her father to notice and understand was what she was going through with her mother. In the analysis she realized that she had to return to that time because something had happened then that had made her life thereafter almost unbearable. She remembered herself before this time as a well-dressed little girl; afterward she felt like a ragamuffin.

When Caroline was four her mother, then recovering from a prolonged depression, had resumed her involvement with the church as an organist and choral leader. The church and the little girl largely made up the boundaries of the mother's restricted world. Even then her mother would often go to bed for the day, saying, "I know I can't get out today." Caroline remembered that during this period she had wanted to learn to play the piano. Taking affront that Caroline might want anyone else to teach her, her mother undertook the task. Caroline recalled that as with everything else, her mother insisted on a strict routine—first, months of finger exercises away from the piano, and only then the real thing. Her mother was overwhelming as a teacher. When Caroline tired and pleaded, "I can't," her mother flew into a rage. Later, Caroline came to understand that the rage was toward her mother's own recalcitrant self, indistinguishable from that of her daughter. The mother desperately wished that her daughter would not give up, as she herself had done, that Caroline would not become a nobody doing the things in the kitchen no one else wanted to do. She insisted that Caroline did not care about her, did not value her. Caroline could see that her mother believed this, and it scared her. But then she told herself perhaps her mother was right, perhaps she would never be able to care for anyone (as she was also told) if she couldn't care for her mother. It was so frightening to think that her mother didn't understand her that she found it a relief to believe that she herself was bad.

Why couldn't she practice, her mother would ask. It was just a matter of moving her fingers. Her mother would demonstrate and then take Caroline's fingers and show her. It could only be rebelliousness, she was always so stubborn. Then, her mother would get out the whip as the little girl froze and cowered. It was a black, braided leather affair with a number of thongs, perfect equipment for not spoiling the child. Although it was only used three or four times, Caroline would remember her fear and humiliation for the rest of her life. That ended her career in music.

One of the most terrifying aspects of these childhood experiences was that something was glaringly wrong, but nobody seemed to know it or do anything about it. When Caroline went to her father, he would change the subject. When she went to the maid, she was told how it was to be an orphan as the maid had been. Caroline had to find some way to live with her mother, so she made herself responsible, telling herself that if she were better her mother would love her. "It is terrifying to be in the power of another person," she observed. This feeling, that something was wrong and nobody seemed to know or do anything about it, was replicated in the analysis when the analyst failed to respond to Caroline's assertions of the threat to herself posed by many of his interpretations.

There was something even worse than whipping, Caroline realized one day. One of the major methods by which her mother controlled her was by continuously threatening to leave her. That was always and still remained the ultimate whip, both with her husband and in the transference. *She realized that the threat may have been completely false objectively, but it was very real to her.* Even now, anyone she needed could reduce her to submission by threatening to leave her. Her mother had simply walked away from her when the little girl had "misbehaved" or acted cranky. "It is almost as if you have a choice of existing or your mother existing, but not both," Caroline explained. The meaning of a remark at the beginning of the analysis was now more understandable: "I have had to be able to hate my mother in order to stay alive!"

Caroline recalled that the family had a small house near the ocean, at the mouth of a river. Her mother was afraid Caroline would drown and so insisted on teaching her to swim—not in the small river but in the ocean. Yet her mother herself could barely swim. Caroline remembered her terror when her mother approached her. She couldn't let her mother near her! She couldn't tolerate looking at her because she knew that just the touch or the look would immediately cause her to lose herself, not feel herself. Her mother frequently said, "If you could just see yourself through somebody else's eyes." Caroline realized how much she had needed for someone to see through her eyes. In the water she would scream, "I'll do it myself; please let me do it myself!" Her mother would stand over her, coldly retorting, "When are you going to do it; when are you going to do it?"

Caroline often imagined running away from her mother's ruthless training. One day, in the analysis, she spoke of this, remarking, "If I had had a father to run to, I would have." It was when she saw all her little friends playing and going places with their fathers that she began to feel like a ragamuffin. She remembered so much wanting to run away, but she was concerned about not having any food. She began to think about packing food in small packages. She collected Tarzan books, and she recalled being fascinated because he was able to survive in the jungle with only a knife; he didn't have to depend on or submit to anyone. Eventually, however, her daydreams of escaping from her mother collapsed. She was too aware of reality and knew that she would have to come back, so she made her peace.

At this stage of the analysis, Caroline remarked on a feeling of being better integrated. The analyst had allowed her to revive in the transference the longed-for selfobject bond to an idealized father, who would help her understand and separate from her pathological enmeshment with her mother. Everything she thought about now seemed more vivid, she commented. Her thoughts and feelings made more sense to her. She felt more self-confidence, although she was still worried that this would disappear and not return. Still, she felt she was stronger, as she put it, than the threat to her was. Moreover, she noted an increased ability to stick to her moderated diet. Slowly but noticeably, she began to lose weight. There was much more to be done, she realized, but she felt that a corner had been turned, as indeed it had.

To summarize this case: Caroline's adult "borderline" characteristics and paranoidlike distrust had arisen in the intersubjective field consisting of her vulnerable, fragmentation-prone self and a failing, archaic selfobject (her husband). These borderline characteristics remained and were periodically intensified in the new intersubjective field of the psychoanalytic situation when the analyst's incorrect interpretive stance and faulty responsiveness unwittingly triggered and exacerbated her states of self-fragmentation. The failures in her marital relationship and in the first phase of the analysis replicated the specific, traumatogenic failures of her original selfobjects. Caroline had adapted to these failures by attempting to become a selfobject for her mother and pushing herself even harder when her mother found her wanting in that role. This was repeated with the analyst. In contrast, in the second phase of the analysis, when the analyst became able to empathically comprehend the actual meaning of Caroline's archaic subjective states and needs, thereby permitting her to revive and establish with him the specific selfobject ties that she required, her so-called borderline features dropped away.

Conclusion

We have criticized the view that the term "borderline" designates a distinct pathological character structure, rooted in pathognomonic instinctual conflicts and primitive defenses. Instead, we propose an alternative conceptualization of so-called borderline phenomena from a psychoanalytic developmental and self-psychological perspective. In particular, we believe that the clinical evidence cited for the operation of primitive defenses against pregenital aggression is better understood as an indication of needs for specific modes of relatedness to archaic selfobjects and the empathic failures of these selfobjects. As the case of Caroline suggests, the psychological essence of what is called "borderline" does not rest in a pathological condition located solely in the patient. Rather, it lies in phenomena arising in an intersubjective field, consisting of a precarious, vulnerable self and a failing, archaic selfobject.

REFERENCES

Adler, G. (1980), Transference, real relationship and alliance. *Int. J. Psycho-Anal.*, 61:547–558.

——— (1981), The borderline-narcissistic personality disorder continuum. *Amer. J. Psychiat.*, 138:40–50.

Brandchaft, B. (1983), The negativism of the negative therapeutic reaction and the psychology of the self. In: *The Future of Psychoanalysis*, ed. A. Goldberg. New York: International Universities Press, pp. 327–359.

Kernberg, O. (1975), *Borderline Conditions and Pathological Narcissism.* New York: Aronson.

Kohut, H. (1971), *The Analysis of the Self.* New York: International Universities Press.

——— H. (1972), Thoughts on narcissism and narcissistic rage. In: *The Search for the Self*, Vol. 2, ed. P. Ornstein. New York: International Universities Press, 1978, pp. 615–658.

———. (1977). *The Restoration of the Self.* New York: International Universities Press.

Modell, A. (1976), The "holding environment" and the therapeutic action of psychoanalysis. *J. Amer. Psychoanal. Assn.*, 24:285–307.

Stolorow, R. & Lachmann, F. (1980), *Psychoanalysis of Developmental Arrests: Theory and Treatment.* New York: International Universities Press.

Sugarman, A. & Lerner, H. (1980), Reflections on the current state of the borderline concept. In: *Borderline Phenomena and the Rorschach Test*, ed. J. Kwawer, H. Lerner, R. Lerner, & A. Sugarman. New York: International Universities Press, pp. 11–37.

Tolpin, P. (1980), The borderline personality: Its makeup and analyzability. In: *Advances in Self Psychology*, ed. A. Goldberg. New York: International Universities Press, pp. 299–316.

Winnicott, D. W. (1965), *The Maturational Processes and the Facilitating Environment*. New York: International Universities Press.

Discussion

GERALD ADLER, M.D.

THE BORDERLINE CONCEPT will probably always remain controversial. Not only is it difficult to agree on the criteria for making the diagnosis, but the intensity of the affect and the primitive nature of borderline patients, as well as the countertransference responses elicited in their therapists or analysts, add fuel to the theoretical debate. Moreover, theory is often dependent on observations made by clinicians and the very nature of these observations may be determined by the clinicians' varying empathic capacities and different theoretical frameworks.

Bernard Brandchaft and Robert Stolorow provide a challenging opportunity to examine aspects of these issues. They conclude that "the psychological essence of what is called 'borderline' does not rest in a pathological condition located solely in the patient. Rather, it lies in phenomena arising in an intersubjective field, consisting of a precarious, vulnerable self and a failing, archaic selfobject." They believe that serious treatment difficulties occur with patients who have severe self pathology and who "fall within the moderate to severe range of self disorder." According to their discussion and clinical descriptions, the therapist of such a vulnerable person may repeatedly fail him (or her), not only through misunderstanding, but also through a failure to acknowledge this misunderstanding. Instead, the therapist may insist on the correctness of his interpretations and force the patient to conform as a condition for remaining in treatment. Under these circumstances, Brandchaft and Stolorow contend, "so-called" borderline features may appear.

As I understand Brandchaft and Stolorow's position, they use the term "borderline" to refer to an entirely iatrogenic illness and believe that the borderline personality disorder does not exist outside of an intersubjective field of a failing, archaic selfobject in the presence of a moderately to severely vulnerable self. In other words, the patients they describe are more primitive narcissistic personality disorder patients who only look "borderline" secondary to the analyst's empathic failures. Brandchaft and Stolorow emphasize that the analyst's responses to his patient, his countertransference difficulties, his empathic capacities, and the vicissitudes of his own omnipotence play important roles in the degree of fragmentation that such fragmentation-prone patients exhibit.

Although I would agree that in the hands of some clinicians, a narcissistic personality disorder patient can appear to be much sicker and that some patients who are somewhere on the continuum between borderline and narcissistic personality disorder can seem borderline with these clinicians, it seems an oversimplification of a very complex subject to state that the borderline personality disorder is an "iatrogenic myth." Brandchaft and Stolorow make a useful contribution in pointing to the empathic failures of and countertransference difficulties in therapists and analysts who treat fragmentation-vulnerable patients. Nevertheless, I believe there are problems with their conceptualizations, and the consequences of their formulations may adversely affect the work of clinicians who treat sicker patients, some of whom are borderline.

DSM-III (American Psychiatric Association, 1980) recognizes borderline personality disorder as a diagnostic entity, in contrast to *DSM-II* and *DSM-I*. The *DSM-III* description stresses the impulsivity of these patients; their intense, unstable relationships; their inappropriate anger; as well as their mood swings. In addition, *DSM-III* emphasizes their tendency for physically self-damaging acts, chronic feelings of emptiness or boredom, and an "intolerance of being alone, e.g., frantic efforts to avoid being alone [and] depressed when alone" (pp. 322–323).

Kernberg (1975) has defined the criteria for the diagnosis of borderline personality organization through descriptive features, a "structural analysis," and a "genetic-dynamic analysis." In his discussion of the structural analysis, Kernberg stresses nonspecific and specific defenses, as well as characteristic difficulties with internalized object relations. His work focuses on the concept of splitting as a major defense in borderline patients. He distinguishes between the regressive fusion of self- and object images seen in psychosis and the splitting found in borderline personality organization, which results from a failure to integrate "self and object images built up under the influence of libidinal drive derivatives with the corresponding self and object images built up under the influence of aggressive drive derivatives" (p. 26). Kernberg thus differentiates psychosis-prone individuals with "blurring of the ego boundaries in the area of differentiation between self and nonself" (p. 27) from borderline personalities, who utilize splitting and manifest blurred ego boundaries only transiently when under severe stress.

In their discussion of splitting in "so-called borderline states," Brandchaft and Stolorow's use of the term differs from that of Kernberg. They describe splitting both as "a defense actively employed to ward off ambivalence conflicts" and as a "lack of synthesis of self- and object experiences," thereby losing Kernberg's distinction between borderline personality organization and psychosis. They also use the term "splitting" to describe the manifestations of chronic fragmentation, which is different from Kernberg's detailing of the separation of self- and object images developed under libidinal drive derivatives from those formed under aggressive drive derivatives.

I believe that Kernberg's distinctions are valid. Borderline patients, as Kernberg describes, have a relatively stable capacity to maintain self and object differentiation, except when under stress. In addition, I would emphasize that the *fear* of this loss of ego boundaries plays an important role in borderline patients' psychopathology (Adler and Buie, 1979; Buie and Adler, 1982–1983). Their longings for closeness and fusion are followed by avoidance and panic when faced with a potentially gratifying and nurturing dyadic relationship. Nevertheless, splitting is not as ubiquitous a phenomenon as Kernberg indicates. Some borderline patients manifest it only as a relatively minor or transient part of their psychopathology. On the other hand, some narcissistic personality disorder patients also utilize splitting as a defense, as *DSM-III* recognizes.

There is evidence that the vulnerability to states of aloneness described in *DSM-III* is characteristic of patients with borderline personality disorders and helps to distinguish between borderline and narcissistic personality disorders (Adler and Buie, 1979; Adler, 1981; Buie and Adler, 1982). In contrast to patients with narcissistic personality disorders, whose primary concerns are self-worth issues, borderline patients have a specific structural vulnerability related to feelings of aloneness. Specifically, they cannot depend on inner resources to tolerate separation anxiety. Their deficiencies involve an inability to maintain holding introjects of important people, especially when under stress. Characteristic of borderline patients is the intensity of their anger, which inevitably emerges in treatment when the therapist's imperfections become manifest. At the same time, their awakened neediness, as well as their wishes for and fears of closeness and merger, unfolds in the dyadic therapeutic situation. Although an analyst who erroneously insists on the correctness of his interpretations can precipitate a borderline patient's decompensation, such a major empathic failure is not a prerequisite for the emergence of the patient's anger and vulnerability to the loss of holding introjects. This vulnerability is intrinsic to borderline patients, and inevitably emerges in treatment, even with therapists who do not fail the patient in the ways that Brandchaft and Stolorow describe. The anger of the narcissistic personality patient can sometimes be intense, but does not lead to aloneness experiences. When the latter occur, the patient probably belongs somewhere in the borderline personality disorder spectrum. These aloneness issues, by definition, are part of a severe regression, which has gone beyond the fragmentation experiences of patients in the narcissistic personality disorder segment of the borderline-narcissistic personality disorder continuum (Adler, 1981).

Why do clinicians who work with primitive patients disagree about the characteristic features of borderline patients; why do they question whether "borderline" is largely or entirely an iatrogenic concept, or whether the concept exists at all? Part of the difficulty lies in the utilization of different theoretical frameworks in evaluating clinical material, as well as the clinician's success in eliciting the patient's psychopathology and working with it constructively. Moreover, this process may be more difficult than usual when working with primitive patients because the therapist is likely to be more vulnerable to countertransference responses, which can seriously impede the work, as well as affect the observations made.

Brandchaft and Stolorow use two patients to illustrate their thesis: Jeff and Caroline. As with all clinical material, much has to be omitted in order to illustrate the points the authors wish to make. They may have data that would clarify that these two patients are borderline. However, according to Brandchaft and Stolorow's description, both patients were able to tolerate the analytic situation, and Jeff's work with his analyst did not suffer from the analyst's failure in understanding that the first half of Caroline's analysis demonstrated. If these patients are borderline, they must be closer than most to the narcissistic personality disorder on the borderline-narcissistic personality disorder continuum (Adler, 1981), for they were able to tolerate the deprivation of lying on a couch without seeing the analyst, something particularly difficult for patients with severe aloneness vulnerability. It is particularly impressive that Caroline could tolerate three years of feeling misunderstood and still remain in analysis without a major decompensation to aloneness issues.

Caroline's first three years of analysis recapitulated the empathic failures of her parents. In her first dream, she took the trunk of a frozen corpse with no limbs out of a freezer and showed it to the analyst and her husband, who tossed it around, laughing. This dream is reminiscent of those Guntrip (1971) describes with schizoid patients. It reveals an extremely vulnerable person who feels frozen, mutilated, and dead; she appears to be telling the analyst that in order to become alive and whole, the overwhelming issues of shame and humiliation will have to be faced and resolved. We do not have the analyst's immediate response to the dream. However, his formulations do not acknowledge this fear of shame and humiliation, and, for this reason, may well have been experienced by her as a failure to be understood. The analyst's response to her "spending spree," which he saw as excessive and lacking in control, seemed to confirm her fears of humiliation, shame, and punishment that the dream addressed. Her response, consistent with her childhood story, was one of conformity in order to keep the analyst at all costs, and chronic fragmentation. Caroline's survival need to conform is very much like Winnicott's descriptions of a "false self" (1960). Her chronic state of fragmentation, anger, and depression seems to have repeated her childhood experiences, including both her struggles and identification with her mother. The account of the last three years of the analysis, in which the analyst was able to understand his failure to grasp these difficulties, clearly and beautifully describe the changes in Caroline and her growth in the analysis.

Brandchaft and Stolorow are correct in stating that Caroline's difficulties in the first three years of analysis "had arisen in the intersubjective field consisting of her vulnerable, fragmentation-prone self and a failing, archaic selfobject (her husband)." But is Caroline borderline? She was able to maintain the intersubjective field with her analyst in spite of his serious empathic failures during the first three years of the analysis. Her chronic fragmentation and conforming behavior were not splitting phenomena as defined by Kernberg (1975). Although she felt alone in the first half of the analysis, it did not seem to be an aloneness that related to the borderline's threatened loss of holding introjects. Instead, it related to experiences from her childhood in which she felt misunderstood. She was also threatened by abandonment, which she knew was not objectively correct, and was enmeshed in a relationship with her mother in which she served as an extension of the mother's wishes, fears, disappointments, anger, and longing. She experienced the treatment as similar to the angry struggle with her mother, which she felt was necessary to remain sufficiently separate and alive.

Caroline did not develop the intense neediness, coupled with fears of closeness, that borderline patients experience. It could be argued that her conformity and chronic fragmentation in the face of being misunderstood and feeling humiliated were evidence of great strength in a narcissistically vulnerable patient in analysis. The loss of her husband as a sustaining selfobject seemed to be an important precipitant in Caroline's decompensation and increasing symptoms of fragmentation before analysis. The episode of "frightening delusions about her husband harming, poisoning, or killing her," which lasted several weeks, might be what Brandchaft and Stolorow label a borderline state—i.e., a transitory decompensation in a narcissistically vulnerable person, which is different from the long-term manifestations of patients who have a borderline personality disorder.

On the other hand, Jeff, in the material presented, did not exhibit characteristics of a borderline personality disorder. What he did exhibit was a narcissistic vulnerability. He felt he had to conform in order to maintain a relationship with his analyst. At the same time, he appeared to be struggling with late adolescent issues of dependency and autonomy, which were recapitulated in the transference. In the careful and empathic work of the analysis, the fragmentation and conformity manifestations were analyzed. The analyst correctly did not interpret these experiences as splitting; there was no evidence that this was splitting as defined by Kernberg.

What are the implications of a disagreement about the existence of borderline personality disorder as a distinct entity? If, as Brandchaft and Stolorow contend, empathic failures in an intersubjective field of narcissistically vulnerable patients form the basis of "so-called borderline" pathology, what impact could this formulation have on therapists who work with these patients? As increasing longings, fears of closeness, disappointments, and anger emerge in treatment, borderline patients devalue their therapists and utilize projection and projective identification, and sometimes splitting. In response, the therapist may feel helpless, confused, worthless, and often furious (Adler, 1970, 1972). Frequently, the therapist's feelings are of such intensity that he may even believe the patient is correct in his devaluing assessment and feel truly deserving of the patient's blame. Of course, as Brandchaft and Stolorow point out, the therapist may have significantly failed the patient; he then has to be able to hear and acknowledge his failures if he is to work successfully with his patient.

If, however, he has not seriously failed the patient, but is the recipient of the intense, inevitable transference experiences of borderline patients, often brought to the surface by the expected empathic failures of the "good-enough therapist" (Adler, 1975), what are his options? Using Brandchaft and Stolorow's formulations, the therapist will believe that his empathic failures are much greater than he thought or that he misunderstands his patient in ways that are unclear to him. Under these circumstances, the therapist may attempt to explore his empathic failures further with his patient and may even feel that the patient's indictments of his competence are valid.[1] Not only may the therapist feel utterly worthless and defeated, but his attempts to explore his "failures" with a borderline patient may frighten the patient, who may experience this as unbearable closeness and warmth. At the same time, the patient may see it as evidence of more vacillation and vulnerability in the therapist than he can tolerate and, therefore, as another significant empathic failure. He may feel that the therapist did not understand the inevitability of his anger. Some patients require the transference experience, as one patient stated, that "the abandoned child must have its due."

From the therapist's vantage point, if the belief becomes firmly established in the psychoanalytic literature that the manifestations of a borderline personality disorder are *always* evidence of the therapist's significant empathic failures, then a potentially serious danger exists: instead of feeling that support is available from colleagues, supervisors, consultants, or published papers in his painful work with the rage of a borderline patient, he will feel blamed, unsupported, and not understood. For the therapist, then, this experience may seem an empathic failure, leading to his own feelings of shame, humiliation, and worthlessness.

Kohut's concepts (1971, 1977) have played an important role in understanding the therapeutic problems of fragmentation-prone people, including the harmful effects on treatment when an omnipotent therapist is convinced of the correctness of his answers and does not hesitate to tell them to the patient, as Brandchaft and Stolorow so well describe. As discussed, the patient with such a therapist feels blamed,

---

[1]It is important to emphasize that good therapists always ask themselves how much a specific decompensation is inevitable as part of the borderline personality disorder, how much is a reflection of their failures to understand the patient, and to what extent optimal support and frustration can be utilized to help the patient relive something important in the transference without more suffering than is necessary.

shamed, and humiliated, with the result that therapy becomes a negative or stalemated experience.

Yet, as I have argued, Brandchaft and Stolorow's formulations may present another dilemma, this time for the therapist. To reiterate: utilizing their formulations, the therapist, when working with borderline patients, may be more likely to feel blamed and to blame himself in therapeutic crises, which may result primarily from the nature of the patient's psychopathology rather than the therapist's own failures. I believe that it is important to use Kohut's valuable contributions to see these issues from the therapist's perspective as well as from the patient's, thus avoiding the possible iatrogenic component of the therapist's self-blame.

REFERENCES

Adler, G. (1970), Valuing and devaluing in the psychotherapeutic process. *Arch. Gen. Psychiat.*, 22:454–461.

——— (1972), Helplessness in the helpers. *Brit. J. Med. Psychol.*, 45:315–326.

——— (1975), The usefulness of the "borderline" concept in psychotherapy. In: *Borderline States in Psychiatry*, ed. J. E. Mack. New York: Grune & Stratton.

——— (1981), The borderline-narcissistic personality disorder continuum. *Amer. J. Psychiat.*, 138:46–50.

——— & Buie, D. H. (1979), Aloneness and borderline psychopathology: The possible relevance of child development issues, Part 1. *Int. J. Psycho-Anal.*, 60:83–96.

American Psychiatric Association (1980), *Diagnostic and Statistical Manual of Mental Disorders*, 3rd Ed. Washington, D.C.: American Psychiatric Association.

Buie, D. H. & Adler, G. (1982–1983), Definitive treatment of the borderline patient. *Int. J. Psychoanal. Psychother.*, 9:51–87.

Guntrip, H. (1971), *Psychoanalytic Theory, Therapy and the Self.* New York: Basic Books.

Kernberg, O. (1975), *Borderline Conditions and Pathological Narcissism.* New York: Aronson.

Kohut, H. (1971), *The Analysis of the Self.* New York: International Universities Press.

——— (1977), *The Restoration of the Self.* New York: International Universities Press.

Winnicott, D. W. (1960), Ego distortion in terms of true and false self. In: *The Maturational Process and the Facilitating Environment.* New York: International Universities Press, 1965, pp. 29–36.

Reply

BERNARD BRANDCHAFT, M.D., and ROBERT D. STOLOROW, Ph.D.

In his synopsis of our viewpoint, Gerald Adler states that we "use the term 'borderline' to refer to an *entirely* iatrogenic illness" (our italics), which he believes is "an oversimplification of a very complex subject." We believe that this is an oversimplified characterization of our views. We have conceptualized borderline phenomena as arising in an intersubjective field consisting of a precarious, vulnerable self and a failing, archaic selfobject. This formulation could not possibly be compatible with a claim that the term "borderline" refers to an "*entirely* iatrogenic illness" for at least two reasons. First, as seen in the case of Caroline, the failing, archaic selfobject is not always a therapist or an analyst, although this will become increasingly more likely as the patient's selfobject needs are engaged in the therapeutic transference. Second, and most important, the claim of an entirely iatrogenic illness would be markedly at variance with our concept of an *intersubjective* field and would completely overlook the contribution of the patient's archaic states, needs, and fragmentation-prone self to the formation of that psychological field. If we view the therapeutic situation as an intersubjective field, then we must see that the patient's manifest psychopathology is always *codetermined* by the patient's self disorder *and* the therapist's ability to understand it.

Our claim is not that borderline symptomatology is entirely iatrogenic, but that the *concept* of a "borderline personality organization" is largely, if not entirely, an iatrogenic myth. We have argued that the idea of a borderline character structure rooted in pathognomonic conflicts and defenses is symptomatic of the difficulty therapists have in comprehending the archaic intersubjective contexts in which borderline pathology arises (Stolorow, Brandchaft, and Atwood, 1983).

Adler criticizes us for failing to adequately take into account the deficiency in object constancy—the "inability to maintain holding introjects of important people" and thus to tolerate separation anxiety—that is characteristic of borderline functioning. In our view, once again, such impaired object constancy cannot be understood apart from the intersubjective context in which it occurs. In the case of Caroline, for example, intolerance of separation was most in evidence when the analyst's faulty interpretive approach consistently prevented her from establishing the selfobject transference relationship she required. As the analyst's comprehension of her selfobject needs improved, so did her ability to maintain a "holding introject"—i.e., a sense of the continuity of the selfobject tie—during separations. Deficient object constancy, in other words, is not *solely* a condition within the patient. It is a property of the self-selfobject unit and indicates the existence of significant disjunctions or asynchronies within that intersubjective system.

Moreover, we differ with Adler in our belief that "vulnerability to aloneness" is *not* an indication of a discrete pathological entity. In our view, it is a symptom experienced by a person who is unable to maintain basic self-regulatory functions in the absence of the required archaic selfobject tie.

Adler has cautioned that our formulation of borderline pathology could have a damaging impact on the self-confidence and self-esteem of therapists, that they may become excessively self-blaming and self-critical and develop serious doubts about their professional competence. It is true that we have sometimes encountered such tendencies in therapists we have supervised. These reactions, however, indicate that the essence of our formulation has not been fully comprehended. To claim that borderline phenomena arise in an intersubjective field is not to place blame on the therapist, but rather to recognize that the manifest pathology is *codetermined* by the patient's archaic states and needs *and* the therapist's often quite understandable difficulty in comprehending and properly responding to them. To blame the therapist for this state of affairs would be completely to neglect the patient's history of early, traumatic selfobject failures and the ways in which these are revived in the therapeutic situation. Even more important, the therapist who feels blamed and indicted by our point of view has not understood the critical difference between an empathic failure and a technical mistake (Schwaber, 1981). The concept of an empathic failure refers to a *subjective experience of the patient* and is certainly not to be seen as an objective index of a therapist's technical competence. When we acknowledge and analyze the patient's experience of empathic failure and accept its "perceptual validity" (Schwaber, 1979), we do so from a position *within the psychic reality of the patient*—i.e., from within the archaic frame of reference created by the engagement in the transference of the patient's early selfobject needs. It is the understanding of this frame of reference, its contribution to the intersubjective field of the therapeutic situation and to the therapist's impact on the patient, that helps the therapist see that he is not "truly deserving of the patient's blame." If the therapist's self-confidence is impaired and if he becomes excessively self-critical because of an increased awareness of unintended effects of the application of theoretical concepts to his patients, then, in our view, that is not a situation to be averted. Rather, what is required in such circumstances is a shift in the basis of the therapist's self-esteem from the presumed correctness of his theoretical ideas to a more broadly based pride in his ability to expand those concepts as empirically indicated.

We are fully aware that from the standpoint of the archaic nature of needs revived in the transference, it is inevitable that the therapist will fail the patient, and that under such circumstances borderline symptoms may appear. In our experience, it is only when the subjective validity and meaning for the patient of these failures and disjunctions go chronically unrecognized, thereby preventing the reestablishment of the therapeutic bond, that borderline phenomena become encrusted into what has been described as a "borderline personality organization."

We are in complete agreement with Adler's plea for a balanced view that keeps in mind the contributions of both patient and therapist. We believe that the concept of intersubjectivity, when correctly understood, provides the basis for just such a balanced view.

REFERENCES

Schwaber, E. (1979), On the 'self' within the matrix of analytic theory—Some clinical reflections and reconsiderations. *Int. J. Psycho-Anal.*, 60:467–479.

——— (1981), Empathy: A mode of analytic listening. *Psychoanal. Inquiry*, 1:357–293. Reprinted here as Chapter 20.

Stolorow, R., Brandchaft, B., & Atwood, G. (1983), Intersubjectivity in psychoanalytic treatment: With special reference to archaic states. *Bull. Menninger Clinic*, 47:117–128.

Author Index

Numbers in *italics* denote pages with bibliographic information.

Subject Index

A

B

C

D